CHAMBERS

Key-Word
DICTIONARY

CHAMBERS
English

CHAMBERS
An imprint of Chambers Harrap Publishers Ltd
7 Hopetoun Crescent
Edinburgh EH7 4AY

A CIP catalogue record for this book is available from the British Library.

ISBN 0550 14080 8

We have made every effort to mark as such all words which we
believe to be trademarks. We should also like to make it clear that
the presence of a word in the dictionary, whether marked or
unmarked, in no way affects its legal status as a trademark.

The British National Corpus is a collaborative initiative
carried out by Oxford University Press, Longman,
Chambers Harrap, Oxford University Computing Services,
Lancaster University's Unit for Computer Research in the
English language, and the British Library.
The project received funding from the UK Department
of Trade and Industry and was supported by additional
research grants from the British Academy and the British Library.

Typeset in Great Britain by Chambers Harrap Publishers Ltd, Edinburgh
Printed in Singapore by SNP Printing Pte Ltd

Contents

Contributors   iv

Preface   v

Organization of entries   vi

Guide to word types   viii

Dictionary   1

Irregular verbs   341

Contributors

Publishing Manager
Elaine Higgleton

Senior Editor
Penny Hands

Editor
Kay Cullen

Assistant Editor
Fiona McPherson

Illustrator
Jenny Cantwell

Preface

Chambers Key-Word Dictionary is for students who have already begun to learn English. It aims to help them learn more about words they already know, as well as to continue to expand their knowledge of vocabulary. The dictionary lists 3500 key vocabulary items, defining them in clear, full sentences that show how they are used grammatically.

Learners who are in the early stages of learning a language need information presented in a clear, uncomplicated way. But short, one- or two-word definitions do not show how words are used, and coding or abbreviated labels are often passed over, since their meaning is not immediately understood.

By recognizing these needs, *Chambers Key-Word Dictionary* has been able to combine a high level of simplicity with many of the useful features that appear in other Chambers learner dictionaries.

- Definitions are given in clear, full sentences which show how the word is used.
- Eight different parts of speech are used. These are given in full and are explained on page viii.
- Parts of verbs, plural forms and comparative and superlatives are shown.
- Examples, supported by the British National Corpus®, show how the word is commonly used in everyday English.
- Help, in the form of a simple re-spelling system, is given for words with difficult pronunciations.
- Words with the same meaning and words with the opposite meaning are given for many words.
- Notes tell learners about contractions and give extra information about the ways in which words are used.
- Illustrations help with new words and words with more than one meaning.
- Idioms and phrasal verbs are listed and defined at the end of many entries.

We hope that learners will enjoy using this dictionary, not only for looking up words that they come across in their everyday lives, but also as a way of expanding their knowledge of English in general.

Organization of entries

nail *noun*: **nails**

1 A **nail** is a thin piece of metal with a sharp end, which you hit into a surface with a hammer: *He fixed the boards to the floor with long nails.*

definition

Definitions are written in full sentences, to show you how a word is used.

2 A **nail** is one of the hard coverings at the end of your fingers and toes: *She has very long fingernails.*

example

Examples show you how words are used in everyday English.

nail

nail

pictures

Pictures help with new words, and words with more than one meaning.

naked *adjective*

Someone who is **naked** isn't wearing any clothes: *Naked children were playing in the sea.*

different parts of the verb

name *verb*: **names, named, naming, has named**

1 You **name** someone or something when you give them a name: *They named their son Samuel.*

The different **parts of the verb** are always given in the same order. These are:

1. **present** (*he, she, it* form)
2. **past**
3. **continuous**
4. **present perfect**

comparative and superlative forms

narrow *adjective*: **narrower, narrowest**

Something is **narrow** if there is not a large distance from one side of it to the other: *The road is too narrow for that truck.*

the opposite is **wide** or **broad**

Comparative and superlative forms follow the *adjective* marker.

hamburger *noun*: **hamburgers**

A **hamburger** is a flat round piece of chopped beef, which is fried and eaten, often in a bread roll.

note

▶ often shortened to **burger**

Notes in boxes tell you more about how words are used.

lit *verb*

see **light**: *She lit the candles on the dinner table.*

plural form

litre *noun*: **litres**

A **litre** is a unit of measurement for liquids: *Try to drink a litre of water every day.*

word type or part of speech

little *adjective*: meaning 3: **less, least**

1 Something that is **little** is small: *He slept in a little room at the back of the house.*

2 You were **little** when you were a young child: *I was scared of the dark when I was little.*

3 Little also means 'not much': *I had very little money, and couldn't afford the plane fare.*

idiom

▷ **a little**

A **little** means 'a small amount': *'Would you like some more wine?' 'Yes please, just a little.'*

line *verb*: **lines, lined, lining, has lined**

People **line** a road when they stand next to each other to form a row along it.

phrasal verb

▷ **line up**

People **line up** when they form a line or queue; you **line** things **up** when you put them next to each other in a row.

live *verb*: **lives, lived, living, has lived**

1 You **live** in a particular place when you have your home there: *She lives in New York. □ They live in Peel Street. □ Have you lived here all your life?*

2 To **live** is to be alive: *She lived till she was 101. □ These animals don't live for long.*

pronunciation

'liv'

word with opposite meaning

meaning 2: the opposite is **die**

Irregular verb forms have their own sections with examples. They direct you to the main section for that verb.

Plural forms follow the *noun* marker.

The word type or **part of speech** shows you which group the word belongs to. See page viii for an explanation of word types.

Idioms and **phrasal verbs** are given at the ends of sections.

Help is given with **pronunciation**.

Words with the **same meaning**, and words with the **opposite meaning** help you to increase your English vocabulary.

Guide to word types

All words are divided into types. These are called **parts of speech**. In *Chambers Key-Word Dictionary*, the words are divided into eight different parts of speech. These are:

word type	used for...	examples are...
noun	names of people or things	child, work, house, dog
verb	talking about what people are doing and what's happening	go, be, eat, walk, think
adjective	telling you more about people and things	green, big, sweet, soft
adverb	(i) telling you more about how things are done. (ii) telling you more about adjectives.	quickly, well, loudly, very
pronoun	replacing nouns to avoid repetition	I, you, he, she, it, we, they, me, him, her, us, them
preposition	placing before nouns and pronouns to tell you about such things as movement or position	on, at, by, to, in
conjunction	joining two parts of a sentence together	and, but, or
determiner	placing before nouns to show which person or thing you are talking about	a, an, the, many

Aa

a or **an** *determiner*
1 You use **a** or **an** when you talk about one person or thing: *You have four fingers and a thumb on each of your hands.* ❏ *It cost a million dollars.* ❏ *I've lost a sock.* ❏ *Would you call a doctor, please?*
2 You also use **a** or **an** when you want to show that you mean any or every thing of the kind mentioned: *Harry put the papers in an envelope.* ❏ *A dog is a good pet.*
3 People also use **a** or **an** to mean 'for each': *He earns £100 a day.* ❏ *The train was travelling at 180 kilometres an hour.*

▸ **an** is used before words that begin with **a**, **e**, **i**, **o**, **u**: *an angry man* ❏ *an earring* ❏ *an idea* ❏ *an old car* ❏ *an umbrella.*
▸ **an** is also used before words that begin with **h** when the word is pronounced so that you don't hear the **h**: *an hour* ❏ *an honest man.*
▸ **a** is used before words that begin with all other letters: *a dictionary* ❏ *a house* ❏ *a beautiful island* ❏ *a yacht.*
▸ **a** is also used before words beginning with **u** when the **u** is pronounced like **you**: *a uniform* ❏ *a useless object.*

---

ability *noun*: **abilities**
1 Someone has the **ability** to do something when they are able to do it: *She's lost the ability to speak.*
2 Someone has **ability**, or an

ability, when they have enough skill, or are clever enough, to do something: *He has enough ability to pass the exam, but he's too lazy to study.* ❏ *These birds have a natural ability to find their way home again.* ❏ *She has abilities that she doesn't use.*

---

meaning 1: the opposite is
inability

---

able *adjective*: meaning 2: **abler, ablest**
1 You are **able** to do something when you have the knowledge, skill, strength, time or money to do it: *She wasn't able to answer all the questions.* ❏ *Is the baby able to walk yet?* ❏ *I don't think you'll be able to lift that heavy suitcase.* ❏ *He will be able to come home next month.* ❏ *Will we be able to pay the rent?*
2 An **able** person is clever, and good at what they do: *He was the country's ablest lawyer.*

---

meaning 1: the opposite is
unable

---

about *preposition and adverb*
1 A book, film or play is **about** a particular thing when that is its subject; you talk, write or think **about** a subject: *What's the book about?* ❏ *Tell me about your new job.* ❏ *He often thought about his family.*
2 You do something **about** a situation when you do something to deal with it or change it: *It was raining heavily but there was nothing he could do about it.*

3a You move **about** when you move from one place to another; you move things **about** when you move them from one place to another: *He was rushing about, shouting orders.* ❑ *Don't wave that sharp knife about!* **b** People or things are **about** a place when they are in different places in it: *We stood about waiting for something to happen.* ❑ *Papers were scattered about the room.*
4 About is used before a number or measurement to mean 'not exactly, but nearly': *It happened about ten years ago.* ❑ *The boy was about twelve.* ❑ *They have about forty cows.*

meanings 3 and 4: same as **around**

▷ **about to**
You say you were **about to** do something if you were just going to do it; something is **about to** happen if it is going to happen soon: *I was about to get into bed, when the telephone rang.* ❑ *It looks as if it's about to snow.*

above *preposition and adverb*
One thing is **above** another thing when it is higher than that other thing: *Your forehead is above your eyes.* ❑ *He lives in the apartment above ours.* ❑ *She could just see the bird flying high above.* ❑ *They had to work in temperatures of 80 degrees and above.*

the opposite is **below** or **beneath**

abroad *adverb*
Someone is **abroad** when they are in another country; they go **abroad** when they go to another country: *He's returned to Singapore after five months abroad.* ❑ *Have you ever been abroad?*

absent *adjective*
A person or thing is **absent** from a place when they are not there: *Half of our class was absent from school today.*.

the opposite is **present**

accept *verb*: **accepts, accepted, accepting, has accepted**
1 You **accept** something that someone is offering to give you when you take it: *Will you accept payment by cheque?* ❑ *Henri accepted the cup of tea she offered him.*
2 You **accept** an invitation when you say 'yes' to it: *They invited me to the party, and I accepted.*

the opposite is **refuse**

accident *noun*: **accidents**
An **accident** is something that wasn't meant to happen; accidents cause people to be hurt or things to be broken: *He broke his leg in an accident.* ❑ *I didn't mean to break the vase — it was an accident.*

▷ **by accident**
Something happens **by accident** when it happens by chance, or when you weren't expecting it: *She found the house by accident.* ❑ *Peter and I met by accident.*

accurate *adjective*
Something that is **accurate** is true or correct: *Is that an accurate statement?* ❑ *He said that all the measurements were accurate.*

the opposite is **inaccurate**

accuse *verb*: **accuses, accused, accusing, has accused**
Someone **accuses** you of doing something wrong when they say that you have done it: *She accused her neighbour of killing her cow.* ❏ *Both men are accused of murder.*

ache *verb*: **aches, ached, aching, has ached**
Part of your body **aches** when there is a pain there that lasts for a long time: *Our feet were aching after the long walk.* ❏ *My head aches.*

rhymes with **take**

ache is also a noun: *She's been complaining of a stomach ache.*

achieve *verb*: **achieves, achieved, achieving, has achieved**
You **achieve** something that you want to do when you succeed in doing it: *If you don't work hard you won't achieve anything.*

across *preposition and adverb*
1 To go **across** something is to go from one side of it to the other side: *ships sailing across the Atlantic* ❏ *How can we get across the city in ten minutes?* ❏ *He walked across the room towards me.* ❏ *We can walk across the river here — it's quite shallow.*
2 Something is **across** a surface when it stretches from one side of the surface to the other side: *He had a scar across his left cheek.*
3 You say that something is **across** a road, a river or a line, when it is on the other side: *My cousin lives in the house across the street.* ❏ *Their farm is just across the border in Switzerland.*
4 You also use **across** to talk

about how wide something is: *The field is 150 metres across and 200 metres long.*

act *verb*: **acts, acted, acting, has acted**
1 You **act** when you do something for a purpose: *You'll have to act quickly to avoid losing everything.*
2 You **act** in a particular way when you behave in that way: *He was acting in a very strange way.* ❏ *She knew she was acting like a fool, but she couldn't help it.*
3 A person who **acts** is an actor or actress: *He's acting in a Shakespeare play.* ❏ *I think he used to act a bit when he was at school.*

▷ **act on**
You **act on** someone's orders or advice when you do what they order or advise you to do: *He acted on the advice of his bank manager.* ❏ *They were acting on the orders of their government.*

act *noun*: **acts**
1 An **act** is something that is done: *It was an act of great courage.*
2 An **act** is also a performance: *His act is the funniest thing I have ever seen.*

action *noun*: **actions**
1 Action, or an **action**, is something that you do, usually for a reason: *We must take some action if we want to stop the criminals.* ❏ *Those were the actions of a frightened man.*
2 An **action** is also a movement that you make: *The song has both words and actions.*

activity *noun*: **activities**
1 There is **activity** when people

or things are moving about or doing things: *There's lots of activity in the city centre at night.*
2 An **activity** is something, such as a sport or hobby, that you do for pleasure: *Playing tennis is one of his favourite activities.*
3 A person's or group's **activities** are the things that they do regularly: *Their criminal activities were discovered by the police.*

actor *noun*: **actors**
An **actor** is a person, either a man or a woman, who performs in plays or films: *He was one of the greatest actors who ever lived.*

actress *noun*: **actresses**
An **actress** is a woman who performs in plays or films.

add *verb*: **adds, added, adding, has added**
1 You **add** one thing to another when you put the one with the other: *Before you serve the sauce, add some cream.* ❑ *Salt is added to many foods.*
2 You **add** when you find out the total that two or more numbers make when they are put together: *Some children know how to add before they go to school.* ❑ *If you add one half and three quarters, what answer do you get?*

---

meaning 2: the opposite is **subtract**

▷ **add up**
You **add up** two or more numbers when you put them together to find the total that they make: *She added up the cost of all the new furniture.* ❑ *You'll need a calculator to add all those figures up.*

addition *noun*
Addition is the part of arithmetic in which two or more numbers are put together to find what the total is.

---

the opposite is **subtraction**

---

address *noun*: **addresses**
Your **address** is the place where you live, or where your business is. When you give your address you usually include the number and name of the street, followed by the town or city and the area or country: *Is that your business address or your home address?* ❑ *My aunt's address is 14 Maryland Drive, Sydney, Australia.* ❑ *Do you have an address in London?*

admire *verb*: **admires, admired, admiring, has admired**
1 You **admire** something when you look at it with great pleasure, or when you say that you like it very much: *I was just admiring the beautiful flowers in your garden.*
2 You **admire** someone when you like them very much or respect what they have done: *He admired her courage.*

admit *verb*: **admits, admitted, admitting, has admitted**
1 A person **admits** that they have done something bad or wrong when they say that they have done it: *The boy admitted that he had stolen fruit from the old man's garden.*
2 You **are admitted** to a public place when you enter it: *He was admitted to hospital last night.*

adult *noun*: **adults**
An **adult** is a grown-up person: *This is a film for both adults and children.*

the opposite is **child**

advertise *verb*: **advertises, advertised, advertising, has advertised**
1 You **advertise** when you put a notice in a public place, telling people that you need something, or that you have something you want to sell: *That company is advertising for salesmen.* ❑ *Houses are advertised for sale in this newspaper.*
2 Businesses **advertise** their products when they try to get the public to buy them using advertisements: *They increased their sales by advertising on television.*

advertisement *noun*: **advertisements**
1 An **advertisement** is a notice that you put in a newspaper telling people that you need something or have something to sell: *The best way to sell your old computer is to put an advertisement in the paper.*
2 An **advertisement** is also a big notice in a public place, or a short film on television, that tries to get you to buy a particular product: *Did you see the advertisement for that new car on television?*

> ▸ **advertisement** is often shortened to **ad** or **advert**: *He put an ad in this week's Herald.* ❑ *There are too many adverts on television.*

advice *noun*
When someone gives you **advice** they give you helpful ideas about what you should do; you take their **advice** when you do what

they suggest: *Can you give me any advice about careers?* ❑ *Take my advice and wear a warm coat.*

advise *verb*: **advises, advised, advising, has advised**
Someone **advises** you when they give you advice; they **advise** you to do something when they say they think you should do it: *No-one could advise him on the best way to solve the problem.* ❑ *My father advised me to save my money.*

aeroplane *noun*: **aeroplanes**
An **aeroplane** is a vehicle with wings, that flies through the air. It carries passengers or goods.

also called a **plane**

affect *verb*: **affects, affected, affecting, has affected**
1 One thing **affects** another when it causes something to happen to that other thing: *The decision will affect the whole village.* ❑ *This exam will affect your whole future.*
2 A disease **affects** you when it makes you ill, or damages part of your body: *The disease often affects patients' sight.*

meaning 1: same as **influence**

> ▸ One thing **affects** another thing. The change it makes on that other thing is its **effect**.

afford *verb*
You can **afford** something when you have enough money to buy it: *We can't afford to go on holiday this year.* ❑ *He's quite rich, so he can afford an expensive car.*

afraid *adjective*
You are **afraid** when you are not happy because you think that

something bad or dangerous could happen to you: *She's too afraid to go out at night.* ❑ *He's afraid of the dark.*

afraid

after *preposition, adverb and conjunction*
1a One thing happens **after** another thing when it happens at a later time: *I've got a lot of things to do after breakfast.* ❑ *Their plane arrived after midnight.* ❑ *He went to hospital but died soon after.* ❑ *After he left school, he travelled round the world.* **b** One thing comes **after** another if it follows the other thing: *In the alphabet, M comes after L.*
2 After also means 'behind': *Close the door after you.* ❑ *One after the other, people left the room.*
3 You go **after** someone or something when you try to catch up with them: *The dog ran after the bus.* ❑ *If you go after him now, you might catch him.*

meaning 1: the opposite is **before**

afternoon *noun*: **afternoons**
Afternoon is the part of the day between midday and evening: *Are you working this afternoon?* ❑ *I'll meet you tomorrow afternoon.* ❑ *Harry spends his afternoons in the garden.*

afterwards *adverb*
You do something **afterwards**

when you do it later, or after something else: *They went to the theatre, and afterwards had a meal in a restaurant.* ❑ *I won't eat the chocolates now — I'll have them afterwards.*

again *adverb*
Something that happens **again** happens for a second time: *Could you show me again please?* ❑ *He phoned on Monday and again on Tuesday.* ❑ *He's done it wrong again.*

▷ **again and again**
Something that happens **again and again** happens many times: *She shouted his name again and again.*

against *preposition and adverb*
1 Something is **against** another thing when it is touching it: *He was leaning against the wall.* ❑ *Don't put anything against the heater.*
2 You are **against** something when you don't agree with it: *I wanted to go to art college but my parents were against it.*
3 You play **against** someone in a game or competition when you try to beat them: *In the football final, Manchester United will play against Barcelona.*

age *noun*: **ages**
Your **age** is the number of years you have lived: *What age are you?* ❑ *He died at the age of fifty.* ❑ *People of all ages enjoy playing tennis.*

ago *adverb*
Something that happened a certain amount of time **ago** happened at that time in the past: *Ten years ago, very few people had computers in their*

homes. ❏ *How long ago did this happen?*

agree *verb*: **agrees, agreed, agreeing, has agreed**
1 You **agree** with someone when you think the same as they do: *He said he didn't like the colour, and I agreed with him.* ❏ *She always agrees with everything he says.*
2 You **agree** to something when you say 'yes' to it: *It was the wrong thing to do and we were stupid to agree to it.*
3 You **agree** to do something when you say that you will do it: *They agreed to meet the next day.*

meaning 1: the opposite is **disagree**

agreement *noun*: **agreements**
An **agreement** is something that has been agreed: *We made an agreement to buy their products.*

ahead *adverb*
Something is **ahead** when it is in front, in position or in time: *He was able to stay ahead of the other runners.* ❏ *You have six months of hard work ahead of you.*

the opposite is **behind**

aim *verb*: **aims, aimed, aiming, has aimed**
1 You **aim** a weapon, such as a gun, when you point it at someone or something: *The robber aimed his gun at the policeman's head.* ❏ *He aimed at the circle on the board but missed.*
2 You **aim** to do something when you try to achieve it: *He aims to finish the work this afternoon.* ❏ *If you're aiming to make a profit, you'll have to ask for more money.*

air *noun*
1 The **air** is what we breathe; it is all around us: *He came to the surface of the water for air.* ❏ *The air was full of smoke.*
2 Something that is up in the **air** is in the space above you, or in the sky: *The balloons went up, high into the air.*

▷ **by air**
You travel **by air** when you travel in an aeroplane or helicopter.

aircraft *noun*: **aircraft**
An **aircraft** is any vehicle that flies, such as an aeroplane or helicopter: *passenger aircraft.*

airline *noun*: **airlines**
An **airline** is a business that uses aeroplanes to carry people and goods from place to place: *Which airline are you using to go to Japan?*

airliner *noun*: **airliners**
An **airliner** is a large aeroplane for carrying passengers: *The airliner had more than 300 passengers on its first flight.*

airport *noun*: **airports**
An **airport** is a place where aircraft land and take off from: *London's largest airport is called 'Heathrow'.*

alarm *noun*: **alarms**
1 An **alarm** is something that warns people of danger: *The fire alarm went off and everyone had to leave the building.* ❏ *Do you have a burglar alarm in your house?*
2 Alarm is a frightened or anxious feeling: *She jumped back in alarm when the door opened suddenly.*

alarm *verb*: **alarms, alarmed, alarming, has alarmed**

Something **alarms** you when it frightens you or makes you feel anxious: *The strange noises in the forest alarmed him.*

alarm clock *noun*: **alarm clocks**
An **alarm clock** is a clock with an alarm that makes a loud noise to wake you up.

album *noun*: **albums**
1 An **album** is a book in which you put photographs or stamps that you have collected: *She has a special album for her wedding photographs.*
2 An **album** is also a collection of music on a record, cassette or CD: *The group's new album comes out in the spring.*

alike *adjective and adverb*
1 People or things that are **alike** behave in the same way, or look like each other: *You and your sister are very alike.* ❑ *They looked so alike, you never knew which one you were talking to.*
2 Alike also means 'in the same way': *We think alike.* ❑ *The boys were dressed alike, in shorts and T-shirts.*

---

meaning 1: same as **similar**

---

alive *adjective*
A person, animal or plant that is **alive** is living, not dead: *He was still alive when the ambulance arrived.* ❑ *Are these plants alive or dead?*

---

the opposite is **dead**

▸The adjective **alive** always comes after the noun. Before a noun, you use **live**: *We use these lorries to carry live animals to the market.*

all *determiner, pronoun and adverb*
1 All of something is the whole of it: *Have you spent all the money I gave you?* ❑ *We waited all day for news.* ❑ *The snow has all gone.* ❑ *This is all very interesting.*
2 All also means 'every one': *We were all very excited.* ❑ *I put all your letters on your desk.* ❑ *Have you eaten all the biscuits?* ❑ *I didn't eat them all.*
3 You also use **all** to mean 'completely': *She was all alone on the island.* ❑ *He tried his best, but it went all wrong.*

▷ **all over**
1 All over means 'in every part' or 'in every place': *There was water all over the floor.* ❑ *The company has offices all over the world.*
2 Something is **all over** when it is completely finished: *When this is all over, you'll be able to have a holiday.*

▷ **all right**
1a You say **all right** to mean 'yes' when you are agreeing with something someone else has said: *'I'll see you later.' 'All right.'*
b You also say '**all right?**' to check that the person you are speaking to agrees with you: *I'll meet you at four o'clock. All right?*
2 You are **all right** when you are not hurt, or when you are well: *He fell down the steps, but he was all right.* ❑ *You look unhappy. Is everything all right?*

▸ write **all right**, not **alright**

▷ **all that**
A situation that is not **all that**

good or bad is not very good or bad: *The illness wasn't all that serious.* ❑ *He isn't all that keen on sports.*

allow *verb*: **allows, allowed, allowing, has allowed**
You **allow** someone to do something when you give them permission to do it; you **allow** something to happen when you let it happen: *They don't allow us to go out after nine o'clock.* ❑ *Do you allow animals in your hotel?* ❑ *Smoking is not allowed in this restaurant.*

same as **permit**

almost *adverb*
Almost means 'nearly': *He's almost eleven years old.* ❑ *We almost won.* ❑ *'Have you finished reading that book yet?' 'Almost.'*

alone *adjective and adverb*
You are **alone** when no-one else is with you; you do something **alone** when you do it without other people: *His wife had died and he was alone.* ❑ *She lived alone.* ❑ *She was alone when her car broke down.* ❑ *Please leave me alone.*

along *preposition and adverb*
1 People or things move **along** something, such as a road, when they travel from one end of it towards the other end: *They were walking along the river bank.*
2 You go **along** in a particular way when you move in that way: *He was running along next to the car.* ❑ *Hurry along now, or you'll be late.*
3 Things are **along** something when they form a line beside or on it: *She planted flowers along*

the path.
4 Something is **along** a road or other surface when it is in a position beside it or on it: *The cinema is somewhere along this street.* ❑ *Is the bathroom along this corridor?*
5 Someone comes **along** when they come with you; you take someone or something **along** when you take them with you: *We're going to a party tomorrow. Would you like to come along?* ❑ *Can I bring my friend along?* ❑ *You'll have to wait, so take a magazine along.*

aloud *adverb*
You say something **aloud** when you say it loudly enough for people to hear: *Each of the children had to read aloud in front of the class.*

alphabet *noun*: **alphabets**
The **alphabet** of a language is the set of letters it uses for writing, arranged in a particular order: *Which letter comes after R in the alphabet?* ❑ *Do you know the Greek alphabet?*

❛**al**-fa-bet❜

already *adverb*
1 Something that has happened **already** has happened before now: *Jane has seen this photograph already.* ❑ *We've already learnt the names of the months.*
2 You also use **already** to mean 'so soon' to show that you are surprised: *Have you finished that book already?* ❑ *I can't believe it's November already!*

also *adverb*
Also means 'too' or 'as well': *He sings, and he also plays the piano.*

❏ *It's difficult to understand, and it's also very long.*

although *conjunction*
Although means 'even when' or 'even though': *Although she didn't agree, she said nothing.* ❏ *I tried to talk to them, although my French is very bad.*

altogether *adverb*
1 Altogether means 'completely': *The old village has disappeared altogether.* ❏ *She stopped working altogether when the second child was born.*
2 Altogether also means 'in total': *We've invited twelve people altogether.* ❏ *How much did the holiday cost altogether?*

always *adverb*
1 You **always** do something when you do it regularly: *We always have a meal with friends at the weekend.* ❏ *He always arrives home at 6 o'clock.*
2 Always means 'at all times': *He's always cheerful.* ❏ *Why is it always so cold in here?*
3 Always also means 'again and again': *She's always doing silly things like that.*

am *verb*
Am is the form of the verb **be** that is used with **I**: *I am a policeman.* ❏ *I am feeling hot.* ❏ *Am I right?*

▶You can shorten **I am** to **I'm**.
▶ In questions, you can turn **am not** into **aren't**: *I'm right aren't I?*
---

amaze *verb*: **amazes, amazed, amazing, has amazed**
Something **amazes** you when it surprises you very much: *Their stupid behaviour amazed me.*

amazing *adjective*
You say something is **amazing** when you think it is wonderful or very surprising: *That was an amazing show.* ❏ *The pictures from the spacecraft were amazing.* ❏ *It's amazing how much they've learnt.*

ambulance *noun*: **ambulances**
An **ambulance** is a vehicle that is used to take sick and injured people to hospital: *Call an ambulance! This man's very ill.*

'amb-you-lans**'**

among or **amongst** *preposition*
1 Among or **amongst** mean 'in the middle of' or 'surrounded by': *Can you see the little house among the trees?* ❏ *You'll find the letter amongst the papers on my desk.*
2 You divide something **among** or **amongst** a number of people when you give some of it to each of them: *The money was divided among his children.*
3 Something is found **among** or **amongst** a particular group when people in that group are affected by it: *Bad teeth are common among children who eat a lot of sweets.*

amount *noun*: **amounts**
An **amount** of something is how much there is of it: *He doesn't earn a large amount of money.* ❏ *There's only a small amount of milk left.*

same as **quantity**

an *determiner*
see **a**: *an electric light* ❏ *You can have an apple or an orange.*

and *conjunction*
1 And is used to join words or

parts of a sentence together:
*Would you like some bread and
butter?* ❑ *We got out of bed and
got dressed.* ❑ *Come inside and
close the door.* ❑ *They have two
children, a girl and a boy.*
2 And also means 'added to': *Two
and six is eight.*

anger *noun*
Anger is the strong feeling you
have when something has
annoyed you very much: *You
must try to control your anger.*

angry *adjective*: **angrier, angriest**
You are **angry** when you feel
anger: *He was so angry he threw
the book on the floor.* ❑ *If you say
that, she'll just get angrier.*

angry

animal *noun*: **animals**
An **animal** is any living creature
that is not a human being or a
plant: *I think it's cruel to keep wild
animals in a zoo.* ❑ *What kind of
animal is a giraffe?* ❑ *cows, sheep
and other farm animals.*

ankle *noun*: **ankles**
Your **ankles** are the two parts of
your body where your feet join
your legs: *Bill fell and broke his
ankle.* ❑ *She wore a long skirt that
covered her ankles.*

annoy *verb*: **annoys, annoyed,
annoying, has annoyed**
Someone or something **annoys**
you when they make you angry:
*It annoys me when people are
late.* ❑ *The dog was annoying me;
it was making so much noise.*

annoyed *adjective*
You are **annoyed** when you are
rather angry: *She's annoyed
because he was late for work
again.*

another *determiner and pronoun*
1 Another person or thing is a
different one: *She's got a job in
another company.* ❑ *I didn't like
the book, so I started reading
another.*
2 Another person or thing is
one more: *Would you make
another copy of this letter, please?*
❑ *'That cake was delicious.' 'Would
you like another?'*

answer *verb*: **answers,
answered, answering, has
answered**
1 You **answer** a question when
you say something to the person
who asked it: *I asked Helen where
she was going but she didn't
answer.* ❑ *Could you answer a few
questions for me, please?*
2 You **answer** a ringing
telephone when you lift it up and
talk to the person who has called:
*Could you answer the phone
please?*
3 You **answer** a letter when you
write a letter back to someone
who has written to you: *She
didn't answer the last letter I wrote
to her.*

'an-ser **'**

answer *noun*: **answers**
1 Your **answer** is what you say or
write to someone who has asked
you a question, or who has told
you something, or who has
written you a letter: *He wants to
know why you won't play with
him, and I think you should give
him an answer.* ❑ *The police*

*weren't satisfied with the answers
he gave.* ❑ *Have you had an
answer to your letter yet?*
2 An **answer** is what you write
or say to a question in a test or
puzzle: *That's the wrong answer.*
❑ *He knew all the right answers.*
❑ *Write your answers down on a
sheet of paper.* ❑ *The answers to
the puzzle are on page 10.*

meaning 1: same as **reply**
the opposite is **question**

ant *noun*: **ants**
Ants are small insects that live
together in very large groups.

ants

anxious *adjective*
When you are **anxious** you feel
worried or nervous about
something: *She's feeling a little
anxious about the operation.* ❑ *Try
not to be too anxious about the
exam.*

'ang-shus **'**

any *determiner and pronoun*
1 Any means 'one' or 'some': *Is
there any tea left in the teapot?* ❑
*You said you didn't want birthday
presents so we didn't buy you any.*
2 Any also means 'it doesn't
matter which': *You can have any
of those books you want.* ❑ *'Which
pen would you like?' 'Any one will
do'.*
3 Any also means 'every': *You'll be
able to find this dictionary in any
library.*

▷ **any more**
1 Something that does not

happen any more no longer
happens: *He said he didn't love
her any more.*
2 Something that will not happen
any more will not happen ever
again: *If Annie leaves the country,
we won't be able to visit her any
more.*

anybody or **anyone** *pronoun*
You use **anybody** or **anyone** to
talk about any person, rather
than one person in particular:
Has anybody found my scarf?
❑ *Anyone can learn to drive, as
long as they are old enough.*

anything *pronoun*
1 You can use **anything** to talk
about any or every thing: *He said
he would do anything they wanted
him to do.* ❑ *He was ready for
anything that might happen.* ❑ *I'll
take what you can give me.
Anything's better than nothing.*
2 You can also use **anything**
instead of 'something' in
questions, with a negative, and
after words like 'if' and 'hardly': *Is
anything going to happen?* ❑ *No, I
don't think anything will happen
now.* ❑ *If anything happens, phone
me.* ❑ *You look worried. Is
anything wrong?* ❑ *There's hardly
anything left in the food cupboard.*

▷ **anything like**
You ask if a person or thing is
anything like another, when
you want to know if they are like
that other person or thing in
some way: *She isn't anything like
her sister.* ❑ *Is New York anything
like Sydney?*

anyway *adverb*
1 Anyway is used to give another
reason for something you have
just said: *He didn't like the suit;*

anyway, it was too expensive.
2 You do something **anyway** when you do it even though you shouldn't: *She knew it was very dangerous, but she did it anyway.* ❑ *They told him not to go, but he went anyway.*
3 You also use **anyway** to show that you want to change the subject of a conversation: *Anyway, let's not talk about it any more.*

> ▸ Note that the two words **any way** mean 'any method or way', as in: *Do it any way you want.* ❑ *Is there any way we can help?*

anywhere *adverb*
1 Anywhere is used instead of 'somewhere' in questions, or with a negative, and before words like 'if' and 'hardly': *Can we take you anywhere?* ❑ *I don't have anywhere to go.* ❑ *This type of forest is found hardly anywhere any more.*
2 Anywhere also means 'it doesn't matter where': *Can we sit anywhere or will you show us where to sit?*

apart *adverb*
1 People or things are **apart** when they are not together, or are separated from each other: *The couple have been living apart for two years now.* ❑ *We had to keep the two dogs apart to stop them fighting.*
2 Things are a certain distance **apart** when that is the distance between them: *Stand with your feet about 30 centimetres apart.*
3 Something comes **apart** when it separates into pieces: *The lions were pulling the body of the deer*

apart. ❑ *Do these two pieces come apart?*

▷ **apart from**
Apart from means 'except for' or 'not including': *There was no-one on the beach apart from a few fishermen.* ❑ *There's the extra cost of travelling, quite apart from the other costs of living so far from the city.*

apartment *noun*: **apartments**
An **apartment** is a set of rooms for living in, usually on one floor of a large building.

same as **flat**

apologize *verb*: **apologizes, apologized, apologizing, has apologized**
You **apologize** when you say sorry to someone for something you have said or done: *I didn't mean to hurt your feelings, and I apologize.* ❑ *I apologize for not writing to you earlier.*

apology *noun*: **apologies**
You make an **apology** when you say sorry for something you have said or done: *Mr Wong sends his apologies for not being able to come to the meeting.*

appear *verb*: **appears, appeared, appearing, has appeared**
1 Something **appears** when it becomes visible, or it arrives: *The moon suddenly appeared from behind a cloud.* ❑ *He hasn't appeared yet, and we don't know why he's late.*
2 Something **appears** in a certain way when that is how it seems: *There appears to be a mistake here.* ❑ *He appeared to be no different from before.*

appearance *noun*
Someone's or something's
appearance is what they look
like or how they seem: *His untidy
appearance didn't help when he
tried to get a job.* ❑ *She had the
appearance of someone who was
used to hard work.*

appetite *noun*: **appetites**
A person's **appetite** is their wish
for food: *You haven't eaten much.
Don't you have any appetite?*
❑ *The children all have very
healthy appetites.*

apple *noun*: **apples**
An **apple** is a round fruit with a
red, yellow or green skin and
sweet white flesh. Apples grow on
trees.

apply *verb*: **applies, applied,
applying, has applied**
You **apply** for something, such
as a job, when you formally ask
someone to consider you for it:
*Elizabeth has applied for several
jobs already.* ❑ *Are you going to
apply for a place on that course?*
2 Something **applies** to you
when it affects you: *This new rule
doesn't apply to people under the
age of eighteen.*

April *noun*
April is the fourth month of the
year: *Jane's birthday is on April
the tenth.* ❑ *He's going to Japan
next April.*

are *verb*
Are is the form of the verb **be**
used with **you**, **we** and **they**, and
when you talk about two or more
people or things: *You are a very
kind person.* ❑ *We are friends.*
❑ *They are all living in tents.* ❑ *Are
you cold?* ❑ *The houses are all
painted white.* ❑ *These people are*

from Scotland. ❑ *His parents are
both still alive.*

▸You can shorten **you are** to
you're, **we are** to **we're** and
they are to **they're**.

area *noun*: **areas**
1 The **area** of a flat surface is
how big it is: *What's the area of a
football pitch?*
2 An **area** is a place that forms
part of a town or a country: *They
live in a wealthy area of the city.*
❑ *What's this area called?* ❑ *The
dust was spread over a large area.*

aren't *verb*
1 Aren't is short for **are not**:
Those aren't the shoes I wanted.
❑ *Aren't you coming with us?*
2 In questions, **aren't** can also be
used as a short form of **am not**:
Aren't I silly! ❑ *I'm getting thinner,
aren't I?*

argue *verb*: **argues, argued,
arguing, has argued**
You **argue** with someone when
you fight with them using words;
two people who disagree with
each other **argue** when they fight
using words: *I argued with him
but I couldn't make him change his
mind.* ❑ *They're always arguing.*

argument *noun*: **arguments**
You have an **argument** with
someone when you fight with
them using words: *They don't
seem to like each other very
much. They're always having
arguments.*

arithmetic *noun*
Arithmetic is the part of
mathematics that has to do with
adding, subtracting, multiplying
and dividing numbers: *My son is
very good at arithmetic.*

arm *noun*: **arms**
1 Your **arms** are the two parts of your body that are attached to your body at your shoulders. Your hands are at the end of your arms: *Lift your arms above your head.* ❑ *He has broken his arm.*

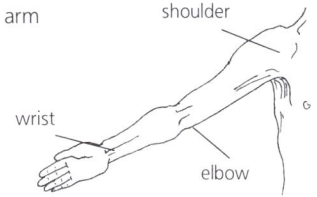

arm shoulder
wrist
elbow

2 A chair with **arms** has two parts on which you can rest your arms: *Don't sit on the arm of the chair — you might break it.* [see picture at **chair**]

armchair *noun*: **armchairs**
An **armchair** is a comfortable chair with arms: *The cat likes to sleep on the armchair nearest the fire.* [see picture at **chair**]

army *noun*: **armies**
An **army** is a large group of soldiers whose job it is to protect or fight for their country: *the Indian army* ❑ *He wants to join the army.* ❑ *The two armies met near Calais.*

around *adverb and preposition*
1 People or things are **around** you when they are on all sides of you: *They gathered around the woman, asking questions.* ❑ *There were trees planted around the lake.*
2 People or things are **around** an area when they are in several places there; they move **around** somewhere when they move from

one place to another: *Do you think there are any wild animals around here?* ❑ *Please don't leave your clothes lying around like that.* ❑ *We've been travelling around the country for the last two weeks.*
3 You move something **around** when you move it in different directions: *He was pushing the food around his plate with his fork.*
4 You turn **around** when you turn to face in the opposite direction: *The teacher told the boy to turn around and face the front.*
5 Something is **around** a particular amount when it is not exactly, but nearly, that amount: *A new car will cost around $20000.*

same as **about**

arrange *verb*: **arranges, arranged, arranging, has arranged**
1 You **arrange** things when you put them in order or set them out in a certain way: *The chairs were arranged in a circle.* ❑ *She arranged the flowers in a large glass vase.*
2 You **arrange** something when you make plans for it: *The school is arranging a trip to France.* ❑ *Let's arrange a time to meet next week.*

meaning 2: same as **organize**

arrangement *noun*: **arrangements**
1 Arrangement is the arranging of something or putting it in order: *The arrangement of the furniture took longer than we thought.*
2 Arrangements are plans, or

the things you do to prepare for something: *Who will be making the travel arrangements?* ❑ *They made an arrangement to meet the following week.*

arrest *verb*: **arrests, arrested, arresting, has arrested**
The police **arrest** someone when they stop them and take them to the police station, because they believe that the person has done something wrong: *The police came to his house to arrest him.* ❑ *The three men were arrested for burglary.*

arrive *verb*: **arrives, arrived, arriving, has arrived**
You **arrive** when you reach the place you have been travelling to: *When does the next train arrive at this station?* ❑ *They arrived just before midday.* ❑ *They will probably arrive home before us.*

same as **reach**
the opposite is **depart**

arrow *noun*: **arrows**
1 An **arrow** is a stick with a sharp point at one end; arrows are shot from a bow: *The boys played with toy bows and arrows.*
2 An **arrow** is also a sign shaped like the pointed end of an arrow, that shows direction: *You have to follow the arrows until you reach a big green door.*

arrows

art *noun*
Art is drawing and painting: *Are you doing art at school this year?* ❑ *My cousin is very good at art.*

artist *noun*: **artists**
An **artist** is a person who draws and paints pictures: *Her favourite artist is Rembrandt.* ❑ *He's a very good artist and can draw almost anything.*

as *preposition and conjunction*
1 As means 'when', or 'during the time that': *The telephone rang just as I was going out.* ❑ *As time passed, they became more friendly.* ❑ *As a child, he was always getting into trouble.*
2 As also means 'in the same way': *They were dressed as policemen.*
3 You can use **as** to mean 'for that reason' or 'since': *As I'm driving past your house, why don't I take you in the car?*
4a You work **as** something when that is the job you do: *Toby was working as a cook during the holidays.* **b** A thing is used **as** something when that is what it is used for: *You could use this piece of wood as a shelf.*
5 You also use **as** when you are comparing two things: *Her hands were as cold as ice.* ❑ *The surface of the lake was as smooth as glass.*

ashamed *adjective*
1 You feel **ashamed** when you feel sorry because you have done something wrong: *I don't know why I said that. I feel so ashamed.*
2 You are **ashamed** of something about yourself when you are worried that people will think you are not a good person: *Stephen was ashamed of his dirty old clothes.*

▸You are **ashamed** when you feel **shame**.

aside *adverb*
1 You move **aside** when you move to one side to allow someone else to pass you: *He stepped aside to let us pass.*
2 You move something **aside** when you put it beside you: *She put her newspaper aside and joined in the conversation.*

ask *verb*: **asks, asked, asking, has asked**
1 You **ask** something when you put a question to someone: *I don't know if we can have lunch now. I'll ask.* □ *He asked me the way to the station.* □ *'When's your birthday?' she asked.*
2 You **ask** for something when you say that you want it: *Sally asked me for a piece of paper.*

asleep *adjective*
You are **asleep** when you are sleeping: *The children are all asleep in bed.* □ *He was so tired that he fell asleep at his desk.*

the opposite is **awake**

assist *verb*
Someone **assists** another person when they help them: *The patient will need someone to assist him when he is getting out of bed.* □ *One of the young doctors will be assisting during the operation.*

assistant *noun*: **assistants**
An **assistant** is a person who helps people, or one person in particular: *The shop assistant asked me if he could help me.* □ *He has an assistant who helps him in the office.*

astronaut *noun*: **astronauts**
An **astronaut** is a person who is trained to travel in spacecraft: *How many astronauts have landed on the moon?*

at *preposition*
1 You use **at** before a noun that refers to a place: *We are living at my aunt's house.* □ *I was at work when I heard the news.* □ *Is that someone at the door?*
2 You use **at** before an expression of time: *We usually have dinner at 8 o'clock.* □ *I'll pay you at the end of the month.* □ *At holiday time the town's streets become very busy*
3 You also use **at** to show direction: *The tiger was looking straight at me.* □ *Is that man waving at us?*
4 You talk about someone being good or bad **at** something to show that they do it well or badly: *Georgie is excellent at making speeches.*

▷ **at all**
You use **at all** with 'not' to make 'not' seem stronger; 'not **at all**' means 'not at any time', 'not in any way', or 'not any': *He's not at all clever.* □ *It wasn't wet at all when we were on holiday.* □ *He didn't have any food at all.*

ate *verb*
see **eat**: *We ate a whole chicken each.*

athlete *noun*: **athletes**
An **athlete** is a person who takes part in any of the sports involving running, jumping and throwing: *an Olympic athlete.*

athletics *noun*
Athletics is the part of sport that includes running, jumping and throwing: *an athletics competition.*

attach *verb*: **attaches, attached, attaching, has attached**
1 You **attach** one thing to another when you fix it to that other thing: *Dad attached a hook to my fishing line.*
2 Two things **are attached** when they are joined together: *The two parts of the shell are attached here.*

attack *verb*: **attacks, attacked, attacking, has attacked**
1 Someone **attacks** you when they suddenly come towards you and try to hurt you: *He was attacked by a large dog.*
2 A place **is attacked** by an enemy in a war when the enemy tries to destroy it: *The enemy attacked the town at night.*

attack *noun*: **attacks**
1 An **attack** is a violent attempt to hurt someone or to damage something: *The attack left the city in ruins.* ❑ *There were several attacks of this kind last year.*
2 An **attack** of an illness is a period of suffering from that illness: *She took a long time to recover from the last attack of flu.* ❑ *We think he has had a heart attack.*

attempt *verb*: **attempts, attempted, attempting, has attempted**
You **attempt** to do something when you try to do it: *He's attempting to break the world record.*

attempt *noun*: **attempts**
An **attempt** is a try: *After three attempts to pass my driving test, I gave up.*

attend *verb*: **attends, attended, attending, has attended**
You **attend** something when you go there, and are present there: *She doesn't attend school regularly.* ❑ *My parents are attending a dinner to celebrate New Year.*

attention *noun*
1 You pay **attention** when you carefully listen to, or watch what is happening: *He wasn't paying attention to the traffic, so he didn't see the lorry.*
2 Someone or something attracts your **attention** when they cause you to look in their direction: *He was waving his arms, trying to attract our attention.*

attract *verb*: **attracts, attracted, attracting, has attracted**
Something **attracts** things when it causes those things to come towards it: *The flower's scent attracts insects.* ❑ *I was attracted to the place because it was near the sea.*

attractive *adjective*
An **attractive** person or thing is pleasant to look at: *They had a very attractive view from their hotel window.* ❑ *She's an attractive girl, with long black hair.*

audience *noun*: **audiences**
An **audience** is a group of people watching a play, a film or a television programme, or listening to a speech, a concert or radio programme: *His TV show had one of the largest audiences ever.*

August *noun*
August is the eighth month of the year, between July and September: *His little brother was born last August.* ❑ *We're having two weeks' holiday in August.*

aunt *noun*: **aunts**
Your **aunt** is the sister of one of your parents, or the wife of your uncle: *This is a picture of my aunt, and those are my cousins.*

rhymes with **plant**

author *noun*: **authors**
The **author** of a book or play is the person who has written it: *Who is your favourite author?*

autumn *noun*
Autumn is the season of the year between summer and winter: *The weather starts to get a little colder in autumn.* ❏ *Autumn is called 'fall' in the United States.*

available *adjective*
Something is **available** when it is there for you to take, use or buy: *Are there any seats available for tonight's concert?* ❏ *I'm sorry, there are no available seats.*

average *noun*: **averages**
An **average** is a number you get when you add several quantities together, and divide the result by the number of quantities: *Find the average of 10, 15, and 50.* ❏ *This figure is an average of the amounts paid in each of the last three years.*

average *adjective*
An **average** person is not better or worse, or bigger or smaller, than most others: *The average person earns about $20 dollars an hour.* ❏ *He's an average pupil.*

avoid *verb*: **avoids, avoided, avoiding, has avoided**
You **avoid** someone or something when you keep away from them: *I think he's avoiding me because I shouted at him.* ❏ *She had to drive on the* pavement to avoid the water on the road. ❏ *Try to avoid eating too many sweets.*

awake *adjective*
You are **awake** when you are not sleeping: *He often stays awake all night.* ❏ *Why aren't the children awake yet?*

the opposite is **asleep**

away *adverb*
1 Someone is **away** from a place when they are not there: *He'll be away from home for two months.*
2 A person or thing is a particular distance **away** when that is how far they are from you: *He was standing about three metres away from the edge.* ❏ *How far away is the nearest town?*
3a You go **away** when you leave: *The dog wouldn't go away.* ❏ *The boys walked away, laughing.* **b** You look or turn **away** from someone or something when you look or turn in another direction: *He looked away for a moment and didn't see her smile.*
4 Something that has been present goes **away** when it disappears: *The doctor said the pain would go away in a few days.* ❏ *My headache's gone away.*

awful *adjective*
When you say that something is **awful** you mean it is very bad: *What awful weather this is!* ❏ *She has an awful cold.* ❏ *The food was awful.*

same as **terrible**

axe *noun*: **axes**
An **axe** is a heavy tool with a square metal blade that is used for cutting wood.

Bb

baby *noun*: **babies**
1 A **baby** is a very young child: *Babies need a lot of sleep.*
2 A **baby** animal is a very young animal: *The baby giraffe was only about one metre tall.*

back *noun and adjective*: **backs**
1a Your **back** is the part of you that is behind you when you walk forward: *Jenny felt the sun on her back.* **b** An animal's **back** is the part of it which is on top when it stands: *Bob put the saddle on the horse's back.*
2 The **back** of something is also the side that is opposite to, or furthest away from, the front: *The shop had a little bar at the back where people could sit.* ❏ *The price is on the back of the book.*
3 Back describes things that are on the opposite side to the front: *She heard him go through the kitchen and leave by the back door.*

the opposite is **front**

back *adverb*
1a You go **back** to a place when you go to the same place again: *I went back to the shop.* **b** You give something **back** when you give it to the person who first gave it to you: *She gave me my bicycle back.*
2 You lie **back**, or sit **back**, when you lie or sit with your back against something: *He lay back in the big chair and closed his eyes.*

background *noun*
The **background** in a picture is the part of it that is behind the main objects in it: *We had a view of the lake with the hills in the background.*

backwards *adverb*
1 You move **backwards** when you move with your back facing in the direction you are going: *He fell backwards down the stairs.*
2 You do something **backwards** when you do it in the opposite way to the usual way: *Can you say the alphabet backwards?*

▷ **backwards and forwards**
A person or thing goes **backwards and forwards** when they move in one direction and then in the opposite direction: *The dog ran backwards and forwards behind the fence, barking.*

bacon *noun*
Meat from a pig that has had salt added to it so that it lasts longer is called **bacon**: *For breakfast, we had fresh grapefruit, bacon and eggs, hot coffee and rolls.*

bad *adjective*: **worst, worst**
1 Bad behaviour is wrong or naughty behaviour: *That was a very bad thing to do.* ❏ *His behaviour in class is not as bad as some of the other boys.*
2 Naughty or disobedient children or animals are often described as **bad**: *Don't do that, you bad dog!*
3 You can also describe someone who is wicked or evil as **bad**: *Quilp was a very bad man.* ❏ *She's not really a bad person.*
4 You are **bad** at something

when you cannot do it well: *I'm really bad at remembering peoples' names.* ❑ *His French is pretty bad, but he's good at English.*

5 Something **bad** is nasty or serious: *He has a bad cold and must stay in bed.* ❑ *She made a bad mistake in the exam.* ❑ *We've had some bad news.*

6 Food goes **bad** when it becomes too old to eat: *Within a few days, all the food on the ship had gone bad.*

7 Something that is described as **bad** manners is not polite: *It's bad manners to ask someone how much money they earn.*

meanings 1 and 2: same as **naughty**
meaning 3: same as **evil** or **wicked**
meanings 1, 2, 3, 4 and 7: the opposite is **good**

badly *adverb*
1 Someone does something **badly** when they do not do it well: *People drive so badly here!*
2 You want something **badly**, or you **badly** want it, when you want it very much: *I badly want to win this time.*

bag *noun*: **bags**
A **bag** is an object made of paper, plastic, cloth or leather in which you carry things: *She was carrying two brown paper bags filled with food.* ❑ *Would you like a bag of sweets?* ❑ *a handbag.*

baggage *noun*
The suitcases and bags that you take with you when you travel are your **baggage**: *The passengers' baggage is checked before they board the aeroplane.*

bake *verb*: **bakes, baked, baking, has baked**
You **bake** bread or a cake when you cook it in an oven: *We spent the afternoon baking cakes for the party.*

baker *noun*: **bakers**
1 A **baker** is a person whose job is making bread and cakes.
2 A **baker** or **baker's** is a shop where you can buy bread and cakes: *She buys fresh bread every day at the local baker's.*

balance *noun*
Balance is the skill of stopping yourself from falling: *He lost his balance and fell on to the grass below.*

balance *verb*: **balances, balanced, balancing, has balanced**
You **balance** somewhere when you stop yourself falling; you **balance** something somewhere when you place it so that it stays upright and does not fall: *She was balancing on one leg.* ❑ *He balanced the plate on his nose.*

bald *adjective*: **balder, baldest**
Someone who is **bald** has very little hair or no hair at all on the top of their head: *I remember my grandad's bald head and big moustache.* ❑ *Bob started going bald when he was 25.* ❑ *He's bald, with a long grey beard.*

bald

ball *noun*: **balls**
A **ball** is a round object which

you use for playing games, such as cricket, football and hockey: *He kicked the ball into the goal.*

balloon *noun*: **balloons**
A **balloon** is a very light, coloured ball that you fill with air; balloons float in the air: *Maggie blew up two balloons and gave them to the children.*

bamboo *noun*
Bamboo is a tall plant with hollow stems which are hard and strong like wood: *The table was made of bamboo, and the top was painted with flowers.*

banana *noun*: **bananas**
A **banana** is a long yellow fruit which grows in hot countries: *The streets were crowded with market stalls selling oranges and bananas.*

band *noun*: **bands**
1 A **band** is a group of musicians: *He plays in a rock band.*
2 A **band** is also a thin piece of material that you put round something: *Put a lid on the box and hold it in place with a rubber band.*

bandage *noun*: **bandages**
A **bandage** is a long piece of cloth for tying round a part of your body which has been cut or hurt: *I'll put a bandage on that cut for you.*

bang *noun*: **bangs**
1 A **bang** is a sudden loud noise: *The pilot heard a bang from one of the engines.*
2 A **bang** is also a knock: *Has she had a bang on the head?*

bang is also a verb: *He fell off the ladder and banged his head.*

bank *noun*: **banks**
1 A **bank** is a place where people can leave their money safely: *She pretends to be poor, but she's got lots of money in the bank.* ▫ *He got a loan from his bank to buy a new car.*
2a The **banks** of a river are the areas of ground that are along each side of it: *In the evenings we walked along the river bank, or sat watching the fish jumping.* **b** The **banks** of a lake are the areas of ground around its edge: *New houses started appearing along the banks of the lake.*

bar *noun*: **bars**
1 A **bar** is a long piece of metal or wood: *The man was hit on the head with an iron bar.* ▫ *There were bars on the windows of the prison.*
2 A **bar** of something is a block of it: *You put some money in here, and the chocolate bar comes out down here.* ▫ *I bought a tube of toothpaste and a bar of soap.*
3a A **bar** is a room in a hotel or theatre or any other place, with a counter where drinks are served: *We had a drink at the bar before going through to the restaurant.* ▫ *There are lots of bars and restaurants along this street.* **b** A **bar** is also a shop or counter where other kinds of food or drinks are served: *a coffee bar* ▫ *a snack bar.*

bare *adjective*
1 Something that is **bare** has nothing covering it: *She felt the warmth of the sun on her bare arms.* ▫ *When we took the pictures down, the room looked bare.*
2 Trees that have no leaves are

also described as **bare**: *In winter you can see through the bare trees to the park.*

bargain *noun*: **bargains**
A **bargain** is something that you buy at a cheaper price than usual: *At £3 a bottle, this wine's a real bargain.*

bark *verb*: **barks, barked, barking, has barked**
1 A dog **barks** when it makes a loud short noise in its throat: *The night was still and warm. Somewhere a dog barked.*
2 People **bark** when they speak or give orders in an angry voice: *'Come on!' he barked. 'We haven't got all day!'*

barrel *noun*: **barrels**
A **barrel** is a round container for liquids or other goods, with curved sides and a flat top and bottom: *The water is stored in a big plastic barrel.*

base *noun*: **bases**
1 The **base** of something is the lowest part or point: *An animal has scratched at the base of the tree here.*
2 A **base** is also the part on which something stands: *This lamp needs a good heavy base.*
3 Your **base** is also the place where you stay or work most of the time: *We have a base in Victoria Street, but we sometimes travel around the country.*

base *verb*: **bases, based, basing, has based**
1 One thing **is based** on another when the one uses something from the other: *This story is based on fact.*
2 You **are based** in a particular place when you stay there for

some time, or when you always return there after travelling: *I'm based in London at the moment, but I travel a lot.*

baseball *noun*
Baseball is an American game played by two teams using a long wooden bat and a hard ball: *a baseball cap □ a baseball bat.*

basement *noun*: **basements**
In a building, the **basement** is the level that is below the ground level: *The kitchen was in the basement of the hotel. □ He lives in a dark basement flat.*

basic *adjective*
1 Something that is **basic** is simple and does not include anything that is not necessary: *They have only the basic things they need to live.*
2 **Basic** also means 'at the smallest or simplest level': *basic knowledge □ basic skills.*

basin *noun*: **basins**
A **basin** is a large bowl: *Mix the flour and eggs together in a large basin. □ Each room has a washbasin and a toilet.*

basket *noun*: **baskets**
A **basket** is a container for carrying things; it is made of strips of wood or stems woven together: *a basket full of shopping. □ a picnic basket.*

basketball *noun*
Basketball is a game in which two teams of five players try to throw a large ball through a net on a high post: *Activities will include athletics, swimming and basketball. □ a basketball player.*

bat *noun*: **bats**
1 A **bat** is a piece of wood used for hitting the ball in certain

games, such as cricket and baseball.

2 A **bat** is an animal that flies; bats move around at night: *Most bats hang upside down to sleep.*

bat

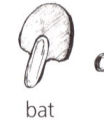

bat

bath *noun*: **baths**
1 A **bath** is a long deep container for water in which you can wash your whole body: *She filled the bath with warm water.* ❑ *All rooms in this hotel have a bath and a shower.*
2 You have a **bath** when you wash your body in a bath: *I had a bath and went to bed early.*

bathe *verb*: **bathes, bathed, bathing, has bathed**
1 You **bathe** when you go swimming: *There were a lot of people bathing in the warm blue sea.*
2 You **bathe** part of the body when you clean it with water or some other liquid: *The nurse bathed the child's knee.*

bathroom *noun*: **bathrooms**
1 A **bathroom** is a room in a house which contains a bath or a shower, a washbasin, and sometimes a toilet: *Many of these houses didn't have a bathroom.*
2 'The **bathroom**' is also another word for 'the toilet': *May I use your bathroom, please?*

battery *noun*: **batteries**
A **battery** is a container which stores electric power and is used to make something work: *Does this radio need batteries?* ❑ *Are batteries included?*

be *verb*: **was** or **were, being, has been**
1 You use **be** to tell people how to behave: *Be careful!* ❑ *I want you to be good while I'm out.*
2 You use **be** to say what you want to do: *I wanted to be an actress when I was younger.* ❑ *She wants to be famous.*
3 You use **be** with **shall** and **will** to say what is going to happen: *I'll be angry if he does that again.* ❑ *You'll be late if you don't leave now.*

> ▸The words **am**, **are**, **is**, **was** and **were** all belong to the verb **be**.

beach *noun*: **beaches**
A **beach** is a strip of land beside the sea, which is covered with sand or small stones: *We lay on the beach while the children played in the sand.*

beak *noun*: **beaks**
A bird's **beak** is the hard pointed part of its mouth which it uses for picking up food: *The bird came out of the water with a fish in its beak.*

bean *noun*: **beans**
Beans are seeds that grow inside long thin cases. There are lots of different kinds of bean, and many are eaten as vegetables: *Leave the beans in water for about twelve hours before cooking them.*

bear *noun*: **bears**
A **bear** is a large wild animal with thick fur and sharp claws: *Bears eat all sorts of things including fruit, meat and fish.*

bear *verb*: **bears, bore, bearing, has borne**
1 To **bear** something is to carry

it: *Will the table bear the weight of all that food?*
2 You **bear** pain when you suffer it: *She had a great ability to bear pain.*
3 You say that you can't **bear** something if you hate or dislike it: *I can't bear slow drivers.* ❏ *I can't bear to see you looking so unhappy.*

beard *noun*: **beards**
A man's **beard** is the hair that grows on his chin and cheeks: *He's growing a beard.* ❏ *Do you think I should shave my beard off?*

beat *verb*: **beats, beat, beating, has beaten**
1 You **beat** someone in a game or a match when you win against them: *They beat us at football six times last year.*
2a When one person **beats**, or **beats up** another person, they hit that person hard several times: *They beat him up and escaped with £500.* **b** You **beat** something when you hit it several times: *He beat a rhythm on the table with his fingers.* ❏ *She was beating the carpet with a bat.*
3 Someone's heart is **beating** when it is making its regular movement inside their chest: *Her heart beat a little faster as the mountains came into view.*

beautiful *adjective*
1 A **beautiful** person is very pretty or handsome: *The photo showed a beautiful young woman.*
2 A **beautiful** thing is very nice to look at: *He bought me a beautiful pair of earrings.*
3 Beautiful weather is very nice pleasant weather: *We had beautiful weather for the boat race.*

meanings 1 and 2: the opposite is **ugly**

beauty *noun*
A person or thing has **beauty** when they are beautiful: *We'll never forget the beauty of the mountains and the wonderful weather.* ❏ *a young woman of great beauty.*

became *verb*
see **become**: *The sky became dark.*

because *conjunction*
You use **because** when you are giving a reason for something: *He did it because he was angry.* ❏ *Because of the snow, they had to stay at home.*

become *verb*: **becomes, became, becoming, has become**
1 You **become** something when you begin to be that thing: *He became famous in 1988.* ❏ *Robert wants to become a doctor.* ❏ *Sue and I became good friends.*
2 You ask what **became** of someone or something when you want to know what happened to them: *What became of Judy?*

bed *noun*: **beds**
A **bed** is a piece of furniture that you sleep on: *I'm going to bed.* ❏ *We usually put the baby to bed at eight.* ❏ *The children make their own beds in the mornings.*

bedroom *noun*: **bedrooms**
A **bedroom** is a room for sleeping in: *There's one large bedroom on the ground floor and two smaller ones on the first floor.*

bee *noun*: **bees**
A **bee** is an insect which makes honey: *Bees get their food from flowers.*

beef noun
Beef is the meat of a bull or cow:
*They serve roast beef, potatoes,
carrots and peas on Sundays.*
❑ *Two beef sandwiches, please.*

been verb
see **be**: *Where have you been?*
❑ *The weather has been bad all
week.* ❑ *Have you ever been to the
USA?* ❑ *We've been living in this
house for five years.* ❑ *Has the car
been repaired?* ❑ *I can't believe
I've been so stupid!*

beer noun
Beer is a strong drink made from
grain, sugar and water: *There was
a choice of beer, wine or orange
juice.*

beetle noun: **beetles**
A **beetle** is an insect with two
hard covers over its wings:
*Hundreds of small black beetles
were crawling up the tree.*

before preposition, conjunction
and adverb
1 You do one thing **before**
another thing when you do that
thing first: *Could you phone me
before you leave?*
2 You do something **before** a
certain time when you do it
earlier than that time: *Please
come before three o'clock.*
3 You do something **before**
someone else when you do it
earlier than them: *I finished
before him.*
4 Before means 'at some time in
the past': *I've seen this film before.*
❑ *Haven't we met before?*

meanings 1, 2 and 3: the
opposite is **after**

beg verb: **begs, begged,
begging, has begged**

1 People **beg** when they ask
other people for money or food:
*More young people are begging in
the streets now.*
2 You **beg** someone to do
something, or you **beg** them for
something, when you ask them
very eagerly: *She begged me to go
with her.* ❑ *'Please, I beg you, help
me.'*

begin verb: **begins, began,
beginning, has begun**
1 Something **begins** when it
starts: *The lesson begins at 9.30.*
❑ *It began to rain.*
2a You **begin** something when
you start it: *She began the long
walk back to the house.* **b** You
begin to do something when you
start to do it: *She began to cry.*

same as **start**
the opposite is **end** or **finish**

beginning noun: **beginnings**
The **beginning** of something is
the place or time when it starts:
*We always have a meeting at the
beginning of the week.* ❑ *The
beginning of the film is set in Paris.*

same as **start**
the opposite is **end**

behave verb: **behaves, behaved,
behaving, has behaved**
1 Someone or something
behaves in a certain way when
they act in that way: *How did the
dog behave when I left the room?*
❑ *He behaved as if he'd never met
me before.*
2 People **behave**, or **behave**
themselves, or **behave** well,
when they act in a good, polite
and obedient way: *The boys were
told to behave themselves.*
3 Someone **behaves** badly if

they act in a rude or disobedient way: *No-one wants a child that behaves badly.*

meaning 2: the opposite is **misbehave**

behaviour *noun*
Your **behaviour** is the way you behave: *What's the best way of teaching children good behaviour? His behaviour has been very strange.*

same as **conduct**

behind *preposition and adverb*
1 Someone or something that is **behind** something else is hidden by it: *The cat always sleeps behind the sofa. He went behind a tree. Behind her smiles, she was really a sad lonely person.*
2 Something that is **behind** another thing is at the back of it: *The car park is behind the supermarket. It has two wheels in front and one behind.*
3 You leave something **behind** if you do not take it with you: *He always leaves his umbrella behind.*

meanings 1 and 2: the opposite is **in front of** or **in front**

being *noun*: **beings**
A **being** is a person or thing that is living: *a human being a strange being from another planet.*

belief *noun*: **beliefs**
A **belief** is something that you believe is true: *a belief in God.*

being *verb*
see **be**: *You're all being so nice to me today!*

believe *verb*: **believes, believed, believing, has believed**
1 You **believe** something when you feel that it is true: *I believe*

her story. Do you? Ask Ken if you don't believe me — he'll tell you it's true.
2 You **believe** in something when you feel sure that it is real: *Do you believe in God? I don't believe in ghosts.*
3 You say that you **believe** something is so if you think that it is so: *I believe he's in a meeting at the moment. I still believe that my decision was right.*

meaning 1: the opposite is **disbelieve**

bell *noun*: **bells**
1 A **bell** is a hollow metal object which has a piece of metal hanging inside it that makes a sound when it hits the sides: *The church bells rang.*
2 A **bell** is also any other object for making a ringing sound: *The doorbell rang. a bicycle bell.*

belong *verb*: **belongs, belonged, belonging, has belonged**
1 Something that **belongs** to you is owned by you: *The house, the car, everything, belongs to her. Does this computer belong to you?*
2 You **belong** to a group if you are a member of it: *Which football club does he belong to?*

below *preposition and adverb*
One thing is **below** another if it is in a lower position than that other thing: *He hurt his leg just below the knee. The plane flew below the clouds. We looked down at the houses below.*

the opposite is **above**

belt *noun*: **belts**
A **belt** is a long piece of leather or cloth that you wear round your waist: *He was wearing a leather*

belt with a knife attached at the side.

bench *noun*: **benches**
A **bench** is a long seat, usually made of wood: *We sat on a bench in the park.*

bend *noun*: **bends**
A **bend** is a curve: *There is a dangerous bend in the road here.*

bend *verb*: **bends, bent, bending, has bent**
1 You **bend** something when you make it form a curve: *Don't do that — you'll bend the spoon.*
2 You **bend** your arm or your leg when you move it so that it is not straight: *It hurts when I bend my arm.*
3 Something **bends** when it forms a curve: *The road bends to the right.*
4 You **bend,** or you **bend** down, when you move the top part of your body downwards: *He bent down and kissed her on the cheek.*

beneath *preposition*
One thing is **beneath** another if it is under or below that other thing: *We sat beneath the apple tree.* □ *They felt the cool wet grass beneath their feet.*

the opposite is **above, over** or **on top of**

bent *verb*
see **bend**: *The strong winds had bent the trees.*

bent *adjective*
Something that is **bent** has a bend or curve in it: *He made a hook for his fishing line with a bent pin.*

the opposite is **straight**

berry *noun*: **berries**
A **berry** is a small juicy fruit such as a strawberry or a raspberry: *We collected berries and made a pie with them.*

beside *preposition*
Someone or something is **beside** another if they are next to that other person or thing: *Come and sit beside me.* □ *I think we should put this table beside the bed.*

besides *preposition and adverb*
1 Besides means 'as well as': *Is anyone coming besides Steve?*
2 Besides means 'also': *I like to go running before breakfast — besides, it gives me an appetite.*

best *adjective and adverb*
The **best** person or thing is the one that is better than all the others: *Tell me your best qualities.* □ *What's the best way to lose weight?* □ *These students work best in small groups.*

the opposite is **worst**

▷ **do your best**
You **do your best** when you try as hard as you can: *Don't worry too much about winning — the important thing is that you do your best.*

better *adjective and adverb*
1 Someone or something that is **better** is good compared with someone or something else: *The new car is better than the old one.* □ *He's become much better at reading recently.*
2 Someone does something **better** than someone else when they do it well compared to the other person: *Older students often do better than younger ones.*
3 Someone who has been ill is

feeling **better** when they are not feeling as bad as before; you also say you are **better** when you are not ill any more: *I'm feeling much better now, thanks.* ❑ *He's been very ill, but he's better now.*

the opposite is **worse**

▷ **had better**

If you say that someone **had better** do something, you mean that it would be a good thing if they did it: *I think we had better tell him what's happened.* ❑ *I'd better not go if the roads are so dangerous.*

between *preposition*
1 Something that is **between** two things is in the space dividing them: *There is a fence between the two gardens.*
2 Something happens **between** two times if it happens after the first one and before the second one: *Could you come between 2 o'clock and 2.30?*
3 Something happens **between** two people when they both take part in it: *There's been a quarrel between two of our workers.*
4 **Between** is also used to talk about differences: *He doesn't understand the difference between right and wrong.*
5 You divide something **between** people when you give each of them some of it: *They divided the money between them.*

beyond *preposition*
1 One thing is **beyond** another if it is on the far side of it: *The post office is just beyond the bank.*
2 Something goes **beyond** a certain point if it goes further than that point: *I won't be able to stay beyond 10 o'clock.*

bicycle *noun*: **bicycles**
A **bicycle** is a vehicle with two wheels. You sit on it and make it go forward by pushing the pedals: *She got on her bicycle and rode away.*

bicycle

big *adjective*: **bigger, biggest**
Something that is **big** is large in size: *They are staying in a big hotel in the city centre.* ❑ *He's a big boy for his age.* ❑ *It is the biggest animal in the forest.*

same as **large**
the opposite is **small** or **little**

bike *noun*: **bikes**
Bike is short for bicycle: *He got a bike for his birthday.*

bill *noun*: **bills**
1 A **bill** is a piece of paper showing how much money you have to pay: *Can we have the bill, please?* ❑ *The telephone bill came this morning.*
2 A **bill** is also a note worth a certain amount of money: *He put a ten-dollar bill in my pocket as I left.*

bin *noun*: **bins**
A **bin** is a container for putting rubbish in: *She put his letter straight in the bin.*

bind *verb*: **binds, bound, binding, has bound**
1 You **bind** something, or you **bind** it up, when you tie it: *Kathy bound up the parcel.* ❑ *The bank robbers bound the bank manager*

to a chair with a rope.
2 You **bind** a part of the body, or you **bind** it up, when you put a bandage on it: *The nurse will bind up your finger.*

bird *noun*: **birds**
A **bird** is an animal with wings and feathers: *Early in the morning the birds sing in the trees.*

birth *noun*: **births**
The **birth** of a baby is its being born: *We went to see Anna in hospital after the birth of her baby.*

birthday *noun*: **birthdays**
Your **birthday** is the day on which you were born, and the same date every year after that: *When is your birthday?* ❑ *My birthday is on February 24th.* ❑ *What do you want for your birthday?* ❑ *Are you having a birthday party?*

biscuit *noun*: **biscuits**
A **biscuit** is a kind of small flat cake which is usually sweet: *Do you like chocolate biscuits?*

‘ **bis**-kit ’

same as **cookie**

bit *noun*: **bits**
1 A **bit** of something is a piece of it: *There is only one bit of cake left.* ❑ *Harry tore a bit of paper out of his notebook.*
2 A **bit** also means ‘rather’ or ‘a little’: *Wait a bit longer.* ❑ *These shoes are a bit too small.*

bite *verb*: **bites, bit, biting, has bitten**
1 You **bite** something when you cut through it with your teeth: *Peter bit off a piece of chocolate.*
2 An animal **bites** when it injures someone with its teeth:

That dog bit me. ❑ *I was bitten by a monkey at the zoo.*

bite is also a noun: *Do you want a bite of my apple?*

bitter *adjective*
Something that is **bitter** is not sweet, and has a sharp taste: *This juice is bitter.*

the opposite is **sweet**

black *noun and adjective*
Black is the darkest colour, the opposite of white: *Black is the colour of the night.* ❑ *She's wearing black shoes today.* ❑ *We watched old black-and-white films all afternoon.*

blade *noun*: **blades**
1 A **blade** is the thin cutting part of a knife or other tool: *I need a knife with a really sharp blade.*
2 The long thin leaves of grass are also called **blades**.

blame *verb*: **blames, blamed, blaming, has blamed**
1 You **blame** someone for something bad when you say that they caused it: *The car driver blamed the cyclist for the accident.* ❑ *I didn't break the window — you can't blame me!*
2 If you tell someone that you don't **blame** them for something, you mean that you don't think that they have done wrong: *I don't blame you for getting angry with Alan — he was very rude to you.*

the opposite is **praise**

▷ **to blame**
A person is **to blame** for something bad that has happened if it is their fault: *You are not to blame for the accident.*

blank *adjective*
Something such as a piece of paper is **blank** if it has nothing written on it: *The teacher gave us each a blank sheet of paper.*

blanket *noun*: **blankets**
A **blanket** is a thick warm cover, usually for a bed: *There's an extra blanket in the cupboard.*

bleed *verb*: **bleeds, bled, bleeding, has bled**
A person or part of their body **bleeds** when blood comes from a part of their body: *Richard's nose is bleeding.* ❑ *Amy's finger bled when she cut it on the knife.*

blew *verb*
see **blow** : *The wind blew very strongly.*

blind *adjective*
Someone who is **blind** cannot see: *Anna helped the blind man to cross the street.*

blink *verb*: **blinks, blinked, blinking, has blinked**
You **blink** when you open and shut both of your eyes at the same time very quickly: *The bright light made me blink.*

block *noun*: **blocks**
1 A **block** is a piece of something solid, such as wood or stone: *I chopped the block of wood into small pieces.*
2 A tall building containing a lot of flats or offices is called a **block**: *We live in a block of flats.* ❑ *My father works in an office block in the city.*
3 A **block** is also a number of buildings arranged in a square with streets along each side: *The taxi driver drove round the block.*

block *verb*: **blocks, blocked, blocking, has blocked**
1 People or things **block** something when they stop things from passing along it: *The lorry broke down, blocking one of the lanes on the motorway.*
2 Something gets **blocked** when it closes up so that things cannot pass through or along it: *My nose gets blocked when I have a cold.*

blood *noun*
Blood is the red liquid that flows inside your body through your veins: *Blood flowed from the injured man's leg.*

blouse *noun*: **blouses**
A **blouse** is a kind of shirt worn by a girl or woman: *We have to wear a blue skirt and a white blouse.*

blow *noun*: **blows**
A **blow** is a hard knock made with a weapon or someone's hand: *The burglar knocked Harry down with one blow of his fist.*

blow *verb*: **blows, blew, blowing, has blown**
1 A wind **is blowing** when the air is moving strongly enough for you to feel it: *A strong wind was blowing when they left the party.*
2 The wind **blows** something somewhere when it carries it there: *The wind blew Mrs Lang's hat off.*
3 You **blow** when you force air out of your mouth: *If you blow too hard the balloon will burst.*
4 You **blow** a whistle, or a musical instrument when you breathe hard into it to make it sound: *Mary tried to blow her father's trumpet.* ❑ *The teacher blew his whistle at the end of the football game.*

▷ **blow up**

1 Someone **blows** something **up** when they destroy it with an explosion: *The soldiers blew up the bridge.* ❑ *The old factory was blown up.*

2 You **blow up** something such as a tyre or a balloon when you fill it with air: *Ben has blown up ten balloons already.*

blue *noun and adjective*: **blues**
Blue is the colour of the sky during the day, when there are no clouds: *Jenny has blue eyes and fair hair.* ❑ *Jack is wearing dark blue trousers and a light blue shirt.*

blunt *adjective*: **blunter, bluntest**
1 Something that you use for cutting is **blunt** if its edge is not sharp: *These scissors are blunt.*
2 A pencil is **blunt** when its point is not sharp any more: *You can't write with a blunt pencil.*

the opposite is **sharp**

blush *verb*: **blushes, blushed. blushing, has blushed**
You **blush** when you become red in the face because you feel ashamed or shy: *He always blushed when he talked to Henrietta.*

board *noun*: **boards**
A **board** is a flat piece of wood: *The head teacher pinned the list on the noticeboard.* ❑ *a cheeseboard* ❑ *All the floorboards were rotten, so we had to replace them.*

board *verb*: **boards, boarded, boarding, has boarded**
You **board** a ship, train or aircraft when you get on it: *Passengers for Bangkok may now board their plane.*

▷ **on board**

You are **on board** a ship, train or aircraft if you are on it, or in it: *The ship left the harbour when all the passengers were on board.*

boast *verb*: **boasts, boasted, boasting, has boasted**
You **boast** when you talk too proudly about yourself: *Gary was always boasting about how rich he was.* ❑ *Sandra boasted that she was the best pupil in her class.*

boat *noun*: **boats**
A **boat** is something in which people can travel over water. A boat is smaller than a ship: *We'll cross the river by boat.* ❑ *The tourists went round the lake in a motorboat.*

body *noun*: **bodies**
1 A person's or animal's **body** is every part of them: *Her whole body ached after the race.* ❑ *A cat's body is covered with fur.*
2 A **body** is also a person's dead body: *The police pulled the body from the river.*

boil *verb*: **boils, boiled, boiling, has boiled**
1 You **boil** liquids when you heat them until they start to bubble and turn into steam: *He boiled the water to make tea.*
2 Liquids **boil** when they get hot and start to bubble and turn into steam: *I'll make tea when the water boils.*
3 You **boil** food when you cook it in boiling water: *Have you boiled the potatoes?*

bolt *noun*: **bolts**
1 A **bolt** is a metal bar that slides across to fasten a door or window: *The bolt on the front door is a bit loose.*

2 A **bolt** is also a thick piece of metal which screws into a nut to hold things together: *There were some nuts and bolts, a hammer and a screwdriver in the box.*

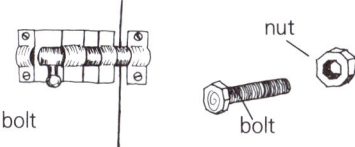

bolt

nut

bolt

bomb *noun*: **bombs**
A **bomb** is a type of weapon which explodes and can cause a lot of damage over a wide area: *The bomb killed five people.*

'**bom**'

bone *noun*: **bones**
A **bone** is one of the pieces of hard white material which makes up a skeleton: *I think I've broken my arm!* ❑ *Remove the bones from the fish before you cook it.*

book *noun*: **books**
1 A **book** is a number of printed sheets of paper joined together between covers: *She's reading a book on gardening.*
2 A **book** is also a number of blank sheets of paper for writing on, joined together between covers: *I got a new address book for my birthday.*
3 A **book** is also a story, or whatever is printed in a book: *Have you read her new book?*

book *verb*: **books, booked, booking, has booked**
You **book** a table, a room or a seat when you ask someone to keep it for you: *We booked a table at the French restaurant.* ❑ *Did you remember to book tickets for the concert?*

bookcase *noun*: **bookcases**
A **bookcase** is a piece of furniture with shelves for books.

boot *noun*: **boots**
A **boot** is a kind of shoe which covers the ankle and sometimes part of the leg: *Penny has bought a new pair of leather boots.*

boots

border *noun*: **borders**
1 The **border** between two countries is the line which separates them: *We crossed the border from France into Germany.*
2 A **border** is a strip round the edge of something: *This handkerchief has a lace border.*

bore *verb*
see **bear**: *She bore the pain without complaining.*

bored *adjective*
You are **bored** when you feel tired because you are doing something that isn't interesting, or because you have nothing to do: *I'm bored. Let's go out for a walk.* ❑ *Matthew was soon bored with his new game.*

boring *adjective*
Something is **boring** if it is not interesting: *The journey was long and very boring.*

born *adjective*
A baby is **born** when it comes out of its mother's body at birth: *Nick was born in 1971.* ❑ *The puppies were born early in the morning.*

borrow *verb*: **borrows, borrowed, borrowing, has borrowed**

You **borrow** something that belongs to someone else when you take it away for a while with their permission and return it later: *I'll ask Joe if we can borrow his car.*

▸ I'm **borrowing** a book **from** Jane. Jane is **lending** the book **to** me.

boss *noun*: **bosses**
Your **boss** is the person who is in charge of you at work: *I'll ask my boss if I can have a few days' holiday.*

both *determiner and pronoun*
Both means each of two people or things: *I know both girls.* ❑ *Can I have both chairs, please?* ❑ *I don't know which colour to pick — I like them both.*

bother *verb*: **bothers, bothered, bothering, has bothered**
1 You don't **bother** doing something if you don't do it because it is not really necessary: *Don't bother making tea — I can't stay long.*
2 You **bother** someone when you disturb them: *Sorry to bother you, but could I ask you something?*
3 Something **bothers** you when it worries you or makes you feel upset: *He can come if he wants — it doesn't bother me.* ❑ *It bothered him that she hadn't telephoned.*

bottle *noun*: **bottles**
A **bottle** is a container made from plastic or glass. Bottles are used to store liquids: *There are three bottles of milk on the table.*

bottom *noun*: **bottoms**
1 The **bottom** of something is the lowest part of it: *Their house is at the bottom of the hill.*
2 Your **bottom** is the part of your body that you sit on: *He slipped and fell on his bottom.*

meaning 1: the opposite is **top**

bought *verb*
see **buy**: *Roy bought a new car last week.*

bounce *verb*: **bounces, bounced, bouncing, has bounced**
1 Something **bounces** when it springs back from a hard surface: *The ball bounced off the wall.*
2 You **bounce** something when you throw it against a hard surface so that it springs back again: *I bounced the ball on the pavement.*

bound *verb*
see **bind**: *The prisoner's hands were bound together behind his back.*

bow *noun*: **bows**
1 A **bow** is a curved piece of wood with a string attached at each end, used to shoot arrows: *The children played outside with their bows and arrows.*
2 A **bow** is a kind of knot with two loops and two loose ends: *She put a piece of ribbon round the box and tied it in a big bow.*
3 A **bow** is a long piece of wood with very fine strings stretched along it, used to play the violin and other similar instruments: *I put my violin and bow back in the case.*

rhymes with **toe**

bow

bow

bow *verb*: **bows, bowed, bowing, has bowed**
1 People **bow** when they bend the top part of their body forward, for example at the end of a performance; or to greet someone very politely: *The actor bowed when the play finished.*

bow

2 You **bow** your head when you bend it downwards: *We all bowed our heads during the prayer.*

rhymes with **now**

bowl *noun*: **bowls**
1 A **bowl** is a deep round dish used for holding food: *We put the salad into a big glass bowl.*
2 A **bowl** of something is the bowl and what is held inside it: *Can I have another bowl of soup?*

box *noun*: **boxes**
1 A **box** is a container made from cardboard, wood or plastic, used for holding things: *We put all the old letters into a box.*
2 A **box** of something is the box and what is held inside: *I ate the whole box of chocolates myself.*

boy *noun*: **boys**
A **boy** is a male child: *Megan has just had a baby boy.*

bracelet *noun*: **bracelets**
A **bracelet** is a chain or band that you wear round your wrist as a piece of jewellery: *Do you like my new silver bracelet?*

brain *noun*: **brains**
Your **brain** is the organ inside your head which controls everything you do, such as thinking, seeing and hearing: *How big is a baby's brain?*

brake *noun*: **brakes**
A **brake** is the handle or pedal that is used to slow down and stop a vehicle: *I put on the brakes quickly when the dog ran in front of my bike.*

branch *noun*: **branches**
A **branch** is a part of a tree that grows out from the trunk: *We found the cat sitting on a branch of the apple tree.*

brave *adjective*: **braver, bravest**
A person who is **brave** is not afraid of danger or pain: *She was very brave; she didn't even cry when she broke her ankle.* ❑ *a brave soldier.*

bread *noun*
Bread is a kind of food made from a mixture of flour and water and baked in the oven: *Do you prefer brown or white bread?*

breadth *noun*
The **breadth** of something is the distance from one side of it to the other: *They searched the length and breadth of the country, but they never found him.*

break *noun*: **breaks**
1 A **break** is a place where something has broken: *He's got a bad break in his leg.*
2 A **break** is also a short rest or pause: *We can have a break at 10 o'clock.*

break *verb*: **breaks, broke, breaking, has broken**
1 You **break** something when you damage it or cause it to separate into pieces: *I broke the chocolate bar in two and gave half to Amy.* ❑ *She threw the ball and*

broke the window. ❏ *Mark has broken his leg.*

2 A machine **breaks**, or **is broken**, when it becomes damaged so that it no longer works: *My watch has broken.*

3 Something **breaks** when it splits into pieces: *The vase broke when it fell on the floor.*

4 You **break** a law or a rule when you disobey it: *You can't do that; you're breaking the law.*

▷ **break down**

A machine or vehicle **breaks down** when it stops working properly: *Our car broke down in the middle of the desert.*

▷ **break in** or **break into**

Someone **breaks in**, or **breaks into** a building, when they enter it by forcing open a door or window: *The thieves broke in during the night.*❏ *Mr Smith forgot his key, and had to break into his own house.*

breakfast *noun*: **breakfasts**

Breakfast is the first meal of the day: *I had tea and toast for breakfast.*

breath *noun*

Breath is the air that goes in and out of your body through your nose or mouth: *I could see my breath in the cold air.*

▷ **out of breath**

You are **out of breath** if you are breathing very quickly, especially because of exercise: *I'm out of breath after climbing all those stairs.*

rhymes with **deaf**

breathe *verb*: **breathes, breathed, breathing, has breathed**

You **breathe** when you take air into your lungs and let it out again: *It was difficult to breathe because the room was full of smoke.*

rhymes with **leave**

breeze *noun*: **breezes**

A **breeze** is a gentle wind: *The cool breeze felt good on that hot day.*

brick *noun*: **bricks**

Bricks are blocks used to build things: *They're using bricks to build the new wall.* ❏ *a brick house.*

bride *noun*: **brides**

A **bride** is a woman who is getting married: *The bride was wearing a long white dress, and carried a bunch of yellow roses.*

bridegroom *noun*: **bridegrooms**

A **bridegroom** is a man who is getting married: *The bridegroom was nervous before the wedding.*

bridge *noun*: **bridges**

A **bridge** is a part of a road or railway which is built over a river or another road, so that you can cross to the other side: *You have to pay to cross the new bridge.*

brief *adjective*: **briefer, briefest**

If something is **brief** it lasts for a short time only: *We had a brief holiday in Greece this year.* ❏ *We had a brief conversation with our son's teacher.*

bright *adjective*: **brighter, brightest**

1 Something is **bright** if it gives out a lot of light: *That light is too bright.*

2 A place is **bright** if it has, or seems to have, a lot of light in it: *We had a nice bright room on the top floor.*

3 A **bright** colour is very strong

and clear: *She was wearing a bright red scarf.*
4 A person is **bright** if they are cheerful or happy: *I feel brighter now after my rest.*
5 A **bright** person is someone who is clever: *Jonathan is very bright for his age.*

meanings 1 and 2: the opposite is **dull** or **dark**

brilliant *adjective*
1 Someone who is described as **brilliant** is very clever: *She was a brilliant student.* ❏ *He has a brilliant mind.*
2 A **brilliant** colour is very bright: *The sea was brilliant blue.*

bring *verb*: **brings, brought, bringing, has brought**
You **bring** someone or something with you if you have them with you when you come: *Can you bring some wine to the party?* ❏ *Are you going to bring your husband to the party?* ❏ *Mrs Marshall says she'll bring her car tonight.*

▷ **bring up**
People **bring up** children, or they **bring** children **up**, when they look after them until they become adults: *Sheila was brought up by her grandparents.* ❏ *I brought my children up to be polite.*

broad *adjective*: **broader, broadest**
Something that is **broad** is wide from one side to the other: *broad shoulders.* ❏ *A broad path led from the house to the lake.*

the opposite is **narrow**

broadcast *verb*: **broadcasts, broadcast, broadcasting, has broadcast**

A company **broadcasts** when it sends out programmes from a television or radio station: *The news was broadcast all through the night.*

broke and **broken** *verb*
see **break**: *I broke my new radio yesterday.* ❏ *She's broken her arm.*

broken *adjective*
Something that is **broken** is in pieces, or is not working: *The washing machine is broken.*

brother *noun*: **brothers**
Your **brother** is a man or boy who has the same parents as you: *My brother is five years younger than me.*

brought *verb*
see **bring**: *Dave brought his mum to the party.*

brown *noun and adjective*:
browns
Brown is the colour of earth: *I've bought a new pair of brown shoes.* ❏ *She's got long dark brown hair.* ❏ *Do you like this green or do you prefer the brown?*

bruise *noun*: **bruises**
A **bruise** is a dark blue or brown mark on the skin, caused by a blow to the body: *I've got a bruise on my knee where I fell.*

brush *noun*: **brushes**
A **brush** is a tool with stiff hairs; you use a brush to paint, tidy your hair, clean things or sweep the floor: *I bought a new toothbrush yesterday.* ❏ *The artist used a narrower brush to paint the child's head and hands.*

brush *verb*: **brushes, brushed, brushing, has brushed**
You **brush** something when you clean it or sweep it using a brush: *He brushed his teeth before he*

went to bed. ❑ *I brushed my hair ten minutes ago and it's untidy again already.*

bubble *noun*: **bubbles**
A **bubble** is a small round clear ball filled with gas or air: *The bath water is full of soap bubbles.*

bubble *verb*: **bubbles, bubbled, bubbling, has bubbled**
Liquid **bubbles** when it forms bubbles on its surface: *When the soup begins to bubble, turn the heat down.*

bucket *noun*: **buckets**
A **bucket** is a container with an open top and a handle, used to carry things: *I carried the coal in a bucket.* ❑ *We'll need water in all these buckets.*

bud *noun*: **buds**
A **bud** is the beginning of a new flower or leaf, growing on a plant: *By early spring, the rose bush was covered with buds.*

build *verb*: **builds, built, building, has built**
You **build** something when you make a building or a road using things like bricks, stones and wood: *When will they finish building the new road?* ❑ *They want to build a garage beside their house.*

builder *noun*: **builders**
A **builder** is a person who builds things, especially houses and other buildings: *The builder is beginning work on the new house today.*

building *noun*: **buildings**
A **building** is a structure with walls and a roof, such as a house or shop: *There are lots of empty buildings in the city centre.* ❑ *The school is the oldest building in the town.*

built *verb*
see **build**: *This church was built in 1862.*

bulb *noun*: **bulbs**
1 A **bulb** is a glass object which fits into an electric lamp and gives out light: *We forgot to buy new bulbs, so we used candles instead.*
2 A **bulb** is also the root of some plants, shaped like an onion: *The bulbs we planted last year are beginning to grow.*

bull *noun*: **bulls**
A **bull** is the male of animals that belong to the cattle family: *They own a few cows and one bull.*

bullet *noun*: **bullets**
A **bullet** is a piece of metal that is fired from a gun: *The bullet hit him in the leg.*

bully *noun*: **bullies**
A **bully** is someone who frightens and hurts other people who are less powerful than themselves: *He's the school bully; all the smaller children are frightened of him.*

bump *verb*: **bumps, bumped, bumping, has bumped**
If you **bump** into something, you hit it by accident: *He bumped into a lamp-post and hurt his head.*

bunch *noun*: **bunches**
A **bunch** is a number of things joined together in some way: *I bought a bunch of bananas and a bunch of grapes.* ❑ *Chris gave me a bunch of flowers.*

a bunch of grapes

a bunch of flowers

burger *noun*: **burgers**
A **burger** is a hamburger: *We had burgers and chips for lunch.*

burglar *noun*: **burglars**
A **burglar** is someone who breaks into buildings in order to steal things: *The burglar broke into the house through a window.*

burglary *noun*: **burglaries**
Someone carries out a **burglary** when they break into a building and steal things: *There was a burglary at the library last night; all the computers were taken.*

buried and **buries** *verb*
see **bury**

burn *noun*: **burns**
A **burn** is a mark or an injury caused by fire or by something hot: *That burn on your leg looks sore.* ❑ *There were cigarette burns all over the carpet.*

burn *verb*: **burns, burnt** or **burned, burning, has burnt** or **has burned**
1 A fire **is burning** when it is making heat, and usually flames and smoke: *The coal fire was burning in the sitting room.*
2 Something **burns**, or **is burning**, when it is making flames: *Gas burns with a blue flame.* ❑ *The school was burning for half an hour before the fire engine arrived.*
3 You **burn** something when you destroy it with fire: *We burnt all the rubbish.*
4 You **burn** food when you cook it too much and it turns black: *Sue's burnt the soup.* ❑ *Turn down the gas; you're burning the sauce.*
5 You **burn** yourself when you injure yourself by touching

something which is too hot: *I burnt myself on the cooker.*

burst *verb*: **bursts, burst, bursting, has burst**
1 You **burst** something, such as a balloon or a bubble, if you suddenly break it: *I burst the balloon.*
2 Something **bursts** if it breaks suddenly: *The balloon burst and gave us all a fright.*
3 You **burst** into a place when you enter it suddenly: *Jim burst into the room.*

bury *verb*: **buries, buried, burying, has buried**
1 You **bury** a dead person when you put their body into the ground: *Mr Potter was buried last week.*
2 You **bury** an object when you cover it with something, such as soil, so that it is hidden: *The dog buried its bone at the bottom of the garden.*

bus *noun*: **buses**
A **bus** is a large vehicle which can carry a lot of passengers: *Does this bus go along Bank Street?*

bush *noun*: **bushes**
A **bush** is a plant which is like a small tree: *They have planted some new rose bushes in the park.*

business *noun*: **businesses**
1 Business is the work of buying and selling, and of producing things which people want to buy: *Mr Johnston has gone into business with his brother.*
2 A **business** is a company which makes or sells things: *He owns a business that makes parts for computers.*

‘**biz**-nis’

bus stop *noun*: **bus stops**
A **bus stop** is a place at the side of the road where people can get on and off buses: *I waited half an hour at the bus stop.*

busy *adjective*: **busier, busiest**
1 You are **busy** if you have a lot of work to do and not much time to do it in: *We are very busy at work just now.* ❑ *I can't meet you at lunchtime — I'm too busy.*
2 A place is **busy** if it has a lot of people or traffic in it: *The town is very busy today.* ❑ *The roads were so busy last night; it took me three hours to get home.*

   ⟨ **biz**-ee ⟩

but *conjunction and preposition*
1 But is used to show that there is a difference between two things: *I'd like to go to the football match but I don't have enough money.*
2 But also means 'except': *We ate nothing but bread for a week.*

butcher *noun*: **butchers**
1 A **butcher** is a person who sells meat: *Ronnie's dad is a butcher.*
2 A **butcher's** is a place where you can buy meat: *I'm going to the butcher's to buy some steaks.*

butter *noun*
Butter is the yellow solid fat that you spread on bread and use in cooking: *She spread butter on her toast.*

butterfly *noun*: **butterflies**
A **butterfly** is an insect with large wings that often have bright colours on them: *The butterfly landed on the rose.*

button *noun*: **buttons**
1 A **button** is a round disc which is used to fasten clothes: *I sewed the button on to my coat.*

2 A **button** is also a flat round disc which you press to make a machine work: *I pressed the button but nothing happened.*

buy *verb*: **buys, bought, buying, has bought**
You **buy** something when you get it by paying for it with money: *I bought a new book yesterday.* ❑ *What shall I buy for dinner?*

the opposite is **sell**

by *preposition*
1 One thing is **by** another if it is next to it: *Richard is sitting in the chair by the window.*
2 Something is done **by** someone or something if they have done it: *They said the painting was by Picasso, but it wasn't.*
3 You travel **by** a kind of vehicle if you use it to go somewhere: *We're going to Spain by car.*
4 By is used to show how something is done: *I sent the letter by post.* ❑ *He paid for the meal by cheque.*
5 Something happens **by** a certain time if it happens at, or before that time: *I'll be at the office by 8 o'clock.* ❑ *I have to finish this book by next week.*
6 You do something **by** day, or you do something **by** night, if you do it during the day or during the night: *We'll drive by day and rest by night.*
7 You use **by** when you are giving measurements of length and width together: *This room is 12 metres by 5.*

bye or **bye-bye**
Bye or **bye-bye** means 'goodbye': *Bye. See you tomorrow.* ❑ *Bye-bye, daddy.*

Cc

cab *noun*
A **cab** is a taxi: *We took a cab to the airport.*

cabbage *noun*: **cabbages**
A **cabbage** is a vegetable made up of lots of thick tightly-packed leaves: *For dinner we had chicken with potatoes and cabbage.*

café *noun*: **cafés**
A **café** is a small restaurant where you can buy drinks and snacks: *We had sandwiches and coffee in the café near the hotel.*

cake *noun*: **cakes**
A **cake** is a sweet food made from a mixture of flour, eggs, sugar and fat, which you bake in an oven: *Can I have another piece of chocolate cake?*

calculate *verb*: **calculates, calculated, calculating, has calculated**
You **calculate** something when you work it out using numbers: *John calculated how much money he would need to buy a car.*

calculator *noun*: **calculators**
A **calculator** is a small machine that you use to add, subtract, multiply and divide numbers: *I had to use a calculator to add up all the figures.*

calendar *noun*: **calendars**
A **calendar** shows the days and months of the year in order: *I'll put this calendar on the wall.*

calf *noun*: **calves**
1 A **calf** is a young cow: *The calf lay in the grass with its mother.*
2 Your **calf** is the back part of your leg, below the knee: *My calves are sore after all that running.*

call *noun*: **calls**
1 A **call** is a shout or cry: *We could hear the calls of the monkeys in the forest.*
2a A **call** is a conversation you have with someone, using the telephone: *I've just had a call from Jenny.* **b** You give someone a **call** when you telephone them: *I'll give you a call next week.*

call *verb*: **calls, called, calling, has called**
1a You **call** someone a particular name when you give them that name; someone **is called** a particular name when they have that name: *Paula has called her son Daniel.* ❑ *What's the new assistant called?* **b** You **call** someone something when you describe them as that: *She called him a liar.*
2 You **call** something a name if you give it that name; something **is called** a name if it has that name: *The house is called 'Rose Cottage'.*
3 You **call** when you shout: *She heard a voice calling 'Help'.* ❑ *'Peter, where are you?' she called.*
4 You **call** someone when you telephone them: *I'll call you next week.*
5 You **call** at a place when you stop there for a short time: *This train calls at Edinburgh, York and London.* ❑ *We called at the post office to pick up our mail.*

▷ **call on**
You **call on** someone when you visit them for a short time: *I'll call on you at about 7 o'clock.*

calm *adjective*: **calmer, calmest**
1 You are **calm** when you are not anxious or angry: *He is usually a very calm person.*
2 The weather is **calm** when it is not windy: *It was windy this morning, but it's calm now.*

came *verb*
see **come**: *I came home early from the party.*

camera *noun*: **cameras**
A **camera** is an instrument that you use to take photographs or to make films: *I need a new film for my camera.* ❑ *a video camera* ❑ *a TV camera.*

camp *noun*: **camps**
A **camp** is a group of tents or huts that people live in for a period of time: *They made their camp near the river.*

camp *verb*: **camps, camped, camping, has camped**
You **camp**, or you **go camping**, when you go and live in a tent, usually for a holiday: *We asked the farmer before we camped in the field.* ❑ *We're going camping again this year.*

can *verb*: **can, could**
1 You **can** do something if you are able to do it: *Can you look after the baby for me on Saturday?*
2 You **can** do something if you know how to do it: *Can you speak French?*
3 You **can** do something if you are allowed to do it, or have permission to do it: *Can we smoke in this room?* ❑ *I'll ask*

Robert if you can come to his party.

the opposite is **cannot**

can *noun*: **cans**
A **can** is a metal container for things such as food, liquid and paint: *a can of soup* ❑ *a can of peas.*

same as **tin**

candle *noun*: **candles**
A **candle** is a stick of wax with a piece of string through it which burns, giving light: *Remember to blow out the candle when you go to bed.*

canned *adjective*
Canned food is food stored in cans: *canned soup.*

same as **tinned**

cannot *verb*
Cannot is the opposite of **can**: *I cannot believe that story.*

can't *verb*
Can't is short for **cannot**: *I can't go to the cinema tonight.*

cap *noun*: **caps**
1 A **cap** is a hat with a curved part at the front that protects your eyes from the sun: *a baseball cap.*

cap

2 A **cap** is also a small lid on something such as a pen or a bottle: *Remember to replace the cap when you've finished.*

capital *noun*: **capitals**
1 The **capital**, or **capital city**, of a country is the city where its government is based: *The capital of Portugal is Lisbon.*

2 A **capital**, or **capital letter**, is a large letter which begins sentences and certain words, such as people's names: *'Paris' begins with a capital letter.*

car *noun*: **cars**
A **car** is a motor vehicle which people can travel in: *Mr White's car broke down yesterday.*

card *noun*: **cards**
1 Card is stiff paper: *She wrote the notice on a large piece of card.*
2 A **card** is a piece of stiff paper which you write a message or greeting on: *I must remember to send Jackie a birthday card.* ❏ *When she was ill all her friends sent cards.*
3 A playing **card** is a piece of card with numbers and symbols on it; playing cards are always in sets of 52, and are used to play games: *card games.*

cardboard *noun*
Cardboard is thick stiff paper used to make boxes and packets: *This child's book is made of cardboard.* ❏ *cardboard boxes.*

care *noun*: **cares**
1 You do something with **care** when you do it carefully: *Treat her with care; she's very nervous.*
2 A **care** is a worry: *He doesn't have a care in the world.*

▷ **take care**
You **take care** when you are careful in a difficult or dangerous situation: *Take care when driving abroad.*

▷ **take care of**
1 You **take care of** someone or something when you look after them: *We're taking care of Tim's dog while he's in France.*
2 You also **take care** of

something when you deal with it: *Don't worry. I'll take care of the bill.*

care *verb*: **cares, cared, caring, has cared**
1 You **care** about something if you are interested in it, or if you think it is important: *He doesn't seem to care about his future.*
2 You **care** about someone if you are fond of them or interested in what happens to them: *She really cares about Matt.*

▷ **care for**
1 You **care for** someone or something when you look after them: *He's caring for his sick grandmother.*
2 You **don't care for** someone or something when you don't like them: *I don't care for him much.*
3 If you ask someone if they would **care for** something you are asking very politely if they would like to have it: *Would you care for another biscuit?*

career *noun*: **careers**
A person's **career** is the job or jobs that they do during their life: *I want to have a career working with animals.*

careful *adjective*
You are **careful** when you make sure that you do something properly without making a mistake or without causing an accident: *Please be careful with the computer.* ❏ *a careful driver.*

carefully *adverb*
You do something **carefully** if you do it properly, without making mistakes: *He doesn't always drive very carefully.*

careless *adjective*
You are being **careless** when you

are not being careful: *I'm so careless — I've lost my purse again.*

carelessly *adverb*
You do something **carelessly** if you don't do it properly or carefully: *He did the work carelessly and they had to ask him to do it again.*

carpet *noun*: **carpets**
A **carpet** is a piece of thick material used to cover a floor: *This carpet is a bit old — we'll have to get a new one.*

carriage *noun*: **carriages**
A **carriage** is a long vehicle which forms part of a train: *We sat in the last carriage of the train.*

carrot *noun*: **carrots**
A **carrot** is a long orange vegetable, pointed at one end.

carrots

carry *verb*: **carries, carried, carrying, has carried**
You **carry** something when you take it somewhere by lifting it with your arms: *She carried the books downstairs.* ❏ *It's too heavy for one person to carry.*

▷ **carry on**
You **carry on** doing something if you continue to do it: *She wants to carry on working after she's sixty.*

▷ **carry out**
You **carry** something **out** when you do it or finish it: *It's a good plan, if we have enough money to carry it out.*

cart *noun*: **carts**
A **cart** is a vehicle with two or four wheels, pulled by a horse.

case *noun*: **cases**
1 A **case** is a suitcase: *Could you take the cases upstairs please?*
2 A **case** is also a container for holding something: *Have you seen my sunglasses case?*

▷ **in case**
You do something **in case** something happens, when you do it because something else may happen: *I'll take my coat in case it gets cold.*

cash *noun*
Cash is money in the form of notes or coins: *They don't accept cheques — we'll have to pay in cash.*

cassette *noun*: **cassettes**
A **cassette** is a plastic case for tape that records and plays music, or for film for a camera.

cat *noun*: **cats**
A **cat** is an animal with soft fur, large eyes, whiskers and a tail; people often keep cats as pets: *The cat lay in front of the fire.* ❏ *Does your cat catch mice?*

catch *verb*: **catches, caught, catching, has caught**
1a You **catch** an animal when you take hold of it and stop it from escaping: *He went fishing yesterday and caught three fish.*
b You **catch** a person when you find them and stop them from escaping: *The police said it would be easy to catch the burglar.*
2 You **catch** something that is falling through the air when you take hold of it with your hands: *I tried to catch the ball.*
3 You **catch** a train or a bus when you get on it before it leaves: *If I miss the bus at 9 o'clock, I'll catch the next one.*

4 You **catch** someone doing something wrong when you discover them doing it: *I caught George sleeping at his desk.*
5 You **catch** an illness when you get it and feel unwell: *He caught a bad cold and had to stay off work for a week.*
6 You **catch** something that someone says when you manage to hear it: *Did you catch his name?* ❑ *Sorry, I didn't catch that.*
7 Something **catches** fire when it begins to burn: *The carpet caught fire when we were in bed.*

caterpillar *noun*: **caterpillars**
A **caterpillar** is a small creature which turns into a butterfly or moth.

cattle *noun*
Cattle are cows and bulls: *He has cattle and sheep on his farm.*

caught *verb*
see **catch**: *I caught the train to London.* ❑ *They caught the burglar as he was trying to break into the house.*

cause *verb*: **causes, caused, causing, has caused**
One thing **causes** another if it makes it happen: *What caused the plane crash?* ❑ *His leg is causing him a lot of pain.*

cause is also a noun: *Do you know the cause of the problem?*

cave *noun*: **caves**
A **cave** is a large natural hole in a cliff, in a mountain or under the ground: *These birds build their nests in caves.*

CD *noun*: **CDs**
A **CD** is a compact disc: *I bought a new CD yesterday.*

'see-**dee**'

ceiling *noun*: **ceilings**
The **ceiling** of a room is its inside roof: *I'm going to paint the ceiling this weekend.*

celebrate *verb*: **celebrates, celebrated, celebrating, has celebrated**
You **celebrate** when you have a party or do something you enjoy because of a special event: *We celebrated my birthday on holiday this year.* ❑ *I've passed my exams so I'm going to celebrate tonight.*

cellar *noun*: **cellars**
A **cellar** is an underground room in a building, used to store things: *a wine cellar.*

cent *noun*: **cents**
A **cent** is a coin. There are a hundred cents in a dollar: *This bar of chocolate costs 50 cents.*

centimetre *noun*: **centimetre**
A **centimetre** is a small measurement of length. There are a hundred centimetres in a metre.

centre *noun*: **centres**
1 The **centre** of something is the middle of it: *It's impossible to park the car in the centre of town.* ❑ *There's a large stone in the centre of this fruit.*
2 A **centre** is a building where a particular activity takes place: *a shopping centre* ❑ *a sports centre.*

century *noun*: **centuries**
A **century** is a period of 100 years: *The house has belonged to his family for three centuries.* ❑ *the twenty-first century.*

cereal *noun*: **cereals**
1 A **cereal** is a type of grain, for example rice or wheat, used as food.
2 **Cereal**, or a **cereal**, is also a kind of food eaten at breakfast:

Would you prefer toast or cereal first? ❑ *This is my favourite breakfast cereal.*

ceremony *noun*: **ceremonies**
A **ceremony** is a formal event carried out because of a special occasion: *The wedding ceremony begins at 3 o'clock.*

certain *adjective and determiner*
1 You are **certain** about something when you are sure about it: *She's certain that she'll pass her exams.* ❑ *I'm certain he'll win.*
2 Certain also means 'some'; you use '**certain**' when you do not want to say exactly who or what you are talking about: *Certain people in our group aren't doing their jobs well.* ❑ *A certain amount of money was stolen from my purse yesterday.*

---
meaning 1: the opposite is
uncertain
---

certainly *adverb*
1 Certainly means 'without doubt': *She's certainly younger than she looks.*
2 Certainly also means 'yes, of course': *'Can I borrow this book?' 'Certainly.'*

chain *noun*: **chains**
A **chain** is a number of metal rings joined together: *She wore a gold chain round her neck.*

chair *noun*: **chairs**
A **chair** is a piece of furniture with four legs and an upright back, used for sitting on: *kitchen chairs.*

 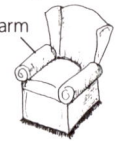 

chair   armchair   wheelchair

chalk *noun*
1 Chalk is a kind of soft white stone.
2 A piece of **chalk** is a stick of this used to write or draw with.

chance *noun*: **chances**
There is a **chance** that something will happen if it is quite probable: *We have a good chance of getting tickets for the concert.*

▷ **by chance**
Something that happens **by chance** has not been planned: *I found out about the job by chance.*

change *noun*: **changes**
1 A **change** is a difference or something new: *I'm bored with my job — I need a change.* ❑ *There have been a lot of changes in the company since 1995.*
2 Change is money in the form of coins rather than notes: *He took some change out of his pocket and gave it to the waiter.*
3 Change is also the money that is given back to you when you pay too much: *I paid with a ten dollar note and got two dollars change.*

change *verb*: **changes, changed, changing, has changed**
1 You **change** something when you make it different: *She's changed many people's lives.* ❑ *He changed his name to Muhammed Ali.* ❑ *You've changed your hairstyle, haven't you?*
2 Something **changes** when it becomes different: *Jane hasn't changed at all.* ❑ *The weather changed and it began to rain.*
3 You **change** something you don't want when you exchange it

for something else: *This skirt is too small — can I change it?*
4 You **change** when you put on different clothes: *I want to change before we go out.*
5 You **change** buses or trains when you get off one and on to another: *This train doesn't go to Stoke — you'll have to change at Crewe.*
6 You **change** money when you exchange it for different notes or coins of the same value: *She's changed her dollars into francs.*

chapter *noun*: **chapters**
A **chapter** is one of the sections that a book is divided into: *She's writing the final chapter.*

character *noun*: **characters**
1 A person's **character** is the qualities that they have: *He's got a very kind side to his character too, you know.*
2 A **character** in a play, book or film is a person who appears in it: *There are six characters in the play.*

charge *noun*: **charges**
1 A **charge** is the price that you pay when you want to buy something: *There will be no charge for the repairs to your washing machine.*
2 The police make a **charge** against someone when they accuse that person of a crime: *The charge made against him was of murder.*

▷ **in charge**
You are **in charge** if you have to look after or manage people and things: *He's in charge of the whole company.*

charge *verb*: **charges, charged, charging, has charged**
1 You **charge** a certain amount of money when you ask for it in return for something: *They charge £1 for a small cup of coffee.*
2 A person **is charged** with a crime when they are accused of it by the police: *He was charged with burglary.*

chase *verb*: **chases, chased, chasing, has chased**
1 You **chase** someone or something when you run after them and try to catch them: *She chased him but she couldn't catch him.*
2 You **chase** someone or something, or you **chase** them **away**, when you make them run away: *I chased the cat from my garden.*

chat *noun*: **chats**
A **chat** is a friendly talk with someone: *If you have any trouble, call me and we can have a chat about it.*

same as **conversation**

chat *verb*: **chats, chatted, chatting, has chatted**
People **chat** when they talk in a friendly way: *They chatted on the phone for hours.*

cheap *adjective*: **cheaper, cheapest**
1 Something is **cheap** if it doesn't cost a lot of money: *This book was cheap — it only cost £1.*
2 You can also say something is **cheap** if it is not good quality: *cheap jewellery.*

meaning 1: the opposite is **expensive**

cheat *noun*: **cheats**
A **cheat** is someone who tries to get a better result for themselves

by doing something that is dishonest: *He accused me of being a cheat.*

cheat *verb*: **cheats, cheated, cheating, has cheated**
Someone **cheats** when they behave in a dishonest way so that they can get a better result: *Mr Reed always cheats at golf.* ▫ *He cheated in the exam.*

check *verb*: **checks, checked, checking, has checked**
You **check** something when you make sure that it is safe or correct: *Can you check these answers, please?* ▫ *She checked that she had switched off the lights.*

cheek *noun*: **cheeks**
Your **cheeks** are the soft parts on the sides of your face, below your eyes: *Mrs Potter's cheeks were red and she was breathing fast.* [see picture at **face**]

cheeky *adjective*: **cheekier, cheekiest**
Someone is **cheeky** when they are rude or too informal with people, especially with those who are older than they are: *Stop being cheeky and answer the question.* ▫ *He's a cheeky little boy.*

cheer *verb*: **cheers, cheered, cheering, has cheered**
You **cheer** when you shout loudly because you are pleased or want to encourage someone: *We all cheered when the goal was scored.*

cheer is also a noun: *The football fans gave a loud cheer when the goal was scored.*

cheerful *adjective*
1 A **cheerful** person is a happy person: *You're very cheerful today.*

2 Something that is **cheerful** makes you feel happy: *a cheerful song.*

cheese *noun*
Cheese is a type of solid food which is made from milk and is usually yellow or white: *goat's cheese.*

cheque *noun*: **cheques**
A **cheque** is a printed piece of paper which you write on and sign; you use cheques instead of money to pay for things: *Can I pay by cheque?*

  rhymes with **neck**

cherry *noun*: **cherries**
A **cherry** is a small red fruit that grows in bunches on a tree: *a cherry pie*

chess *noun*
Chess is a board game played by two people, with 32 pieces.

chest *noun*: **chests**
1 Your **chest** is the front part of your body between your neck and your stomach.
2 A **chest** is a large wooden box, used to store things: *a tea chest* ▫ *The children found the old clothes in a chest under the stairs.*

chew *verb*: **chews, chewed, chewing, has chewed**
You **chew** food when you break it up with your teeth and make it easier to swallow: *You have to chew it well before you can swallow it.*

chick *noun*: **chicks**
A **chick** is a baby bird: *There were three chicks in the nest.*

chicken *noun*: **chickens**
1 A **chicken** is a bird which is kept for its eggs and meat.
2 Chicken is the meat of this

bird, used as food: *chicken and chips.* ❑ *a chicken curry.*

child *noun*: **children**
1 A **child** is a young person who has not yet become an adult: *He's too young for that; he's still a child.* ❑ *The younger children stayed at home.*
2 A person's **child** is their son or daughter: *Mr and Mrs Fowler have three children.* ❑ *Their eldest child is called Sylvie.*

children *noun*
see **child**.

chimney *noun*: **chimneys**
A **chimney** is a narrow tube through which smoke can escape: *a factory chimney.*

chin *noun*: **chins**
Your **chin** is the part of your face below your mouth. [see picture at **face**]

chip *noun*: **chips**
1 Chips are thin strips of fried potato: *fish and chips.*
2 A **chip** is a piece which has broken off something, or the gap that has been left: *There's a chip in this vase.*
3 A **chip** is also a very small device used to make computers work.

chocolate *noun*: **chocolates**
1 Chocolate is a sweet food that is usually dark brown in colour: *a bar of chocolate.*
2 A **chocolate** is a sweet made from chocolate: *a box of chocolates.*

choice *noun*: **choices**
1 You have a **choice** when you have the chance to choose from a variety of things: *We have the choice of going to the cinema or going to the party.*

2 You make a **choice** when you choose between two or more things: *I hope I've made the right choice.*

choose *verb*: **chooses, chose, choosing, has chosen**
1 You **choose** something when you decide to have it, rather than something else: *She chose soup and salad for lunch.*
2 You **choose** to do something when you decide to do it: *He chose to go to Amsterdam.*

 'chooz'

meaning 1: same as **select**

chop *verb*: **chops, chopped, chopping, has chopped**
You **chop** something, or you **chop** it **up**, when you cut it into small pieces: *Can you chop the vegetables, please?* ❑ *Joe has chopped up some wood.*

chopstick *noun*: **chopsticks**
Chopsticks are a set of two sticks held in one hand that are used to serve and eat food.

chose and **chosen** *verb*
see **choose**: *They chose the sofa with the pattern, rather than the plain one.* ❑ *Which colour have you chosen to paint the bathroom?*

 rhymes with **hose**

Christmas *noun*
Christmas is the day on which people celebrate the birth of Jesus Christ. Christmas is on 25 December: *What did you get for Christmas?* ❑ *Christmas Day.* ❑ *'I'd like to wish you all a happy Christmas.'*

church *noun*: **churches**
A **church** is a building where people go to praise God.

cigar *noun*: **cigars**
A **cigar** is a roll of dried tobacco leaves, which people smoke.

cigarette *noun*: **cigarettes**
A **cigarette** is a narrow tube of paper filled with tobacco, which people smoke.

cinema *noun*: **cinemas**
A **cinema** is a building where films are shown on a big screen: *We're going to the cinema tonight.*

circle *noun*: **circles**
A **circle** is a round shape: *Can you draw a circle?*

circular *adjective*
Circular means shaped like a circle: *a circular rug* ❑ *There was a circular mark on the table where the vase stood.*

same as **round**

city *noun*: **cities**
A **city** is a very large town: *I wouldn't like to live in the city; it's too noisy and dirty.*

clap *verb*: **claps, clapped, clapping, has clapped**
You **clap** when you bring your hands together several times, making a noise: *The audience clapped at the end of the play.*

class *noun*: **classes**
1 A **class** is a lesson: *He was late for his history class.*
2 A **class** is also a group of students who learn together: *He's in the same class as my son.*

classroom *noun*: **classrooms**
A **classroom** is a room in a school where classes are taught: *Where is the science classroom?*

claw *noun*: **claws**
1 A **claw** is one of the large sharp nails that certain animals and birds have on their feet: *The*

tiger's claws left deep scratches on the tree.
2 Claws are also the arms of some sea animals, such as crabs.

clean *adjective*: **cleaner, cleanest**
Something is **clean** if it is free of dirt: *She put on a clean T-shirt.* ❑ *The kitchen wasn't very clean.*

clean *verb*: **cleans, cleaned, cleaning, has cleaned**
You **clean** something when you make it free from dirt: *I cleaned the bathroom last night.* ❑ *Have you cleaned your teeth?*

clear *adjective*: **clearer, clearest**
1 Something is **clear** when it is easy to see, hear or understand: *His voice is loud and clear.* ❑ *She gave very clear instructions.*
2 Something is **clear** if you can see through it: *The water in the sea is quite clear here.*
3 A road or path is **clear** if there isn't anything blocking it: *The journey will only take an hour if the roads are clear.*
4 The sky is **clear** if there are no clouds: *It's a bit cold today but the sky is clear.*

▷ **clear up**
1 You **clear up**, or **clear up** a room when you put things away in their proper places: *I'll have to clear up before the guests start arriving.*
2 The weather **clears up** when it stops raining and the clouds move away: *It's raining just now, but I think it will clear up soon.*
3 A headache or illness **clears up** when it gets better: *I had a cold last week but it has cleared up now.*

clearly *adverb*
1 Clearly means 'in a clear way':

He spoke slowly and clearly. ❑ *It was dark and we couldn't see the road very clearly.*
2 You also use '**clearly**' when you want to show that there is no doubt about something: *Clearly, this kind of work is not good enough.*

clever *adjective*: **cleverer, cleverest**
You are **clever** if you are able to learn and understand things quickly: *You're so clever! You passed all your exams!* ❑ *His brother isn't as clever as he is.* ❑ *She's the cleverest girl in the class.*

cliff *noun*: **cliffs**
A **cliff** is a high area of rock, especially on the coast: *We went for a walk along the top of the cliff.*

climb *verb*: **climbs, climbed, climbing, has climbed**
You **climb** something, or you **climb up** something, when you go towards the top of it: *They climbed three mountains in three days.* ❑ *If you climb up the tower, you'll get a good view of the city.*

rhymes with **time**

clinic *noun*: **clinics**
A **clinic** is a hospital, or part of a hospital, where people can go for treatment or advice: *a mother-and-baby clinic.*

clock *noun*: **clocks**
A **clock** is an instrument that shows the time: *The clock showed 9am; I was late.*

close *adjective*: **closer, closest**
1 One thing is **close** to another if it is near that other thing: *Their house is close to the railway station.* ❑ *Come closer; I can't see you clearly.*

2 Two people are **close** if they are very good friends: *Those two girls are very close.*

close *verb*: **closes, closed, closing, has closed**
You **close** something when you shut it: *Can you close the window, please?*

rhymes with **nose**

closed *adjective*
Something is **closed** when it is shut: *I needed to buy some milk, but the shop was closed.*

cloth *noun*: **cloths**
1 Cloth is material used to make clothes and other things: *a cloth cap* ❑ *The wool is used to make cloth.*
2 A **cloth** is a piece of this material used for cleaning, or for some other purpose: *I cleaned the kitchen floor with an old cloth.* ❑ *a new tablecloth.*

clothes *noun*
Clothes are the things that you wear, such as trousers, shirts and skirts: *He's bought himself some new clothes.*

clothing *noun*
Clothing is clothes: *winter clothing.*

cloud *noun*: **clouds**
Clouds are the grey or white collections of small drops of water which float in the sky: *When they arrived at the beach, dark clouds were already visible in the distance.*

club *noun*: **clubs**
1 A **club** is an organized group of people who meet regularly to take part in an activity: *He's joined a tennis club.*
2 A **club** is also the place where

the members of a club meet: *It only takes 5 minutes to walk to the club.*
3a A **club** is one of the metal sticks used to hit the ball in the game of golf. **b** A **club** is a thick heavy stick, used as a weapon: *Someone hit him with a club.*

clue *noun*: **clues**
A **clue** is a piece of information which helps to solve a mystery or a problem: *The police searched the house for clues.*

clumsy *adjective*: **clumsier, clumsiest**
A **clumsy** person often has accidents or breaks things: *I'm so clumsy — I've broken another glass.*

coach *noun*: **coaches**
A **coach** is a large comfortable bus for long journeys: *We went to Frankfurt by coach.*

coast *noun*: **coaches**
The **coast** is the area of land along the side of the sea: *We're going on holiday to a village on the coast.*

coat *noun*: **coats**
1 A **coat** is a piece of clothing which you wear over your other clothes when you go outside.
2 An animal's **coat** is its fur: *This dog has a beautiful shiny coat.*

cobweb *noun*: **cobwebs**
A **cobweb** is a spider's web: *The room was full of cobwebs.* [see picture at **spider**]

cock *noun*: **cocks**
A **cock** is a male bird, especially an adult male chicken.

coconut *noun*: **coconuts**
A **coconut** is a large nut with white flesh and a sweet clear

liquid inside; coconuts grow on a type of palm tree.

coffee *noun*: **coffees**
1 Coffee is a dark brown powder made from roasted beans, which is used to make a hot drink.
2 Coffee is also the hot drink made with this powder: *Do you prefer tea or coffee?*
3 A **coffee** is a cup of coffee: *Can I have three coffees, please?*

coin *noun*: **coins**
A **coin** is a small round piece of metal that is used as money: *You need coins for this telephone.*

cold *adjective*: **colder, coldest**
Something is **cold** when it is low in temperature: *Their house is always cold.* ❑ *Is it cold outside?* ❑ *a cold drink* ❑ *Your hands will get cold if you don't wear your gloves.*

cold *noun*: **colds**
A **cold** is a common illness which makes you cough and sneeze: *She's got a bad cold.*

collar *noun*: **collars**
1 The **collar** of a shirt or jacket is the band of material at the neck.
2 A dog's or a cat's **collar** is a band you put round its neck, to which a lead can be attached.

collect *verb*: **collects, collected, collecting, has collected**
1 You **collect** things when you take them and put them together: *I collected all the old newspapers and put them in the bin.*
2 You **collect** a particular kind of thing when you get more and more of them because you are interested in them: *He collects stamps.*
3 You **collect** someone or something when you fetch them

from somewhere: *I'll collect you at 5 o'clock.*

collection *noun*: **collections**
A **collection** of things is a set of them: *Mr Collins has a large collection of rare paintings.*

college *noun*: **colleges**
A **college** is a place where people study or do training, usually after they have left school: *My brother's going to college to study business.*

collide *verb*: **collides, collided, colliding, has collided**
Two or more things **collide** when they crash or bump into each other: *The two cars collided on the motorway.* ❑ *I collided with Mrs Cox on the stairs.*

colour *noun*: **colours**
The **colour** of something is its appearance in the light of day — whether it is red, yellow or blue, for example: *What's your favourite colour?* ❑ *The sea is such a lovely colour.* ❑ *the colours of the rainbow.*

colour *verb*: **colours, coloured, colouring, has coloured**
You **colour** something, such as a drawing, when you add colour to it: *Colour the sky blue.*

colourful *adjective*
Something that is **colourful** has a lot of bright colours: *He was wearing a very colourful new shirt.*

comb *noun*: **combs**
A **comb** is a piece of plastic or metal with a row of thin points called 'teeth'; you use a comb to tidy your hair.

comb

comb is also a verb: *He quickly shaved and combed his hair before the guests arrived.*

come *verb*: **comes, came, coming, has come**
1a Someone or something **comes** towards you when they move towards you: *He came to my office and gave me a letter.* ❑ *Come here and look at this.* ❑ *The car came round the corner on the wrong side of the road.*
b Someone **comes** with you when they go to a place with you: *Are you coming to the beach with us?* ❑ *We're leaving now. Are you coming?*
2 You **come** to a place when you reach it or arrive there: *Finally, we came to a big old house.* ❑ *The bus comes into Kuala Lumpur at midday.*
3 A date or time **comes** when it arrives or happens: *The wet season will be coming soon.* ❑ *He said he couldn't wait for Friday to come.*
4a A person **comes** from a particular place if that is their home or the place where they were born: *She asked me where I came from.* ❑ *I'm going back to the place I come from.*
b Something **comes** from a particular place if that is where you can find it: *Oil comes from under the ground.* ❑ *These plants come from South America.* ❑ *There's a strange noise coming from the washing machine.*
5a Something **comes** to a certain level if that is the level it reaches: *The water only comes to my knees here.* **b** The cost of a number of things **comes** to a

certain amount when that is the total cost: *The four meals came to just $20.*
6 Something **comes** to be a certain way when it becomes that way: *My wish came true.* ❑ *The box came apart in my hands.*

---

meanings 1 and 2: the opposite is **go**

▷ **come about**
You use **come about** when you are talking about how something happened: *How did this mistake come about?*

▷ **come across**
You **come across** something when you find it by chance: *I came across some old toys in the cupboard.*

▷ **come back**
You **come back** to a place when you return there after being away: *When are you coming back home?*

▷ **come down**
1 Something **comes down** when it moves to a lower position: *Come down from that wall now!*
2 The cost or level of something **comes down** when it gets less: *Fruit and vegetables have come down a lot this month.*

▷ **come on**
1 Something **is coming on** well when it is making good progress: *Your picture is coming on really well.*
2 You say **come on!** to someone when you want them to hurry: *Come on! We're going to miss the bus.*

▷ **come out**
1 The sun or moon **comes out** when it appears from behind the clouds.

2 Marks on cloth **come out** when they disappear because of cleaning: *That red wine won't come out of the carpet.*
3 A photograph **comes out** when it is successful, and you can clearly see the subject.

▷ **come over**
A feeling **comes over** you when it suddenly affects you: *A strange feeling of fear suddenly came over me.*

▷ **come up**
1 Something **comes up** when it happens, often suddenly: *You've got important exams coming up soon.* ❑ *A problem came up and he had to work late at the office.*
2 A subject **comes up** when people mention it in a conversation: *We talked for quite a while, but the subject of work didn't come up.*

comfortable *noun*
1 You are **comfortable** when you feel relaxed: *He looks very comfortable sitting in that chair.*
2 Something is **comfortable** if it makes you feel relaxed: *This chair is so comfortable.*

common *adjective*: **commoner, commonest**
1 Something is **common** if it happens often: *Rain is common in the autumn.*
2 Something is **common** to a group of people or things when they all share it: *There's a common kitchen for all the rooms on this floor.*

---

meaning 1: the opposite is **rare**

---

compact disc *noun*: **compact discs**
A **compact disc** is a small disc

with a lot of information or sound stored on it; you play it using a machine called a 'CD player'.

same as **CD**

company *noun*: **companies**
1 A **company** is a business organization: *She works for an oil company.*
2 You have the **company** of someone when you have them with you: *It will be nice to have your company on the journey.*

compare *verb*: **compares, compared, comparing, has compared**
You **compare** two or more things when you try to see how they are the same, and how they are different: *We compared the books to see which was best.*

compartment *noun*: **compartments**
A **compartment** is a section inside a larger space, which has a particular purpose: *There's a compartment for storing pens and pencils in this desk.*

compete *verb*: **competes, competed, competing, has competed**
You **compete** when you try to win, or try to be better than other people: *He's competing in the 100 metres race.* ☐ *They're always competing against each other, rather than working together.*

competition *noun*: **competitions**
A **competition** is an event in which people try to win by being better than everyone else: *Patrick won the swimming competition.*

complain *verb*: **complains, complained, complaining, has complained**

1 You **complain** when you tell someone that you are not happy or pleased with something: *We complained about the dirty hotel room.*
2 You **complain** of something when you say you are suffering from it: *She had complained of chest pains.*

complete *verb*: **completes, completed, completing, has completed**
You **complete** something when you finish it: *He completed the exam in an hour.*

complete *adjective*
1 Something is **complete** when it is finished, or if all its parts are there: *This jigsaw is complete.*
2 Complete also means 'total': *The party was a complete failure — no-one enjoyed it.*

completely *adverb*
Completely means 'totally': *He looks completely different — I didn't recognize him.*

computer   screen
keyboard   mouse

computer *noun*: **computers**
A **computer** is a machine which can store a lot of information and do many different tasks very quickly.

concert *noun*: **concerts**
A **concert** is a performance of music and singing: *We're going to a rock concert tomorrow.*

condition *noun*
The **condition** of a person or thing is the state that they are in: *The bike is in good condition.*

conduct *noun*
A person's **conduct** is the way in which they behave: *His conduct has got worse over the year.*

'**kon**-dukt'

connect *verb*: **connects, connected, connecting, has connected**
You **connect** two or more things when you join them together: *How do you connect the two parts?* ❑ *You have to connect the red wire to the green wire.*

connection *noun*: **connections**
A **connection** is something which joins or links two or more things: *The connection from the lamp to the plug was loose.* ❑ *Was there any connection between the two events?*

consider *verb*: **considers, considered, considering, has considered**
You **consider** something when you think about it for some time, before making a decision: *He'll consider all your suggestions and then make a decision.*

contact *verb*: **contacts, contacted, contacting, has contacted**
You **contact** someone when you telephone them or write to them: *I'll contact you when I have more information.*

contain *verb*: **contains, contained, containing, has contained**
Something such as a box or a cupboard **contains** things if it has them inside it: *Those boxes contain old books.* ❑ *What does this cupboard contain?*

container *noun*: **containers**
A **container** is an object designed to hold things: *We keep the cake in a plastic container.*

contest *noun*: **contests**
A **contest** is a competition: *Fifty people took part in the cycling contest.*

continent *noun*: **continents**
A **continent** is a large area of land which is divided into smaller countries: *Europe, Asia, America and Africa are continents.*

continue *verb*: **continues, continued, continuing, has continued**
1 You **continue** to do something when you do not stop doing it: *He continued to read until the end of the chapter.*
2 Something **continues** when it begins again; you **continue** something when you begin it again: *The film continues after the news.* ❑ *He continued his studies after his holiday.*

control *verb*: **controls, controlled, controlling, has controlled**
1 Someone **controls** something when they are in charge of it, and make all the important decisions: *She controls the business.*
2 You **control** a vehicle when you guide it or operate it: *It was difficult to control the van on the icy roads.*
3 You **control** a person or an animal when you make them behave properly or well: *Please try to control your dog.* ❑ *Mr Malcolm is a good teacher, but he can't control his students.*

control *noun*
Control is the power that someone has over people or

things: *The government wants to have more control over business.*

conversation *noun*: **conversations**
A **conversation** is a talk you have with someone: *We had a long conversation about music.*

cook *noun*: **cooks**
A **cook** is a person who prepares or cooks food, especially as a job.

cook *verb*: **cooks, cooked, cooking, has cooked**
1 You **cook** food when you prepare it for eating using heat: *I'm cooking fish tonight.*
2 Food **cooks** when it heats up and becomes ready to eat: *The chicken isn't cooking very fast.*

cooked *adjective*
Cooked food has been heated up so that it is ready to eat: *You can eat onions raw or cooked.*

the opposite is **raw**

cooker *noun*: **cookers**
A **cooker** is a device which you use to cook food in, or on: *a gas cooker* ❑ *He put the frying pan on the cooker and started to cook the sausages.*

same as **stove**

cookie *noun*: **cookies**
A **cookie** is a biscuit.

cooking *noun*
Cooking is the activity of preparing food by baking, boiling or frying it: *Who's doing the cooking for the party?*

cool *adjective*: **cooler, coolest**
1 Something is **cool** if it is quite cold, often in a pleasant way: *a cool drink.* ❑ *a cool breeze.*
2 A **cool** person is calm and doesn't often get upset.

meaning 1: the opposite is **warm** or **hot**

copy *verb*: **copies, copied, copying, has copied**
1 You **copy** a piece of work when you make another one that is exactly the same: *He copied the names on the list into his notebook.* ❑ *Can I copy your notes from this morning's lesson?*
2 You **copy** someone when you do exactly the same as they do: *I always copied my older sister when I was younger.*

copy *noun*: **copies**
1 A **copy** of a piece of work is another one that is exactly the same as it: *He made a copy of the report.*
2 A **copy** of a particular book or newspaper is one example of it: *I've just bought a copy of his new book.*

corn *noun*
Several plants that produce grain, such as wheat or maize, are called **corn**: *a field of corn* ❑ *The chickens feed on corn.*

corner *noun*: **corners**
1 A **corner** is the place where two edges meet: *the corner of the table.* ❑ *A cube has eight corners and six sides.*

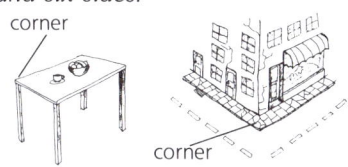

corner

corner

2 A **corner** is also the place where two roads meet or where a road changes direction: *The library is on the corner of Hope Street and Ferry Road.* ❑ *The bus* *was going too fast round the corner.*

correct *adjective*
Something is **correct** if it doesn't have any mistakes: *Who knows the correct answer?* ❑ *Is that the correct spelling?*

same as **right**
the opposite is **wrong** or **incorrect**

correct *verb*: **corrects, corrected, correcting, has corrected**
You **correct** something when you remove the mistakes in it: *Could you correct this letter for me please?*

corridor *noun*: **corridors**
A **corridor** is a long narrow place in a building, usually with rooms on either side.

cost *noun*: **costs**
The **cost** of something is the amount of money that you have to pay to get it: *The cost of petrol is rising.*

cost *verb*: **costs, cost, costing, has cost**
Something **costs** a particular amount of money when you have to pay that much to get it: *This car costs £3000.* ❑ *It cost $100.*

cot *noun*: **cots**
A **cot** is a small bed with high sides, for a young child.

cottage *noun*: **cottages**
A **cottage** is a small house, especially one in a village.

cotton *noun*
Cotton is a type of material which comes from a plant and is used to make cloth: *a cotton shirt.* ❑ *It's made of cotton.*

couch *noun*: **couches**
A **couch** is a sofa.

cough *verb*: **coughs, coughed, coughing, has coughed**
You **cough** when you make a sudden rough noise, forcing air out of your throat: *He coughed to attract the assistant's attention.*

'**kof**'

cough is also a noun: *She's got a bad cough.*

could *verb*
1 see **can**: *She asked if I could speak French.*
2 You use **could** with another verb to say that something is possible: *We could go on Friday evening.*
3 You use **could** with another verb to ask someone for something politely: *Could I have another cup of tea, please?*

rhymes with **good**

couldn't *verb*
Couldn't is short for **could not**: *I couldn't believe my good luck.*

count *verb*: **counts, counted, counting, has counted**
1 You **count** when you say numbers in order, for example 'one, two, three, four': *Count up to a hundred.*
2 You **count** people or things when you find out how many of them there are by adding them up: *I'll quickly count how many people have arrived.*

'**kownt**'

counter *noun*: **counters**
1 A **counter** in a shop is a long narrow table where you pay for things: *If you can't find something, please ask at the counter.*
2 A **counter** is also a small disc used in some board games.

'**kownt**-er'

country *noun*: **countries**
1 A **country** is an area of land in the world with its own government and sometimes its own language: *China is one of the largest countries in the world.*
2 The **country** is land away from the city that does not have many buildings or busy roads: *We went for a drive in the country.*

ꞌ**kunt**-riꞌ

couple *noun*: **couples**
1 Two people who are married, or who have a similar relationship, are often called a **couple**: *They make a nice couple.*
2 A **couple** is also two people who are together for a particular reason: *There were four couples dancing to the music.*
3 A **couple** of people or things is two of them, or a small number of them: *Can I have a couple of those pins, please?* ❑ *I'll join you in a couple of minutes.*

ꞌ**kup**-lꞌ

courage *noun*
You have **courage** if you are willing to do dangerous or difficult things: *He showed great courage, saving the lives of three people.*

ꞌ**kur**-idjꞌ

course *noun*: **courses**
1 A **course** is a number of lessons or lectures on a particular subject: *We're going to do a course in modern art.*
2 A meal can be divided into different **courses**: *We had steak for our main course.*

ꞌ**kors**ꞌ

▷ **of course**
You say '**of course**' when you want to agree to a request in a polite way: *'Can you come to my office this afternoon?' 'Of course.'*

court *noun*: **courts**
1 A **court** is a building where judges make decisions on legal subjects and where people are found guilty or innocent of crimes.
2 A **court** is also an area marked with lines, where a particular game or sport is played: *a tennis court.*

ꞌ**kort**ꞌ

cousin *noun*: **cousins**
Your **cousin** is the child of your aunt and uncle.

ꞌ**kuz**-inꞌ

cover *noun*: **covers**
A **cover** is something that you put over an object to protect or hide it: *a seat cover.* ❑ *a cushion cover.*

cover *verb*: **covers, covered, covering, has covered**
1 You **cover** an object when you put something over it to protect or hide it: *We covered the floor with old newspapers before painting.*
2 An object **is covered** in, or with, something when it has a layer of that thing over it: *My shoes were covered in mud.* ❑ *The ground was covered with snow.*

cow *noun*: **cows**
A **cow** is a female animal which is kept on farms for its milk and meat.

crab *noun*: **crabs**
A **crab** is a sea animal with a hard shell and two large claws.

 crab

crack *noun*: **cracks**
A **crack** is a split forming a thin line in something: *There's a crack in this plate.*

crack *verb*: **cracks, cracked, cracking, has cracked**
Something such as a mirror or a window **cracks** when it gets damaged but it doesn't break into pieces: *The mirror cracked when it fell on the floor.*

cracked *adjective*
Something such as a mirror or a window is **cracked** when it is damaged but is not broken into pieces: *This window is cracked.*

cradle *noun*: **cradles**
A **cradle** is a very small baby's bed, which usually moves from side to side.

crane *noun*: **cranes**
A **crane** is a tall machine with a long arm that swings from side to side; it is used for lifting and moving heavy things.

crash *noun*: **crashes**
1 A **crash** is an accident in which one or more vehicles are damaged: *a plane crash.* ❑ *a car crash.*
2 A **crash** is also a sudden loud noise: *The cup fell to the floor with a crash.*

crash *verb*: **crashes, crashed, crashing, has crashed**
1 A vehicle **crashes** when it hits another vehicle or object: *His car crashed into a lamp-post.*
2 Something **crashes** when it falls and hits something such as the ground, making a loud noise: *The vase crashed to the floor.*

crate *noun*: **crates**
A **crate** is a strong box that is used to carry things: *He was carrying a crate of wine.*

crawl *verb*: **crawls, crawled, crawling, has crawled**
1a Someone **crawls** when they move somewhere on their hands and knees: *The baby crawled across the floor.* **b** Insects or other small creatures **crawl** when they move, especially slowly: *A huge spider crawled out from under a rock.*

crawl

2 Something **crawls** when it moves very slowly: *The traffic crawled along the road.*

crazy *adjective*: **crazier, craziest**
1 A **crazy** person behaves in a strange or foolish way: *You must be crazy to pay £100 for that jacket.*
2 You are **crazy** about someone or something if you like them very much: *She's crazy about football.* ❑ *He's crazy about Yvonne.*

same as **mad**

cream *noun*
1 Cream is a thick yellow food that forms on the top of milk.
2 Cream is also a thick liquid which people rub into their skin to make it soft: *hand cream.*

creature *noun*: **creatures**
A **creature** is an animal or a human being: *a sea creature* ❑ *She was a beautiful creature.*

creep *verb*: **creeps, crept, creeping, has crept**
You **creep** if you move slowly

and quietly, especially when you do not want anyone to notice you: *She crept into the room.*

crew *noun*: **crews**
The **crew** of an aeroplane or ship is the team of people who work on it.

cricket *noun*
Cricket is a sport played by two teams of eleven players, who try to hit a hard ball with a narrow wooden bat.

cried and **cries** *verb*
see **cry**: *The baby cried all day.* ❑ *She always cries when she looks at these photos.*

crime *noun*: **crimes**
Someone carries out a **crime** when they do something that is against the law: *He was accused of the crime of murder.*

criminal *noun*: **criminals**
A **criminal** is a person who carries out a crime.

crisp *adjective*: **crisper, crispest**
Something that is **crisp** is hard, and breaks or cracks easily: *After the frost, the snow felt crisp under our feet.* ❑ *Fry the potatoes until they are crisp.*

crocodile *noun*: **crocodiles**
A **crocodile** is a reptile with rough skin and huge jaws; crocodiles live in and near rivers in hot countries.

crop *noun*: **crops**
Crops are plants that farmers grow: *He grows several different crops on his farm.* ❑ *The only crop we grow here is wheat.*

cross *noun*: **crosses**
1 A **cross** is a shape formed by two lines which cross each other, such as (+).

2 A **cross** is also written like the letter X, and is used to show that something is wrong.

cross *verb*: **crosses, crossed, crossing, has crossed**
1 You **cross** a road or a river when you go from one side of it to the other: *We crossed the river in a boat.*
2 You **cross** your arms, or you **cross** your legs, when you place one of them over the other: *He sat down and crossed his legs.*

▷ **cross out**
You **cross out** a piece of writing when you draw a line through it: *She crossed out all the mistakes in the letter.*

cross *adjective*
You are **cross** when you are rather angry: *He was cross with her for not coming to his party.*

same as **annoyed**

crouch *verb*: **crouches, crouched, crouching, has crouched**
You **crouch**, or you **crouch down**, when you bend down very low with your knees bent: *She crouched down beside the little boy and asked him his name.*

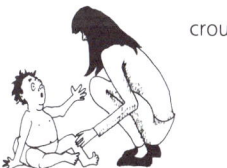
crouch

crowd *noun*: **crowds**
A **crowd** is a large number of people together in the same place: *A crowd gathered in the street and waited for the president to arrive.*

cruel *adjective*: **crueller, cruellest**
A **cruel** person is someone who deliberately causes suffering to others: *He was a cruel and evil man.*

crumb *noun*: **crumbs**
A **crumb** is a tiny piece of bread or cake: *There were bread crumbs all over the floor after the meal.*

crush *verb*
1 You **crush** something when you press it into small pieces: *Crush the garlic and add it to the onions.*
2 Something that **is crushed** has been pressed hard against something else: *Her silk shirt was crushed after the long journey.*

cry *noun*: **cries**
1 A **cry** is a loud shout: *I could hear cries coming from the garden.*
2 A **cry** is also the sound that a bird or animal makes: *the cry of a monkey.*

cry *verb*: **cries, cried, crying, has cried**
1 You **cry** when tears come from your eyes, because you are upset or in pain: *The baby cries every time we put her in bed.*

cry

2 You **cry**, or you **cry out**, when you shout because you are afraid, or to attract someone's attention: *She cried out for help.* ❑ *'Help me', she cried.*

meaning 1: same as **weep**

cube *noun*: **cubes**
A **cube** is a solid square object with six equal sides.

cucumber *noun*: **cucumbers**
A **cucumber** is a long vegetable, with green skin and white or pale green flesh.

cuff *noun*: **cuffs**
A **cuff** is the part at the bottom of a sleeve, which goes round your wrist. [see picture at **sleeve**]

cup *noun*: **cups**
1 A **cup** is a small round container with a handle, which is used for drinking from: *a coffee cup.*
2 A **cup** of something is what is inside the cup, or the amount that a cup will hold: *a cup of tea* ❑ *two cups of sugar.*
3 A **cup** is also a trophy which is given to the winner in some sports competitions: *They've won the cup for a second year.*

cupboard *noun*: **cupboards**
A **cupboard** is a piece of furniture with shelves and a door or doors, used for storing things.

cure *verb*: **cures, cured, curing, has cured**
1 Someone **cures** a disease or an illness when they get rid of it using drugs, medicine or some other method: *The doctors believe they can cure the disease.*
2 A drug or some other medicine **cures** an illness when it gets rid of it: *That pill cured my headache.*

curious *adjective*
1 A person who is **curious** is eager to find things out: *I'm curious to see what their house is like.*
2 Something that is **curious** is strange or unusual: *They have some curious habits.*

curl *noun*: **curls**
A **curl** is a ring of hair: *He brushed his dark curls.*

curly *adjective*: **curlier, curliest**
Curly means having a curl or curls: *curly hair* ❑ *a pig with a curly tail.*

curry *noun*: **curries**
A **curry** is a dish made with meat, vegetables or fish, mixed with spices and often served with rice: *He loves curries.* ❑ *a prawn curry.*

curtain *noun*: **curtains**
A **curtain** is a long piece of cloth which hangs over a window, to stop light from coming into the room.

curve *noun*: **curves**
A **curve** is a bend or a rounded line: *They followed the curve of the road.*

curved *adjective*
Curved means bent or rounded: *They make furniture with soft, curved lines.*

cushion *noun*: **cushions**
A **cushion** is a bag of cloth filled with soft material, which is used to make seats more comfortable.

custom *noun*: **customs**
A **custom** is something that people regularly do, and have usually done for a long time: *It was his custom to go on holiday in winter.* ❑ *He lived there for many years, so he knows about the people and their customs.*

customer *noun*: **customers**
A **customer** is someone who buys something in a shop: *They're trying to attract more customers.*

cut *verb*: **cuts, cut, cutting, has cut**

1 You **cut** something, or you cut it up, when you divide it into parts using a knife or something similar: *I'll cut the cake.*
2 You **cut** something when you make it shorter or tidier, using scissors or some other sharp tool: *I need to have my hair cut.* ❑ *He's cutting the grass.*
3 You **cut** yourself when you hurt yourself on something sharp so that you bleed: *He cut his finger on a kitchen knife.*

▷ **cut back**
You **cut back**, or **cut back** on something, when you use less of it, especially money: *When she lost her job, they had to cut back on spending.*

▷ **cut down**
1 You **cut** a tree **down** when you saw or chop its trunk so that it falls to the ground.
2 You **cut down** on something when you use less of it: *The doctor told him to cut down on cigarettes.*

▷ **cut off**
1 A supply of something **is cut off** when it is stopped: *The electricity was cut off for three days.*
2 People or places **are cut off** when they cannot be reached, often because of bad weather: *The floods destroyed roads and bridges, and many farms were cut off.*
3 You get **cut off** when you are talking to someone on the telephone, if the connection is broken: *We got cut off while we were talking.*

▷ **cut out**
1 You **cut** something **out** when you remove it by cutting: *I cut this advertisement out of yesterday's newspaper.*

2 You **cut** something **out** of a piece of writing when you remove it: *If you cut out these two paragraphs the letter will fit on one page.*

cut *noun*: **cuts**
A **cut** is a hole or injury that is made by cutting: *The cut in his hand is quite deep.*

cycle *verb*: **cycles, cycled, cycling, has cycled**
You **cycle** when you ride a bicycle: *He cycles to work every day.*

cyclist *noun*: **cyclists**
A **cyclist** is a person who is riding a bicycle.

Dd

dad or **daddy** *noun*: **dads** or **daddies**
Your **dad** is your father.

daily *adverb*
1 Something that happens **daily** happens every day: *The park opens daily at 10am.*
2 A **daily** newspaper is one that you can buy each day, usually from Monday to Saturday.

damage *verb*: **damages, damaged, damaging, has damaged**
To **damage** something is to spoil it or harm it in some way: *The storm damaged a few buildings in the town.*

damage *noun*
Damage is harm caused to something: *The storm caused a lot of damage to buildings.*

damp *adjective*: **damper, dampest**
Something is **damp** when it is slightly wet: *damp clothes* ❑ *My hair's still damp from swimming.*

dance *verb*: **dances, danced, dancing, has danced**
You **dance** when you move about in time to music: *Would you like to dance with me?*

dance *noun*: **dances**
1 A **dance** is a set of steps or movements that you do in time to music: *Have you done this dance before?*
2 A **dance** is a party at which people dance: *We're going to the school dance tonight.*

danger *noun*: **dangers**
1 There is **danger** when there is a possibility of damage or injury; a person or thing is in **danger** when they may be damaged, injured or killed: *They told us about the danger of driving on icy roads.* ❑ *The doctors said that his life wasn't in danger.*
2 A **danger** is something which may cause harm or injury: *That busy road is a real danger to pedestrians.*

the opposite is **safety**

dangerous *adjective*
Something is **dangerous** if it can cause harm or injury: *It is dangerous to drive so fast.*

the opposite is **safe**

dare *verb*: **dares, dared, daring, has dared**
You **dare** to do something which is dangerous or frightening when you are brave enough to do it: *I wouldn't dare to fly in such a tiny aircraft.*

dark *adjective*: **darker, darkest**
1 It is **dark** when there is not enough light to allow you to see properly: *They sat in the dark room watching television.* ❑ *It's only 5 o'clock and it's dark already.*
2 A colour is **dark** if it is closer to black than white: *His hair is very dark.* ❑ *dark blue.*

dark *noun*
The **dark** is the lack of light, for example at night: *Don't go out*

after dark. □ *They're using a special camera to take photos in the dark.*

date *noun*: **dates**
The **date** is the day, the month and the year: *What's today's date?* □ *Do you know the dates of the children's birthdays?* □ *He gave me the date and time of the meeting.*

daughter *noun*: **daughters**
A **daughter** is a female child: *They have two daughters and one son.*

rhymes with **water**

dawn *noun*
Dawn is the time of day when the sun rises and the sky begins to get light: *The birds started to sing at dawn.*

day *noun*: **days**
1 A **day** is the 24 hour period between one midnight and the next: *I'm going to Spain for ten days.*
2 The **day** is the time between sunrise and sunset, when it is light: *The animals rest during the day, and hunt at night.*

dead *adjective*
A **dead** person, animal or plant is one that is no longer living: *All the flowers in the garden are dead.* □ *The man was dead when they arrived at the hospital.* □ *a dead body.*

deaf *adjective*: **deafer, deafest**
A **deaf** person is someone who cannot hear; someone goes **deaf** when they lose their ability to hear.

deal *verb*: **deals, dealt, dealing, has dealt**
1 You **deal** with problems,

situations or people when you do with them whatever is necessary: *When are you going to deal with all these bills?* □ *He's very good at dealing with difficult customers.*
2 You **deal** with a particular company when you do business with them: *Our company deals with firms all over the world.*
3 Playing cards **are dealt** when they are shared among the players: *Who's going to deal?*

dear *adjective*: **dearer, dearest**
1 Dear means 'well loved': *a dear friend.*
2 Dear also means 'sweet': *a dear little kitten.*
3 Something that is **dear** is expensive: *That painting was far too dear.*

deceive *verb*: **deceives, deceived, deceiving, has deceived**
You **deceive** someone if you make them believe something that isn't true: *I think they're trying to deceive you.*

December *noun*
December is the twelfth month of the year.

decide *verb*: **decides, decided, deciding, has decided**
You **decide** to do something when you choose to do it: *I've decided to go on holiday in October.*

decision *noun*: **decisions**
You make a **decision** when you choose what to do: *I think he's made the wrong decision.* □ *She has to make important decisions every day.*

decorate *verb*: **decorates, decorated, decorating, has decorated**
1 You **decorate** something when

you make it look nicer, usually by adding things to it: *We decorated the room with balloons.*
2 You **decorate** a room when you put paper or paint on the walls: *We're decorating the house before the baby is born.*

deep *adjective and adverb*: **deeper, deepest**
1 Something that is **deep** goes far down or far back: *This swimming pool isn't very deep.* ❑ *We'll need deeper shelves for these big old books.*
2 Something goes **deep** into something else when it goes a long way down or into it: *They went deeper into the forest.* ❑ *The wheels have gone down deep into the mud.*
3 You also use '**deep**' when you are giving a measurement from the top to the bottom of a container, or from the back to the front of something: *The pool is two metres deep at this end.* ❑ *These shelves are only 10 centimetres deep.*
4 A **deep** colour is strong and dark: *a deep blue sea.*
5 A **deep** sound is a low one: *He's got a very deep voice.* ❑ *Boys' voices get deeper as they get older.*
6 Someone who is in a **deep** sleep cannot be easily woken up.
7 You take a **deep** breath when you take a lot of air into your lungs at one time.

---

meaning 1: the opposite is **shallow**

---

deer *noun*: **deer**
A **deer** is an animal with long thin legs that can run fast. Most types of male deer have horns on their heads.

degree *noun*: **degrees**
1 A **degree** is a unit of temperature: *Water boils at 100 degrees.*
2 A student who has passed his or her final exams at university gets a **degree**.

delay *verb*: **delays, delayed, delaying, has delayed**
1 You **delay** something when you change your plans and decide to do it at a later time: *Can we delay our meeting until next Wednesday?*
2 You are **delayed** when something makes you late: *Our flight was delayed by fog.* ❑ *He was delayed and didn't get to the meeting on time.*

delay *noun*: **delays**
There is a **delay** when you have to wait longer than you expected for something to happen: *There was a ten minute delay before the match started.*

deliberately *adverb*
You do something **deliberately** if you do it intentionally, not by accident: *You broke that glass deliberately!*

delicious *adjective*
Something that is **delicious** tastes very good: *That chocolate cake is delicious — you should try a piece.* ❑ *a delicious meal.*

deliver *verb*: **delivers, delivered, delivering, has delivered**
Something **is delivered** when it is brought to the person it is intended for: *What time is the post usually delivered in the morning?* ❑ *The newspaper is delivered to the house every morning.*

demand *verb*: **demands, demanded, demanding, has demanded**
You **demand** something when you ask for it firmly: *She demanded more money.*

dentist *noun*: **dentists**
A **dentist** is a person whose job is to look after people's teeth.

dentist

depart *verb*: **departs, departed, departing, has departed**
You **depart** from a place when you leave it: *Our train departs from London at 5 o'clock.*

depth *noun*
The **depth** of something is the distance from the top of it to the bottom of it, or from the back to the front: *What is the depth of the swimming pool?*

describe *verb*: **describes, described, describing, has described**
You **describe** something when you say what it is like: *Can you describe the man you saw?* ❑ *He described her as 'strange but beautiful'.*

description *noun*: **descriptions**
A **description** of something or someone is the word or words used to say what it is like: *He gave a description of the thief.*

desert *noun*: **deserts**
A **desert** is an area of land where few or no plants grow and where it doesn't rain very much: *the Sahara desert.*

deserve *verb*: **deserves, deserved, deserving, has deserved**
You **deserve** something when you should have it, or be given it, because of something you have done: *She deserves a holiday after all her hard work.* ❑ *He deserved to fail his exams — he didn't do any work.*

design *noun*: **designs**
1 A **design** is a plan which shows how something will look when it is finished: *He showed me the design for the new theatre.*
2 A **design** is also the pattern on something, such as a piece of material or wallpaper: *I don't like the design on these curtains.*

design *verb*: **designs, designed, designing, has designed**
You **design** something such as a building when you make a plan of how it will look when it is finished: *My father designed the new library.*

desk *noun*: **desks**
A **desk** is a table which you sit at to write, read or use a computer.

dessert *noun*: **desserts**
Dessert is the course that you eat at the end of a meal; desserts are usually sweet: *We had strawberries and cream for dessert.* ❑ *There were several desserts on the menu.*

destroy *verb*: **destroys, destroyed, destroying, has destroyed**
Something is **destroyed** when it is damaged so much that it is completely ruined: *All the*

government buildings were destroyed by the bomb.

detail *noun*: **details**
A **detail** is something small that you don't always notice immediately: *She drew every detail of his face.*

▷ **go into details**
When you **go into details** you describe every small thing about a situation: *He said he was having a party, but he didn't go into details.*

▷ **in detail**
You talk about something **in detail** when you discuss every small thing about it: *We had a meeting to discuss the plan in detail.*

develop *verb*: **develops, developed, developing, has developed**
1 Something **develops** when it grows and changes: *This tiny puppy will soon develop into a very big dog.* ❑ *There's a storm developing out at sea.*
2 You **develop** an illness when you begin to have it: *He's developed a very bad cold.*
3 Camera film **is developed** when photographs are made from it.

device *noun*: **devices**
A **device** is a tool, an instrument or a machine that is designed to do a particular job: *He's invented a device to stop people snoring.* ❑ *You'll need a special device to remove the chain.*

diagram *noun*: **diagrams**
A **diagram** is a simple drawing that explains how something works, or how something is made up: *He showed me a diagram of the car engine.*

dial *verb*: **dials, dialled, dialling, has dialled**
You **dial** a telephone number when you press the buttons or turn the disc on the telephone: *I dialled the wrong number.*

diary *noun*: **diaries**
1 You use a **diary** to write down the things that you plan to do each day.
2 You can also use a **diary** to write down the things that you have done each day.

dictionary *noun*: **dictionaries**
1 A **dictionary** is a book which gives the words of a language in the order of the alphabet, with their meanings.
2 A **dictionary** is also a book which gives the words of a language in the order of the alphabet, with a translation of each word into another language.

did *verb*
see **do**: *I did all the washing-up yesterday.*

didn't *verb*
Didn't is short for did not: *I didn't go to the cinema last night.*

die *verb*: **dies, died, dying, has died**
A person, animal or plant **dies** when they stop living: *The plants all died while we were on holiday.* ❑ *He died of old age.*

the opposite is **live**

▷ **die down**
Something **dies down** when it becomes less strong: *The wind died down during the night.*

▷ **die out**
A kind of plant or animal **dies out** when it becomes very rare and then disappears from the

world: *Tigers are in danger of dying out.*

difference *noun*: **differences**
A **difference** between two or more things is a way in which they are not alike: *I can't see any difference between the two pictures.* ❑ *Young babies don't understand the difference between right and wrong.*

different *adjective*
Two or more things are **different** when they are not the same: *He speaks a different language.* ❑ *These two fruits look the same, but they taste very different.*

difficult *adjective*
Something is **difficult** if it is not easy to do or understand: *These questions are very difficult.*

the opposite is **easy**

dig *verb*: **digs, dug, digging, has dug**
You **dig** when you remove earth from the ground with a spade: *We'll have to dig the garden before we can plant the flowers.*

dim *adjective*: **dimmer, dimmest**
Something is **dim** if it is not very bright, or if it is difficult to see: *The light is too dim for taking photographs.* ❑ *We could see the dim shapes of the boats through the mist.*

dining room *noun*: **dining rooms**
A **dining room** is a room in a house or hotel where you have meals.

dinner *noun*
Dinner is the main meal of the day, usually eaten in the evening: *What's for dinner tonight?*

dip *verb*: **dips, dipped, dipping, has dipped**
You **dip** something into a liquid when you put it in there for a short time: *He dipped his bread in the tomato soup.*

direction *noun*: **directions**
1 The **direction** that you go in is the way that you go to get somewhere: *They drove away in the direction of the city centre.*
2 You ask someone for **directions** when you ask them how to get somewhere: *A tourist asked me for directions to the bus station.*

dirt *noun*
1 Dirt is anything that is not clean, such as mud or dust: *She hates dirt, so she's always cleaning the house.*
2 Dirt is also soil: *We drove along a dirt track.*

dirty *adjective*: **dirtier, dirtiest**
Something is **dirty** when it is not clean: *Your face is very dirty.*

dirty

disagree *verb*: **disagrees, disagreed, disagreeing, has disagreed**
You **disagree** with someone when you have a different opinion from them: *Pat thought it was a good film, but I disagreed with her.*

the opposite is **agree**

disappear *verb*: **disappears, disappeared, disappearing, has disappeared**
1 Something **disappears** when it can no longer be seen: *The plane disappeared behind the clouds.*
2 Someone or something **disappears** when they cannot be found: *The young girl disappeared three weeks ago.* ❏ *My keys have disappeared again.*

the opposite is **appear**

disappointed *adjective*
You **are disappointed** when you feel sad because something has not happened: *His parents were very disappointed when he failed the exam.*

disc *noun*: **discs**
A **disc** is a flat round object: *The moon appeared as a bright disc of light in the sky.*

discover *verb*: **discovers, discovered, discovering, has discovered**
1 You **discover** something when you are the first person to find it: *They realized they had discovered a new planet.*
2 You **discover** something, such as a fact, when you find out about it: *It was many years later that they discovered the truth.*

discuss *verb*: **discusses, discussed, discussing, has discussed**
You **discuss** something when you talk about it with other people: *We discussed our plans for the future.* ❏ *I want to discuss this with my wife before I make a decision.*

disease *noun*: **diseases**
A **disease** is an illness: *Children get different diseases now.* ❏ *heart disease.*

dish *noun*: **dishes**
1 A **dish** is a plate or a bowl for serving food.
2 A **dish** is also food that has been prepared for eating: *We had a rice dish for dinner.*

▷ **wash the dishes**
You **wash the dishes** when you clean all the cups, plates and other things that you have used to cook and serve a meal

dishonest *adjective*
A **dishonest** person tells lies, steals or cheats: *He's careless but he isn't dishonest.*

disk *noun*: **disks**
1 A **disk**, or a **floppy disk**, is a flat piece of plastic on which you can copy information from a computer.
2 A **disk**, or a **hard disk**, is the part of a computer that is used to store information.

dislike *verb*: **dislikes, disliked, disliking, has disliked**
You **dislike** someone or something when you don't like them: *She dislikes rock music.* ❏ *He dislikes getting up early.*

distance *noun*: **distances**
The **distance** between two things or places is the space between them: *What is the distance from here to Paris?*

disturb *verb*: **disturbs, disturbed, disturbing, has disturbed**
You **disturb** someone when you interrupt them: *Sorry to disturb you, but could you help me move this bookcase?* ❏ *Don't disturb her now. She's busy.*

ditch *noun*: **ditches**
A **ditch** is a long narrow area in

the ground, carrying water away from a field.

dive *verb*: **dives, dived, diving, has dived**
1 You **dive** into water when you enter it with your arms and head reaching the water first: *He dived into the swimming pool.*
2 Divers **dive** when they go deep under water, often using equipment to help them breathe.

dive

dive

diver *noun*: **divers**
A **diver** is someone who works under water, often using equipment to help them breathe.

divide *verb*: **divides, divided, dividing, has divided**
1 You **divide** something when you separate it into parts: *We divided the garden in half with a wall.*
2 You also **divide** something when you share it out among a number of people: *Divide the cake so that everyone can have a piece.*
3 You **divide** one number by a smaller number when you find out how many times the smaller number is contained in the larger one: *20 divided by 5 is 4.*

division *noun*: **divisions**
1 The **division** of something is the act of separating it into parts; a **division** is a part that is

separate from others: *The division of the country happened just after the war.* ❏ *a division of the company.*
2 Division is also the act of finding out how many times a smaller number is contained in a larger number.

do *verb*: **does, did, doing, has done**
1a You **do** something when you carry out an action or task: *He's doing the ironing.* ❏ *Peter's doing some work in the garden.* ❏ *Have you nothing to do?* ❏ *I'll find you something to do.* **b** You **have done** a task when you have completed it: *Have you done the cleaning?* ❏ *I've done most of my essay.*
2 You **do** something about a situation when you act or take action: *We'll have to do something to help him.* ❏ *Is there nothing you can do about the noise?*
3a You ask someone what they **do** when you want to know what their job is: *What did you do before you had your children?*
b The subjects you **are doing** at school or college are the subjects you are studying there: *He's doing English, French and German.*
4 Someone or something **does** harm or good when they have that effect: *His remarks did a lot of harm to the government.* ❏ *She became a doctor because she wanted to do some good.*
5 You **do** your hair or your teeth, when you tidy or arrange your hair, or brush your teeth.
6a A vehicle **is doing** a particular speed when that is the speed it is travelling at: *The car was doing 100 miles per hour.* **b** A

vehicle can **do** a particular speed when that is the fastest speed it can travel at.

7 You also use **do** with another verb in sentences with 'not': *I don't like him.* ❑ *She does not know the answer.*

8 You use **do** with another verb in questions, and in some answers: *Do you know what the time is?* ❑ *'You don't have a job yet, do you?' 'Yes, I do.'*

▷ **do without**
You **do without** something when you manage to live without it: *We did without a car for years.*

doctor *noun*: **doctors**
A **doctor** is someone whose job is to treat people who are ill.

> ▸ **doctor** is written **Dr** before a name

doctor

does *verb*
see **do**: *Does Matt want to come to the party?*

'**duz**'

doesn't *verb*
Doesn't is short for **does not**: *He doesn't want to go out tonight.*

dog *noun*: **dogs**
A **dog** is an animal which many people keep as a pet; dogs are also used in hunting and to guard things: *Please keep your dog on a lead.* ❑ *The dog was barking in the night.*

doing *verb*
see **do**: *What are you doing with those boxes?*

doll *noun*: **dolls**
A **doll** is a toy in the shape of a person.

dollar *noun*: **dollars**
The **dollar** is the main unit of money in the USA and other countries.

done *verb*
see **do**: *Have you done that report?*

'**dun**'

donkey *noun*: **donkeys**
A **donkey** is an animal which looks like a small horse with long ears.

don't *verb*
Don't is short for do not: *I don't like carrots.* ❑ *Don't do that!*

door *noun*: **doors**
A **door** is a large flat piece of wood which closes the entrance to a building or room: *Could you close the door please?*

dot *noun*: **dots**
A **dot** is a small round mark: *There should be a dot on the letter 'i'.*

double *adjective*
1 Double means twice the weight or size of something: *I earn double the amount I earnt in my last job.*
2 A **double** room or bed is big enough for two people: *a double room.* ❑ *a double bed.*
3 '**Double**' also refers to things that are made up of two parts: *We have double doors leading into the kitchen.*

doubt *noun*: **doubts**
1 Doubts are feelings that you have when you are not very sure

about something: *I have doubts about her ability to do the job.*
2 Doubt is what you feel when you are not sure about something: *There's no doubt that he loved her.*

doubt *verb*: **doubts, doubted, doubting, has doubted**
You **doubt** something if you think it is not very probable: *I doubt he'll win the prize.*

doughnut *noun*: **doughnuts**
A **doughnut** is a sweet round cake which is fried and covered in sugar.

down *preposition and adverb*
1 You go **down** something when you move towards a lower place: *He climbed down the ladder.*
❑ *She fell down the stairs.*
2 Down means towards or at a lower level: *He sat down and waited for the train.* ❑ *Prices have gone down.*
3 You go **down** a road when you go along it: *We walked down the road to the shops.*

the opposite is **up**

downstairs *adverb*
1 You go **downstairs** when you go to a lower floor: *I'll go downstairs and get that book.*
2 Something that is **downstairs** is on a lower floor: *The toilets are downstairs.*

the opposite is **upstairs**

downwards or **downward** *adverb*
You go **downwards** or **downward** when you move towards a lower level: *The stairs led downwards to the garden.*

the opposite is **upwards** or **upward**

dozen *noun*
1 A **dozen** is a set of twelve: *I'll have a dozen eggs, please.*
2 '**Dozens**' means 'a lot': *He's applied for dozens of jobs.*

drag *verb*: **drags, dragged, dragging, has dragged**
You **drag** something heavy when you pull it: *He dragged the bags across the floor.*

drain *noun*: **drains**
A **drain** is a pipe which carries away water.

drain *verb*: **drains, drained, draining, has drained**
1 You **drain** something when you remove liquid from it: *Could you drain the potatoes, please?* ❑ *The lake was drained and houses were built on the land.*
2 Liquid **drains** when it flows away somewhere: *The waste water drained into the river.*

drank *verb*
see **drink**: *Bill drank all the wine.*

draw *verb*: **draws, drew, drawing, has drawn**
1 You **draw**, or you **draw** a picture, when you make a picture using a pen or pencil: *She loves drawing.*
❑ *He drew a picture of our house.*
2 You **draw** someone's attention to something when you make them notice it: *Jack drew my attention to the marks on the window.*
3 You **draw** something from a place when you take it out: *Draw any card from the pack.*
4 Two teams **draw** when they finish a match with the same score: *They drew 2-2.*
5 You **draw** curtains when you

open or close them: *It's getting dark — we'd better draw the curtains.*

drawer *noun*: **drawers**
A **drawer** is a box that slides in and out of a piece of furniture: *We keep the scissors in the top drawer.*

drawer

drawing *noun*: **drawings**
A **drawing** is a picture done with a pen or pencil: *He did a simple drawing of the church.*

drawn *verb*
see **draw**: *I've drawn a picture of the hills.* ❑ *She's drawn my attention to a few mistakes.*

dream *verb*: **dreams, dreamt** or **dreamed, dreaming, has dreamt** or **has dreamed**
1 You **dream** when you see events in your mind, especially when you are asleep: *Last night I dreamt I was flying.*
2 You **dream** of doing something, or of being something, when you wish it could happen: *He dreams of being a famous writer.*

dream is also a noun: *I had a very strange dream last night.*

dress *noun*: **dresses**
A **dress** is a skirt and top in one piece, worn by women or girls.

dress *verb*: **dresses, dressed, dressing, has dressed**
1 You **dress** yourself, or you **get dressed**, when you put clothes on: *I got dressed and left the house.*

2 You **dress** a wound when you clean it and put a bandage on it: *I cut my hand and had to have it dressed.*

dressing *noun*: **dressings**
1 A **dressing** is a bandage for a wound.
2 A **dressing** is also a sauce that you put on salads: *He made a dressing from oil and vinegar.*

drew *verb*
see **draw**: *Flora drew a picture of an aeroplane.*

dried and **dries** *verb*
see **dry**: *I dried my hair and then got dressed.* ❑ *This paint dries in 3 hours.*

drier and **driest** *adjective*
see **dry**: *It's been much drier this year.* ❑ *This is one of the driest places in the country.*

drink *noun*: **drinks**
A **drink** is a liquid that you swallow, especially when you are thirsty: *Would you like a cold drink?*

drink *verb*: **drinks, drank, drinking, has drunk**
You **drink** a liquid when you swallow it: *You should drink more water in this hot weather.*

drip *verb*: **drips, dripped, dripping, has dripped**
Liquid **drips** when it falls in small drops: *Rain dripped off the roof.*

drive *verb*: **drives, drove, driving, has driven**
1 You **drive** a vehicle such as a car, when you control it and make it go in a particular direction: *I learned to drive three years ago.* ❑ *I've driven a car, but never a lorry.*
2 You **drive** somewhere when

you go there in a car: *I'll have to drive to work tomorrow.*

driver *noun*: **drivers**
A **driver** is a person who drives a vehicle: *He's a train driver.*

drop *verb*: **drops, dropped, dropping, has dropped**
1 You **drop** something when you let it fall, especially by accident: *I dropped the mug but it didn't break.*
2 Something **drops** when it falls: *Three apples dropped off the tree today.*

drop *noun*: **drops**
1 A **drop** is a small amount of liquid that falls from somewhere: *A few drops of rain fell.*
2 A **drop** of liquid is a small amount of it: *There's still a drop of wine left in the bottle.*

drove *verb*
see **drive**: *Chris drove to Liverpool for a meeting yesterday.*

drown *verb*: **drowns, drowned, drowning, has drowned**
Someone **drowns** when they die under water because they cannot breathe: *He fell into the river and drowned.*

drug *noun*: **drugs**
1 A **drug** is a medicine: *The doctor gave him some drugs for his back pain.*
2 A **drug** is also a pill or powder that people take because it makes them feel good; these drugs are usually not allowed by law.

drum *noun*: **drums**
A **drum** is a round, hollow musical instrument with a skin stretched over the top of it; you beat a drum with sticks or with your fingers.

drunk *verb*
see **drink**: *He's drunk all the orange juice.*

dry *adjective*: **drier, driest**
1 Something is **dry** if it doesn't have much, or any, liquid in it: *When the clothes were dry we ironed them and put them away.*
2 The weather is **dry** when it isn't raining.

the opposite is **wet**

dry *verb*: **dries, dried, drying, has dried**
You **dry** something when you remove liquid from it using heat, warm air or a cloth: *Can you dry these glasses, please?* ❑ *He dried his hands on an old rag.* ❑ *This wind should dry your hair quickly.*

duck *noun*: **ducks**
A **duck** is a water bird with short legs, flat wide feet and a broad beak.

duck

dug *verb*
see **dig**: *They dug a hole and put the young tree into it.*

dull *adjective*: **duller, dullest**
1 You can say something is **dull** if it is boring: *That lesson was really dull.*
2 **Dull** colours are not very bright: *The walls were painted a dull red.*
3 The weather is **dull** when the sky is grey and filled with clouds: *It was too dull for taking good photographs.*

dumb *adjective*
Someone who is **dumb** cannot speak.

dump *verb*: **dumps, dumped, dumping, has dumped**
1 You **dump** something when you put it down carelessly: *We dumped the bags on the bed.*
2 You also **dump** something when you get rid of it: *Someone's dumped an old car outside our house.*

during *preposition*
1 Something happens **during** a period of time when it lasts for all of that time: *During the war, it was difficult to get meat and fresh fruit.*
2 Something also happens **during** a period when it happens at some point in it: *It must have rained during the night.*

dusk *noun*
Dusk is the time of the evening when it is just beginning to get dark: *We returned from our walk at dusk.*

dust *noun*
Dust is a layer of dirt which forms on things that haven't been moved for a long time: *The old books were covered in dust.*

dust *verb*: **dusts, dusted, dusting, has dusted**
You **dust** furniture when you clean dust away from it: *We dusted the shelves before putting books on them.*

dustbin *noun*
A **dustbin** is a large container for rubbish.

duty *noun*: **duties**
1 A **duty** is something that you should do: *I feel it's my duty to tell you the truth.*
2 A **duty** is also a job that you have been given: *His duties involved emptying and cleaning the dustbins.*

dying *verb*
see **die**: *All the flowers are dying.*

Ee

each *determiner and pronoun*
Each person or thing in a group
is every one in it: *Each person
has to make a speech.* ❑ *Each of
these students needs to learn
English* ❑ *He gave us a book each.*

▷ **each other**
You use **each other** to show that
someone does something to one
person, and that person does the
same thing back: *They love each
other.* ❑ *We must all help each
other.* ❑ *They read each other's
work.*

eager *adjective*
You are **eager** to do something
when you want to do it very
much: *I'm eager to hear about the
results of the meeting.*

same as **keen**

ear *noun*: **ears**
Your **ears** are the two parts of
your body at each side of your
head, which you use to hear.

early *adjective and adverb*: **early,
earlier, earliest**
1 Someone or something is **early**
if they arrive sooner than
expected: *He came to the party
early.* ❑ *The train left early.*
❑ *You're early. Would you like a
coffee?* ❑ *We took an earlier train.*
2 Early means near the
beginning of the day: *We'll have
to get up early tomorrow.*

the opposite is **late**

earn *verb*: **earns, earned,
earning, has earned**
You **earn** money when you

receive money for work you have
done: *Lawyers can earn a lot of
money.*

earring *noun*: **earrings**
An **earring** is a piece of
jewellery that you attach to your
ear: *She was wearing gold
earrings.*

earth *noun*
1 The **Earth** is the planet that we
live on.
2 Earth is also another word for
'soil': *Use some earth from the
garden to fill the plant pots.*

easily *adverb*
Something is **easily** done if it is
not difficult to do.

east *noun*
The **east** is the direction from
which the sun rises: *The sun rises
in the east and sets in the west.*
❑ *an east wind* ❑ *the east coast.*

easy *adjective*: **easier, easiest**
Something is **easy** if it is not
difficult to do: *These questions are
easy.* ❑ *This is an easy job.* ❑ *It'll
be easier if we go on Tuesday.*

the opposite is **difficult** or **hard**

eat *verb*: **eats, ate, eating, has
eaten**
You **eat** food when you put it in
your mouth and swallow it: *They
eat too many sweet things.* ❑ *Who
has eaten all the sandwiches?*

edge *noun*: **edges**
1 The **edge** of something is the
place where it ends: *That cup is
too near the edge of the table.*
2 The cutting side of something

sharp is its **edge**: *Be careful. It's got a very sharp edge.*

education *noun*
Education is the process of learning things, usually at school or university: *We want our children to have a good education.*

ʻed-ju-**kay**-shunʼ

effect *noun*: **effects**
One thing has an **effect** on another when it causes something to happen to it: *What are the main effects of this drug?*

egg *noun*: **eggs**
1 An **egg** is an oval shell with a developing baby animal inside.
2 An **egg** is one of these laid by a hen, and used as food: *fried eggs.*

eight *noun and adjective*: **eights**
1 Eight is the number or figure 8: *Seven plus one is eight.* ❑ *Two eights are sixteen.*
2 Eight is the time of 8 o'clock: *The film starts at eight.*
3 Eight is also the age of eight; someone who is **eight** is eight years old: *He'll be eight on his birthday.*

eight *determiner and pronoun*
Eight means eight in number: *The tickets cost eight pounds.* ❑ *He already had two computer games, and Peter gave him another eight.*

eighteen *noun and adjective*: **eighteens**
1 Eighteen is the number 18: *Seventeen plus one is eighteen.*
2 Eighteen is also the age of eighteen; someone who is **eighteen** is 18 years old: *Her brother is eighteen.* ❑ *You can vote at eighteen.*

eighteen *determiner and pronoun*
Eighteen means eighteen in number: *The tickets cost eighteen dollars.* ❑ *Twenty people were on the boat when it sank, and eighteen were rescued.*

eighth *determiner and adjective*
The **eighth** person or thing is the one that comes after the seventh.

eighty *noun and adjective*: **eighties**
1 Eighty is the number 80: *Seventy plus ten is eighty.*
2a Eighty is also the age of eighty; someone who is **eighty** is 80 years old: *Her grandmother is eighty.* **b** A person in their **eighties** is between 80 and 89 years old.
3 The years in any century between 80 and 89 are often called 'the **eighties**': *Like many people, he became rich in the eighties.*

eighty *determiner and pronoun*
Eighty means eighty in number: *The tickets cost eighty pounds.* ❑ *Eighty people were hurt in the crash.* ❑ *'How many tickets do you need?' 'At least eighty.'*

either *determiner and pronoun*
1 You use **either** to show that you mean one or the other: *You can take either the bus or the train to the airport.* ❑ *Either jacket would be suitable for a wedding.* ❑ *She applied for two jobs but she didn't get either.*
2 Either also means 'each' when it is clear that there are two: *She was holding a bag of shopping in either hand.*

▷ **either … or**
You use **either … or** to show

that there are two possibilities: *Either she's missed the plane, or she wants to stay in London.* □ *You can have either tea or coffee.* □ *Either turn the TV down or close the door.*

either *adverb*
You use **either** with 'not' to add a second piece of information: *I didn't like him, and my sister didn't like him either.* □ *'Rona's never been to Singapore.' 'I haven't been there either.'*

elastic *noun*
Elastic is material, usually in a long thin form, that stretches easily: *We used elastic to hold our hats on in the wind.*

elbow *noun*: **elbows**
Your **elbow** is the place where your arm bends in the middle: *He knocked his elbow on the table.* [see picture at **arm**]

elder *adjective*
Your **elder** brother or sister is the one that is older than you: *My elder sister's getting married tomorrow.*

eldest *adjective*
The **eldest** child in a family is the oldest one: *My eldest brother lives in Australia.*

electric *adjective*
An **electric** device or machine is worked by electricity: *an electric light.*

electricity *noun*
Electricity is a form of energy which is used to provide heat, light and power: *This machine uses electricity.*

elephant *noun*: **elephants**
An **elephant** is a very large grey animal with a long nose called a 'trunk'.

eleven *noun and adjective*:
elevens
1 Eleven is the number 11: *Seven plus four is eleven.*
2 Eleven is the time of 11 o'clock: *The train leaves at eleven.*
3 Eleven is the age of eleven; someone who is eleven is 11 years old: *His brother is eleven.* □ *At eleven, he was taller than his father.*

eleven *determiner and pronoun*
Eleven means eleven in number: *The shoes cost eleven pounds.* □ *There are eleven books on the table.* □ *'How many players are there in a cricket team?' 'Eleven.'*

eleventh *determiner and adjective*
The **eleventh** person or thing is the one that comes after the tenth.

else *adverb*
Else means 'other than the person or thing mentioned': *Jack can't help us. Who else could we ask?* □ *Someone else can wash the dishes — I did them yesterday.* □ *I love Switzerland. Where else would you get a view like this?* □ *Do you do anything else in your spare time?*

e-mail *noun*
E-mail is the system for sending messages from one computer to another through telephone lines.

employ *verb*: **employs, employed, employing, has employed**
You **employ** someone when you give them money to work for you: *They've employed a cleaner.* □ *How many people are employed by this company?*

employee *noun*: **employees**
An **employee** is someone who works for a company: *They have over 200 employees in their Edinburgh office.*

employer *noun*: **employers**
An **employer** is a person or a company that pays people to work for them.

empty *adjective*: **emptier, emptiest**
1 Something is **empty** if it has nothing inside it: *My glass is empty.*
2 A building is **empty** when there is no-one using it: *That old house has been empty for years.*

meaning 1: the opposite is **full**

empty *verb*: **empties, emptied, emptying, has emptied**
You **empty** something when you take out whatever is inside it: *Please would you empty the dustbin?*

the opposite is **fill**

encourage *verb*: **encourages, encouraged, encouraging, has encouraged**
1 You **encourage** someone when you try to make them feel that they will succeed: *Helen's parents have always encouraged her in her music.*
2 You **encourage** someone to do something when you persuade them to do it: *We encouraged him to talk about his problems.*

end *noun*
The **end** of something is the last part of it: *We left the cinema before the end of the film.* ❑ *Mrs Maxwell lives in the house at the end of the street.*

the opposite is **beginning** or **start**

end *verb*: **ends, ended, ending, has ended**
1 You **end** something when you finish it: *We ended the day with a quick swim.*
2 Something **ends** when it finishes: *The film ends at 11 o'clock.*

the opposite is **begin** or **start**

enemy *noun*: **enemies**
1 An **enemy** is someone who doesn't like you and wants to harm you: *He has made a few enemies at work.*
2 In a war, the **enemy** is the side that you are fighting against: *The enemy is getting closer to the city every day.* ❑ *Two hundred enemy soldiers have been killed.*

meaning 1: the opposite is **friend**

energy *noun*
1 You have **energy** if you are feeling strong and not tired: *I don't have the energy to play rugby tomorrow.*
2 **Energy** is a form of power produced by burning fuel.

engine *noun*: **engines**
1 An **engine** is a machine which produces power to make a vehicle move: *There's something wrong with the car's engine.*
2 An **engine** is also a vehicle that pulls a train.

enjoy *verb*: **enjoys, enjoyed, enjoying, has enjoyed**
You **enjoy** something when you get pleasure from it: *I really enjoyed that play.* ❑ *Did Alan enjoyed the football match?*

▷ **enjoy yourself**
You **enjoy yourself** when you have a good time: *We all enjoyed ourselves at your party.*

enormous *adjective*
Enormous means very large: *An African elephant has enormous ears.* ❑ *The new library is enormous.*

same as **huge**

enough *determiner, pronoun and adverb*
1 Enough of something is as much as you need: *Have you had enough?* ❑ *I haven't got enough money to go out tonight.* ❑ *Is it warm enough for you?* ❑ *He wasn't good enough to get into the team.*
2 You say you have had **enough** when you want something to stop: *She's had enough of long working hours.*

❛ i-**nuf** ❜

enter *verb*: **enters, entered, entering, has entered**
1 You **enter** a place when you go into it: *I entered the house by the back door.*
2 You **enter** a competition when you take part in it: *He's entered the swimming competition.*

meaning 1: the opposite is **leave**

entertain *verb*: **entertains, entertained, entertaining, has entertained**
Someone **entertains** you when they do something that makes you laugh, or that interests you: *Her jokes entertained us for hours.*

entrance *noun*: **entrances**
An **entrance** to a place is a way in, such as door or a gate: *We couldn't find the entrance to the park.*

the opposite is **exit**

entry *noun*
Entry to a place is the act or fact of entering it it: *The sign on the door read 'No entry', so we didn't go in.*

envelope *noun*: **envelopes**
An **envelope** is a paper cover in which you send letters by post.

equal *adjective*
Two or more things are **equal** when they are the same in some way: *She cut the cake into four equal slices.* ❑ *coins of equal value.*

equipment *noun*
Equipment is the tools that you need to carry out a particular job: *He couldn't repair the bicycle without the right equipment.*

eraser *noun*: **erasers**
An **eraser** is a piece of rubber that you use to remove pencil marks.

escape *verb*: **escapes, escaped, escaping, has escaped**
1 You **escape** from a person when you manage to get away from them: *He was trying to escape from the two policemen.*
2 You **escape** from a place when you manage to get away from it: *He escaped from jail three times.*

escape *noun*: **escapes**
An **escape** is an act of getting away: *He made his escape at midnight.* ❑ *You had a lucky escape from the accident.*

especially *adverb*
Especially means 'more than usual' or 'more than other things

mentioned': *I like all sweets but I'm especially fond of chocolates.* ❑ *I get hungry in the middle of the afternoon, especially when it's cold.*

essay *noun*: **essays**
An **essay** is a piece of written work on a particular subject: *We all wrote essays about our holidays.*

even *adjective*
1 A surface is **even** if it is smooth and flat: *Be careful. The path isn't very even.*
2 Two things are **even** if they are the same in height, length and amount: *I've cut the table legs so that they are even.*
3 Even is also used to describe numbers that can be divided by 2, such as 4, 26 and 100.

meanings 1 and 2: the opposite is **uneven**
meaning 3: the opposite is **odd**

even *adverb*
1 You use **even** to draw people's attention to something surprising: *I haven't even started the letter yet.* ❑ *She has even tidied up.*
2 You also use **even** when you are comparing one thing with another: *I'm bad at maths, but he's even worse.* ❑ *It's even hotter today than it was yesterday.*

evening *noun*: **evenings**
The **evening** is the part of the day which comes between the afternoon and the night: *We're going to the cinema tomorrow evening.* ❑ *They spend most evenings at home.*

event *noun*: **events**
1 An **event** is something that happens, especially something

important: *I can still remember the terrible events of last winter.*
2 An **event** is also one of the contests which make up a sports competition: *The next event will be the long jump.*

ever *adverb*
1 You use **ever** to mean 'at any time': *Have you ever been to London?* ❑ *We hardly ever go out during the week.*
2 You also use **ever** to mean 'always': *They lived happily ever after.* ❑ *I'll remember this day for ever.*

every *determiner*
1 Every means each thing or person in a group: *Every house should have a smoke alarm.* ❑ *We went out every night last week.*
2 Every also means each of the days or other times mentioned: *We go out for lunch every Sunday.* ❑ *She goes to the dentist every six months.*

everybody *pronoun*
Everybody means all the people in a certain group, or all people in general: *Everybody was happy with the new arrangements.* ❑ *Everybody thinks he's mad.*

the opposite is **nobody**

everyone *pronoun*
Everyone means all the people in a certain group, or all people in general: *Everyone laughed at the jokes.* ❑ *Everyone enjoyed the party.*

the opposite is **no-one**

everything *pronoun*
Everything means all the things in a certain group, or all things in general: *Have you got everything you need?* ❑ *Everything got wet*

when it started to rain.❏ *They sold everything and moved to France.*

everywhere *adverb*
Everywhere means the whole of a certain area, or all places in general: *I've looked everywhere for my earrings.* ❏ *There is litter everywhere.*

evil *adjective*
Someone who is **evil** is very bad: *an evil man* ❏ *He's not just bad, he's evil.*

exact *adjective*
Something is **exact** if it is correct in every detail: *Do you have the exact measurements of the window?*

exactly *adverb*
1 Exactly means no more or no less than the quantity stated: *The book cost exactly £5.*
2 A person or thing is **exactly** right when they are just what is needed: *He's exactly right for the job.*

exam *noun*: **exams**
Exam is short for 'examination': *I sat my last exam today.*

examination *noun*:
examinations
1 An **examination** is a formal test to find out how much you know about a subject: *He's passed all his examinations.*
2 A doctor does an **examination** when he or she looks carefully at a patient to see how healthy they are.

examine *verb*: **examines, examined, examining, has examined**
1 You **examine** something when you look at it very carefully: *He examined the old book.*
2 A doctor **examines** someone

when he or she looks at a patient to see how healthy they are.

example *noun*: **examples**
An **example** is something that shows you what other things of the same kind are like: *This story is a good example of the writer's work.*

▷ **for example**
You use **for example** when you are about to give an example: *Some cities, for example Paris, are very popular with tourists.*

excellent *adjective*
Excellent means 'very good': *Jackie is an excellent cook.* ❏ *The performance was excellent.*

except *preposition*
You use **except** to show that one person or thing is not included: *Everyone's coming except Mr Woods.* ❏ *I've done my essay, except for the last page.*

exchange *verb*: **exchanges, exchanged, exchanging, has exchanged**
You **exchange** something when you give it away and receive something else in return: *He exchanged the jeans for a pair of cotton trousers.*

excited *adjective*
You are **excited** about something when you have strong feelings that you are going to enjoy it: *She's really excited about going to Barbados.*

exciting *adjective*
Something that is **exciting** gives you strong feelings of pleasure, often because you don't know what is going to happen next: *I'm reading an exciting book at the moment.* ❏ *The sailing trip was really exciting.*

excuse *noun*: **excuses**
An **excuse** is a reason you give to explain why you did something: *His excuse for being late was that he missed the bus.* ❑ *Did she have a good excuse for being late?*

❛ iks-**kyoos**❜

excuse *verb*: **excuses, excused, excusing, has excused**
You **excuse** someone for something they have done when you forgive them: *I excused him for being late.*

❛ iks-**kyooz**❜

▷ **excuse me**
You say **excuse me** when you want to apologize for disturbing someone: *Excuse me, can you tell me where the railway station is, please?* ❑ *Excuse me, can I get past you, please?*

exercise *noun*: **exercises**
1 Exercise is sport, or other movements that you do to stay healthy; an **exercise** is one of these movements: *I need to get more exercise.* ❑ *I do some exercises every morning when I get up.*
2 An **exercise** is a piece of written work that you do to practise what you have learned: *spelling exercises.*

exercise *verb*: **exercises, exercised, exercising, has exercised**
You **exercise** when you play sports, or do special movements with your body to stay healthy: *He should exercise more.*

exist *verb*: **exists, existed, existing, has existed**
Something that **exists** is part of

the real world: *Ghosts don't really exist.*

exit *noun*: **exits**
An **exit** from a place is a way out, such as a door or gate: *Excuse me, where's the exit, please?*

the opposite is **entrance**

expect *verb*: **expects, expected, expecting, has expected**
1 You **expect** something if you know or believe that it will happen: *We're expecting visitors this weekend.*
2 You **expect** that something is true if you think that it is probably true: *I expect he'll want to go out tonight.*

expensive *adjective*
Something that is **expensive** costs a lot of money: *I can't afford these shoes — they're too expensive.* ❑ *an expensive holiday.*

same as **dear**
the opposite is **cheap**

experience *noun*: **experiences**
1 Experience is skill or knowledge gained through practice: *He has a lot of experience in teaching.*
2 An **experience** is an event which affects you in some way: *The crash was a terrible experience for him.* ❑ *My father had many interesting experiences in Kenya.*

explain *verb*: **explains, explained, explaining, has explained**
1 You **explain** something to someone if you make it easy for them to understand: *Dave explained the joke to us.*
2 You also **explain** something

when you give a reason for it: *I can't explain his behaviour.*

explode *verb*: **explodes, exploded, exploding, has exploded**
Something such as a bomb **explodes** when it blows up: *The bomb exploded, killing ten people.*

explore *verb*: **explores, explored, exploring, has explored**
You **explore** a place when you search it to try and discover things about it: *They explored the jungle, looking for rare birds.*

explosion *noun*: **explosions**
An **explosion** is the loud noise that a bomb makes when it blows up: *People in the next town heard the explosion.*

expression *noun*: **expressions**
An **expression** is a word, or group of words that have a particular meaning.

extra *adjective*
Extra means more than usual, or more than necessary: *I'll need extra help with the party.* ❑ *I've taken an extra pair of socks.*

eye *noun*: **eyes**
Your **eyes** are the parts of your body that you use to see: *Close your eyes.* ❑ *He's got blue eyes.*

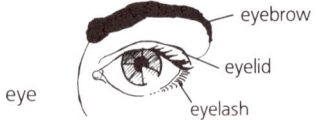
eyebrow
eyelid
eye
eyelash

eyebrow *noun*: **eyebrows**
Your **eyebrows** are the curved lines of hair above your eyes.

eyelash *noun*: **eyelashes**
Your **eyelashes** are the hairs that grow along the edges of your eyelids.

eyelid *noun*: **eyelids**
Your **eyelids** are the pieces of skin that cover your eyes when you close them.

Ff

face *noun*: **faces**
1 Your **face** is the front of your head where your eyes, nose and mouth are: *He's got a scar across his face.*

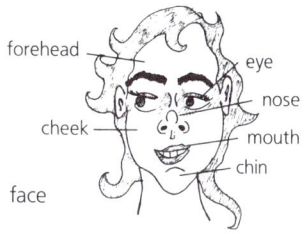

forehead
eye
nose
cheek
mouth
chin
face

2 The **face** of a clock or a watch is the part with the numbers and hands on it.

face *verb*: **faces, faced, facing, has faced**
One thing **faces** another if it looks towards it: *Their house faces the park.* ❏ *He turned to face me.*

fact *noun*: **facts**
A **fact** is something that you know is true: *When we get all the facts, we can decide what to do.*

▷ **in fact**
You use **in fact** when you want to be more exact: *They know each other well; in fact they went to school together.*

factory *noun*: **factories**
A **factory** is a building where goods are made in large numbers: *She works in a biscuit factory.*

fail *verb*: **fails, failed, failing, has failed**
1 You **fail** when you don't manage to do something: *They*

failed to arrive in time. ❏ *His attempt to persuade them failed.*
2 You **fail** an examination when you are not good enough to pass it: *He's failed his driving test for the third time.*

meaning 1: the opposite is **succeed**
meaning 2: the opposite is **pass**

failure *noun*: **failures**
1 Failure is lack of success: *Their first attempt ended in failure.*
2 A **failure** is someone who is unsuccessful: *He thinks he's a failure because he hasn't got a job.*

faint *adjective*: meaning 1: **fainter, faintest**
1 Something that is **faint** is weak and difficult to notice: *There's still a faint mark on the carpet.*
2 You feel **faint** when you feel as if you are going to fall down and become unconscious: *She feels faint when she sees blood.*

faint *verb*: **faints, fainted, fainting, has fainted**
You **faint** when you suddenly become unconscious: *A lot of people fainted in the heat.*

fair *adjective*: **fairer, fairest**
1 You are **fair** if you treat everyone in the same way: *Mum was always very fair with us.*
2 Someone who is **fair** has pale yellow hair: *Sharon is fair, but her sister is dark.*

fall *noun*: **falls**
1 Someone has a **fall** when they have an accident and hit the ground: *He had a bad fall and*

broke his leg.
2 Fall is the American word for autumn.

fall *verb*: **falls, fell, falling, has fallen**
1 You **fall** when you have an accident and hit the ground: *He fell down the stairs.* ❑ *The path is icy — be careful not to fall.*
2 Something **falls** when it drops down: *The apples fell from the tree.*
3 An amount **falls** when it goes down: *The price of a cinema ticket has fallen by 20p.*
4 A temperature **falls** when it goes down: *The temperature fell to 0°.*

false *adjective*
1 Something that is **false** is not true or correct: *That's a false signature.*
2 False also means 'not real': *false teeth.*

family *noun*: **families**
1 A **family** is a group of people who are related to each other: *There are five children in the family next door.* ❑ *I'm spending the weekend with my family.*
2 A **family** is also a group of related things, such as animals, plants or languages: *Lions belong to the cat family.*

famous *adjective*
A **famous** person or thing is known by a lot of people: *Robert De Niro is a famous actor.* ❑ *Scotland is famous for its whisky.*

fan *noun*: **fans**
1 A **fan** of an actor or singer is someone who admires that person very much: *She's a fan of Elvis Presley.*
2 A **fan** is also someone who

likes a particular sport very much: *The football fans shouted and sang songs.*
3 A **fan** is a flat object that you move in front of your face to make you cool when you are hot.
4 A **fan** is also a machine with thin blades which turn round very fast and make a place cooler.

fan

fan

far *adjective and adverb*:
meaning 1: **far, farther** or **further, farthest** or **furthest**
meaning 2: **far, further, furthest**
1a Something that is **far**, or **far** away is a long distance away: *'Are the shops far from your house?' 'No, not far.'* ❑ *The bank is further away than the post office.* ❑ *Which planet is furthest from the Sun?* **b** You ask how **far** it is to a place when you want to know what the distance is to that place: *How far is it to London from here?*
2 You use **far** when you are talking about the progress someone has made: *He hasn't got very far with English yet — he only knows a few words.* ❑ *How far have you got with that book?*
3 The **far** end of something is the end that is the greatest distance away from you: *Their house is at the far end of the village, near the school.* ❑ *The mountains are in the far north of the country.*
4 You also use **far** to mean 'very much' when you are comparing two people or things: *He's a far better dancer than I am.* ❑ *I'm feeling far more cheerful today.*

meaning 1: the opposite is **near**

▷ as far as
You go **as far as** a certain point when you go to it, but not beyond it: *We walked as far as the old church.* ❏ *Have you read as far as page 60 yet?*

▷ far away or far off
Something that is **far away** or **far off** is a long distance away: *Paul lives far away in Australia.*

▷ so far
So far means 'up to the present time': *So far, I've read ten pages.* ❏ *It's 10 o'clock now, and so far he hasn't phoned.*

fare *noun*: **fares**
A **fare** is the price of a journey by bus, train or aeroplane: *The bus fare to the centre of town is 80p.*

farm *noun*: **farms**
A **farm** is an area with buildings and fields, that is used to grow food and to keep animals.

farmer *noun*: **farmers**
A **farmer** is a person who owns and works on a farm.

farming *noun*
Farming is the business of running a farm.

farther *adjective and adverb*
see **far**: *It was farther to the next town than we thought.*

farthest *adjective and adverb*
see **far**: *Which is the farthest, London or Paris?* ❏ *Bill ran the farthest.*

fashion *noun*: **fashions**
Fashion is the way of dressing that a lot of people like at a certain time: *Short skirts are in fashion again.* ❏ *ladies' fashions.*

fast *adjective and adverb*: **faster, fastest**

1a A **fast** person or thing moves quickly; something happens **fast** when it happens quickly: *Sharon is a fast swimmer.* ❏ *This car is very fast.* ❏ *Time seemed to go by really fast.* **b** You ask 'how **fast**...?' in questions about speed: *How fast can you type?*
2 A watch or clock is **fast** when it shows a time that is later than the correct time: *That clock is five minutes fast.*

the opposite is **slow**

fasten *verb*: **fastens, fastened, fastening, has fastened**
1 You **fasten** something when you tie it or close it: *Please fasten your seatbelts.* ❏ *Could you help me fasten my dress?*
2 You **fasten** one thing to another when you join them together: *I fastened the lead to the dog's collar.*

the opposite is **unfasten**

fat *noun*: **fats**
1 Fat is a layer under the skin that keeps your body warm.
2 Fat is a kind of solid oil found in animals or plants, and which is used in cooking.

fat *adjective*: **fatter, fattest**
A **fat** person has a large round body: *When he was a child, he was rather fat.*

the opposite is **thin** or **slim**

father *noun*: **fathers**
A **father** is a male parent: *He looks like his father.*

fault *noun*: **faults**
1 A **fault** is something that has gone wrong: *There's a fault in my computer.*
2 Something that has gone wrong

is your **fault** if you caused it: *It's my fault we're late — I couldn't find my purse.* ❑ *Don't be angry with him — it's not his fault.*

favour *noun*: **favours**
You do someone a **favour** when you do something to help them: *Could you do me a favour and lend me ten dollars?*

favourite *adjective*
Your **favourite** thing of a particular kind is the one that you like most: *My favourite film is 'Casablanca'.* ❑ *What's your favourite colour?*

fax *noun*: **faxes**
1 A **fax**, or a **fax machine**, is a machine which sends and receives copies of letters using telephone lines: *I'll send it to you by fax.*
2 A **fax** is also the copy that you send or receive: *I got a fax from him this morning.*

---

fax is also a verb: *I'll fax you a copy of the letter.*

---

fear *noun*: **fears**
1 Fear is an anxious feeling you get when you feel that you are in danger: *He tried to hide his fear.*
2 A **fear** is an anxious or frightened feeling you have about something: *She has a fear of spiders.*

feather *noun*: **feathers**
A **feather** is one of the long light objects that grow from a bird's skin and cover its body: *We cleaned the oil off the bird's feathers.*

feather

February *noun*
February is the second month of

the year, between January and March.

fed *verb*
see **feed**: *Have you fed the dog?* ❑ *He fed the chickens.*

▷ **fed up**
You are **fed up** if you are bored or unhappy with something: *I'm fed up being poor.* ❑ *He looks a bit fed up.*

feed *verb*: **feeds, fed, feeding, has fed**
1 You **feed** animals or people when you give them food: *I must remember to feed the cat.*
2 An animal or bird **feeds** on a particular thing when they eat that thing: *Sheep feed on grass.*

feel *verb*: **feels, felt, feeling, has felt**
1 You **feel** something when you touch it with your fingers, or you touch it to find out what it is like: *Can you feel the lump on my head?* ❑ *The blind man felt the object carefully.*
2 You **feel** something touching you, or happening to you, when your senses tell you that something is touching you or happening to you: *Suddenly, she felt a hand on her shoulder.* ❑ *He could feel himself slipping slowly downwards.*
3 You **feel** a particular way, such as sad, tired, ill or angry, when you have that feeling: *He felt very tired.* ❑ *Do you feel better today?* ❑ *Alice was feeling happy.*
4 Something **feels** a particular way when that is how it seems to you when you touch or hold it: *Your forehead feels hot.* ❑ *A baby's skin feels soft.*
5 You use 'it **feels**...' to say how the weather seems to you: *It feels*

colder this morning.
6 The way you **feel** about someone or something is the opinion you have of them: *How do you feel about the new boss?*
7 You **feel** like having or doing something when you want to have or do it: *Do you feel like having some of this cake?* ❏ *I feel like a swim.*

feeling *noun*: **feelings**
A **feeling** is something that you experience, such as sadness, hunger and happiness: *He had a great feeling of happiness.*

feet *noun*
see **foot**

fell *verb*
see **fall**: *Chris fell down the stairs and cut his head.*

felt *verb*
see **feel**: *He felt sad when his grandfather died.*

female *adjective*
Female describes any animal which can give birth or lay eggs: *a female lion is called a lioness.*

the opposite is **male**

female *noun*: **females**
A **female** is a female animal.

fence *noun*: **fences**
A **fence** is a line of wooden or metal posts around a piece of land: *He jumped over the fence and into the garden.*

ferry *noun*: **ferries**
A **ferry** is a boat that can carry people and vehicles across water: *We took the ferry to Calais.*

fetch *verb*: **fetches, fetched, fetching, has fetched**
You **fetch** something when you go somewhere to get it, and then

bring it back: *Could you fetch the newspaper for me please?*

few *determiner and pronoun*
Few means 'not many': *Few people know about his work.*
❏ *They're spending the next few weeks in New Zealand.* ❏ *Very few people came to the meeting.*

▷ **a few**
A few means 'a small number' or 'some': *I've only received a few letters.* ❏ *He lent me a few of his books.* ❏ *'Did you take any photos?' 'Yes, a few.'*

the opposite is **a lot**

fewer *determiner and pronoun*
Fewer means 'not as many': *Fewer people work on farms now.* ❏ *He made fewer mistakes this time.*
❏ *'More than a hundred people came to the party.' 'No, there were fewer than that.'*

the opposite is **more**

fewest *determiner*
The **fewest** number of people or things is the smallest number of them: *This region has the fewest number of people.*

field *noun*: **fields**
1 A **field** is an area of land used for growing food crops and keeping animals: *The cows and sheep are kept in separate fields.*
2 A **field** is an area of grass used to play sports.

fierce *adjective*: **fiercer, fiercest**
A **fierce** animal always wants to attack: *a fierce dog.*

fierce

fifteen *noun and adjective*:
fifteens
1 Fifteen is the number 15: *Ten plus five is fifteen.*
2 Fifteen is also the age of fifteen; someone who is **fifteen** is fifteen years old: *He was fifteen last week.* ❑ *He left school at fifteen.*

fifteen *determiner and pronoun*
Fifteen means fifteen in number: *The book cost fifteen pounds.* ❑ *This book costs ten dollars, and that one costs fifteen.*

fifth *determiner and adjective*
The **fifth** person or thing is the one that comes after fourth.

fifty *noun and adjective*: **fifties**
1 Fifty is the number 50: *Ten plus forty is fifty.*
2a Fifty is also the age of fifty; someone who is **fifty** is fifty years old: *She was fifty last month.* ❑ *She's taking more exercise at fifty than she did when she was twenty.* **b** A person in their **fifties** is between 50 and 59 years old.
3 The years in any century between 50 and 59 are often called 'the **fifties**': *They were both born in the fifties.*

fifty *determiner and pronoun*
Fifty means **fifty** in number: *The vase cost fifty pounds.* ❑ *He paid seventy dollars for the necklace, but I wouldn't pay more than fifty.*

fight *noun*: **fights**
People have a **fight** when they hit each other or shout at each other in an angry way: *Three young men were injured in the fight.*

fight *verb*: **fights, fought, fighting, has fought**

1 People or animals **fight** when they use their strength to try to hurt each other.
2 People also **fight** when they argue.

figure *noun*: **figures**
1 A **figure** is one of the numbers between 0 and 9.
2 A **figure** is also the shape of a person: *I saw a dark figure at the end of the street.*

file *noun*: **files**
1 A **file** is an envelope or box for keeping papers together: *She keeps all her letters in a file.*
2 A **file** is a tool with a rough edge, used for making things smooth: *Have you got a nail file? My nail's broken.*

fill *verb*: **fills, filled, filling, has filled**
1 You **fill** a container when you make it full: *He filled our glasses with wine.*
2 Something **fills** when it becomes full: *The concert hall quickly filled with people.* ❑ *His eyes filled with tears.*

film *noun*: **films**
1 A **film** is a set of moving pictures that tell a story; you watch films at a cinema or on television: *I saw a good film on television last night.*
2 A **film** is a strip of material you put in a camera to take photographs: *I need a new film for my camera.*

final *adjective*
Something that is **final** comes at the end: *In the final chapter of the book, Kit and Barbara get married.*

finally *adverb*
1 Something **finally** happens

when it happens at the end of a long period of time: *We waited for him for three hours, and he finally arrived at 10pm.*
2 You use **finally** before the last in a series of things: *Finally, I would like to wish everybody a good holiday.*

find *verb*: **finds, found, finding, has found**
1 You **find** something when you get it after looking for it: *I found my pen under the table.*
2 You also **find** something when you discover it by accident: *Clive found a watch in the street yesterday.*
3 You use **find** when you want to describe how you feel about someone or something: *I found him rather rude.* ❑ *He finds crime books exciting.*

meaning 1: the opposite is **lose**

▷ **find out**
1 You **find** something **out** when you discover a piece of information: *I'll find out what time the party starts.*
2 Someone **finds** you **out**, or you are **found out**, when they discover that you have done something wrong: *He was lying; we found him out.*

fine *adjective*: meanings 3, 4 and 5: **finer, finest**
1 You feel **fine** if you are healthy or well: *I was tired yesterday, but I'm fine now.*
2 You say that something is **fine** if it is good: *'Is four o'clock a good time to meet you?' 'Yes, fine.'*
3 You describe something as **fine** when you think it is excellent: *He gave a fine performance as Macbeth.*

4 The weather is **fine** if the sky is clear and it is sunny.
5a Fine threads are very thin: *She has fine hair.* **b Fine** sand or soil is made of very small pieces: *a fine powder.*

finger *noun*: **fingers**
Your **fingers** are the five separate parts at the end of your hand: *He cut his finger on a kitchen knife.* [see picture at **hand**]

finish *verb*: **finishes, finished, finishing, has finished**
1 You **finish** something when you come to the end of it: *I've finished my book.* ❑ *She finished the race in the fastest time.*
2 Something **finishes** when it comes to an end: *The film finished at 10.30.*
3 You **finish** food or drink when you eat or drink the last bit of it: *I'll just finish my drink and then we can go.*

the opposite is **start** or **begin**

fire *noun*: **fires**
1 A **fire** is something that is burning by accident: *There was a fire at the school last night.*
2 A **fire** is also a pile of wood or other fuel that is burning to give warmth.
3 A **fire** is a gas or electric heater: *I'm cold — I think I'll switch on the fire.*

▷ **on fire**
Something that is **on fire** is burning: *That house is on fire.* ❑ *A man came out of the burning building with his clothes on fire.*

▷ **set fire to**
You **set fire to** something when you make it start burning: *He set fire to the leaves with a match.*

fire *verb*: **fires, fired, firing, has fired**
1 You **fire** a gun when you shoot a bullet from it: *He raised the gun and fired.*
2 A person **is fired** when they are told by their employer that they no longer have a job: *He was fired for stealing from the company.*

fire alarm *noun*: **fire alarms**
A **fire alarm** is a loud bell which rings to warn people when there is a fire: *When the fire alarm goes off, please leave the building immediately.*

fire engine *noun*: **fire engines**
A **fire engine** is a vehicle which carries firefighters and their equipment.

firefighter *noun*: **firefighters**
A **firefighter** is a person who is trained to put out fires.

fireplace *noun*: **fireplaces**
A **fireplace** is a space for a fire in the wall of a room.

firework *noun*: **fireworks**
Fireworks are containers filled with powder, which explode and make bright flashes in the sky: *a firework show* □ *There are always a lot of fireworks at Chinese New Year celebrations.*

firm *noun*: **firms**
A **firm** is a company: *He works for a firm of lawyers.*

firm *adjective*: **firmer, firmest**
1 Something is **firm** if it feels hard and does not bend easily: *Try sleeping on a firmer mattress.*
2 **Firm** also means strong and steady: *Place the Christmas tree on a firm base.*

first *determiner and pronoun*
1 The **first** person or thing comes before all the others: *The first person to arrive was Philip.* □ *He was the second person to reach the South Pole, but who was the first?*
2 The **first** of any month is the first day of the month: *Her birthday is on the first of March.* □ *We won't get there till the first.*

first *adverb and adjective*
1 You do something **first** if you do it before anyone else: *I finished the exam first.*
2 You do something **first** if you do it before you do anything else: *I'll clean the windows first.*
3 You are first, or you come **first**, in a competition when you do better than everyone else: *He came first in the class again.* □ *John was first in the race.*

the opposite is **last**

▷ **at first**
At first means 'at the beginning of a period of time': *I didn't like him at first.* □ *At first, we thought that he was joking.*

fish *noun*: **fish** or **fishes**
1 A **fish** is a creature that lives in the water. Fish travel through the water by moving flat parts on their bodies called 'fins': *There aren't many fish in this river.*
2 **Fish** is also the flesh of this creature, eaten as food: *fish and chips.*

fish *verb*: **fishes, fished, fishing, has fished**
You **fish** when you try to catch fish: *We fished all day, but we didn't catch anything.*

fisherman *noun*: **fishermen**
A **fisherman** is a person who

fishes either as a job or as a hobby.

fishing *noun*
Fishing is the job or hobby of catching fish.

fishmonger *noun*: **fishmongers**
A **fishmonger** is a person who sells fish for eating.

fist *noun*: **fists**
Your **fist** is the shape of your hand when you close it tightly: *The men were fighting with their bare fists.* ▫ *The baby waved its little fists about.*

fit *verb*: **fits, fitted, fitting, has fitted**
1 Clothes **fit** you if they are the correct size for you: *Those trousers fit you really well.*
2 You **fit** something when you attach it: *We need to fit a new lock to the door.*

fit *adjective*: **fitter, fittest**
You are **fit** if you are healthy and able to do exercises without feeling tired.

five *noun and adjective*: **fives**
1 Five is the number or figure 5: *Three plus two is five.* ▫ *Three fives are fifteen.*
2 Five is the time of 5 o'clock: *The plane leaves at five.*
3 Five is also the age of five; someone who is **five** is five years old: *He was five last week.* ▫ *Many children start school at five.*

five *determiner and pronoun*
Five means five in number: *The flowers cost five dollars.* ▫ *They have five children.* ▫ *There were twenty people on the bus, and then five got off.*

fix *verb*: **fixes, fixed, fixing, has fixed**
1 You **fix** one thing to another

when you attach it: *Jack fixed the notice to the wall.*
2 You **fix** something when you repair it: *Could you fix the washing machine?*

flag *noun*: **flags**
A **flag** is a piece of cloth with a design on it, which is used to represent a country or an organization: *The flag of the European Union is blue with a circle of gold stars.* ▫ *People were waving flags and cheering.*

flame *noun*: **flames**
A **flame** is a bright light which is produced by something which is burning: *We could see the flames and smoke from far away.*

flash *noun*: **flashes**
A **flash** is a sudden bright light: *A flash of lightning lit up the sky.*

flash *verb*: **flashes, flashed, flashing, has flashed**
A light **flashes** if it shines for a very short time: *The driver flashed his lights as a warning.*

flat *noun*: **flats**
A **flat** is a set of rooms for living in, usually on one floor of a large building: *Their flat is on the second floor.*

flat *adjective and adverb*: **flatter, flattest**
1 A **flat** surface is a level one: *The top of Table Mountain is almost flat.*
2 A **flat** tyre has lost all its air.
3 Batteries are **flat** when there is no more power in them.
4 You lie **flat** when you lie with your whole body close to a surface: *He was lying flat on the ground, and he wasn't breathing.*

flesh *noun*
1 Flesh is the muscle and fat

under the skin of animals and humans.

2 Flesh is also the soft part inside the skin of a fruit.

flew *verb*
see **fly** : *A bird flew in through the window.*

flight *noun* : **flights**
1 A **flight** is a journey that you make in an aeroplane: *How long does the flight take?*
2 Flight is the action of flying: *birds in flight.*
3 A **flight** of stairs is a set of stairs: *They climbed up six flights of stairs.*

float *verb* : **floats, floated, floating, has floated**
Something **floats** when it stays on the surface of a liquid: *Pieces of wood and plastic bottles were floating on the river.*

flock *noun* : **flocks**
A **flock** is the name for a group of certain animals or birds: *a flock of sheep.* ❑ *a flock of birds.*

flood *noun* : **floods**
There is a **flood** when an area of land is suddenly covered by a large amount of water.

flood *verb* : **floods, flooded, flooding, has flooded**
Water **floods** a place when it covers it in large amounts: *The radiator leaked and flooded the bedroom.*

floor *noun* : **floors**
1 A **floor** of a room is the surface that you stand on: *There was a beautiful Indian rug on the bedroom floor.*
2 A **floor** of a building is one of the levels in it: *We live on the first floor.*

flour *noun*
Flour is a white or brown powder used to make bread and cakes.

flow *verb* : **flows, flowed, flowing, has flowed**
Liquid flows when it moves steadily along: *The river flows very slowly here.*

flower *noun* : **flowers**
A **flower** is a plant which has parts with coloured petals.

flown *verb*
see **fly** : *The birds have flown south for the winter.*

flu *noun*
Flu is an illness which causes pains in your muscles, a headache and a sore throat: *He's in bed with flu.*

flute *noun* : **flutes**
A **flute** is a musical instrument in the form of a pipe with holes; it is played by blowing across a hole at one end.

fly *noun* : **flies**
A **fly** is an insect with wings.

a fly

fly *verb* : **flies, flew, flying, has flown**
1 Birds **fly** when they move through the air using their wings: *Hundreds of birds flew over our heads.*

to fly

2 An aeroplane **flies** when it travels through the air: *The plane flew above the clouds.*
3 You **fly** when you travel by aeroplane: *She's flying to Frankfurt today.*

fog *noun*
Fog is a thick cloud near the surface of the ground. It is difficult to see through fog.

fold *verb*: **folds, folded, folding, has folded**
1 You **fold** paper or cloth when you move one part of it over the other, so that it covers the other part: *He folded the newspaper in half.*
2 You **fold** your arms when you cross them over your chest.

follow *verb*: **follows, followed, following, has followed**
1 You **follow** someone when you go along behind them: *He followed me into the room.*
2 One thing **follows** another if it happens after it: *The meal was followed by a dance.*
3 You **follow** a road when you go along it: *Follow the path to the end and then turn right.*
4 You **follow** what someone is saying to you when you understand it: *I tried to follow the story, but I was too sleepy.*
5 You **follow** advice or instructions when you obey them: *I followed his advice and bought a more expensive computer.*

meaning 1: the opposite is **lead**

fond *adjective*: **fonder, fondest**
You are **fond** of someone or something if you like them a lot: *They are very fond of each other.* ❏ *He's fond of chocolate ice cream.*

food *noun*
Food is anything that humans or animals eat: *We buy most of our food at the supermarket.* ❏ *These nuts are the monkeys' favourite food.*

fool *noun*: **fools**
A **fool** is a stupid person: *He's a fool if he thinks I believe his excuse.*

fool *verb*: **fools, fooled, fooling, has fooled**
You **fool** someone when you make them believe something that isn't true: *He managed to fool us all with his false beard and glasses.*

foolish *adjective*
A person is **foolish** if they behave in a silly way: *Stop being foolish and listen to me.* ❏ *His foolish behaviour caused the accident.*

the opposite is **wise** or **smart**

foot *noun*: **feet**
1 Your **feet** are the two parts at the lower ends of your legs, that you use to stand and walk on: *I've got sore feet from all that dancing.*

foot   toe   heel

2 The **foot** of something is the lowest part of it: *The village is at the foot of the hill.* ❏ *He sat at the foot of the stairs.*
3 A **foot** is a unit of length, equal to about 30 centimetres: *He's six feet tall.*

▷ **on foot**
You go somewhere **on foot** if you walk there: *We cycled most of the way, and completed the journey on foot.*

football *noun*: **footballs**
1 Football is a game played between two teams; each team tries to kick a ball into the other team's goal.

2 A **football** is also the ball used in this game.

for *preposition*
1 Something is **for** someone if it is intended for them: *I've brought that book for you.*
2a Something goes on **for** a certain period of time when it lasts that long: *I've worked here for over two years.* **b** You go on **for** a certain distance when you cover that distance: *They walked for another two kilometres.*
3 You use **for** when you are talking about how much things cost: *What can I buy for $10?* ❑ *I only paid £2.50 for it.*
4 Something is **for** a particular purpose if that is how it is used: *Can you lend me money for the bus fare?* ❑ *We used this room for sleeping in.* ❑ *What's that switch for?*
5 You do something **for** someone when you help them: *She made a meal for us.*
6 You work **for** a company if they employ you: *He works for a building firm.*
7 You feel something **for** someone if that is how you feel towards them: *We all felt very sorry for him.*
8 You use **for** to talk about the direction a person or vehicle is travelling in: *Is this the train for Paris?* ❑ *He's leaving for Hong Kong tomorrow morning.*
9a Something is good or bad **for** someone when it has a good or bad effect on them: *Exercise is good for you.* **b** Something is difficult or easy **for** someone when they find it difficult or easy: *It will be easy for him to find another job.*

10 For is used in several other ways: *Are you going for a walk?* ❑ *He asked me for my name and address.* ❑ *the patients' need for medicine.* ❑ *There's no time for a snack.* ❑ *She spoke too fast for me.*

forbid *verb*: **forbids, forbade, forbidding, has forbidden**
You **forbid** someone to do something when you tell them that they must not do it: *I forbid you to go out tonight.* ❑ *We were forbidden to run in the school buildings.* ❑ *Her parents forbade her to see the boy again.*

the opposite is **permit**

force *verb*: **forces, forced, forcing, has forced**
1 You **force** someone to do something when you make them do it: *He forced me to give him money.*
2 You **force** your way into a place when you use all your strength to enter it: *We forced the door open and entered the room.*

force *noun*
1 Force is power or strength: *The force of the wind blew some branches off the tree.*
2 Force is also violent action: *The thieves got into the bank by force.*

forehead *noun*: **foreheads**
Your **forehead** is the part of your face above your eyebrows: *She has a scar on her forehead.* [see picture at **face**]

foreign *adjective*
Something is **foreign** if it belongs to a country that is not your own: *How many foreign languages can you speak?*

forest *noun*: **forests**
A **forest** is a large area of land which is covered with trees.

forever or **for ever** *adverb*
Forever means 'always': *He said he would love her forever.* ❑ *Are you leaving for ever?*

forgave *verb*
see **forgave**: *He forgave me for being so rude.*

forget *verb*: **forgets, forgot, forgetting, has forgotten**
You **forget** something when you don't remember it: *Phone me tomorrow. Don't forget!* ❑ *She's always forgetting people's names.*

forgive *verb*: **forgives, forgave, forgiving, has forgiven**
You **forgive** someone who has done something wrong when you stop being angry with them: *I'll forgive you this time, but don't do it again.* ❑ *Have you forgiven me yet?*

forgot and **forgotten** *verb*
see **forget**: *I forgot to telephone her yesterday.* ❑ *I've forgotten my purse again.*

fork *noun*: **forks**
A **fork** is a narrow piece of metal with points that you use to lift food to your mouth: *He dropped his fork on the floor.*

form *noun*: **forms**
1 A **form** is a shape: *A dark form came out of the shadows.* ❑ *The table was in the form of a triangle.*
2 A **form** of something is a kind or type of it: *This is a Japanese form of poetry.*
3 A **form** is a class at school: *He's in the sixth form.*
4 A **form** is a piece of paper with questions and spaces for answers

printed on it: *He had to fill in a lot of forms to get a passport.*

form *verb*: **forms, formed, forming, has formed**
1 Something **forms**, or **is formed**, when it is made: *How was the Earth formed?* ❑ *During the storm, many small lakes formed in the valley.*
2 People **form** a shape when together they make that shape: *We formed a queue outside the cinema.*
3 People **form** a club when they begin it: *She's forming a film club at school.*

formal *adjective*
A **formal** letter or occasion follows certain rules of behaviour or style: *He received a formal letter from his boss.*

the opposite is **informal**

fortnight *noun*: **fortnights**
A **fortnight** is a period of fourteen days: *We're going to Greece for a fortnight.*

fortune *noun*: **fortunes**
1 A **fortune** is a lot of money: *His uncle left him a fortune.* ❑ *Their new car cost a fortune.*
2 Fortune is good or bad luck: *He had the good fortune to win first prize.*

forty *noun and adjective*: **forties**
1 Forty is the number 40: *Ten plus thirty is forty.*
2a Forty is the age of forty; someone who is **forty** is forty years old: *He was forty last week.*
b A person in their **forties** is between 40 and 49 years of age.
3 The years in any century between 40 and 49 are often called 'the **forties**'.

forty *determiner and pronoun*
Forty means forty in number:
The table cost forty pounds.
❑ *Why pay fifty dollars when you can have it for forty?*

forwards or **forward** *adverb*
You move **forwards** or **forward** when you go in the direction that is in front of you: *They pushed the car forward.*

fought *verb*
see **fight**: *He fought in the war.*

found *verb*
see **find**: *I found my pen under the desk.*

four *noun and adjective*: **fours**
1 Four is the number or figure 4: *Three plus one is four.* ❑ *Three fours are twelve.*
2 Four is the time of 4 o'clock: *The train leaves at four.*
3 Four is also the age of four; someone who is **four** is four years old: *Her daughter was four last week.*

four *determiner and pronoun*
Four means four in number: *The plant cost four pounds.* ❑ *'How many children have you got?' 'Four.'*

fourteen *noun and adjective*:
fourteens
1 Fourteen is the number 14: *Twelve plus two is fourteen.*
2 Fourteen is also the age of fourteen; someone who is **fourteen** is fourteen years old: *Her niece was fourteen last week.*

fourteen *determiner and pronoun*
Fourteen means fourteen in number: *The jumper cost fourteen pounds.* ❑ *There are seven days in a week, and fourteen in a fortnight.*

fourth *determiner and adjective*
The **fourth** person or thing is the one that comes after third.

fraction *noun*: **fractions**
A **fraction** is an amount, such as $\frac{1}{2}$ or $\frac{1}{4}$, that is part of a whole number.

free *adjective and adverb*:
meaning 1: **freer, freest**
1 A person is **free** if they are allowed to do what they want: *You are free to do what you like.*
2 A person is also **free** if they are not a prisoner: *The prisoner was set free after three years.*
3 You are **free** if you are not busy: *I can't come today, but I'm free tomorrow.*
4 Something is **free** if no-one is using it: *Is this seat free?*
5 Something that is **free** doesn't cost any money: *They're giving away free books at the library.*
❑ *We got the tickets free.*

freeze *verb*: **freezes, froze, freezing, has frozen**
1 Liquid **freezes** when it gets very cold and turns into ice: *The river always freezes in winter.*
2 You **freeze** food when you store it at a very cold temperature, so that you can use it later.
3 It **is freezing** when the weather is very cold: *It's freezing today — I'd better put my gloves on.*

frequent *adjective*
Something that is **frequent** happens often: *Tim makes frequent visits to Edinburgh.*

frequently *adverb*
Something that happens **frequently** happens a lot: *He is frequently late for work.*

same as **often**

fresh *adjective*: **fresher, freshest**
1 Food is **fresh** if it has just been made: *I love the smell of fresh bread.*
2 Food is also **fresh** if it is not old and dry: *This bread is still fresh — I bought it only yesterday.*
3 Fresh fruit and vegetables have not been frozen or stored in a can.
4 Something is **fresh** if it is clean: *I've put fresh sheets on the bed.*
5 Something is **fresh** if it is pleasantly cool: *a fresh breeze.*
6 Water is **fresh** if it is not salty: *We get fresh water from the stream.*

Friday *noun*
Friday is the fifth day of the week, the day after Thursday.

fridge *noun*: **fridges**
Fridge is short for **refrigerator**

fried and **fries** *verb*
see **fry**: *Have you fried the chicken yet?* ❏ *She fried the fish in a little butter.*

friend *noun*: **friends**
A **friend** is someone whom you know very well and like to spend time with: *He's a good friend of mine.* ❏ *This is my friend Sue Lin.*

friendly *adjective*: **friendlier, friendliest**
Someone is **friendly** if they are kind and make friends easily: *She's a very friendly person.*

the opposite is **unfriendly**

fright *noun*: **frights**
1 Fright is a sudden feeling of fear: *He was shaking with fright.*
2 You have a **fright** when you have a shock or when someone suddenly scares you: *You gave me such a fright!*

frighten *verb*: **frightens, frightened, frightening, has frightened**
Something **frightens** you when it makes you scared: *The loud bang frightened the dog.*

frightened *adjective*
You are **frightened** when you are nervous because you think that something dangerous could happen to you: *He was tired and frightened when the police finally found him.*

frog *noun*: **frogs**
A **frog** is a small animal that lives by the water; frogs have strong back legs which they use for jumping.

frog

from *preposition*
1 From shows the place that someone leaves when they move: *She's driving up from London tonight.*
2 From shows who gave or sent something: *I got a letter from Ian today.* ❏ *Who did you get that bracelet from?*
3 From shows when something starts: *The shop is open from 7 o'clock in the morning.*
4 You say you come **from** a place if that is where you were born: *She comes from London.*
5 You take something **from** a person or place when you remove it from them: *Take those sweets from him before he eats them all!* ❏ *He took a notebook from the drawer.*

6 You get something **from** a place if that is where you find it: *He's gone to get some bread from the supermarket.*

7 Something is made **from** a particular material if that material is used to make it: *Plastic is made from oil.*

8 You use **from** after certain verbs to show what has caused a state or condition: *He is suffering from a cold.*

front *noun and adjective:* **fronts**
The **front** of something is the part of it that faces forwards: *The front of the house was painted red.* ▢ *There's someone at the front door.* ▢ *He's lost his front teeth.*

the opposite is **back**

▷ **in front of**
Someone or something is **in front of** someone or something else if they are facing it: *He stood in front of the crowd.*

the opposite is **behind**

frost *noun*
Frost is a very thin layer of ice which forms on outside surfaces when it is very cold: *The window was covered with frost.*

frown *verb:* **frowns, frowned, frowning, has frowned**
You **frown** when you move your eyebrows together, for example, when you are thinking about something: *He frowned and tried to remember.*

frown

froze and **frozen** *verb*
see **freeze**: *The river froze during the night.* ▢ *The water in the pipes has frozen.*

fruit *noun:* **fruit** or **fruits**
A **fruit** is the part of a plant that has flesh which you can eat: *We had fresh fruit for pudding.*

fry *verb:* **fries, fried, frying, has fried**
You **fry** food when you cook it in hot fat: *Shall I fry some fish?*

frying pan *noun:* **frying pans**
A **frying pan** is a shallow pan with a handle that you use to fry food in.

fuel *noun:* **fuel**
Fuel is material such as coal, wood or petrol which you burn in order to get heat or power: *We need to get some more fuel for the fire.*

full *adjective:* **fuller, fullest**
1 Something that is **full** is holding as much as possible: *Is there a full bottle in the cupboard?* ▢ *We couldn't go to the cinema last night; it was full.*
2 You say you are **full**, or you are **full up**, when you have had enough to eat.
3 Full means 'complete': *He told me the full story.*

meaning 1: the opposite is **empty**

▷ **full up**
Something is **full up** if there is no more space left for anything else: *The bus was full up, so we waited for the next one.*

full stop *noun:* **full stops**
A **full stop** is a mark (.) used to show where a sentence ends.

fun *noun*
You have **fun** when you enjoy yourself: *We had a lot of fun at the party.*

funeral *noun*: **funerals**
A **funeral** is a ceremony held before a dead person is buried or burned.

funny *adjective*: **funnier, funniest**
1 Something that is **funny** makes you laugh: *That joke wasn't very funny.*
2 Funny also means strange or odd: *We heard a funny noise coming from the cupboard.*

fur *noun*
Fur is the thick hair that grows on animals: *Their dog has very soft fur.*

furniture *noun*
Furniture is a general word for things like beds, sofas, tables and chairs: *They've just bought new furniture for the bedroom.*

further *adverb and adjective*
1 Further means 'a greater distance': *Which is further from here, London or Bristol?*
2 Further also means 'more': *Can I have further information about the plans?*

furthest *adverb and adjective*
Furthest means 'the greatest distance': *He threw the furthest, so he won the prize.* ❑ *What's the furthest distance people have travelled from the earth?*

future *noun*
The **future** is the time that comes after now: *I wonder what will happen in the future?*

the opposite is the **past**

▷ **in future**
Something that will be done **in future** will be done after now: *You must be kinder to him in future.*

Gg

gain *verb*: **gains, gained, gaining, has gained**
1 You **gain** something when you get it: *He gained a lot of experience working abroad.*
2 You also **gain** something when you get more of it: *The car gained speed as it travelled down the road.*

game *noun*: **games**
1 A **game** is an activity which people do for fun: *The children were playing some kind of game.*
2 A **game** is also a sport or a contest with rules, that you try to win: *She's very good at card games.*
3 A **game** is also a match: *Would you like a game of football?*

gang *noun*: **gangs**
1 A **gang** is a group of criminals: *The gang made plans to rob the bank.*
2 A **gang** is also a group of young people, who are all friends.

gap *noun*: **gaps**
A **gap** is a small space between two things: *We squeezed through the narrow gap in the fence.*

garage *noun*: **garages**
1 A **garage** is a building in which you put a car when you are not using it: *The garage is attached to the house.*
2 A **garage** is also a place where you go to buy petrol, or where cars can be repaired: *The car's in the garage. There's something wrong with the engine.*

garden *noun*: **gardens**
A **garden** is an area of land beside a house, where flowers, plants and vegetables are grown: *We spent the afternoon in the garden.*

garlic *noun*
Garlic is a small vegetable with a white bulb, which has a strong taste and smell; garlic is used in cooking.

gas *noun*
1 Gas is a type of fuel which is used for heating and cooking: *We've got a new gas oven.*
2 Gas is also the American word for petrol.

gate *noun*: **gates**
A **gate** is a door in an outside wall or fence: *The gates were closed so we had to climb over the wall.*

gather *verb*: **gathers, gathered, gathering, has gathered**
1 You **gather** things when you bring them together in one place: *He gathered all the papers together and put them in the bin.*
2 People or animals **gather** when they come together in one place: *All the students gathered outside the library.*

gave *verb*
see **give**: *He gave me a ring for my birthday.*

gaze *verb*: **gazes, gazed, gazing, has gazed**
You **gaze** when you look at something for a long time: *She gazed out of the window.*

geese *noun*
see **goose**

general *adjective*
'**General**' refers to most people or situations: *There's a general feeling that things are getting better.*

▷ **in general**
Things **in general**, are all or most things.

generous *adjective*
A **generous** person is kind, and willing to help other people: *He's very generous. How can we thank him?.*

the opposite is **selfish** or **mean**

gentle *adjective*: **gentler, gentlest**
1 Gentle things are soft and light, and not rough in any way: *A gentle breeze blew through the garden.*
2 Gentle also means 'kind and quiet': *'It's all right,' he replied, in a gentle voice.*

gentleman *noun*: **gentlemen**
1 Gentleman is a polite word used to refer to a man that you don't know: *These two gentlemen have some questions to ask you.*
2 A **gentleman** is a man who is very polite and kind: *Mr Gallagher is a real gentleman.*

gently *adverb*
Gently means 'in a gentle way': *The teacher spoke gently to the little girl.*

germ *noun*: **germs**
Germs are tiny living things that make people ill: *I'm staying at home; I don't want to pass germs on to you.*

get *verb*: **gets, got, getting, has got**
1 You **get** something when someone gives it to you, or you buy it: *What did you get for your birthday?* ❑ *I got a new dress*
yesterday.
2 You've **got** something if you have it: *She's got black hair.*
3 You **get** something for someone when you fetch it for them: *Could you get me a newspaper when you go out?*
4 You **get** somewhere when you arrive there: *We got home about midnight.* ❑ *They will probably get to the hotel before us.*
5 You **get** someone to do something when you persuade them to do it: *I'll get my brother to meet us.*
6 You **get** a bus, or another type of public vehicle, when you travel somewhere on it: *I'll get the last bus home.*
7 You **get** a disease or illness when you catch it: *I don't want to get another cold.*
8 You **get** tired or angry when you become tired or angry: *Can we stop for five minutes? I'm getting tired.*

▷ **get along with**
You **get along** with someone if you are friendly with them and enjoy their company: *I get along with him much better now.*

▷ **get away**
You **get away** when you escape: *The thieves got away with all the money.*

▷ **get away with**
You **get away** with dishonest behaviour when you escape being punished for it: *He got away with stealing all that money.*

▷ **get hold of**
1 You **get hold** of something when you grab it: *He got hold of her arm and pulled her back.*
2 You **get hold** of something

when you manage to find it: *I've finally got hold of that book you wanted.*

3 You **get hold** of someone when you manage to speak to them, especially by phone: *I need to get hold of Jeremy — is he in his office?*

▷ **get in**
A bus or train **gets in** when it arrives at its final stop: *What time does your train get in?*

▷ **get into**
You **get into** something such a car when you climb inside it: *Get into the car and wait for me — I'll only be a few minutes.*

▷ **get off**
You **get off** a train or a bus when you climb down from it: *I'll get off outside the school.*

▷ **get on**
1 You **get on** with someone if you are friendly with them and like to spend time with them: *Those two get on well together.*
2 You ask how someone **is getting on** when you want to know how their work is progressing: *How are you getting on in your new job?*
3 You **get on** with something when you continue to do it: *I must get on with my work.*
4 You **get on** a bus or a train when you climb inside it: *I got on the train at Manchester.*

meaning 4: same as **board**

▷ **get out**
You **get out** of something when you leave it: *The car broke down, so we all had to get out and push.*

▷ **get out of**
You **get out of** doing something you don't like if you manage to

avoid doing it: *I got out of making the tea every day last week.*

▷ **get through**
You **get through** something that you have to do when you complete it: *I got through all the questions in one hour.*

▷ **get up**
1 You **get up** when you get out of bed: *I get up at 7 o'clock every morning.*
2 You **get up** when you stand up: *Everyone got up when she entered the room.*

ghost *noun*: **ghosts**
A **ghost** is the shape of a dead person, which some people believe they have seen: *He says he saw a ghost last night.*

gift *noun*: **gifts**
A **gift** is a present that you give to someone: *We've bought her some flowers as a gift.*

giggle *verb*: **giggles, giggled, giggling, has giggled**
People, especially children **giggle** when they laugh in a silly way: *We all giggled at her silly jokes.*

ginger *noun*
Ginger is a kind of root which is peeled and cut up, or made into a powder; ginger is used in cooking.

giraffe *noun*: **giraffes**
A **giraffe** is a tall African animal with a very long neck and long legs.

girl *noun*: **girls**
A **girl** is a female child: *They have three children — two boys and one girl.*

give *verb*: **gives, gave, giving, has given**
1 You **give** something to

someone when you pass it to them: *Could you give me the newspaper?*
2 You also **give** something to someone when you pass it on to them as a present: *He gave me a bracelet for my birthday.*
3a You **give** a party when you organize it: *She's giving a party, and we're all invited.* **b** You **give** a performance when you perform to an audience.
4 You use **give** to talk about certain things that people do: *He gave me a push.* ❑ *She gave a yell of excitement.*

▷ **give away**
1 You **give** something **away** when you give it to someone else, because you don't need or want it anymore: *She gave most of her toys away.*
2 You **give** secret information **away** when you tell it to someone: *He's been giving secrets away to other companies.*

▷ **give back**
You **give** something **back** when you return it to its owner: *I forgot to give that book back.*

▷ **give up**
1 You **give up** doing something when you decide to stop doing it: *She wants to give up smoking.* ❑ *He says he's given up trying to lose weight.*
2 You **give up** when you admit that you cannot do something: *I give up — what's the answer?*

▷ **give way**
1 Something **gives way** when it breaks: *The chair gave way under his weight.*
2 You **give way** to something when you agree to do it, even

though you don't really want to: *I had to give way to their wishes.*

glad *adjective*: **gladder, gladdest**
You are **glad** when you are happy or pleased: *I'm glad you're feeling better now.*

glass *noun*: **glasses**
1 Glass is a hard transparent material which can break quite easily: *Windows are made from glass.* ❑ *a glass door.*
2 A **glass** is a container made from this material, used to drink from: *We've bought some new wine glasses.* ❑ *I'll have a glass of wine, please.*

a glass

glasses
(or spectacles)

glasses *noun*
Glasses are spectacles: *He can't see anything without his glasses.*

glove *noun*: **gloves**
You wear **gloves** on your hands to protect them, or to keep them warm: *It was a very cold day, so she put on her woollen gloves.*

glow *verb*: **glows, glowed, glowing, has glowed**
Something **glows** when it sends out heat or light, without any flames: *The coal glowed in the fire.*

glue *noun*
Glue is sticky stuff used to stick things together: *He stuck the pieces of wood together with glue.*

glue is also a verb: *They glued the two pieces of wood together.*

go *verb*: **goes, went, going, has gone**
1 You **go** somewhere when you

travel or move there: *I'm going to Amsterdam next week.*

2 You **go** to a particular place when you attend it regularly: *They go to the pub every Saturday.* ❏ *Do you want to go to the cinema?* ❏ *Which school does he go to?*

3 Someone or something **goes** when they leave: *I have to go at nine o'clock.* ❏ *Has Amy gone yet?*

4 A road **goes** somewhere when it leads to that place: *This road goes to the station.*

5 Something **goes** somewhere when that is the place where it is kept: *Where do the knives go?* ❏ *The books go in the other room.*

6 You can also use **go** to mean 'become': *My dinner's gone cold.* ❏ *His hair is beginning to go grey.*

7 You can also use **go** when you talking about doing an activity: *I'm going for a walk.* ❏ *They're all going swimming later.*

▷ **go ahead**
1 You **go ahead** with something when you do it as you planned: *He went ahead with his plan and made lots of money.*

2 Something **goes ahead** if it happens as planned: *The match went ahead even though it was raining.*

3 You **go ahead** of someone when you move in front of them: *He went ahead of us to get everything ready.*

▷ **go off**
1 A bomb or a gun **goes off** when it explodes or it is fired: *The gun went off by accident.*

2 Food **goes off** when it becomes rotten or sour: *The fridge broke down and all the food went off.*

3 An alarm bell **goes off** when it starts ringing.

▷ **go on**
1 You **go on** doing something when you continue to do it: *He went on talking even when most people had left.*

2 You ask what is **going on** when you want to know what is happening: *What's going on here?*

▷ **go out**
1 Someone **goes out** when they leave the room or building they are in: *He went out of the room and came back holding something.*

2 A light **goes out** when it is switched off; a fire or a flame **goes out** when it stops burning: *The lights suddenly went out.* ❏ *The door slammed and the candle went out.*

3 You **go out** when you go to a restaurant or a party, for example: *We're going out tonight — do you want to come with us?*

▷ **go over**
You **go over** something when you read it carefully: *He went over his essay checking for mistakes.*

▷ **go with**
Two things **go with** each other if they look attractive together: *The blue tie doesn't really go with the green shirt.*

▷ **going to**
1 You say you **are going to** do something when you are intending to do it soon: *I'm going to have a bath.*

2 You say something **is going to** happen when you feel sure that it will happen: *It's going to be sunny tomorrow.*

go *noun*: **goes**
1 You have a **go** when you make

an attempt at doing something: *I don't know if I'll be able to do it, but I'll have a go now.*

2 A **go** is also a person's turn to play, in a game, for example: *Can I have a go?* ❑ *It's my go now.*

goal *noun*: **goals**

1 In games such as football and hockey, the **goal** is the area into which you must put the ball, in order to score a point.

2 A **goal** is also the point that you score for doing this: *Liverpool beat Manchester United by three goals to one.*

goat *noun*: **goats**

A **goat** is an animal of the sheep family, with horns and a hairy coat.

God *noun*

God is the name given to the being which, many people believe, made the world and also controls the world: *Do you believe in God?*

god *noun*: **gods**

A **god** is one of several beings which many people believe have some kind of power over nature: *the Greek god of war.*

gold *noun*

Gold is a yellow precious metal which is used to make jewellery; something that is **gold** is made of this metal or is the pale yellow colour of this metal: *This bracelet is made of gold.* ❑ *gold earrings* ❑ *gold paint* ❑ *Is this real gold?*

golden *adjective*

Something that is **golden** is the pale yellow colour of gold: *We lay on the warm golden sand.*

gone *verb*

see **go**: *He's gone to Spain.*

good *adjective*: **better, best**

1 You say that something is **good** if you think it is pleasant or if you enjoy it: *I had a good time last night.* ❑ *This book is really good.*

2 Good behaviour is correct and proper behaviour: *That was a very good thing to do.* ❑ *His behaviour in class has been better this year.*

3 Well-behaved children or animals are often described as **good**: *Since you've been so good, we can go the park.* ❑ *Go and fetch the stick, there's a good dog.*

4 You can also describe someone who is kind or helpful as **good**: *She's a very good person — always thinking of others.*

5 You are **good** at something when you can do it well: *I'm not very good at remembering people's names.* ❑ *His English is pretty good.*

6 Something **good** is pleasing: *We've just received some good news.*

7 Good manners are correct manners: *It is not good manners to speak with your mouth full.*

8 Good is also used in several forms of greeting: *Good afternoon, how can I help you?* ❑ *Good evening sir. Your table is ready.* ❑ *Good morning, everyone.*

goodbye

You say **goodbye** when you are leaving someone, or they are leaving you: *Goodbye. See you on Thursday.*

goodnight

You say **goodnight** when you are leaving someone, especially when you are going to bed: *Goodnight. See you in the morning.*

goods *noun*

Goods are things that people

buy and sell: *They sell their goods at the local market.* ❑ *leather goods.*

goose *noun*: **geese**
A **goose** is a bird with a long neck, similar to a large duck.

got *verb*
see **get**: *I got a letter from Brian this morning.*

▷ **have got**
You **have got** something when you have it: *He's got blue eyes.* ❑ *Have you got a cold?*

government *noun*: **governments**
The **government** of a country is the group of people who are in charge of that country.

grab *verb*: **grabs, grabbed, grabbing, has grabbed**
You **grab** something when you take hold of it suddenly with one or both of your hands: *She grabbed the newspaper from me.*

same as **snatch**

graceful *adjective*
1 A **graceful** person moves in a smooth way that is pleasant to watch: *a graceful dancer.*
2 Something is **graceful** if it has an attractive shape or if it is made up of smooth lines: *tall graceful trees.*

grade *noun*: **grades**
1 A **grade** is a mark or level of quality: *We sell three grades of petrol.*
2 In the USA, a **grade** is a class in a school: *Mr Bergman teaches the fourth grade.*

gradual *adjective*
Something that is **gradual** happens very slowly, so that you hardly notice it: *There's been a*

gradual increase in prices over the past six months.

gradually *adverb*
Something that happens **gradually** happens very slowly: *He gradually pulled himself up to the top branch of the tree.* ❑ *The room gradually became lighter.*

grain *noun*
Grain is the seed of crops such as wheat and rice.

gram or **gramme** *noun*: **grams** or **grammes**
A **gram** is a unit of weight: *One thousand grams equal one kilogram.*

grand *adjective*: **grander, grandest**
Something that is **grand** is large and has the best or most expensive things in it: *The wedding was rather grand.* ❑ *a grand house.*

grandchild *noun*: **grandchildren**
Someone's **grandchild** is the child of their son or daughter: *They have three grandchildren.*

granddaughter *noun*: **granddaughters**
Someone's **granddaughter** is the female child of their son or daughter: *Mr Clark has only one granddaughter.*

grandfather *noun*: **grandfathers**
Your **grandfather** is the father of your mother or father: *Her grandfather died eight years ago.*

grandmother *noun*: **grandmothers**
Your **grandmother** is the mother of your mother or father: *His grandmother is nearly eighty.*

grandparents *noun*
Your **grandparents** are the

parents of your mother or father: *My grandparents live in France.*

grandson *noun*: **grandsons**
Someone's **grandson** is the male child of their son or daughter: *Mrs Davis only has two grandsons.*

grape *noun*: **grapes**
A **grape** is a small round fruit that grows in bunches and is used to make wine: *These grapes don't have seeds in them.* □ *This wine is made from French grapes.*

grapefruit *noun*: **grapefruits**
A **grapefruit** is a yellow or pink fruit, like a large orange, but with a sharper taste: *grapefruit juice.*

grass *noun*
Grass is a green plant which covers fields and gardens; grass is eaten by animals such as cows.

grasshopper *noun*:
grasshoppers
A **grasshopper** is an insect with long back legs that it uses to jump very high.

grateful *adjective*
You are **grateful** when you feel that you want to thank someone for the help they have given you: *I'm grateful for all your help.*

grave *noun*: **graves**
A **grave** is a place where a dead body is buried: *He laid flowers on his grandmother's grave.*

grease *noun*
Grease is thick oil, especially the kind that is put in machines to make their parts work more smoothly.

great *adjective*: **greater, greatest**
1 Great means 'very large': *There was a great crowd of people at the football match.*
2 Great also means 'a lot of':

Andrew took great care of his new watch.
3 You describe someone as **great** if they are very important or special: *He is one of the greatest writers of all time.*
4 Something is **great** if it is excellent or very good: *That was a great joke.* □ *We had a great time at the party.*

rhymes with **plate**

greedy *adjective*: **greedier, greediest**
Someone who is **greedy** wants more than they need, especially food: *Don't be greedy — you've had enough to eat now.*

green *noun and adjective*
Green is the colour of fresh grass: *Pale green is a nice colour for a bedroom.* □ *He's wearing a green shirt.*

greet *verb*: **greets, greeted, greeting, has greeted**
You **greet** someone when you welcome them: *Mr Fraser greeted all his guests as they arrived at the party.*

greeting *noun*: **greetings**
1 A **greeting** is what you say when you welcome someone.
2 A **greeting** is a message which you send someone, often written in a card: *Birthday greetings from the Smith family.*

grew *verb*
see **grow**: *We grew cabbages and potatoes in the garden.*

grey *noun and adjective*
Grey is the colour of rain clouds: *Mr Crosbie's hair is grey.* □ *a pair of grey trousers* □ *The hall was decorated in greys and browns.*

grill *verb*: **grills, grilled, grilling, has grilled**
You **grill** food when you cook it under a strong heat: *We grilled the sausages and burgers.*

grind *verb*: **grinds, ground, grinding, has ground**
You **grind** something when you crush it into a powder: *I'll grind some coffee beans and we can have coffee.*

grip *verb*: **grips, gripped, gripping, has gripped**
You **grip** something when you hold it tightly in your hand: *He gripped the rope and pulled himself up.*

groan *verb*: **groans, groaned, groaning, has groaned**
You **groan** when you make a deep sound, because you are unhappy or in pain: *He put his head in his hands and groaned.*

grocer *noun*: **grocers**
1 A **grocer** is a person who sells food and things for use in the home.
2 A **grocer** or **grocer's** is a shop where you can buy food and things for the home: *There was just a church, a post office and a small grocer's when we first came to live here.*

ground *noun*
1 The **ground** is the solid surface of the earth which you walk on: *He easily jumped the 3 metres to the ground.*
2 A **ground** is an area of land that is used for a special purpose: *a football ground.*
3 The **grounds** of a large house are the areas of land around it that belong to it: *They showed us round the grounds of the palace.*

ground
see **grind**: *He ground the beans to make coffee.*

group *noun*: **groups**
1 A **group** of people or things is a number of them together in one place: *There was a small group of trees in the field.* ❑ *The teacher divided the class into groups of four.*
2 A **group** is a band of musicians who play pop music together: *He's the singer in a group.*

grow *verb*: **grows, grew, growing, has grown**
1 Someone or something **grows** when it becomes bigger: *Their puppy has grown a lot in two weeks.*
2 You **grow** plants when you look after them and help them to get bigger: *We're trying to grow roses this year.*
3 You **grow** your hair when you don't cut it so that it becomes longer.
4 You can use **grow** to mean 'become': *The sky grew dark and it began to rain.* ❑ *We forget that she's growing older.*

growl *verb*: **growls, growled, growling, has growled**
An animal **growls** when it makes a deep rough noise in its throat, usually because it is angry: *The dog growled at the postman.*

grown *verb*
see **grow**: *Jackie's grown a lot since we last saw her.*

grown-up *noun*: **grown-ups**
A **grown-up** is an adult person.

growth *noun*
Growth is the process of getting bigger: *Children's growth is fastest at around the age of thirteen.*

guard *noun*: **guards**
1 A **guard** is someone whose job is to protect people or things from danger: *The guard walked beside the president at all times.* ❑ *The guards didn't see the three men entering the bank.*
2 A **guard** is also someone whose job is to stop prisoners from escaping: *He works as a guard in a prison.*
3 A **guard** on a train is the person who is in charge of all the passengers: *The guard checked everyone's ticket.*

guard *verb*: **guards, guarded, guarding, has guarded**
You **guard** a person or place when you protect them from danger: *Two policemen guarded the main entrance to the building.* ❑ *We took turns to guard the money.*

guess *verb*: **guesses, guessed, guessing, has guessed**
1 You **guess** the answer to something when you say what you think the answer might be: *He tried to guess her age.* ❑ *If you don't know the answer, just guess.*
2 'I **guess**' also means 'I think': *I guess I should go now.*

meaning 2: same as **suppose**

guess *noun*: **guesses**
A **guess** is an answer that you think might be right, but you don't know for sure: *I don't know if it's right — it's just a guess.*

guest *noun*: **guests**
1 A **guest** is someone whom you have invited to your home: *Some of the guests arrived early, and we weren't ready.*
2 In a hotel, the **guests** are the people who pay to stay there.

guide *noun*: **guides**
1 A **guide** is someone who shows people round a place: *We hired a guide to show us round the old town.*
2 A **guide** is also a book which tells you about a particular subject or place: *a guide to camping in Scotland.*

rhymes with **side**

guide *verb*: **guides, guided, guiding, has guided**
1 You **guide** someone when you give them directions or take them somewhere: *I don't know the way to the library — I'll need someone to guide me.* ❑ *The boy was guiding the blind man across the road.*
2 You also **guide** someone when you help or advise them: *Thanks for guiding me through my first months here.*

guilty *adjective*: **guiltier, guiltiest**
1 You feel **guilty** when you feel bad because you have done something wrong: *She felt guilty about arguing with her mother.*
2 A person who is **guilty** has broken the law: *He was found guilty of murder.*

meaning 2: the opposite is **innocent**

guitar *noun*: **guitars**
A **guitar** is a musical instrument with six strings which you play with your fingers: *He's teaching me to play the guitar.*

guitar

gum *noun*: **gums**
1 Gum is a kind of glue.
2 Your **gums** are the soft pink areas of flesh that hold your teeth.

gun *noun*: **guns**
A **gun** is a weapon which fires bullets: *The policeman carried a gun at the side of his belt.*

gymnastics *noun*
Gymnastics is a sport in which people do difficult exercises and movements, sometimes using special equipment.

Hh

habit *noun*: **habits**
A **habit** is something that you do regularly, often without realizing that you are doing it: *She has a habit of biting her nails.*

had *verb*
see **have**: *I had soup for my lunch.* ❑ *We all had a great time at the party.*

▶You can shorten **I had**, **you had**, **he had**, **she had**, **we had and they had** to **I'd**, **you'd**, **he'd**, **she'd**, **we'd** and **they'd**.

hadn't *verb*
Hadn't is short for had not: *She was very excited because she hadn't been to the zoo before.*

hair *noun*: **hairs**
1 A **hair** is one of the fine threads that grow from your skin, especially on your head: *He's got a few grey hairs.*
2 Your **hair** is all the hairs on your head: *He's got dark brown hair.*

hairdresser *noun*: **hairdressers**
1 A **hairdresser** is a person whose job is to wash and cut people's hair.
2 A **hairdresser** or **hairdresser's** is a place where you go to have your hair cut: *She's going to the hairdresser's tomorrow.*

hairstyle *noun*: **hairstyles**
Your **hairstyle** is the way that your hair is cut or arranged: *I think it's time to change my hairstyle.*

hairy *adjective*: **hairier, hairiest**
Something that is **hairy** is covered with hairs: *He's got a hairy chest.*

half *noun*: **halves**
A **half** of something is one of two equal parts of it: *It took half an hour to get to the station.* ❑ *We'll cut these cakes into halves.*

▷ **half past**
When it is **half past** an hour, it is thirty minutes past that hour: *Tell me when it's half past five.*

half past five

▷ **in half**
You cut something **in half** when you cut it into two equal parts: *She cut the cake in half and gave me a piece.*

half *adverb*
1 Half means 'to the level or point of one half': *The kettle is half full of water.*
2 You also use **half** to mean 'partly': *This cup is only half full.* ❑ *He was half dead with hunger and thirst.*

hall *noun*: **halls**
1 A **hall** is a room in a house, which has other rooms leading from it: *You can hang your coats up in the hall.*
2 A **hall** is also a large room in a building, used for events such as meetings or concerts: *The meeting was held in the school hall.*

halve *verb*: **halves, halved, halving, has halved**
You **halve** something when you divide it into two equal parts: *He halved the cake and shared it with his sister.*

ham *noun*
Ham is salty meat which comes from the back leg of a pig: *We had ham and eggs for tea.*

hamburger *noun*: **hamburgers**
A **hamburger** is a flat round piece of chopped beef, which is fried and eaten, often in a bread roll.

▶ often shortened to **burger**

hammer *noun*: **hammers**
A **hammer** is a tool with a heavy metal head which you use to hit nails into wood, or to break things.

hammer

hammer *verb*: **hammers, hammered, hammering, has hammered**
You **hammer** something when you hit it hard using a hammer: *We hammered the tent pegs into the ground.*

hand *noun*: **hands**
1 Your **hands** are the parts of your body at the end of your arms: *He was holding something in his hands.* □ *She had a ring on the third finger of her left hand.* □ *Which hand do you write with?*

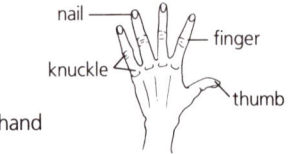
nail — finger
knuckle
thumb
hand

2 The **hands** of a clock or a watch are the parts which move round and point to the numbers.
3 You give someone a **hand** when you help them: *I'll give you a hand to move that bookcase.*

▷ **shake hands**
Two people **shake hands** when they greet each other by holding each other's right hand and moving it up and down: *The two men shook hands.*

hand *verb*: **hands, handed, handing, has handed**
You **hand** something to someone when you pass it to them: *Would you hand me the scissors please?*

handbag *noun*: **handbags**
A **handbag** is a woman's small bag.

handkerchief *noun*: **handkerchiefs**
A **handkerchief** is a piece of cloth or soft paper which you use to wipe your nose.

handle *noun*: **handles**
1 A **handle** is the part of an object that you use to pick it up or hold it: *The handle on my bag has broken.*
2 The **handle** on a door is the part that you hold when you open it or close it.

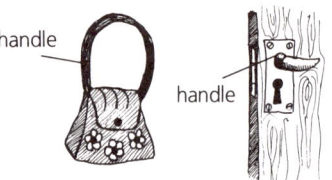
handle
handle

handsome *adjective*: **handsomer, handsomest**
A man who is **handsome** has an attractive face: *He was a*

handsome man with a soft, gentle voice.

handy *adjective*: **handier, handiest**
Something that is **handy** is useful: *It's a handy little dictionary that you can carry in your bag.*

hang *verb*: **hangs, hung, hanging, has hung**
1 You **hang** something on a hook when you attach its top part, leaving the rest held loosely above the ground: *The children hung their coats on hooks outside the classroom.*
2 Something **is hanging** when it is held loosely in this way: *The washing was hanging on the line.*

happen *verb*: **happens, happened, happening, has happened**
1 Something **happens** when it takes place: *Where did the accident happen?* ❏ *I don't remember what happened next.*
2 Something, often something bad, **happens** to a person or thing when they are affected by it: *Did something bad happen to you at school today?* ❏ *Something's happened to the lights — they don't work.* ❏ *What's happened to your hand?*

▷ **happen to**
1 You use '**happen to**' to talk about something that takes place by chance: *I happened to see him coming out of the house.* ❏ *If you ever happen to be in New York, you must come and visit us.*
2 You also use '**happen to**' to talk about something that other people do not know about: *She happens to be a good friend of*

mine. ❏ *Do you happen to know what time it is?*

happiness *noun*
Happiness is the good feeling that you have when you are enjoying your life: *They've had years of happiness together.*

happy *adjective*: **happier, happiest**
1 You are **happy** when you feel pleased: *She gave him a happy smile.*
2 You are **happy** to do something if it gives you pleasure or you are very willing to do it: *I'd be happy to drive you to work tomorrow.*

meaning 1: the opposite is **sad**

harbour *noun*: **harbours**
A **harbour** is a place where ships can shelter.

hard *adjective and adverb*: **harder, hardest**
1 Something is **hard** if it is very firm and solid: *I need a cushion — this chair is too hard.*
2 A **hard** task or question is not easy to do or answer: *These puzzles are too hard for the children.*
3 You work **hard** when you work quickly with a lot of energy: *He's worked very hard all day.*

meaning 2: same as **difficult**

hardly *adverb*
1 Hardly means 'almost no …' or 'almost never': *I hardly ever go out.* ❏ *There's been hardly any rain so far this year.*
2 Hardly also means 'only just': *My feet are so sore. I can hardly walk.*

harm *verb*: **harms, harmed, harming, has harmed**

1 Someone or something **harms** you when they hurt you or injure you: *Don't worry — the dog won't harm you.*

2 Something **harms** something else if it spoils that other thing: *This government's actions will harm our children's future.*

harm *noun*
Harm is injury or damage: *I'm sure he did them no harm.*

harmful *adjective*
Something that is **harmful** is bad for you: *Smoking is harmful to the health.*

harmless *adjective*
Something that is **harmless** is safe and not dangerous: *This snake is harmless.*

harvest *noun*: **harvests**
1 The **harvest** is the time when farmers gather in ripe crops: *The whole village helped with the harvest.*

2 The **harvest** is also the crops that are gathered: *We had a very good harvest this year.*

has *verb*
see **have**: *He has blue eyes.* ❑ *Roy has two brothers and one sister.* ❑ *Has the programme finished yet?*

▶You can shorten **he has**, **she has** and **it has** to **he's**, **she's** and **it's**.
▶You can also shorten **what has** and **that has** to **what's** and **that's**.
▶You can also shorten, for example, **Jane has** to **Jane's**.

hasn't *verb*
Hasn't is short for **has not**: *He hasn't telephoned me yet.*

hat *noun*: **hats**
A **hat** is a piece of clothing that

you wear on your head: *She bought a warm woollen hat for the winter.*

hate *verb*: **hates, hated, hating, has hated**
You **hate** someone or something when you dislike them very much: *I hate cabbage.* ❑ *I hate him — he tried to hurt our dog.*

the opposite is **love**

have *verb*: **has, had, having, has had**
1 You use **have** when you want to talk about experiences in the past, or things that began in the past and have some importance now: *Have you been to Paris before?* ❑ *I have never read that book.* ❑ *He has gone home early.*

2 You **have** or **have got** something when it is yours, or is part of you: *They have a dog called Tina.* ❑ *I've got brown eyes.* ❑ *Does he have a car?*

3 You **have** or **have got** an illness when you are suffering from it: *I've got a headache.* ❑ *Mr Rogers has a cold.*

4 You **have** food or drink when you eat it: *I had chicken for dinner.*

▶You can shorten **I have**, **you have** and **we have** to **I've**, **you've** and **we've**.

▷ have to or have got to
If you **have to**, or **have got to** do something you must do it: *I have got to finish this before 5 o'clock.*

haven't *verb*
Haven't is short for **have not**: *I haven't seen him today.*

hay *noun*
Hay is grass that has been cut

and dried; hay is usually used to feed cattle.

he *pronoun*
You use **he** to talk about a man, boy or male animal that has already been mentioned: *Brian telephoned — he can't come tonight.* ❑ *Don't worry — he's just being friendly.* ❑ *'This boy says he's your brother.' 'Yes, he is.'*

head *noun*: **heads**
1 Your **head** is the part at the top of your body, where your face and brain are: *She shook her head.* ❑ *He couldn't see over the people's heads.* ❑ *I've got a sore head.*
2 The **head** of an organization is the person who is in charge of it: *Mr Shepherd is the school's head.*
3 The **head** of something is the top or front part of it: *The title is printed at the head of the first page.* ❑ *He went to the head of the queue.*

headache *noun*: **headaches**
A **headache** is a pain in your head: *She's got a bad headache and has gone to bed.*

headteacher *noun*: **headteachers**
A **headteacher** is a teacher who is in charge of a school: *The boys had to go to the headteacher to be punished.*

heal *verb*: **heals, healed, healing, has healed**
A cut or other wound **heals** when it closes up and gets better: *The cut on my finger has healed now.*

health *noun*
Your **health** is the way that you feel and how well your body is:

The doctor said I was in good health.

healthy *adjective*: **healthier, healthiest**
1 You are **healthy** when you feel well and you are not ill: *You would be healthier if you took more exercise.*
2 Something is **healthy** if it is good for you: *Exercise is very healthy.*

the opposite is **unhealthy**

heap *noun*: **heaps**
A **heap** of something is a rough pile of it: *There was a heap of books on the table.*

hear *verb*: **hears, heard, hearing, has heard**
1 You **hear** sounds when you notice them using your ears: *I can't hear you.* ❑ *I don't think he heard what you said.*
2 You **hear** something about someone or something when you receive information about them: *Have you heard the news?* ❑ *I hear you've got a new job.*

heart *noun*: **hearts**
1 Your **heart** is the part inside your chest which pumps blood around your body: *He could feel his heart beating fast.*
2 The **heart** of something is the centre of it: *We live in the heart of London.*

heat *noun*
Heat is warmth that comes from something hot, such as a fire or the sun: *The heat from the fire soon dried their clothes.* ❑ *I can't work in this heat.*

heat *verb*: **heats, heated, heating, has heated**
You **heat** something when you

make it hot: *I'll just heat the milk in this pan.*

▷ **heat up**
1 You **heat** something **up** when you make it hot: *I'll heat the soup up now.*
2 Something **heats up** when it becomes hotter: *The water is heating up for your bath.*

heater *noun*: **heaters**
A **heater** is a device for heating a room, or for heating water: *It's cold in here — I'll switch on the heater.*

heating *noun*
The **heating** in a building is the system that keeps the rooms warm: *They switch the heating off at 5pm.*

heavy *adjective*: **heavier, heaviest**
1 Something that is **heavy** weighs a lot: *Those bags are heavy. Let me carry one.*
2 You ask how **heavy** something is if you want to know how much it weighs: *How heavy is this suitcase?*
3 Heavy also means 'a lot of': *We're expecting heavy snow tonight.*
4 Something that lands with a lot of weight is **heavy**: *He gave the rock a heavy blow with the hammer.*

the opposite is **light**

he'd *verb*
He'd is short for **he had** or **he would**: *Mike said he'd already seen the film.*

heel *noun*: **heels**
1 Your **heel** is the back part of your foot: *These shoes are hurting my heels.* [see picture at **foot**]

2 The **heel** of a sock is the part of it that covers the heel of your foot: *There's a hole in the heel of your sock.*
3 The **heel** of a shoe or a boot is the part of it under the heel of the foot: *The heel has come off my boot.* ❑ *shoes with high heels.*

height *noun*: **heights**
The **height** of something is the distance from the top to the bottom of it: *What is the height of that building?* ❑ *The walls are all of different heights.* ❑ *He couldn't join the police because of his height.*

held *verb*
see **hold**: *She held the large plate in one hand.*

helicopter *noun*: **helicopters**
A **helicopter** is a type of aircraft with large blades attached to the top; the blades turn round very fast and lift the helicopter off the ground.

he'll *verb*
He'll is short for **he will**: *I'm sure he'll help if you ask him.* ❑ *He'll be here in two hours.*

hello
You say **hello** when you meet someone you know: *Hello Louise, how are you?*

helmet *noun*: **helmets**
A **helmet** is a hard hat made from metal or plastic, which you wear to protect your head: *a motorbike helmet.*

help *verb*: **helps, helped, helping, has helped**
1 You **help** someone when you make it easier for them to do something: *Could you help me move this bookcase?* ❑ *He says he'll help me later.*

2 You can't **help** something if you are not able to stop it happening: *I couldn't help laughing when he fell over the cat.* ❑ *I can't help it if he arrives late.*

▷ **help yourself**
You **help yourself** to food or drink when you serve yourself rather than waiting for someone to serve you: *Please help yourself to wine.*

help *noun*
1 You give someone **help** when you help them: *Thanks for all your help.*
2 People shout '**Help!**' when they are in danger and want to attract attention.

helpful *adjective*
Something or someone is **helpful** when they give you help: *I found this book very helpful when I was studying.*

helpless *adjective*
You are **helpless** when you are not able to do anything for yourself: *a helpless baby.*

hem *noun*: **hems**
The **hem** of a piece of clothing is the bottom edge of it, which has been turned up and sewn to stay in position.

hen *noun*: **hens**
A **hen** is a female chicken: *Have you fed the hens and collected the eggs today?*

her *pronoun and determiner*
1 You use **her** to talk about a woman, girl or female animal who has already been mentioned: *I'll ask Stephanie when I see her.* ❑ *She's a stranger. No-one here knows her.* ❑ *He picked up the cat and put her back in the basket.*
2 Her means belonging to a

woman or girl: *I'll ask if I can borrow her car.* ❑ *It's her book, not yours.*

herb *noun*: **herbs**
Herbs are plants which are used in cooking and also to make medicines.

herd *noun*: **herds**
A **herd** of animals, such as deer, cows or horses, is a group of them: *a herd of cows.*

here *adverb*
Here means at or to this place: *We can have the party here.* ❑ *I'll wait here for you.* ❑ *Here's your coat.* ❑ *Come here. I want to speak to you.* ❑ *My arm hurts here, just above the wrist.*

the opposite is **there**

▷ **here and there**
Things are **here and there** when they are in several different places: *Books were lying here and there about the room.*

hers *pronoun*
You use **hers** to talk about something that belongs to a woman, girl or female animal that had already been mentioned: *'It's not my shirt. Is it hers?'* ❑ *I gave her my address and she gave me hers.* ❑ *He's a relative of hers.*

herself *pronoun*
1 You use **herself** after the verb when the woman or girl who does an action is the same woman or girl who is affected by that action: *She hurt herself when she fell downstairs.*
2 A woman or girl does something **herself** if she does it without help from anyone else: *Did she really do that herself?*
3 You can use **herself** to show

who you mean more clearly: *I wanted to speak to Elaine herself, but instead I spoke to her assistant.*

he's
He's is short for **he is** or **he has**: *He's my husband.* □ *He's gone to Greece on holiday.*

hi
Hi is a friendly way of saying hello: *Hi, how are you?*

hide *verb*: **hides, hid, hiding, has hidden**
1 You **hide** something when you put it in a secret place so that other people can't find it: *I'll hide his present under the bed.*
2 You **hide** when you go to a secret place so that people can't find you easily: *The children were hiding in a cupboard.*

high *adjective*: **higher, highest**
1 Something is **high** if it reaches a long way above the ground: *What's the name of the highest mountain in Scotland?*
2 You use **high** when you are talking about what something measures from top to bottom: *The fence is six feet high.*
3 High means more than is normal: *He has a high temperature.* □ *She got a very high mark in the exam.*
4 A sound is **high** if it is not deep: *She sang in a high voice.*

the opposite is **low**

highway *noun*: **highways**
A **highway** is a main road.

hill *noun*: **hills**
1 A **hill** is a piece of land that rises above the land around it: *We went for a walk up the hill before lunch.*

2 A **hill** is also a slope on a road: *A lot of cars were stuck in the snow at the bottom of the hill.*

him *pronoun*
You use **him** when you are talking about a man, boy or male animal that has already been mentioned: *Simon asked us to telephone him.* □ *Can you take the dog for a walk today? I took him yesterday.*

himself *pronoun*
1 You use **himself** after the verb when the man or boy who does an action is the same man or boy who is affected by that action: *He hurt himself when he fell downstairs.*
2 A man or boy does something **himself** if he does it on his own without help from anyone else: *Did he really do that himself?*
3 You can use **himself** to show who you mean more clearly: *I wanted to speak to Robert himself, but instead I spoke to his wife.*

hinge *noun*: **hinges**
A **hinge** is a piece of metal which is used to attach a door to a wall, so that it can be opened or closed: *The hinges on this door are a bit loose.*

'hin-j**'**

hint *noun*: **hints**
A **hint** is a piece of information that you give to someone to help them to do something: *I gave him a few hints on gardening.*

hip *noun*: **hips**
Your **hips** are the parts on each side of your body, between your waist and the top of your legs: *She stood with her hands on her hips.*

hire *verb*: **hires, hired, hiring, has hired**
You **hire** something when you pay to use it for a certain period of time: *We've hired a car for a few days.* ❑ *This machine can be hired for £10 a day.*

his *pronoun and determiner*
You use **his** to talk about about something that belongs to a man, a boy or a male animal that has already been mentioned: *It's not my book. Is it his?* ❑ *Mr Bruce has lost his keys.*

history *noun*
1 History is all the things that have happened in the past: *All these people or events are part of our history.*
2 History is the study of events that happened in the past: *George got a good grade in history last year.*

hit *verb*: **hits, hit, hitting, has hit**
1 Someone **hits** another person when they strike them hard: *He hit me on the side of my face.* ❑ *One man was hitting the other with a piece of wood.* ❑ *Don't wave that stick about — you might hit someone with it.*
2 One thing **hits** another when it strikes it: *The bullet hit the target.*

meaning 2: the opposite is **miss**

hobby *noun*: **hobbies**
A **hobby** is an activity that you enjoy doing in your spare time: *His favourite hobby is fishing.*

hockey *noun*
Hockey is a game played by two teams; each team tries to hit a ball into a goal using long curved sticks.

hold *verb*: **holds, held, holding, has held**
1 You **hold** something when you have it in your hand: *He was holding the bag.*
2 One things **holds** another if it contains it: *Will this bookcase hold all of our books?*
3 You **hold** something when you keep it in a particular position for a while: *Could you hold the picture just there, please?*
4 You **hold** an event, such as a party, when you organize it: *She's holding a party next week.*

▷ **hold on**
1 You **hold on** to something when you grip it with your hands or arms: *Hold on to the rope and you won't slip.*
2 You **hold on** when you wait for a while: *Hold on a minute, I've forgotten my wallet.*

▷ **hold up**
1 Someone or something **holds** you **up** when they delay you: *Sorry we're late — we were held up in traffic.*
2 Something that **is held up** is supported by something: *The bed is held up with a couple of bricks.*

hold *noun*
You have a **hold** on something when you are holding it: *He lost his hold on the rope.*

▷ **get hold of**
1 You **get hold of** something when you manage to catch it and hold it: *I couldn't get hold of the branch.*
2 You **get hold of** someone when you manage to see them or speak to them: *I can't get hold of him on the phone — he must be out.*

hole *noun*: **holes**
A **hole** is a tear or a gap in something: *I've got a hole in my trousers.* ❑ *We had to fix the hole in the fence.*

holiday *noun*: **holidays**
1 A **holiday** is a period of time when you are not at work: *We get five weeks' holiday a year.*
2 A **holiday** is also a period of time when you go away to another place to enjoy youself: *We've just come back from a holiday in Australia.*

▷ **on holiday**
You are **on holiday** when you don't have to go to work: *Tim's been on holiday all week.*

hollow *adjective*
Something that is **hollow** has an empty space inside it: *The tree trunk was hollow.*

home *noun*: **homes**
1 Your **home** is the place where you live, often with your family: *They have a lovely new home.* ❑ *He doesn't have a proper home.*
2 Your **home** is also the place where you were born: *He lives in Edinburgh but his home is London.*

home *adverb*
Home means 'to or at the place where you live': *I'm going home now.* ❑ *He usually gets home at about 7 o'clock.* ❑ *Hi! I'm home!*

homeless *adjective*
A **homeless** person doesn't have anywhere to live.

homesick *adjective*
A person is **homesick** when they are feeling sad because they are not at home with their family and friends: *At first she was homesick,* but she soon started to make new friends in London.

homework *noun*
Homework is extra work that teachers give to students to do at home: *I can't go out tonight — I've got too much homework.*

honest *adjective*
An **honest** person always tells the truth and doesn't cheat: *Always try to be honest when you're dealing with children.*

honesty *noun*
Honesty is the state of being honest.

honey *noun*
Honey is a sticky golden food, made by bees: *He spread honey on his toast.*

hoof *noun*: **hoofs** or **hooves**
Hooves are the hard parts of the feet of animals such as goats, horses and cows.

hook *noun*: **hooks**
A **hook** is a curved piece of metal or plastic that you use to hang things on: *I hung my coat on the hook behind the door.* ❑ *a fish hook.*

hop *verb*: **hops, hopped, hopping, has hopped**
1 You **hop** when you jump up and down on one foot: *He hopped across the room.*
2 Birds and animals **hop** when they move using their legs, or only their back legs.

hope *verb*: **hopes, hoped, hoping, has hoped**
You **hope** that something you want will happen when you believe that it can happen: *I hope my visitors arrive soon.* ❑ *She hopes to go on holiday to America.*

hope *noun*: **hopes**
Hope is the feeling you have when you think that something you want may happen; a **hope** is something that you want to happen: *Don't give up hope — things will get better.* ❑ *His hopes for the future were wrecked when he was injured in the accident.*

hopeful *adjective*
You are **hopeful** if you believe that what you want will happen: *He was hopeful that he would pass his driving test.*

hopeless *adjective*
You describe something as **hopeless** if it is impossible and is not likely to get better: *It's hopeless to try and find him after so long.*

horn *noun*: **horns**
1 Horns are the two hard points that grow from the heads of animals such as cows and goats.
2 A vehicle's **horn** is its device which makes a loud noise as a warning to others: *The driver sounded his horn as he came round the corner.*
3 A **horn** is also a musical instrument which you blow into.

horrible *adjective*
Something **horrible** is very nasty, unpleasant or ugly: *There's a horrible smell coming from that room.* ❑ *The monster's face was horrible.*

horse *noun*: **horses**
A **horse** is a large animal with long hair on its neck and tail; people use horses to pull carts and to ride on: *The horses were in their stables.*

hose *noun*: **hoses**
A **hose** is a long rubber tube that you use to put water on to things: *The firefighters used their hoses to put the fire out.*

hospital *noun*: **hospitals**
A **hospital** is a place where people go when they are ill or injured: *I had to go to hospital when I broke my foot.*

hot *adjective*: **hotter, hottest**
1 Something is **hot** if it feels very warm: *Is the water hot yet?* ❑ *This coffee's too hot to drink.*
2 The weather is **hot** when it is sunny and the air temperature is high: *We had a very hot summer last year.*
3 Hot food is spicy and gives you a burning feeling in your mouth: *a hot curry.*

---

meaning 1 and 2: the opposite is **cold**

---

hot dog *noun*: **hot dogs**
A **hot dog** is a hot sausage served inside a long bread roll.

hotel *noun*: **hotels**
A **hotel** is a building where people pay to stay for a period of time: *They arrived at the hotel at about midnight.*

hour *noun*: **hours**
An **hour** is a period of time which lasts sixty minutes: *It took me over an hour to finish my work.* ❑ *There are 24 hours in a day.*

house *noun*: **houses**
A **house** is a building in which people live: *Mr and Mrs Evans have bought a new house.*

housework *noun*
Housework is all the jobs that you have to do to keep a house clean, such as dusting, washing dishes and cleaning floors.

how *adverb and conjunction*
1 You use **how** to ask about the way to do something: *How do you get to the station?* ❑ *How did you get here so quickly?*
2 You also use **how** in questions about size, quantity, time and distance: *How tall are you?* ❑ *How much money have you got?* ❑ *How long will the meeting last?* ❑ *How far is London from here?*
3 You can use **how** to show that you are surprised: *How strange!*

▷ **how about**
You use **how about** when you want to suggest something: *How about a drink?* ❑ *How about going to the cinema tonight?*

▷ **how are you?**
You say '**how are you?**' when you meet someone you know, and you want to know how they are feeling: *Hello Lynne — how are you?*

▷ **how do you do?**
A polite way of greeting someone whom you haven't met before is to say '**How do you do?**'

however *adverb and conjunction*
1 You use **however** when you mention something that will make a difference to what you have already said: *I'll try to get there by 10 o'clock. However, I may be later if there's a lot of traffic.*
2 However also means 'it doesn't matter how': *Do it however you like, as long as it's done.*

howl *verb*: **howls, howled, howling, has howled**
Animals such as dogs or wolves **howl** when they make a loud crying sound: *The dog howled when we left him out in the cold.*

hug *verb*: **hugs, hugged, hugging, has hugged**
You **hug** someone when you put your arms around them and hold them tight: *She hugged her mother, said goodbye, and got on the train.*

hug

huge *adjective*
Something that is **huge** is very large: *There was a huge crowd at the football match.* ❑ *Mr Grant's new house is huge.*

same as **enormous**
the opposite is **tiny**

hum *verb*: **hums, hummed, humming, has hummed**
You **hum** when you sing with your lips closed: *Danny didn't know the words so he just hummed the tune.*

human or **human being** *noun*: **humans** or **human beings**
A **human** or a **human being** is a person.

hundred *noun and adjective*: **hundreds**
1 A **hundred** or one **hundred** is the number 100: *Fifty plus fifty is a hundred.*
2 One **hundred** or a **hundred** is also the age of 100; someone who is a **hundred** is one hundred years old: *He'll be a hundred on his next birthday.*

hundred *determiner and pronoun*
A **hundred** means one hundred in number: *The painting cost a hundred pounds.* ❑ *There were a hundred people waiting outside.* ❑ *He spent two hundred dollars and I spent a hundred.*

▷ hundreds of
Hundreds of means two or more hundred, or a very large number: *Hundreds of people came to the concert.* ❑ *He receives hundreds of letters every day.*

hung *verb*
see **hang**: *He hung his scarf on the hook.*

hunger *noun*
Hunger is the uncomfortable feeling you get when you haven't eaten for a while: *She tried to ignore the feelings of hunger.*

hungry *adjective*: **hungrier, hungriest**
You are **hungry** when you have the feeling that you want something to eat: *I didn't have any lunch, so I'm really hungry now.*

hunt *verb*: **hunts, hunted, hunting, has hunted**
People **hunt** when they chase and kill wild animals, either for food or for sport.

hurry *verb*: **hurries, hurried, hurrying, has hurried**
1 You **hurry** when you do something or go somewhere quickly: *We'll have to hurry if we want to get there on time.* ❑ *They hurried to the harbour to see the ships coming in.*

2 You **hurry** someone when you make them move or work quickly: *If you hurry me, I'll make mistakes.*

▷ hurry up
You tell someone to **hurry up** when you want them to move faster: *Hurry up Helen, or we'll be late.*

▷ in a hurry
1 You do something **in a hurry** when you do it quickly: *She finished her dinner in a hurry.*
2 You are **in a hurry** when you need to do something or go somewhere quickly: *I can't stop and chat — I'm in a hurry.*

hurt *verb*: **hurts, hurt, hurting, has hurt**
1 You **hurt** yourself, or a part of your body, when you injure yourself: *I fell and hurt my ankle.* ❑ *Did you hurt yourself when you fell?*
2 You **hurt** someone when you injure them: *I hope I didn't hurt you.*
3 A part of your body **hurts** when it is painful: *My ankle hurts when I walk.*
4 You **hurt** someone's feelings when you upset them: *I think you hurt his feelings when you said that he was selfish.*

husband *noun*: **husbands**
A woman's **husband** is the man she is married to: *Is she bringing her husband to the party?*

hut *noun*: **huts**
A **hut** is a small house or shed, often made of wood: *We slept in a wooden hut on the beach.*

Ii

I *pronoun*
I is a word you use when you are talking about yourself: *I feel ill.*
□ *'I want to go to the cinema tonight.' 'So do I.'*

ice *noun*
Ice is frozen water: *It's so cold — the lake is covered with ice.*

ice cream *noun*
Ice cream is a sweet frozen food, made from milk or cream: *strawberry ice cream.*

ice skate *noun*: **ice skates**
Ice skates are boots with blades attached, used for skating on ice.

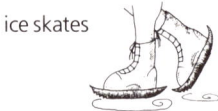
ice skates

icy *adjective*
Icy means covered with ice or as cold as ice: *icy roads* □ *an icy wind.*

I'd *verb*
I'd is short for **I should**, **I would** or **I had**: *I'd love to go out tonight.* □ *I'd just gone to bed when the telephone rang.*

idea *noun*: **ideas**
An **idea** is a thought that you have, or a suggestion that you make: *I've got a good idea for a birthday present for Lucy.* □ *That's a good idea!*

identify *verb*: **identifies, identified, identifying, has identified**
You can **identify** someone or something if you are able to say who or what they are: *Would you be able to identify the men who attacked you?* □ *I can't identify this plant.*

if *conjunction*
1 You use **if** when you are talking about something which may happen: *If we take the train, it'll be less expensive.*
2 If also means 'whether': *I'll ask Tom and see if he knows.* □ *Do you know if the train has left yet?*

ignore *verb*: **ignores, ignored, ignoring, has ignored**
1 Someone **ignores** you when they pretend you are not there and do not speak to you: *I said hello but they just ignored me and walked away.*
2 Someone **ignores** you when they do not follow your advice: *He ignored my advice and borrowed more money.*

ill *adjective*
You are **ill** when your health is not good, or when you are sick: *Jack is ill in bed.* □ *I think I'm going to be ill.*

I'll *verb*
I'll is short for **I shall** or **I will**: *I'll telephone you tomorrow.*

illness *noun*: **illnesses**
An **illness** is a disease or a period of bad health: *He died after a short illness.* □ *Many of the students are absent through illness.*

I'm *verb*
I'm is short for **I am**: *I'm going to India tomorrow.* □ *I'm twenty-five.*

imagine *verb*: **imagines, imagined, imagining, has imagined**
You **imagine** something when you see it in your mind: *I'm sure I saw something, but maybe I imagined it.*

imitate *verb*: **imitates, imitated, imitating, has imitated**
You **imitate** someone or something when you copy exactly what they do or say: *The parrot could imitate the old lady's laugh.*

immediately *adverb*
You do something **immediately** when you do it at once, without waiting: *We must leave immediately or we'll miss the train.*

important *adjective*
1 Something is **important** if it matters a lot: *They've got some important news to tell you.* ❑ *There's an important meeting next week.*
2 An **important** person is a powerful person: *She's a very important member of the government.*

impossible *adjective*
Something is **impossible** if it cannot be done: *These questions in the exam were impossible.* ❑ *It is impossible to sing and drink at the same time.*

improve *verb*: **improves, improved, improving, has improved**
Something **improves** if it becomes better: *I hope the weather improves tomorrow.* ❑ *His behaviour has improved over the last few weeks.*

in *preposition*
1 Someone or something is **in** something else, such as a container, when it is inside it: *The wine is in the cellar.* ❑ *Are there any matches in that box?* ❑ *He keeps his keys in the drawer.*
2 You put something **in** a place when you put it into that place: *He put his books in the bookcase.* ❑ *She put the meat in the fridge.*
3a You use **in** to talk about something that happens during a certain period of time: *She's going on holiday in October.* ❑ *He'll come round in the evening.* **b** You also use **in** to show that something happens at the end of a particular period of time: *He's going away but he'll be back in a month.*
4 You are **in** certain clothes when you are wearing them: *She was in jeans and a jumper.*
5 In is used to talk about many different actions and states: *I'm in a hurry.* ❑ *He's in uniform.* ❑ *This letter is in Japanese.* ❑ *I think he's in his sixties.* ❑ *Don't walk in that puddle!* ❑ *That was when long dresses were in fashion.* ❑ *She tied the ribbon in a bow.*

in *adverb*
1 You are **in** when you are at home or at your place of work: *Is Lisa in?* ❑ *Is the manager in yet?* ❑ *He got in at midnight.*
2 A train or bus gets **in** when it arrives: *The train doesn't get in until eleven o'clock.*
3 Something is **in** when it is in fashion: *Are short skirts in again?*

inch *noun*: **inches**
An **inch** is a unit of measurement which is equal to 2.5 centimetres: *The curtains measure 40 inches in length.*

include *verb*: **includes, included, including, has included**
A person or thing is included when they are part of a larger group or amount: *Did you remember to include Andy?* ❑ *The price of the ticket includes dinner.*

including *preposition*
You use **including** when you want to draw attention to one thing amongst others: *We went to all the museums, including the new one.*

increase *verb*: **increases, increased, increasing, has increased**
1 Something **increases** when it becomes bigger: *Prices have increased a lot this year.*
2 You **increase** something when you make it bigger or greater: *She increased her speed and passed the lorry.*

indoor *adjective*
Indoor describes things that are inside a building rather than outside: *an indoor swimming pool.* ❑ *If it's raining we can play indoor games.*

the opposite is **outdoor**

indoors *adverb*
Indoors means inside a building: *Let's go indoors. It's starting to rain.*

the opposite is **outdoors**

infectious *adjective*
An **infectious** disease is one that can be passed from one person to another: *Flu is a very common infectious disease.*

influence *noun*: **influences**
1 Something is, or has, an **influence** on you if it changes you in some way: *The weather has a strong influence on the way I feel.* ❑ *Those boys are a bad influence on him.*
2 Someone who has **influence** has the power to make others do things: *He uses his influence with the press.*

influence *verb*: **influences, influenced, influencing, has influenced**
One person or thing **influences** another when they have an effect on them: *Who influenced you most when you were a child?* ❑ *The weather influences our activities.*

informal *adjective*
1 Informal things are done in a relaxed or easy way: *The first meeting will be short and informal.*
2 You wear **informal** clothes to relax, in places where there are no rules about how to dress.

information *noun*
Information is facts or news: *I got all the information I needed at the library.*

injection *noun*: **injections**
You have an **injection** when a doctor uses a hollow needle to put a liquid medicine into you: *We stood in a queue waiting to have our injections.*

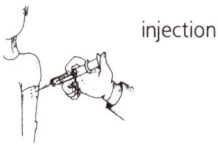

injection

injure *verb*: **injures, injured, injuring, has injured**
You **injure** a part of your body when you damage it: *The athlete fell, injuring his ankle.* ❑ *Many*

*people are injured on the roads
every year.*

injury *noun* : **injuries**
You have an **injury** when a part
of your body is damaged: *All the
passengers had serious injuries.*
❑ *Is the injury serious?*

ink *noun*
Ink is a coloured liquid that you
put in a pen and use to write:
There's no ink left in this pen.

inner *adjective*
1 Inner means 'on the inside': *The
inner walls of the house were
painted white.*
2 Inner also means 'towards the
centre' or 'towards the middle':
She lives in inner London.

innocent *adjective*
A person is **innocent** of a
crime if they have not carried it
out: *She was innocent of the
charges against her.* ❑ *an innocent
man.*

the opposite is **guilty**

insect *noun* : **insects**
An **insect** is a small creature
with six legs: *There were insects
crawling over the floor.*

inside *preposition and adverb*
1 One thing is **inside** another
when it is within it: *What's inside
the box?* ❑ *Open the box and look
inside.* ❑ *The boy carried the
puppy inside his jacket.*
2 You are **inside** when you are
within a building; you go **inside**
when you go into a building: *The
bear was inside the cave.* ❑ *It's wet
out there. Come inside.* ❑ *Let's go
inside.*

the opposite is **outside**

inside *noun* : **insides**
The **inside** of something is the
part contained within it: *The
inside of this pear is too hard.*

the opposite is **outside**

▷ **inside out**
Something is **inside out** when
the surface that is usually on the
inside is on the outside: *You've
got your jumper on inside out.*
inside *adjective*
1 Inside is used to describe
things that are on the inner
surface, or are not outside: *He
put his wallet in the inside pocket
of his jacket.*
2 Inside is also used to describe
people or things that are part of
your group: *The information came
from an inside source.*

the opposite is **outside**

instant *noun*
An **instant** is a moment: *It only
took him an instant to answer the
question.* ❑ *You press this button
and your food is cooked in an
instant.*

instant *adjective*
Something that is **instant**
happens, or is made,
immediately: *The film was an
instant success.* ❑ *We usually drink
instant coffee.*

instantly *adverb*
Something that happens
instantly happens immediately:
*When the fire alarm rings, please
leave the building instantly.*

instead *adverb*
You do one thing **instead** of
another when you do it in place
of that other thing: *They all went
to the cinema but I went to the
theatre instead.* ❑ *Can I have*

water instead of orange juice, please?

instruct *verb*: **instructs, instructed, instructing, has instructed**
1 You **instruct** someone to do something when you order them to do it: *They instructed me to come home at once.*
2 You also **instruct** someone when you teach them: *The girls were instructed in cookery and sewing.*

instruction *noun*: **instructions**
Instructions tell you how to do something: *Follow the instructions on the packet, but add more milk.*

instrument *noun*: **instruments**
1 An **instrument** is a tool, especially one used by a doctor.
2 An **instrument**, or a musical **instrument**, is an object such as a flute or piano, that you use to make music.

intelligent *adjective*
An **intelligent** person or animal is clever and able to understand things quickly: *He's a very intelligent student.* □ *Our dog is very intelligent and can do lots of tricks.*

intend *verb*: **intends, intended, intending, has intended**
You are **intending** to do something if you have decided that you will do it: *I'm intending to finish work early this afternoon.*

interest *noun*: **interests**
1 You have an **interest in something**, or you take an **interest** in something, when it attracts you and you want to find out more about it: *I have no interest in cricket.*

2 An **interest** is a hobby: *His main interests are football and rugby.*

interest *verb*: **interests, interested, interesting, has interested**
Something **interests** you if it attracts you or makes you feel curious: *Music doesn't interest him at all.*

interested *adjective*
You are **interested** when you want to find out more about something: *He had an interested look on his face.*

interesting *adjective*
Something is **interesting** if it attracts you and makes you want to find out more about it: *This is a very interesting book.*

Internet *noun*
The **Internet** is an information system which links computers everywhere in the world; anyone who has a computer that is connected to the Internet can get information, or contact other users.

interrupt *verb*: **interrupts, interrupted, interrupting, has interrupted**
1 You **interrupt** someone when you stop them talking or doing something: *I'm sorry to interrupt, but your husband's on the phone.*
2 You **interrupt** an activity when you stop it for a while: *He interrupted the meeting to make a phone call.*

interview *noun*: **interviews**
An organization holds **interviews** for a job when they meet the people interested in getting the job to find out who is the most suitable person:

I'm going for an interview next week.

into *preposition*

1 One thing goes **into** another when it goes inside it: *The couple went into the house together.* ❏ *The bananas were packed into wooden crates.*

2 You get **into** a vehicle when you climb inside it: *We all got into the car.*

3 One thing goes **into** another when it hits it: *The car behind ran into the back of our car.*

4 Something changes or turns **into** a different thing when it becomes that thing: *This caterpillar will change into a beautiful butterfly.* ❏ *His books have been translated into many different languages.*

5 You use **into** when you are talking about dividing one number by another: *Seven into fourteen goes twice.* ❏ *How many times does two go into fourteen?*

introduce *verb*: **introduces, introduced, introducing, has introduced**

You **introduce** two people who don't know each other when you tell each of them what the other's name is: *I introduced my guests to each other.* ❏ *I must introduce you to Mr Morris.*

‘in-tro-**djoos**’

invent *verb*: **invents, invented, inventing, has invented**

1 A person **invents** something when they make something that no-one else has ever made: *Thomas Edison invented the electric light bulb.*

2 You **invent** a story when you make it up: *He invented an excuse but no-one believed him.*

investigate *verb*: **investigates, investigated, investigating, has investigated**

You **investigate** something when you try to find information about it: *The police are investigating the burglary at the shop.*

invisible *adjective*

Something that is **invisible** cannot be seen: *The gas is invisible and has no smell.*

invitation *noun*: **invitations**

An **invitation** is a request to come to an event such as a wedding or a party: *We sent out all the invitations yesterday.*

invite *verb*: **invites, invited, inviting, has invited**

You **invite** someone to an event when you ask them to come to it: *I'd like to invite Julian to the party.*

involve *verb*: **involves, involved, involving, has involved**

1 You **are involved** in a situation when you play a part in it: *She's involved in politics.* ❏ *This man was involved in the crime.*

2 Something that you do **involves** certain things when those are the things that are needed to do it: *My daughter wants a job that involves a lot of travelling.*

iron *noun*: **irons**

1 Iron is a hard metal used to make tools, railings and other things: *The gates are made of iron.* ❏ *There were iron bars across the window.*

2 An **iron** is an electric device with a flat surface that you heat and press on to clothes to make them smooth.

iron *verb*: **irons, ironed, ironing, has ironed**
You **iron**, or **iron** clothes, when you use an iron to make them smooth: *I'd better iron my shirt tonight.* ◻ *Do you have anything that needs to be ironed?*

irregular *adjective*
An **irregular** verb is a verb that does not follow the usual rules of grammar.

is *verb*
You use **is** with **he, she** and **it**, when you are talking about a single person or thing, or a particular person or thing: *Penny is asleep.* ◻ *Is it time to go yet?* ◻ *His father is a doctor.* ◻ *The dog is barking.* ◻ *Soup is usually served hot.*

> ▸ **is** belongs to the verb **be**.
> ▸ You can shorten **he is, she is** and **it is** to **he's, she's** and **it's**; **that is** to **that's**; **there is** to **there's**; **what is** to **what's**; **where is** to **where's**.

island *noun*: **islands**
An **island** is a piece of land that is completely surrounded by water: *Australia is the largest island in the world.*

'eye-land**'**

isn't *verb*
Isn't is short for **is not**: *That isn't fair.* ◻ *Nick is very handsome, isn't he?*

it *pronoun*
1 You use **it** to talk about an animal, a baby or a thing: *This is a great book — do you want to read it?* ◻ *Look at that dog; it can't walk properly.*
2 You also use **it** to talk about a fact: *It's very expensive to travel*

by air.
3 You can use **it** to talk about the weather, time or distance: *I hope it's a nice day tomorrow.* ◻ *How far is it to London from New York?* ◻ *What time is it?*
4 You can also use **it** to say what you think about a place or a situation: *It's very peaceful here, isn't it?*

itch *verb*: **itches, itched, itching, has itched**
Part of your body **itches** when you have a feeling that you want to scratch it: *These socks make my feet itch.*

itchy *adjective*: **itchier, itchiest**
Your skin is **itchy** when it gives you the feeling that you want to scratch it: *I've got an itchy back.*

it'll *verb*
It'll is short for **it will**: *It'll be late before we get home.*

its *determiner*
Its describes something that belongs to the thing, animal or child already mentioned: *This bag has lost its handle.* ◻ *The dog was barking at its owner.* ◻ *The baby smiled at its mother.*

it's *verb*
It's is short for **it is** or **it has**: *It's three o'clock and he still isn't here.* ◻ *It's been raining.*

itself *pronoun*
1 You use **itself** when you talk about the same animal or small child that you have just mentioned: *The baby looked at itself in the mirror.* ◻ *The lion can make itself almost invisible in the long grass.*
2 If an animal or child does something **itself**, it does it without any help: *The cat licked*

itself in front of the mirror.
3 You use **itself** to show the thing you mean more clearly: *The house itself was fine, but I don't like the town much.*

I've *verb*
I've is short for **I have**: *I've never been to Spain.*

Jj

jack *noun*: **jacks**
A **jack** is a tool that you use to lift a car off the ground.

jacket *noun*: **jackets**
A **jacket** is a short coat: *She's got a new leather jacket.*

jail *noun*: **jails**
A **jail** is a prison: *He's been in jail for ten years.*

jam *noun*: **jams**
Jam is a sweet food made from fruit and sugar, which you spread on bread: *He spread some strawberry jam on his toast.*

jam *verb*: **jams, jammed, jamming, has jammed**
1 Something **jams** when it sticks tightly in a space and can't be moved: *My key jammed in the lock.*
2 You **jam** something when you cause it to get stuck: *He jammed his fingers in the door.*
3 A place **is jammed** when it becomes full of people or vehicles so that movement is difficult: *The city centre was jammed with traffic.*

January *noun*
January is the first month of the year, coming after December and before February: *They are getting married in January.*

jar *noun*: **jars**
A **jar** is a glass container, used to keep food in: *a jam jar* □ *a jar of honey.*

jaw *noun*: **jaws**
1 Your **jaw** is one of the two bones in your mouth which hold your teeth: *He broke his jaw in a fight.*
2 An animal's sharp teeth are its **jaws**: *The crocodile had the animal's leg in its jaws.*

jealous *adjective*
Someone is **jealous** of you if they dislike you because you have something that they haven't got: *She's jealous of her successful sister.* □ *He's jealous that James has so many friends.*

jeans *noun*
Jeans are trousers made from heavy cotton, with pockets at the front and back: *All the young people were dressed in t-shirts and jeans.*

jeep *noun*: **jeeps**
A **jeep** is a vehicle which can travel over rough ground.

jerk *verb*: **jerks, jerked, jerking, has jerked**
1 You **jerk** something when you pull it with a short sudden movement: *Don't jerk the horse's head like that.*
2 Something **jerks** when it makes a short sudden movement: *His whole body jerked with the shock.*

jersey *noun*: **jerseys**
A **jersey** is a warm piece of clothing for the top part of your body.

same as **jumper** or **sweater**

jet *noun*: **jets**
1 A **jet** is an aeroplane with engines which suck in air and force it out behind.

2 A **jet** is also a strong stream of liquid or gas which is forced through a narrow opening: *jets of water.*

jewel *noun*: **jewels**
A **jewel** is a precious stone, often used to make up a necklace or a ring.

jewellery *noun*
Jewellery is things such as necklaces, bracelets and rings: *She doesn't wear much jewellery — just a wedding ring.*

jigsaw *noun*: **jigsaws**
A **jigsaw** is a puzzle made up of a lot of pieces that fit together to make a picture.

job *noun*: **jobs**
1 Your **job** is the work that you do regularly for money: *He hasn't had a job since he left school.*
2 A **job** is also a task that you have to do: *There are a few jobs I have to do in the garden this weekend.*

jockey *noun*: **jockeys**
A **jockey** is a person who rides horses in races.

join *verb*: **joins, joined, joining, has joined**
1 Two or more things **are joined** when they are connected; you two or more things when you connect them: *The dolls' heads are joined to the bodies with glue.* ❑ *Could you join those wires together, please?*
2 You **join** a particular group when you become a member of it: *He wants to join the police.* ❑ *She's joined a chess club.*
3 You **join** someone when you meet them: *I'll join you later in the restaurant.*
4 Two roads or rivers **join** when they come together: *This road joins the main road at the next junction.*

joke *noun*: **jokes**
1 A **joke** is a funny story that makes people laugh: *He told us a joke about a man and a parrot.*
2 A **joke** is also anything you do which makes people laugh: *He dressed up as a ghost for a joke.*

joke *verb*: **jokes, joked, joking, has joked**
You **joke** when you say something funny: *They spent the evening laughing and joking together.*

journey *noun*: **journeys**
You make a **journey** when you travel from one place to another: *The train journey lasts 4 hours.*

joy *noun*
Joy is great happiness: *I couldn't hide my joy at the good news.*

judge *noun*: **judges**
1 A **judge** is a person whose job is to decide what happens to people when they are found guilty of a crime: *The judge told the man he would go to prison for five years.*
2 A **judge** is also a person who chooses the winner of a competition: *The judge looks closely at each dog before making a decision.*

judge *verb*: **judges, judged, judging, has judged**
You **judge** a competition when you choose the winner: *Mr Atkins is judging the poetry competition.*

jug *noun*: **jugs**
A **jug** is a container with a handle and a shaped part at the top for pouring: *Could you pass the milk jug, please?*

juice *noun*: **juices**
1 Juice is the liquid which comes from fruit or vegetables when you squeeze them: *Squeeze some lemon juice over the fish.* ❑ *carrot juice.*
2 Juice is also a drink made from this liquid: *I'll have a glass of orange juice.*
3 Juice is the liquid that comes out of meat when you cook it: *Use the juices from the meat to make the sauce.*

rhymes with **goose**

juicy *adjective*: **juicier, juiciest**
A piece of fruit is **juicy** if it contains a lot of juice: *a juicy pear.*

July *noun*
July is the seventh month of the year, between June and August: *We are going on holiday in July.*

jump *verb*: **jumps, jumped, jumping, has jumped**
1 You **jump** when you suddenly move your body upwards or forwards: *He jumped off the wall.* ❑ *The cat jumped on to the kitchen table.* ❑ *Can you jump over this wall?* ❑ *There's no bridge across the stream. We'll have to jump across.*
2 Something makes you **jump** when it gives you a sudden fright: *I heard a sound that made me jump.*

jumper *noun*: **jumpers**
A **jumper** is a warm piece of clothing which you pull over your head and wear on the top part of

your body: *It looks cold outside — you'll need a jumper.*

same as **jersey** or **sweater**

junction *noun*: **junctions**
A **junction** is the point at which two or more roads or railway lines come together: *Turn left at the next junction.*

June *noun*
June is the sixth month of the year, between May and July: *He was born in June.*

jungle *noun*: **jungles**
A **jungle** is an area of thick forest in hot countries: *Many kinds of snake live in the jungle.*

just *adverb*
1 Something has **just** happened when it happened a very short time ago: *'Would you like a biscuit?' 'No thanks. I've just had my dinner.'*
2 You are **just** doing something when you are doing it at the moment: *I won't be long — I'm just brushing my teeth.*
3 Just means 'only': *He was just two years old when his mother died.*
4 Just also means 'exactly': *He looks just like his father.* ❑ *You sound just like your mum on the phone.*

▷ **just about**
You use **just about** to mean 'around' or 'almost': *It was just about midnight when we heard a loud bang.* ❑ *'Have you finished reading the newspaper yet?' 'Just about.'*

Kk

keen *adjective*: **keener, keenest**
1 You are **keen** to do something when you want to do it very much: *He's keen to learn more about his family's history.*
2 You are **keen**, or are **keen** on something, if you like it very much: *She's keen on football.* ❑ *He's a keen tennis player.*

meaning 1: same as **eager**

keep *verb*: **keeps, kept, keeping, has kept**
1 You **keep** something when you continue to have it: *You can keep the book if you want.*
2 You **keep** things when you don't throw them away: *She's kept all the old photographs.*
3 You **keep** something in a place if that is where you put it when you are not using it: *We keep all our old toys in a box in the cupboard.*
4 You **keep** doing something if you continue to do it: *I keep forgetting to buy him a birthday card.*
5 You **keep** something in a particular state when you make it stay that way: *Keep the door closed.*
6 You **keep** animals when you have them and look after them: *They keep cattle and sheep on the farm.*
7 Food **keeps** when it stays fresh and doesn't go bad: *I hope this meat keeps until the weekend.*

▷ **keep away**
You **keep away** from a place when you don't go near it: *Everyone was told to keep away from the old mine.*

▷ **keep off**
You **keep off** an area when you do not go into it: *Keep off the grass.*

▷ **keep on**
You **keep on** doing something if you continue to do it, or if you do it a lot: *We kept on walking, even when it started to rain.* ❑ *He kept on asking when we could go home.*

▷ **keep out**
You **keep out** of an area if you do not enter it: *They were told to keep out of the park.*

▷ **keep up**
1 You **keep up** with someone or something else when you make progress at the same speed as them: *She walks too fast; I can't keep up with her.* ❑ *He finds it difficult to keep up with the rest of the class.*
2 You **keep up** with something if you continue to do it: *He tried very hard to keep up with his music classes.*

kerb *noun*: **kerbs**
A **kerb** is the row of stones along the edge of a pavement: *He parked the car close to the kerb.*

ketchup *noun*
Ketchup is a cold red sauce made from tomatoes and vinegar: *Do you want ketchup on your chips?*

kettle *noun*: **kettles**
A **kettle** is a container with a handle and a spout, used to boil water: *Could you fill the kettle up? — we're all having tea.*

key *noun*: **keys**
1 A **key** is a small metal device which you use to open and close a lock: *I've lost my key.* ❑ *She carries her car keys in her pocket.*
2 A **key** is also one of the buttons on a typewriter or computer keyboard which you press to print a letter or number.
3 A **key** on a musical instrument is one of the parts that you press to make a sound: *A piano has black and white keys.*

keys
keys keys

keyboard *noun*: **keyboards**
1 The **keyboard** of a musical instrument is the part which holds the keys.
2 The **keyboard** of a typewriter or computer is the part which holds all the keys. [see picture at **computer**]

kick *verb*: **kicks, kicked, kicking, has kicked**
You **kick** something when you hit it with your foot: *He kicked the ball along the road.* ❑ *The horse kicked me on the leg.*

kick *noun*: **kicks**
A **kick** is a blow made with the foot: *He gave me a kick on the knee.*

kid *noun*: **kids**
1 A **kid** is a child: *Is it okay if we bring the kids?*
2 A **kid** is also a baby goat: *The kid ran about the field with its mother.*

kill *verb*: **kills, killed, killing, has killed**
A person, animal or plant **is killed** when someone or something causes them to die: *The cold winter killed all the young plants.* ❑ *No-one was killed in the train crash.* ❑ *The disease has already killed 220 people.*

kilo *noun*: **kilos**
A **kilo** is a kilogram: *Two kilos of apples, please.*

kilogram or **kilogramme** *noun*: **kilograms** or **kilogrammes**
A **kilogram** is a unit of weight, equal to 1000 grams: *He weighs 50 kilograms.*

▸ written **kg** for short

kilometre *noun*: **kilometres**
A **kilometre** is a unit of length, equal to 1000 metres: *We have to drive for another 20 kilometres and then we'll be there.*

▸ written **km** for short

kind *noun*: **kinds**
A **kind** of something is a type or a variety of that thing: *What kind of car would you like?* ❑ *They sell most kinds of cheese in this shop.*

kind *adjective*: **kinder, kindest**
A **kind** person is generous and helpful: *It's very kind of you to help me like this.*

the opposite is **cruel** or **unkind**

kindness *noun*
Kindness is being kind: *We thanked them for all their kindness.*

king *noun*: **kings**
A **king** is the male ruler of a

country: *He'll become king when his mother, the queen, dies.*

kiss *verb*: **kisses, kissed, kissing, has kissed**
You **kiss** someone when you touch them with your lips, as a greeting or to show that you love them: *She kissed us all before she left.*

kitchen *noun*: **kitchens**
A **kitchen** is a room where you cook food: *There was a lovely smell coming from the kitchen.*

kitten *noun*: **kittens**
A **kitten** is a young cat: *The kittens were playing in the garden.*

> ▶ Note that if a word begins with **kn**, you do not pronounce the **k**.

knee *noun*: **knees**
Your **knee** is the part in the middle of your leg which bends: *He hurt his knee when he fell.* [see picture at **leg**]

'**nee** '

kneel *verb*: **kneels, knelt** or **kneeled, kneeling, has knelt** or **has kneeled**
You **kneel** when you bend your legs so that your knees are touching the ground: *She knelt down next to the child's bed.*

'**neel** '

kneel

knew *verb*
see **know**: *I knew the answers to most of their questions.*

'**nyew** '

knife *noun*: **knives**
A **knife** is a tool with a sharp blade that is used to cut things: *He cut the rope with a sharp knife.*
❑ *Could I have a clean knife, please?*

rhymes with **wife**

knit *verb*: **knits, knitted, knitting, has knitted**
You **knit** when you make something from woollen thread using long needles: *She's knitting a jumper.*

'**nit** '

knock *verb*: **knocks, knocked, knocking, has knocked**
1 You **knock** when you make a tapping noise with your fist on a hard surface, such as a door or a window: *He knocked on the door.*
❑ *I can hear someone knocking at the front door.*
2 You **knock** something when you bump it, usually damaging it or causing it to fall: *I knocked the glass and it fell off the table.*

'**nok** '

▷ **knock out**
Someone **is knocked out** when they are hit so hard that they become unconscious: *He was knocked out in a fight.*

knock *noun*: **knocks**
1 A **knock** is the sound of someone or something knocking on a door or a window: *We heard a knock at the door.*
2 A **knock** is also a blow or an injury caused by bumping against something: *He got a knock on the head when he fell.*

knot *noun*: **knots**
A **knot** is a join in a piece of string or rope, made by tying the

ends together: *She tried to loosen the knot in the piece of string.*

‘ **not** ’

know *verb*: **knows, knew, knowing, has known**
1 You **know** something when you have information about it: *How do you know when the car needs more petrol?* ❏ *'Do you know where Joe is?' 'I'm sorry, I don't know.'* ❏ *I know you're tired, but could you look at this, please?* ❏ *He told us everything he knew about it.*
2 You **know** something when you have learned about it: *He knows a lot about films.* ❏ *Do you know the alphabet?*
3 You **know** someone if you have met and talked to them before: *I know James well.* ❏ *I didn't know anyone at the party.*

‘ **no** ’

knowledge *noun*
Knowledge is information or understanding about something: *Her knowledge of sport is very good.*

‘ **no**-lidj ’

known *verb*
see **know**: *I've known them for years. They are friends of my mother.*

rhymes with **bone**

knuckle *noun*: **knuckles**
Your **knuckles** are the parts on your hands where your fingers bend: *She scraped her knuckles against the wall.* [see picture at **hand**]

‘ **nuk**-el ’

LI

label *noun*: **labels**
A **label** is a small written note which you attach to something: *The label on the suitcase has our name and address on it.*

labourer *noun*: **labourers**
A **labourer** is a person who does hard work, such as digging roads or carrying heavy things.

lace *noun*: **laces**
1 A **lace** is a shoelace: *He's learning to tie his laces.*
2 Lace is a kind of material which looks like fine net: *a lace tablecloth.*

lack *noun*
There is a **lack** of something when there is not enough of it: *The biggest problem is lack of time.* ❑ *There's a lack of fresh water in the camp.*

ladder *noun*: **ladders**
A **ladder** is a set of steps between two long pieces of wood or metal: *We had to climb up the ladder to get on to the roof.*

lady *noun*: **ladies**
1 Lady is a polite word for a woman: *Who's that lady over there?*
2 A **lady** is a woman who has good manners.

laid *verb*
see **lay**: *We laid the table before dinner.*

lain
see **lie**: *She had lain awake all night.*

lake *noun*: **lakes**
A **lake** is a large area of water surrounded by land: *We went for a walk round the lake.*

lamb *noun*: **lambs**
1 A **lamb** is a young sheep: *The lambs were born in the spring.*
2 Lamb is also meat from a young sheep: *We're having lamb for dinner tonight.*

lamp *noun*: **lamps**
A **lamp** is an electric light that you put on a table or on the floor: *I'll switch the lamp on — it's dark in here.*

lamp-post *noun*: **lamp-posts**
A **lamp-post** is a tall pole with a light at the top, which lights up the streets at night.

land *noun*: **lands**
1 Land is the part of the Earth that is not covered by water.
2 Land is also an area of ground: *The land here is very good for growing crops.*
3 A **land** is a country: *I was always attracted to foreign lands.*

land *verb*: **lands, landed, landing, has landed**
1 You **land** when you come down to the ground, or part of your body comes down on the ground: *He jumped out of the tree, and landed on his feet.*
2 An aeroplane or spacecraft **lands** when it comes down to the ground after a flight: *The plane landed on time.* ❑ *Apollo 11 was the first spacecraft fo land on the monn.*
3 Something that has been travelling through the air **lands** when it comes down: *A tennis ball came through the window and*

landed on my plate. ❑ *If that tree falls it will land on our roof.*

lane *noun*: **lanes**
1 A **lane** is a narrow road: *The farm is at the end of a small country lane.*
2 A **lane** is one of the parts marked on a road for a single line of traffic: *The new road has four lanes.*

language *noun*: **languages**
A **language** is the words and speech of a particular country, or of a particular group of people: *How many languages do you know?* ❑ *the French language.*

lap *noun*: **laps**
Your **lap** is the flat area formed by your thighs when you sit down with your legs together: *The cat jumped on to my lap.*

lap *verb*: **laps, lapped, lapping, has lapped**
An animal **laps** liquid when it drinks it using its tongue: *The puppy lapped up the water.*

large *adjective*: **larger, largest**
Something is **large** if it is not small in size or amount: *They live in a large house.* ❑ *He earned a large amount of money last year.*

---

same as **big**

---

last *adjective*
1 You use **last** to talk about what came before: *We went to the cinema last night.* ❑ *Our last house had a bigger garden than this.*
2 The **last** of a number of things comes at the end: *We missed the last train home.* ❑ *He came last in the race.*
3 The **last** thing is the only one that remains: *Who drank the last*

bottle of orange juice? ❑ *I spent my last pound in the sweet shop.*

---

meaning 1: same as **previous**
meaning 2: the opposite is **first**

▷ **at last**
Something happens **at last** when it happens after a long wait: *The bus arrived at last.*

last *verb*: **lasts, lasted, lasting, has lasted**
Something **lasts** for a particular amount of time when it continues for that amount of time: *The film lasts for 2 hours.*

late *adjective and adverb*: **later, latest**
1 Someone or something is **late** if they come after the expected time: *We had a late breakfast on Sunday.* ❑ *The bus was late this morning.* ❑ *She arrived late and missed the beginning of the concert.*
2 Late also means 'near the end of the day': *It was very late when we got home.*

▷ **too late**
It is **too late** for something when it is no longer possible to do it: *It's too late to help him now.* ❑ *Is it too late to apply?*

lately *adverb*
Lately means 'recently': *I haven't seen Anne lately. How is she?*

later *adjective and adverb*
1 One thing happens **later** than another if it happens after it: *We were delayed and had to take a later train.* ❑ *Jack will probably arrive later than me.*
2 You say that you will do something **later**, or **later on**, when you plan to do it some time

in the future: *I'll phone you later.* ❏ *He says he'll come later on.*

latest *adjective*
Latest means 'most recent': *Have you heard the latest news? He's getting married.*

laugh *verb*: **laughs, laughed, laughing, has laughed**
You **laugh** when you smile and make a sound with your voice which shows that you think something is funny: *We all laughed at her jokes.*

laughter *noun*
Laughter is the sound of people laughing: *We could hear laughter from the next room.*

laundry *noun*: **laundries**
1 Laundry is clothes and other things that need to be washed: *I did all the laundry yesterday.*
2 A **laundry** is a place where clothes are washed: *He sends his shirts out to a laundry.*

law *noun*: **laws**
1 The **law** is a set of rules by which people live: *Murder is against the law.*
2 A **law** is a rule that you must obey: *New laws have been introduced by the government.*

lawyer *noun*: **lawyers**
A **lawyer** is a person who knows about the law, and who advises people about it: *I think you should see a lawyer about this.*

lay *verb*
see **lie**: *The dog lay on its blanket and went to sleep.*

lay *verb*: **lays, laid, laying, has laid**
1 You **lay** something on a flat surface when you put it down on it carefully: *She laid the clothes on the bed.*

2 You **lay** the table when you arrange the knives, forks and plates on it before eating a meal: *He laid the table for dinner.*
3 A bird or reptile **lays** eggs when it produces them: *The hens laid six eggs this morning.*

layer *noun*: **layers**
A **layer** is a covering, or something between two things: *The ground was covered with a layer of snow.* ❏ *The wedding cake was made up of three layers.*

lazy *adjective*: **lazier, laziest**
A **lazy** person doesn't like doing things which require effort: *Colin is too lazy to walk to the shops.*

lead *verb*: **leads, led, leading, has led**
1 You **lead** when you go in front of someone or something: *You lead; I'll follow.*
2 You **lead** someone when you guide them or take them somewhere: *He led the blind man across the busy road.*
3 A road **leads** somewhere if it goes to that place: *This motorway leads to Perth.*
4 A person **is leading** in a race when they are in front of everyone else: *She was leading from the beginning of the race.*
5 One thing **leads** to another if it causes it: *His foolish behaviour led to his death.*

rhymes with **need**

meaning 1: the opposite is
follow

▷ **lead up to**
Events that **lead up to** another are events that come before, and sometimes cause, that final event

to happen: *Let's look at the events leading up to the war.*

lead *noun*: **leads**

1 The **lead** is the front position in a race or competition: *Chris is in the lead.*

2 A **lead** is a long strap or chain which you attach to a dog's collar so that you can control the dog when you take it for a walk: *He kept the dog on a lead until he got to the park.*

rhymes with **need**

lead *noun*: **leads**

1 **Lead** is a type of heavy grey metal: *The pipes are made from lead.*

2 **Lead** is the thin stick of grey material in the middle of a pencil: *The lead in this pencil is always breaking.*

rhymes with **head**

leader *noun*: **leaders**

A **leader** is a person who is in charge of a group: *The leaders of all the European countries met in Dublin today.*

leaf *noun*: **leaves**

A **leaf** is one of the flat green parts which grow from the stems of plants or the branches of trees: *The leaves all began to fall off the trees.*

leak *noun*: **leaks**

1 A **leak** is a small hole which lets gas or liquid through it: *We'd better fix that leak in the roof.*

2 A **leak** is also the gas or liquid that is allowed to pass through such a hole: *a gas leak.*

leak *verb*: **leaks, leaked, leaking, has leaked**

1 Something **leaks** when it lets gas or liquid pass through it: *This pipe is leaking.*

2 Gas or liquid **leaks** when it passes through a small hole: *Water is leaking from that pipe.*

lean *verb*: **leans, leant** or **leaned, leaning, has leant** or **has leaned**

1 You **lean** when you bend your body in a particular direction: *I leant across to close the window.*

2 You **lean** on something when you rest all, or most of your weight on it: *Don't lean on that table. It's broken.* ❑ *He was leaning against a wall.*

3 Something that is usually upright or straight **leans**, or **leans over**, when it lies or slopes to one side: *The trees were leaning over in the wind.*

leap *verb*: **leaps, leapt** or **leaped, leaping, has leapt** or **has leaped**

You **leap** when you jump: *The burglar leapt over the wall and ran away.*

rhymes with **keep**

leap *noun*: **leaps**

A **leap** is a jump: *The horse got over the fence in one leap.*

leapt *verb*

see **leap**: *The dancer leapt into the air.*

rhymes with **kept**

learn *verb*: **learns, learnt** or **learned, learning, has learnt** or **has learned**

1 You **learn** something when you study it and find out how to do it: *Jackie is learning to play the piano.*

2 You also **learn** something, such as a poem, when you study it so that you can say it from memory: *I've got to learn these words before tomorrow.*

the opposite is **teach**

least *adjective and adverb*
1 Least means the smallest in amount or number: *He does the least work but gets paid the most money.*
2 Least also means less of a particular quality than all the others: *She is the least clever in her family.*

the opposite is **most**

▷ **at least**
1 You use **at least** to mean 'not less than': *It'll cost at least £10 each.*
2 You also use **at least** when there is a good point that you want to draw to people's attention: *Our car may be old, but at least it works.*

leather *noun*
Leather is the skin of an animal, used to make things such as shoes and bags: *Are these shoes made of leather?*

rhymes with **weather**

leave *verb*: **leaves, left, leaving, has left**
1 You **leave** a place when you go away from it: *She leaves home at 8.30 every morning.*
2 You also **leave** a place when you go away from it for ever: *She left school three years ago.*
3 You **leave** something somewhere when you don't take it with you: *I've left my car keys on the kitchen table.* ◻ *We left the dog with friends when we went on holiday.*
4 You **leave** something in a particular state when you let it remain in that state: *We left the*

kitchen in a mess this morning. ◻ *Make sure you don't leave the door open when you go out.*
5 You **leave** something when you don't use it, or don't use all of it: *I left the wine. It tasted funny.*

▷ **leave out**
You **leave** someone or something **out** when you don't include them: *Sally was very upset when we left her out of our plans.*

lecture *noun*: **lectures**
A **lecture** is a formal talk, usually given to students: *He's giving a lecture at 12 o'clock.*

led *verb*
see **lead**: *She led us into a dark room.*

left *verb*
see **leave**: *They left about an hour ago.*

▷ **left over**
Something is **left over** when it is extra and it has not been used: *There's some salad left over if you want it.* ◻ *I've got some money left over from my holiday.*

left *adjective and adverb*
The **left** side is the opposite side to the one which has the hand that most people write with; you turn **left** when you turn in the direction of your left side: *I wear my watch on my left hand.* ◻ *Drive down this road and turn left at the post office.*

the opposite is **right**

left *noun*
Something that is on or to the **left** is on or to the left side: *The house is on the left as you go down the street.* ◻ *He looked to his left.*

leg noun: **legs**
1 Legs are the limbs that animals and people use to walk: *He broke his leg playing football.* ❑ *This creature has several pairs of legs.*
2 A **leg** is also one of the upright parts of a table or chair which support it: *A stool usually has three legs.*

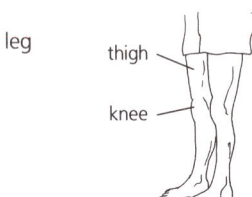

leg
thigh
knee

legal adjective
Legal means 'allowed by law': *Is it legal to park the car here?*

leisure noun
Leisure is time when you don't have to work, when you can do what you want: *He spends all his leisure time gardening.*

rhymes with **pleasure**

lemon noun: **lemons**
A **lemon** is a yellow fruit with a thick skin and a sour taste.

lend verb: **lends, lent, lending, has lent**
You **lend** something to someone when you let them use it for a certain period of time: *I'll lend you my new tape.*

> ▸ I'm **lending** a book **to** Jane. Jane is **borrowing** the book **from** me.

length noun: **lengths**
The **length** of something is the distance from one end of it to the other: *The swimming pool is 25*

metres in length. ❑ *He swam two lengths of the pool.*

lent verb
see **lend**: *Ian lent me his new book.* ❑ *He has lent it to me for a week.*

less determiner, pronoun and adverb
1 Less means a smaller amount of something: *They've got less money since the baby was born.* ❑ *Next time I make soup, I'll put less salt in it.* ❑ *She eats less than she used to.*
2 Less is used to compare things or people: *He is less intelligent than his brother.* ❑ *He thought the exams were less difficult this year.*

▷ **less and less**
1 Something happens **less and less** when it happens less often: *We saw each other less and less over the next few months.*
2 You have **less and less** of something when you have a smaller and smaller amount of it: *We've got less and less time to spend together.*

lesson noun: **lessons**
A **lesson** is a period of time when you are taught a subject by a teacher: *The first lesson of the day was maths.*

let verb: **lets, let, letting, has let**
1 You **let** someone do something when you allow them to do it: *Mary's mum doesn't let her go out after dark.*
2 Someone **lets** a house or room when they allow someone else to use it in return for money: *We let the cottage in the summer.*

▷ **let down**
You **let** someone **down** when you do not do what you said you

would do: *I'm sorry I let you down, but I was ill.*

same as **disappoint**

▷ **let go**
You **let go** of something when you stop holding it: *Let go of my hand.* ❑ *He let go of the rope.*

let's *verb*
Let's is short for **let us**: *Let's go on holiday.*

letter *noun*: **letters**
1 A **letter** is a written message that you send by post: *I sent them a letter, but they haven't replied yet.*
2 A **letter** is also one of the written or printed signs used in writing: *Z is the·last letter of the English alphabet.*

letter box *noun*: **letter boxes**
1 A **letter box** is a container in the street where you can post letters.
2 A **letter box** is also a hole in the door of a house, through which a postman puts letters.

lettuce *noun*: **lettuces**
Lettuce is a vegetable with large green leaves, used in salads: *Can I have some more lettuce, please?* ❑ *I'll have three lettuces, please.*

❝ **let**-is ❞

level *adjective*
A **level** surface is flat and does not slope: *The surface of this table isn't very level.*

lever *noun*: **levers**
A **lever** is a handle that you push or pull to work a machine: *If you pull this lever, the back of the lorry lifts up.*

liar *noun*: **liars**
A **liar** is a person who tells lies.

library *noun*: **libraries**
A **library** is a building where a lot of books are kept for people to read or borrow: *You have to be a student to use this library.*

lick *verb*: **licks, licked, licking, has licked**
You **lick** something when you pass your tongue over it: *He licked the stamp and stuck it on the envelope.* ❑ *We found the dog in the kitchen, licking the plates clean.*

lick

lid *noun*: **lids**
A **lid** is a cover for a container such as a pot or box: *Does this saucepan have a lid?*

lie *noun*: **lies**
A **lie** is something that someone says that is not true: *He said he was ill, but it was a lie.*

lie *verb*: meaning 1: **lies, lied, lying, has lied**
meaning 2: **lies, lay, lying, has lain**
1 A person **lies** when they don't tell the truth: *Have you ever lied about your age?*
2 You **lie** somewhere when you get into a flat position, with your body and legs resting on something: *The dog lay on the floor and fell asleep.* ❑ *I'm going to lie on my bed and read.*

▷ **lie down**
You **lie down** when you get into a flat position, with your body and legs resting on something, usually to rest or go to sleep: *He*

*lay down on the grass and fell
asleep.*

life *noun*: **lives**
Your **life** is the time that you are
alive, between your birth and
your death: *He had a long and
happy life.*

lift *verb*: **lifts, lifted, lifting, has
lifted**
1 You **lift** something when you
raise it up: *They lifted the table
and carried it downstairs.*
2 Something **lifts** when it rises:
*The mist lifted and we could see
the hills again.*

lift *noun*: **lifts**
A **lift** is a type of machine which
moves up and down between the
floors of a building, carrying
people: *The lift was broken so we
had to use the stairs.*

light *noun*: **lights**
1 Light is the bright rays that
come from the sun, or from a
lamp inside, which help you to
see things: *There's not enough
light in here — I'll open the
curtains.*
2 A **light** is also an electric lamp:
*Switch the light off when you
leave, please.*

light *verb*: **lights, lit, lighting, has
lit**
1 You **light** something when you
make it start to burn: *We lit the
fire and warmed our hands in
front of it.*
2 A place **is lit** when something
such as a lamp gives light to it:
The church was lit by candles.

light *adjective*: **lighter, lightest**
1 It is **light** when there is enough
light to allow you to see properly:
This is a very light room. ❑ *It gets
light very early in the summer.*

2 A colour is **light** if it is closer
to white than black: *light blue.*
3 Something is **light** if it doesn't
weigh very much and you can lift
it easily: *My bag is much lighter
than yours.*
4 Light also means gentle: *A
light breeze was blowing through
the trees.*
5 A **light** meal is one made up of
a small amount of food: *We had a
light lunch.*

meanings 1 and 2: the opposite
is **dark**
meaning 3 and 5: the opposite
is **heavy**

lightning *noun*
Lightning is bright flashes of
light that go across the sky during
storms: *The lightning flashed, and
I looked at the white faces around
me.*

like *preposition*
1 One thing is **like** another if it is
similar to it: *She looks like her
sister.* ❑ *He walks like a duck.*
2 You ask what something or
someone is **like** when you want a
description of them: *What is your
new boss like?* ❑ *What was Texas
like?*

like *verb*: **likes, liked, liking, has
liked**
1 You **like** something if you enjoy
it, or enjoy doing it, or think it's
nice: *Ian likes football.* ❑ *I don't
really like cabbage.* ❑ *I like your
new dress.*
2 You **like** someone if you are
fond of them and you enjoy their
company: *I like Helen — she's a
good friend.*
3 You say that you would **like** to
do something if you want to do it;
you say that you would **like**

something if you want to have it:
I'd like to go out tonight. ❏ *Do you think she'd like a bracelet for her birthday?*

likely *adjective*: **likelier, likeliest**
You say that something is **likely**, or **likely** to happen, if you think that it probably will happen: *Some rain is likely this afternoon.* ❏ *He's not likely to arrive after midnight, is he?*

limb *noun*: **limbs**
A **limb** is an arm or a leg: *Several people suffered broken limbs in the accident.*

limp *noun*: **limps**
Someone walks with a **limp** when they put more weight on one leg than on the other because they have injured one foot or leg.

limit *noun* **limits**
There is a **limit** when the amount or number of something is controlled: *There is a limit to the amount of money we can spend.*

---

limit is also a verb: *They've limited the amount of money we can spend.*

---

line *noun*: **lines**
1 A **line** is a long thin mark: *She drew a line through his mistake.*
2 A **line** is also a row of people or objects standing next to each other: *The crowd organized themselves into a long line.* ❏ *There was a line of trees at the edge of the field.*
3 A **line** is a row of printed or written words: *a poem with fourteen lines.*
4 An actor's **lines** are the words that they have to learn for their

part in a film or play.
5 A **line** is a long piece of string, wire or rope, used for a particular purpose: *He hung the clothes on the washing line.* ❏ *a fishing line.*

line *verb*: **lines, lined, lining, has lined**
People **line** a road when they stand next to each other to form a row along it.

▷ **line up**
People **line up** when they form a line or queue; you **line** things **up** when you put them next to each other in a row.

link *verb*: **links, linked, linking, has linked**
You **link** two things when you connect them: *They linked arms and walked down the street.* ❏ *The cities were linked by the motorway.*

lion *noun*: **lions**
A **lion** is a large animal which belongs to the cat family; the male has long thick hair around its head.

lip *noun*: **lips**
Your **lips** are the two pieces of red flesh that form the edges of your mouth.

liquid *noun*: **liquids**
Water, milk, blood and other things that flow are **liquids**: *There was a thick liquid on the floor that looked like oil.* ❏ *The ice cream has turned to liquid.*

list *noun*: **lists**
A **list** is a set of names or other things, written down, one after another: *He took out the list of names and began to read.*

list *verb*: **lists, listed, listing, has listed**
You **list** names or other things

when you write or say them one after the other: *She listed all her favourite hobbies and pastimes.*

listen *verb*: **listen, listened, listening, has listened**
You **listen** when you pay attention to a sound, so that you hear it well: *Sorry, what did you say? — I wasn't listening.* ❑ *He was in his bedroom listening to pop music.*

lit *verb*
see **light**: *She lit the candles on the dinner table.*

litre *noun*: **litres**
A **litre** is a unit of measurement for liquids: *Try to drink a litre of water every day.*

litter *noun*: **litters**
1 Litter is rubbish that people drop in the street: *He picked up all the litter and put it in the bin.*
2 A number of baby animals born at the same time is called a **litter**: *There were five puppies in the litter.*

little *adjective*: meaning 3: **less, least**
1 Something that is **little** is small: *He slept in a little room at the back of the house.*
2 You were **little** when you were a young child: *I was scared of the dark when I was little.*
3 Little also means 'not much': *I had very little money, and couldn't afford the plane fare.*

▷ **a little**
A little means 'a small amount': *'Would you like some more wine?' 'Yes please, just a little.'*

live *verb*: **lives, lived, living, has lived**
1 You **live** in a particular place when you have your home there:

She lives in New York. ❑ *They live in Peel Street.* ❑ *Have you lived here all your life?*
2 To **live** is to be alive: *She lived till she was 101.* ❑ *These animals don't live for long.*

❛ **liv** ❜

meaning 2: the opposite is **die**

live *adjective*
see **alive**.

live *adverb*
Something is broadcast **live** when it is shown on television at the same time as it is happening: *We watched the match live on TV.*

rhymes with **five**

living *noun*
You do something for a **living** when you do it to earn money: *He drives a taxi for a living.*

living room *noun*: **living rooms**
The **living room** is the room in a house where you relax: *We sat in the living room and watched TV.*

lizard *noun*: **lizards**
A **lizard** is a type of reptile. Most lizards have four short legs, toes and a tail.

load *noun*: **loads**
A **load** is something heavy that is carried somewhere: *The lorry was carrying a load of wood.*

load *verb*: **loads, loaded, loading, has loaded**
1 You **load** a vehicle when you put things into it: *They loaded the car, ready for the long journey.*
2 You **load** a gun when you put bullets into it.

loaf *noun*: **loaves**
A **loaf** is bread which has been baked into a regular shape.

loan *noun*: **loans**
A **loan** is an amount of money that a person has borrowed: *They got a loan to buy a new car.*

local *adjective*
Local means belonging to a particular area: *Mr Melville works in the local library.* ❑ *the local newspaper.*

lock *noun*: **locks**
1 A **lock** is a device that is used to fasten things such as doors, windows and drawers; you need a key to open and close a lock: *He put his key in the lock and opened the door.*
2 A **lock** is also a piece of hair: *She kept a lock of his hair.*

lock *verb*: **locks, locked, locking, has locked**
1 You **lock** something, such as a door, a window or a case when you fasten it with a key: *Don't forget to lock the door.*
2 A door or window **locks** when it can be fastened using a key: *This window doesn't lock.*

log *noun*: **logs**
A **log** is a thick piece of wood cut from a tree: *She threw another log on to the fire.*

lonely *adjective*: **lonelier, loneliest**
1 You are **lonely** if you are unhappy because you don't have anyone to be with or talk to: *He was very lonely living by himself.*
2 A **lonely** place is far from other places where people live: *They live on a lonely island.*

long *adjective and adverb*: **longer, longest**
1 Something that is **long** is an unusually large distance from one end to the other: *The queue wasn't very long so he stood and waited.* ❑ *He wore a long coat that touched the ground.*
2 A **long** event or activity takes up a lot of time: *Is it a long film?* ❑ *It doesn't take a long time to get there.*
3 Something is a certain distance **long** when it measures that distance; something is a certain time **long** when it takes that time: *The ruler is 30 cm long.* ❑ *The film is about two and a half hours long.*
4 Long means 'a long time' or 'for a long time': *Have you been waiting long?* ❑ *Dinner won't be long.* ❑ *How long did the parcel take to arrive?*

▷ **all day long**
You do something **all day long** when you do it through the whole day: *He stayed indoors all day long and finished his work.* ❑ *It rained all day long.*

▷ **no longer**
You use **no longer** to mean 'not any more': *We no longer love each other.*

long *verb*: **longs, longed, longing, has longed**
You **long** for something when you want it very much: *She longed for a holiday.*

look *verb*: **looks, looked, looking, has looked**
1 You **look** at something when you use your eyes to see it: *Look at this.* ❑ *He was looking out of the window.*
2 Something **looks** a certain way if it appears that way: *The sky looks very black over there.* ❑ *Mr Anderson doesn't look very happy.*
3 You **look** for something when

you try and find it: *Can you help me look for my book?* ❑ *I'm looking for Claire — do you know where she is?* ❑ *I've looked everywhere, but I still can't find the scissors.*

▷ **look after**
You **look after** someone or something when you take care of them: *We're looking after their dog while they're in France.* ❑ *She doesn't look after her toys; lots of them are broken.*

look forward to
You **look forward to** something in the future when you feel happy that it is going to happen: *They were looking forward to the party.*

▷ **look into**
You **look into** something when you investigate it: *I'll look into the problem and tell you what's wrong.*

▷ **look out**
You say **look out!** to warn someone about a danger: *Look out! There's a car coming.*

▷ **look round**
1 You **look round** when you turn your head to look at something behind you: *She looked round and saw the car.*
2 You **look round** a place when you visit it to look at the things in it: *They spent the afternoon looking round the old town.*

▷ **look up**
You **look** information **up** when you look for it in a book: *If there's a word you don't understand, look it up in your dictionary.*

look *noun*: **looks**
1 You have a **look** at something when you examine it: *I had a look at the newspaper, but there wasn't anything interesting in it.*

2 The **look** of something or someone is the way they appear to you; someone has a certain **look** when that is the appearance they have: *She had a scared look in her eye.* ❑ *I didn't like the look of the weather.*

loose *adjective*: **looser, loosest**
1 Something is **loose** if it is not fastened very tightly: *The button on your shirt is loose.*
2 Clothes are **loose** if they don't fit very tightly: *This dress is too loose.*
3 Animals or things are **loose** when they are not tied to anything and they are free: *He let the dogs loose in the park.* ❑ *She wears her hair loose.*

meaning 2: the opposite is **tight**

loosen *verb*: **loosens, loosened, loosening, has loosened**
You **loosen** something, or something **loosens**, if you make it, or it becomes, less tight: *He loosened his trousers.* ❑ *The screw loosened and fell out.*

lorry *noun*: **lorries**
A **lorry** is a large vehicle used to carry heavy loads by road.

same as **truck**

lorry

lose *verb*: **loses, lost, losing, has lost**
1 You **lose** something when you can't find it: *I've lost my keys.*
2 You **lose** a match or a contest when you don't win it: *He lost the game.*

3 You **lose** weight when you reduce the amount of fat on your body so that you weigh less: *He's lost 10 kilos already.*

loss *noun*: **losses**
1 A **loss** is the act of losing something: *Have you told the police about the loss of your purse?*
2 A **loss** is also the money that you lose when you sell something for less money than you paid for it: *He made a loss of $100 when he sold his bike.*

---

meaning 2: the opposite is **profit**

---

lost *verb*
see **lose**: *I've lost my keys.*

lost *adjective*
1 Something is **lost** when it is missing: *Everyone searched for the lost ticket.*
2 A person is **lost** if they don't know where they are, and they don't know how to get to where they want to go: *The boy was lost and had to ask for directions.*

lot *noun*
The **lot** is the whole of something: *She wanted a slice of cake, but her dad had eaten the lot.*

▷ **a lot** or **a lot of**
You can use **a lot**, or **a lot of**, when you are talking about a large number: *Some people are leaving but a lot are staying.* ❑ *She has a lot of friends.*

▷ **lots of**
If there are **lots of** things there are many of them; if there is **lots of** a particular thing, there is a large amount of it: *There were lots*

of people at the party. ❑ *There's lots of ice cream left.*

loud *adjective and adverb*: **louder, loudest**
Something is **loud** if it makes a lot of noise: *Can you turn the music down? It's too loud.* ❑ *She laughed so loud that people in the next room could hear her.* ❑ *Could you speak a little louder?*

---

the opposite is **quiet**

---

love *noun*
1 Love is the feeling of being very fond of someone: *Everyone can see her love for her children.*
2 Love is the feeling of liking something very much: *She has a great love of music.*

love *verb*: **loves, loved, loving, has loved**
1 You **love** someone when you are very fond of them: *She told him she loved him.*
2 You **love** something when you like it very much: *I love reading.* ❑ *She loves chocolate.*

---

the opposite is **hate**

---

lovely *adjective*: **lovelier, loveliest**
Something that is **lovely** is beautiful: *He has a lovely smile.* ❑ *It's a lovely day.*

low *adjective and adverb*: **lower, lowest**
1 Something is **low** when it is close to the ground: *He hit his head on the low ceiling.* ❑ *You have hung the painting too low.* ❑ *The helicopter flew low over the trees.*
2 Something is also **low** when it is not high: *The temperature is low for this time of year.* ❑ *low prices.* ❑ *If the temperature falls*

too low, these plants will die.
3 Sounds are **low** when they are not very loud: *The music was on so low we could hardly hear it.* ❑ *He turned the sound on the TV down low.*

rhymes with **toe**

meanings 1 and 2: the opposite is **high**
meaning 3: the opposite is **high** or **loud**

lower *adjective*
1 One thing is **lower** than another if it is not so high: *The prices here are much lower than in the city.*
2 Lower is also used to describe something that is below another similiar thing: *The child cut its lower lip.* ❑ *The lower part of the ship was soon flooded.*

luck *noun*
1 Luck is success that comes through chance: *It was luck that he got the job.*
2 Luck is also good or bad fortune: *It was a bit of luck winning that money.*

lucky *adjective*: **luckier, luckiest**
1 You are **lucky** when good things happen to you by chance:

I know I'm very lucky to have this job .
2 Something is **lucky** if you believe it brings good fortune: *What's your lucky number?*

luggage *noun*
The suitcases and bags that you take with you when you travel are your **luggage**: *We didn't have much luggage when we went on holiday.*

lump *noun*: **lumps**
1 A **lump** is a solid piece of something: *a lump of earth.*
2 A **lump** is also a place on someone's body that is swollen: *He's got a big lump on his head where the ball hit him.*

lunch *noun*
Lunch is the meal that you eat in the middle of the day: *I've got sandwiches for lunch.*

lung *noun*: **lungs**
Your **lungs** are the two organs inside your chest which fill with air when you breathe in, and empty when you breathe out.

lying *verb*
see **lie**: *The cat was lying under the tree.* ❑ *He has been lying to us.*

Mm

machine *noun*: **machines**
A **machine** is a device that is designed to do a certain kind of work: *We've got a new washing machine.*

mad *adjective*: **madder, maddest**
1 A **mad** person is crazy; someone goes **mad** when they become ill in their mind and start to behave strangely: *Poor woman; she went mad in the last years of her life.*
2 Mad also means angry: *He was mad with me for not finishing my work.*
3 You are **mad** about something when you like it very much: *He's mad about football.*

Madam *noun*
Madam is a polite form that people such as shop assistants or waiters use when they are speaking to a woman: *This way, madam.*

made *verb*
see **make**: *I made the dinner last night so it's your turn to make it tonight.*

magazine *noun*: **magazines**
A **magazine** is a paper that you can buy every week or month; magazines usually have reports, stories and advertisements in them: *She bought a magazine at the newsagents.* ❑ *a fashion magazine.*

magic *noun*
1 People refer to an event as '**magic**' when they cannot explain it, and they believe that a strange power caused it to happen: *The door opened as if by magic.*
2 Magic is also the skill of performing tricks, such as making things seem to disappear: *He did some magic to entertain the children.* ❑ *a magic trick.*

maid *noun*: **maids**
A **maid** is a woman who does cleaning and other work in a hotel, or in someone's house.

mail *noun*
Mail is letters and parcels which are delivered by post: *Did you get any mail today?*

main *adjective*
Main means 'most important': *We went into the building by the main entrance.* ❑ *The main character in the play is called Blanche.*

mainland *noun*
The **mainland** of a country or a continent is the biggest area of land in it, rather than nearby islands which also belong to it: *Last year we went on holiday to the Greek islands, so this year we're going to the mainland.*

mainly *adverb*
Mainly means 'most of the time' or 'usually': *We mainly go out at weekends.* ❑ *It's mainly French that's spoken in this part of Canada.*

maize *noun*
Maize is a cereal plant which produces small yellow seeds.

make *verb*: **makes, made, making, has made**

1 You **make** something when you produce it or prepare it: *They make steel in this factory.* ❑ *I've made a cup of tea for you.*

2 You **make** someone do something when you force them to do it: *She made me take piano lessons twice a week.*

3 Someone or something **makes** you do something when it causes you to do it: *His remarks made her feel very unhappy.*

4 You **make** money when you earn it: *He makes £250 a week, cleaning windows.*

5 You use **make** to talk about doing certain actions: *I'm sorry, I think you've made a mistake.* ❑ *They made a difficult decision.* ❑ *I have to make a phone call and then I'll be ready.*

6 Two or more quantities added together **make** a particular amount: *5 plus 7 makes 12.*

▷ **made from** or **made of** or **made out of**

Something is **made from**, **made of** or **made out of**, a particular material if it is produced from it: *Paper is made from wood.* ❑ *He'd made the shelter out of branches.* ❑ *This dress is made of silk.*

▷ **make out**

You can **make out** what something is when you can just see or hear it: *We could just make out the shape of a building through the fog.*

▷ **make up**

1 You **make** something **up** when you invent it: *He made up a story to tell his children.*

2 You also **make** something **up** when you pretend that is true: *He made up an excuse and his boss*

believed him.

3 People **make up** when they become friends again after an argument: *Have you and Simon made up yet?*

4 Something is **made up** of the various things that form it: *The team is made up of students of all ages.*

male *noun*: **males**
A **male** is a man or boy, or an animal which does not give birth: *Our cats are both males.*

male *adjective*
Male is used to describe men or boys, or animals which do not give birth: *male behaviour.*

the opposite is **female**

man *noun*: **men**
A **man** is an adult male human being: *He's a very nice man.* ❑ *There were more women than men at the meeting.*

manage *verb*: **manages, managed, managing, has managed**
1 You **manage** to do something when you are able to do it: *Will you manage to carry all those bags?*

2 You **manage** an organization when you are in charge of it: *Mr Evans manages the local football team.* ❑ *She manages a large supermarket.*

manager *noun*: **managers**
A **manager** is a person in charge of a business or a team: *I'd like to speak to the manager please.*

manner *noun*
1 Someone's **manner** is the way that they talk and behave: *He has a strange manner.*

2 The **manner** in which you do

something is the way that you do it: *He greeted me in a friendly manner.*

meaning 2: same as **way**

manners *noun*
You have good **manners** when you behave in a polite way towards others: *Their children have such good manners.* ❑ *It is bad manners to speak with your mouth full.*

many *determiner and pronoun*: **more, most**
Many people or things is a large number of them: *Not many people came to the party.* ❑ *There were too many people on the bus.* ❑ *I haven't got many clothes.*

the opposite is **few**

▷ **how many**
You ask 'how **many**…' when you want to know the number of people or things: *How many people are coming tonight?* ❑ *How many chairs will we need?*

map *noun*: **maps**
A **map** is a drawing of a particular area, seen from above: *We looked at the map to find out where we were.*

march *verb*: **marches, marched, marching, has marched**
People **march** when they walk with regular steps, often in time to music: *The soldiers marched along the street.*

March *noun*
March is the third month of the year, between February and April: *He started his job last March.*

margarine *noun*
Margarine is a soft yellow fat, similar to butter, which you can

spread on bread and use for baking: *Do you want margarine or butter on your toast?*

mark *noun*: **marks**
1 A **mark** is a stain: *You've got a red mark on your skirt.*
2 You are given **marks** for an exercise or task when someone decides how well you have done it, and gives you points: *He got full marks in the test.* ❑ *I didn't get a very good mark for my last essay.*
3 A **mark** is a written or printed sign: *There's a mark on the map, showing where the church is.*

mark *verb*: **marks, marked, marking, has marked**
1 Something **marks** a surface when it makes a dirty stain on it or damages it: *Don't put your hot cup down on the table. It'll mark it.*
2 You **mark** a student's task or exercise when you decide how well they have done it and give them points for it: *She spent the evening marking students' essays.*
3 You **mark** something when you put a label on it: *On the map, the church is marked with a cross.*

market *noun*: **markets**
A **market** is a place where goods are sold, usually outside on stalls: *We bought some fruit and vegetables at the market.*

marriage *noun*: **marriages**
1 A **marriage** is a wedding: *The marriage ceremony lasted two hours.*
2 **Marriage** is also the state of being married to someone: *They seem to have a happy marriage.*

marry *verb*: **marries, married, marrying, has married**

1 You **marry** someone when you become their husband or wife: *He asked her if she would marry him.*

2 Someone **marries** two people when he or she performs the ceremony that makes them man and wife: *The priest married the couple.*

▷ **get married**
Two people **get married** when they become husband and wife: *They got married three weeks ago.*

marvellous *adjective*
You say something is **marvellous** when you think it is very good: *That was a marvellous film.* ❑ *Paul has just had a marvellous idea.*

mask *noun*: **masks**
A **mask** is a covering that you put over your face, so that other people don't recognize you: *Everyone had to wear masks at the party.*

mast *noun*: **masts**
The **mast** of a ship is the tall pole which the sails are attached to.

mat *noun*: **mats**
1 A **mat** is a piece of cloth, plastic or other material which you put under a plate on a table: *a set of six table mats.*

2 A **mat** is also a thick piece of material, used to protect a floor: *We wiped our feet on the mat before going into the house.*

match *noun*: **matches**
1 A **match** is a short thin piece of wood which catches fire when you rub the end against a rough surface: *Use a match to light the fire.*

2 A **match** is also an organized game between two people or teams: *Who won the match?* ❑ *She lost the tennis match.*

match *verb*: **matches, matched, matching, has matched**
Two things **match** when they are the same in colour or shape: *That scarf matches the colour of your eyes.* ❑ *Those socks don't match.*

material *noun*: **materials**
1 Material is cloth: *The curtains were made out of orange material.*
2 Materials are things that you use to write or to make things: *building materials.* ❑ *This shop sells artists' materials.*

mathematics *noun*
Mathematics is the subject in which you study numbers.

maths *noun*
Maths is short for **mathematics**: *a maths exam.* ❑ *He's got a degree in maths.*

matter *noun*
1 A **matter** is a subject: *This is a matter for the police.*
2 Something is the **matter** when something is wrong: *You look worried. Is anything the matter?* ❑ *What's the matter with this lock? I can't turn the key.*

matter *verb*: **matters, mattered, mattering, has mattered**
Something **matters** when it is important: *It doesn't matter if you can't answer all the questions.* ❑ *The weather matters to people like farmers and fishermen.*

mattress *noun*: **mattresses**
A **mattress** is a large thick cushion that fits on a bed.

may *verb*: **may, might**
1 You ask if you **may** do something when you want to know if you have permission to

do it: *May we smoke in this room?*
2 You use **may** to talk about
something that is possible but not
certain: *He may come tomorrow.*
❑ *I think it may rain.*

May *noun*
May is the fifth month of the
year, between April and June:
Her sister was born in May.

maybe *adverb*
Maybe means 'perhaps': *Maybe I
should go by car.* ❑ *'Are you going
to the cinema tonight?' 'Maybe.'*

▸ write **maybe**, not **may be**

me *pronoun*
Me is a word that you use when
you are talking about yourself:
Could you give me my bag please?
❑ *No-one asked me.* ❑ *I'll bring Joe
with me.*

meal *noun*: **meals**
A **meal** is the food that you eat
at a particular time of the day:
*The price includes a double room
for one night, breakfast and an
evening meal.*

mean *verb*: **means, meant,
meaning, has meant**
1 You say what a word **means**
when you explain it so that other
people can understand it:
'Vacation' means 'holiday'. ❑ *What
does 'organize' mean?*
2 You ask someone what they
mean when you want them to
explain more clearly what they
have just said: *What do you mean
by that?*
3 You **mean** to do something if
you have decided to do it: *I
meant to telephone you last night,
but I fell asleep.*

mean *adjective*: **meaner, meanest**
1 A **mean** person doesn't like

sharing things with other people:
They aren't poor — just mean.
2 Mean also means 'unkind':
Don't be so mean to Joe.

meaning *noun*: **meanings**
The **meaning** of a word is what
people understand by it: *What is
the meaning of 'ashamed'?* ❑ *Many
words have several different
meanings.*

meant *verb*
see **mean**: *I meant to telephone
you, but I forgot.*

rhymes with **sent**

meanwhile *adverb*
1 Meanwhile means 'in the time
before something happens':
*They're coming round at 8 o'clock;
meanwhile, we can watch television.*
2 Meanwhile also means 'at the
same time': *We prepared the dinner.
Meanwhile, Brian was finishing the
painting in the living room.*

measure *verb*: **measures,
measured, measuring, has
measured**
1 You **measure** something when
you find out what size it is: *We
measured the length of the room.*
2 Something **measures** a
particular amount when that is its
size: *The curtains measure 2.5
metres.*

meat *noun*
Meat is the flesh of animals, used
as food: *The meat of the cow is
called beef.*

medical *adjective*
Medical means having to do
with medicines and treating
illness: *medical care.* ❑ *When you
join the army, you have to pass a
medical examination.*

medicine *noun*: **medicines**
Medicine is liquid that you swallow to make you feel better when you are ill: *He has to take his medicine before every meal.* ❑ *cough medicine.*

❛**med**-sin❜

medium *adjective*
Medium is neither large nor small, but somewhere in between: *He was a man of medium height.* ❑ *'Six eggs please.' 'Small, medium or large?'*

meet *verb*: **meets, met, meeting, has met**
1 Two people who know each other **meet** when they find themselves together by chance: *I met Robin on my way to work today.* ❑ *We met in the corridor, but we didn't speak.*
2 You also **meet** someone when you arrange to join them in a certain place at a certain time: *I'm meeting Nick tonight.* ❑ *I'll meet you at 7 o'clock.*
3 You **meet** someone when you are introduced to them for the first time: *Come and meet my mother.*
4 Two things **meet** when they come together or join: *The accident happened where the two roads meet.*

meeting *noun*: **meetings**
A **meeting** is a time when people come together for a particular reason, usually to discuss things: *The meeting lasted three hours.*

melt *verb*: **melts, melted, melting, has melted**
Something **melts** if it becomes soft or turns to liquid because it has been heated: *The ice melted in the sun.* ❑ *Melt some butter in the frying-pan.*

member *noun*: **members**
A **member** of a group or club is someone who takes part in its activities: *We are members of the local football club.*

memory *noun*: **memories**
1 Your **memory** is the ability you have to remember things: *He has an excellent memory.*
2 A **memory** is an event that you remember: *Tell me about your first childhood memories.*

men *noun*
see **man**: *There were twelve men in the room.*

mend *verb*: **mends, mended, mending, has mended**
You **mend** something when you repair it: *They've mended the leak in the roof.*

mention *verb*: **mentions, mentioned, mentioning, has mentioned**
You **mention** something when you say it: *He didn't mention that he was going on holiday.* ❑ *I mentioned our plan to her, but she didn't like it.*

menu *noun*: **menus**
A **menu** is a list of the dishes that you can have in a particular restaurant: *Can we see the menu, please?*

❛**men**-yew❜

mess *noun*: **messes**
A place or a thing is a **mess** when it is untidy: *The wind has made a mess of my hair.* ❑ *This cupboard is in a terrible mess.* ❑ *Your room is a mess.*

message *noun*: **messages**
A **message** is a piece of

information that is sent from one person to another: *When I returned, there was a message on my desk.*

messenger *noun*: **messengers**
A **messenger** is someone who passes a message from one person to another.

met *verb*
see **meet**: *They met at university.*

metal *noun*
Metal is a hard material such as iron, steel or gold: *Keys are made of metal.*

method *noun*: **methods**
A **method** is a particular way of doing something: *We learnt about different teaching methods.*

metre *noun*: **metres**
A **metre** is a unit of measurement, equal to 100 centimetres: *'How tall are you?' '1.83 metres.'*

  'mee-ter**'**

▸ written **m** for short

mice *noun*
see **mouse**: *He keeps mice as pets.*

midday *noun*
Midday is twelve o'clock in the middle of the day: *They arranged to meet at midday.*

midday

middle *noun*
The **middle** of something is the centre of it: *We had seats in the middle of the cinema.*

midnight *noun*
Midnight is twelve o'clock in the middle of the night: *By midnight, everyone was asleep.*

midnight

might *verb*
1 see **may**: *He asked if he might borrow the car.*
2 You use **might** with another verb to show that something is possible: *I think it might rain later.* ❑ *He thinks he might not be able to come.*

mild *adjective*: **milder, mildest**
1 The weather is **mild** when it is not very cold: *It's mild for December.*
2 Mild also means 'not very bad': *It's just a mild cold, so I'll probably still go to work.* ❑ *He only got a mild punishment.*

mile *noun*: **miles**
A **mile** is a unit of length which is equal to 1.6 kilometres: *We were three miles from home when the car broke down.*

milk *noun*
1 Milk is the white liquid produced by cows and other female animals as food for their babies; milk is also drunk by humans: *Milk is used to make cheese and butter.*
2 Milk is the white liquid produced by female humans as food for their babies.

mill *noun*: **mills**
1 A **mill** is a building where grain is made into flour.
2 A **mill** is also a device used to grind things, such as coffee beans and pepper: *a pepper mill.*

3 A **mill** is a large factory which produces goods, such as cotton, steel and iron: *Most of these women work in the cotton mill.*

millimetre *noun*: **millimetres**
A **millimetre** is a measurement of length. There are one thousand millimetres in a metre.

▸ written **mm** for short

million *noun*: **millions**
A **million** is the number 1 000 000: *A thousand times a thousand is a million.*

million *determiner and pronoun*
A **million** means 1 000 000 in number: *There are more than seven million people living in London.*

mind *noun*: **minds**
Your **mind** is your brain and the power it has to think and understand: *For an old lady she had a very quick mind.*

▷ change your mind
You **change your mind** when you decide to do something different: *I was going to go to the party, but I changed my mind.*

▷ make up your mind
You **make up your mind** when you decide to do something: *He made up his mind to ask his father for help.*

mind *verb*: **minds, minded, minding, has minded**
1 You ask someone if they **mind** something when you want to know if they would be angry about it: *You don't mind if I use this pen, do you?* ❑ *Would you mind if I closed the window?*
2a You **mind** about something when you care about it: *I don't mind about the money - pay me*

back when you can. **b** You also **mind** something when you are careful about it: *Mind you don't cut yourself on the broken glass.*
3 You **mind** something when you look after it: *We're minding their dog while they go on holiday.*

▷ never mind
Never mind means 'don't worry' or 'it is not important': *Never mind, you tried hard.* ❑ *'I don't have any nice clothes to wear.' 'Oh, never mind, wear your jeans.'*

mine *pronoun*
You use **mine** to talk about something that belongs to you: *The book is mine, but you can borrow it.* ❑ *Give me back the ball — it's mine.*

mine *noun*: **mines**
A **mine** is a place under the ground where coal and precious metals are dug up: *a gold mine.*

minus *preposition and adjective*
1 You use **minus** when you are taking one number away from another: *Ten minus three is seven (10 – 3 = 7).*
2 Minus means 'less than zero': *The temperature outside was minus 10° (–10°).*

minute *noun*: **minutes**
1 A **minute** is one of the sixty units of time which make up an hour: *I'll meet you outside the school in ten minutes.*
2 A **minute** is also a short period of time: *Can you wait for me? I'll only be a minute.*

‘**min**-it ’

mirror *noun*: **mirrors**
A **mirror** is a flat piece of glass in which you see yourself when

you look at it: *She looked in the mirror to see if her hair was tidy.*

miserable *adjective*
Someone is **miserable** when they feel very unhappy: *She was miserable when she heard the news.*

Miss *noun*
Miss is a title that you use before the name of a girl or woman who is not married: *Miss Smith will be teaching you English this year.*

miss *verb*: **misses, missed, missing, has missed**
1 You **miss** something if you don't hit it or catch it: *She missed the ball and it fell to the ground.* □ *He threw the can at the bin, but missed.*
2 You also **miss** something if you arrive too late for it: *I missed the bus, so I had to walk home.*
3 You **miss** something if you don't hear or see it: *Sorry I missed that — What did you say?*
4 You **miss** someone or something when you are sad because they are no longer with you: *I'll miss you when you go.*

▷ **miss out**
You **miss** something **out** when you don't include it: *He missed out the third question in the exam.*

missing *adjective*
Something or someone is **missing** if you cannot find them: *Their dog has been missing for four days.* □ *I never found the missing book.* □ *There's a button missing from this coat.*

mist *noun*
Mist is a kind of light fog: *It was difficult to see because of the mist.*

mistake *noun*: **mistakes**
A **mistake** is something which is not correct: *I've made a mistake.* □ *He got on the wrong bus by*

mistake. □ *How many mistakes did you make?*

mistake *verb*: **mistakes, mistook, mistaking, has mistaken**
You **mistake** one person or thing for another when you think that they are that other person or thing: *I always mistake Matt for his father on the phone.* □ *I think Helen has mistaken my coat for hers.*

mix *verb*: **mixes, mixed, mixing, has mixed**
1 You **mix** things when you shake or stir them together: *Mix the eggs with the flour.*
2 You **mix** with other people when you talk to them or get to know them: *He needs to mix with more people of his own age.*

model *noun*: **models**
A **model** is a small copy of something: *They made a model of the ship.* □ *a model aeroplane.*

modern *adjective*
Something is **modern** if it is new and belongs to the present time: *Would you prefer an old house or something more modern?* □ *modern teaching methods.*

moment *noun*: **moments**
1 A **moment** is a very short period of time: *A moment later, there was a huge explosion.*
2 A **moment** is also a particular point in time: *At that moment, I knew I had made a mistake.*

▷ **at the moment**
You use **at the moment** in the same way as 'now': *I'm busy at the moment — could you come back later?*

▷ **in a moment**
Something that will happen **in a moment** will happen very soon: *I'll finish that letter in a moment.* □ *The film begins in a moment.*

Monday noun
Monday is the first day of the week, the day after Sunday.

money noun
Money is coins or notes that you use to pay for things: *I haven't got enough money to go out tonight.*

monkey noun: **monkeys**
A **monkey** is an animal with a long tail, which is similar to a small human being.

monster noun: **monsters**
A **monster** is a huge ugly creature, especially one that is found in stories: *The child had a bad dream about a huge green monster.* ❑ *The monster opened its huge jaws.*

month noun: **months**
A **month** is one of the twelve parts into which a year is divided: *September, April, June and November are the months which have 30 days.* ❑ *I'm going to France next month.*

monthly adverb and adjective
Something happens **monthly** if it happens once every month: *That magazine comes out monthly.* ❑ *The staff here are paid monthly.* ❑ *a monthly salary.*

mood noun: **moods**
The **mood** that someone is in is the way that they feel at a particular time: *Richard is in a bad mood.*

moon noun
The **moon** is the round object that you see shining in the sky at night; the moon moves round the Earth: *There's a full moon tonight.* ❑ *When did men first land on the moon?*

mop noun: **mops**
A **mop** is a bunch of cloth attached to a long handle, used to clean floors: *She was standing in the kitchen holding a mop and a bucket.*

more determiner, pronoun and adverb
1 More means a greater amount or number of something: *They've got more friends than us.* ❑ *I thought I had more money than that.* ❑ *'Were there a lot of people there?' 'Yes, more than usual.'*
2 More also means 'an extra amount': *Can I have some more coffee please?* ❑ *Do you think we need more chairs?* ❑ *Take these envelopes, and there are more here if you need them.*
3 More is used to compare things or people: *She is more intelligent than her sister.* ❑ *The exams were more difficult this year.* ❑ *He eats more than I do.*

---

meaning 1: the opposite is **less** or **fewer**
meaning 3: the opposite is **less**

▷ **more and more**
You use **more and more** to talk about an increase: *She became more and more upset.* ❑ *More and more people now own cars.*

▷ **more or less**
More or less means 'almost' or 'not exactly, but nearly': *I've more or less finished.* ❑ *It'll take three hours, more or less.*

morning noun: **mornings**
The **morning** is the time of day from midnight to midday: *Mr Price takes his dog for a walk every morning.* ❑ *I got up late this morning.* ❑ *I woke up at two in the morning.*

mosque noun: **mosques**
A **mosque** is a building where Muslims go to pray.

'mosk'

mosquito *noun*: **mosquitos**
A **mosquito** is a small insect which pricks your skin and sucks your blood.

'mos-kee-toe'

most *determiner, pronoun and adverb*
1 Most means 'nearly all': *Most people voted for him.* □ *Most of the eggs were cracked.* □ *He spends most of the week in London.*
2 'The **most**' means 'the greatest amount or number': *Who has done the most work?* □ *She has read the most books.* □ *We each ate a lot of biscuits, but Dad ate the most.*
3 Most is also used to show that one person or thing has more of a particular quality than all the others: *She is the most helpful person I know.* □ *That was the most boring meeting I've ever attended.*

meanings 2 and 3: the opposite is **least**

moth *noun*: **moths**
A **moth** is an insect with large wings, similar to a butterfly.

mother *noun*: **mothers**
A person's or animal's **mother** is their female parent: *She looks like her mother.* □ *After a few weeks, the baby horse spends less time with its mother.*

motor *noun*: **motors**
A **motor** is the part of a machine or vehicle which produces power to make it work: *The washing machine has an electric motor.*

motorbike or **motorcycle** *noun*: **motorbikes** or **motorcycles**
A **motorbike** is a road vehicle with two wheels and an engine: *He comes to work on his motorbike.*

motorist *noun*: **motorists**
A **motorist** is a person who is driving a car.

motorway *noun*: **motorways**
A **motorway** is a wide road with two or more lanes, on which vehicles can travel at high speeds.

mountain *noun*: **mountains**
A **mountain** is a very high hill: *Ben Nevis is the highest mountain in Britain.*

mouse *noun*: **mice**
1 A **mouse** is a small animal with white, brown or grey fur and a long tail: *A mouse ran across the kitchen floor.*

mouse

2 A **mouse** is also a device that you use to point to places on a computer screen; it has a button that you can press to instruct the computer to do something. [see picture at **computer**]

moustache *noun*: **moustaches**
A **moustache** is the line of hair which grows above a man's top lip: *He's got a beard and a moustache.*

'mus-tash'

mouth *noun*: **mouths**
Your **mouth** is the part of your face that contains your teeth and tongue; you use your mouth to speak and eat: *He opened his mouth to speak.* □ *Don't put your dirty fingers in your mouth!* [see picture at **face**]

move *verb*: **moves, moved, moving, has moved**
1 You **move** something when you put it in a different place: *Who*

has moved my book? □ *We need to move this table.*

2 Something **moves** when it changes position or goes from one place to another: *The trees moved in the breeze.* □ *I could hear someone moving about upstairs.*

3 People **move**, or **move house**, when they leave one home and go and live in another: *They're moving to Liverpool.* □ *When did the Simpsons move house?*

▷ **move in** or **move into**
People **move in**, or **move into** a building when they put the things that belong to them there, and begin to live or work there: *'We've bought a house.' 'Great! When are you moving in?'*

▷ **move off**
A vehicle **moves off** when it starts moving: *Put your seatbelt on before we move off.*

▷ **move out**
People **move out** when they leave a building that they have been living or working in, and take the things that belong to them: *We moved out of that flat three months ago.*

movement *noun*: **movements**
A **movement** is an act of moving: *He made a quick movement with his hand.*

movie *noun*: **movies**
A **movie** is a film: *We saw a great movie last night.*

Mr *noun*
Mr is the title used before a man's name: *I'd like to introduce Mr George O'Boyle.*

‘**mis**-ter ’

Mrs *noun*
Mrs is the title used before a

married woman's name: *I'd like to introduce Mrs Marjorie Stewart.*

‘**mis**-iz ’

Ms *noun*
Ms is a title that you can use before the name of a girl or woman whether she is married or not: *In her report, Ms Digby described the event as 'horrible'.*

‘**miz** ’

much *determiner, pronoun and adverb*
1 Much means 'a great amount': *I haven't got much time.* □ *She has too much work to do.* □ *You haven't eaten much.*

2 Much also means 'a certain amount': *How much money have you got?* □ *How much time do we have?* □ *How much was that skirt?* □ *How much did the skirt cost?*

3 Much is used in comparing, to show that something has a lot of a particular quality: *She is much happier today.* □ *I'm feeling much better, thank you.* □ *This computer works much more quickly than the old one.*

mud *noun*
Mud is soft wet soil: *The boys were covered in mud after their game of football.*

mug *noun*: **mugs**
A **mug** is a deep cup: *She was drinking tea from a mug.*

multiply *verb*: **multiplies, multiplied, multiplying, has multiplied**
You **multiply** a number when you add it to itself a certain number of times: *7 multiplied by 3 equals 21 (7 x 3 = 21).* □ *Multiply 4 by 5.*

mum or **mummy** *noun*: **mums** or **mummies**
A person's **mum** is their mother; **mummy** is a child's word for mother: *I'll ask my mum if we can go.* ◻ *Mum, what's for dinner?* ◻ *I've lost my mummy.*

murder *verb*: **murders, murdered, murdering, has murdered**
One person **murders** another person when they kill that other person on purpose: *An old man was murdered in his own home last night.*

muscle *noun*: **muscles**
A **muscle** is one of the pieces of flesh that are attached to bones inside your body; your muscles make your body move: *Arnold has very strong muscles in his arms.*

 'mus-el **'**

museum *noun*: **museums**
A **museum** is a place where people can go and look at old and interesting objects: *We went to a small museum in the village and looked at old jewellery.*

 'myew-**zee**-um **'**

mushroom *noun*: **mushrooms**
A **mushroom** is a plant that you can eat, with a short stem and a top shaped like an umbrella: *mushroom soup* ◻ *fried mushrooms.*

music *noun*
Music is the sounds made by people playing instruments or singing: *There wasn't anything interesting on television, so we listened to some music.*

musical *adjective*
1 Musical means 'connected with music': *musical instruments.*
2 A **musical** person is someone who is good at playing music: *Nicholas is very musical — he can play the piano and the flute.*

musician *noun*: **musicians**
A **musician** is a person who can play a musical instrument well: *Her brother is a musician.*

must *verb*
1 You use **must** to show that something is necessary: *We must leave the house by 8 o'clock.* ◻ *You must remember to bring the keys.*
2 You also use **must** to say that something is probable: *You must be tired after such a long journey.*

> ▸You can shorten **must not** to **mustn't**.

my *determiner*
My means 'belonging to me': *Have you seen my book?* ◻ *I've hurt my leg.* ◻ *He asked if he could borrow my car.*

> ▸This is **my** book. This book is **mine**.

myself *pronoun*
1 You use **myself** to show that you are affected by your own action: *I fell and hurt myself.*
2 'I did it **myself**' means 'I did it without any help': *I did all the work myself.*

mystery *noun*: **mysteries**
A **mystery** is a strange event which cannot be explained: *The flashing lights on top of the hill have always been a mystery to us.*

Nn

nail *noun*: **nails**
1 A **nail** is a thin piece of metal with a sharp end, which you hit into a surface with a hammer: *He fixed the boards to the floor with long nails.*
2 A **nail** is one of the hard coverings at the end of your fingers and toes: *She has very long fingernails.*

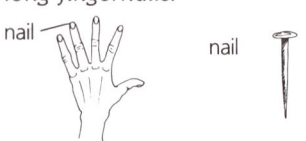

naked *adjective*
Someone who is **naked** isn't wearing any clothes: *Naked children were playing in the sea.*

name *noun*: **names**
The **name** of a person, place or animal is the word that you use when you are speaking about, or to them: *My dog's name is Sparky.* □ *The name of this street is Rodenhurst Road.* □ *What's his name?*

name *verb*: **names, named, naming, has named**
1 You **name** someone or something when you give them a name: *They named their son Samuel.*
2 You **name** something when you say its name: *Can you name all the presidents of the USA since Kennedy?*

narrow *adjective*: **narrower, narrowest**
Something is **narrow** if there is not a large distance from one side of it to the other: *The road is too narrow for that truck.*

the opposite is **wide** or **broad**

nasty *adjective*: **nastier, nastiest**
1 Something that is **nasty** is horrible or unpleasant: *That soup has a nasty taste.*
2 A **nasty** person behaves in a mean and cruel way: *He's a really a nasty man.* □ *That was a nasty thing to do.*

natural *adjective*
1 Something is **natural** if it is normal and not surprising: *It's natural to feel tired when you've been so ill.*
2 **Natural** materials are made by nature and not by humans: *Coal and oil are natural fuels.*

nature *noun*
1 **Nature** refers to plants and animals, the weather, and anything that has not been made by humans: *We watched a nature programme on television last night.*
2 A person's **nature** is the sort of person that they are: *She has a very kind nature.*

naughty *adjective*: **naughtier, naughtiest**
A **naughty** child or animal behaves badly: *a naughty puppy* □ *a naughty child.*

'naw-tee '

near *adverb and preposition*: **nearer, nearest**
1 **Near** means 'a short distance

away': *The young deer stayed near its mother.* ❏ *Our office is near the railway station.* ❏ *He was standing near me.*

2 Something is **near** when it will happen soon: *As the exams got nearer, he began to feel nervous.*

3 Near also means 'almost': *Her hands were shaking and she was near to tears.* ❏ *'It's about fifty miles away.' 'No, it's nearer to a hundred miles away.'*

same as **close**
meaning 1: the opposite is **far**

near *adjective*: **nearer, nearest**
Something is **near** when it is not far away: *The park is very near.*

nearly *adverb*
Nearly means 'not quite' or 'not completely': *It's nearly midnight.* ❏ *'Have you finished yet?' 'Nearly.'* ❏ *I nearly crashed the car yesterday.*

same as **almost**

neat *adjective*: **neater, neatest**
Someone or something is **neat** if they are very tidy: *She wore a neat blouse and skirt.*

necessary *adjective*
Something that is **necessary** is needed: *Is it really necessary to use the car?*

the opposite is **unnecessary**

neck *noun*: **necks**
Your **neck** is the part of your body between your head and your shoulders: *He wore a scarf round his neck.* ❏ *Giraffes have very long necks.*

necklace *noun*: **necklaces**
A **necklace** is a piece of jewellery which you wear round

your neck: *A gold necklace was stolen in the robbery.*

need *verb*: **needs, needed, needing, has needed**
1 You **need** something when it is important that you have it: *I need some help to move the bookcase.* ❏ *I'll need the money by tomorrow.*

2 You **need** to do something if you have to do it: *I need to finish this report tonight.*

need *noun*: **needs**
1 A **need** is something which you must or should have: *They talked about the need for change.*

2 You say there is no **need** for something when you want to show that it is not needed or there is no reason for it: *There's no need to worry — everything will be fine.* ❏ *He said he'd bring his car, but I said there was no need.*

needle *noun*: **needles**
1 A **needle** is a very thin piece of metal, with a sharp point at one end and a hole at the other; a needle is used for sewing: *a needle and thread.*

2 A **needle** is also a long thin rod which is used for knitting: *a pair of knitting needles.*

negative *noun and adjective*: **negatives**
A **negative**, or a **negative** answer or statement, is one which means 'no': *His suggestions received negative answers.* ❏ *'No' and 'never' are negatives.*

neighbour *noun*: **neighbours**
Your **neighbour** is the person who lives in the house next to yours, or near yours: *Mr Miller is our next-door neighbour.*

'nay-ber **'**

neither *determiner and pronoun*
Neither person or thing means not one nor the other of two: *Neither Penny nor Chris came to the party.* ❑ *Neither room has a large window.* ❑ *Neither of us can drive so we took the bus.*

nephew *noun*: **nephews**
Your **nephew** is the son of your brother or sister: *Her nephew is called Sam.*

nervous *adjective*
Someone who is **nervous** feels anxious: *I get really nervous before exams.* ❑ *He's always been nervous about flying.*

nest *noun*: **nests**
1 A **nest** is a bird's home that it builds using twigs, grass and leaves: *A bird is building its nest in the tree at the bottom of the garden.*
2 A **nest** is also a home that some insects make for themselves: *There is a wasps' nest in this tree.*

net *noun*: **nets**
1 Net is a kind of light material that you can see through: *The kitchen curtains are made from net.*
2 A **net** is a piece of this material, used for a particular purpose: *Mike caught several fish in his fishing net.* ❑ *Try to hit the ball over the net.*

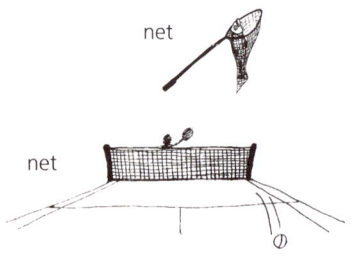

net

net

never *adverb*
Never means 'not ever' or 'at no time': *I've never been to South America.* ❑ *Jackie has never met my mother.*

new *adjective*: **newer, newest**
1 Something is **new** if it has never been used before or if it has just been made: *We can collect our new car this afternoon.* ❑ *She's bought a new dress for the wedding.*
2 New also means 'different from the last one': *Have you met your new boss yet?*

the opposite is **old**

news *noun*
1 News is information about things which have happened recently: *I've got some good news for you.* ❑ *Is there any news about George?*
2 The **news** is a report about recent events on the television or radio, or in newspapers: *We listened to the news at 9 o'clock.*

newsagent *noun*: **newsagents**
1 A **newsagent** is a person who manages a shop where you can buy newspapers and magazines, and other things such as sweets.
2 A **newsagent** or **newsagent's** is a shop where you can buy newspapers and magazines, and other things such as sweets: *He bought some chocolate at the newsagent's.*

newspaper *noun*: **newspapers**
A **newspaper** is a set of folded pages which have news printed on them: *I forgot to buy a newspaper this morning.*

▸ also called a **paper**

next *determiner and pronoun*
1 The **next** thing follows straight

after the present one: *They called the next person on the list.* ❑ *I'll see you next Saturday.* ❑ *He ate one bar of chocolate and then started on the next.*
2 Next also means 'nearest': *Take the next street on the right.*

next *adverb*
Next means 'immediately afterwards': *Paul arrived first and Angela came in next.* ❑ *What happened next?*

▷ **next door**
Someone who lives **next door** to you lives in the next house or flat to yours: *Mr Moran lives next door to us.*

▷ **next to**
One thing is **next to** another if it is beside it without anything else in between: *He sat next to me.* ❑ *They went into the shop next to the bakers.*

nice *adjective*: **nicer, nicest**
1 A **nice** person, place or thing is pleasant and attractive: *She has a nice smile.* ❑ *He's such a nice man.* ❑ *It's nice here, isn't it?*
2 Nice also means 'kind': *It was very nice of you to buy me flowers.*

niece *noun*: **nieces**
Your **niece** is the daughter of your brother or sister: *My niece is coming to stay during the holidays.*

night *noun*: **nights**
1 Night is the time when it is dark: *The wind blew all night.*
2 Night is also late evening: *We often go to the cinema on Saturday nights.*

nine *noun and adjective*: **nines**
1 Nine is the number or figure 9: *Seven plus two is nine.*
2 Nine is the time of 9 o'clock:

The film ends at nine.
3 Nine is also the age of nine; someone who is **nine** is nine years old: *He'll be nine on his next birthday.*

nine *determiner and pronoun*
Nine means nine in number: *It's my birthday in nine days.* ❑ *It'll take us nine years to pay the money back.* ❑ *Nine of the players were injured.*

nineteen *noun and adjective*: **nineteens**
1 Nineteen is the number 19: *Seventeen plus two is nineteen.*
2 Nineteen is also the age of nineteen; someone who is **nineteen** is nineteen years old: *Her nephew is nineteen.*

nineteen *determiner and pronoun*
Nineteen means nineteen in number: *The lamp cost nineteen pounds.* ❑ *Nineteen people died in the crash.* ❑ *Out of twenty-five people, nineteen died.*

ninety *noun and adjective*: **nineties**
1 Ninety is the number 90: *Seventy plus twenty is ninety.*
2a Ninety is also the age of ninety; someone who is **ninety** is ninety years old: *Her grandmother is ninety.* **b** A person in their **nineties** is between 90 and 99 years old.
3 The years in any century between 90 and 99 are often called 'the **nineties**'.

ninety *determiner and pronoun*
Ninety means ninety in number: *The plane tickets cost ninety pounds each.* ❑ *Ninety people were arrested by the police.*

ninth *determiner and adjective*
The **ninth** person or thing is the one that comes after eighth.

no
1 You say **no** when you want to give a negative reply: *I asked if there were any tickets left, but the woman said no.* ◻ *'Have you met Christine before?' 'No, I haven't.'*

no *determiner and adverb*
1 No also means 'not any': *There are no biscuits in the tin.* ◻ *There is no other person who can do it.*
2 No is used to show that something is not allowed: *The sign read 'No smoking'.*

nobody *pronoun*
Nobody means 'not anyone': *Nobody knew the answer to the question.* ◻ *Nobody lives in that house.*

nod *verb*: **nods, nodded, nodding, has nodded**
You **nod** when you move your head up and down, to show that you agree: *He asked if he could leave and I nodded.*

noise *noun*: **noises**
1 A **noise** is a sound: *I heard a strange noise in the night.*
2 A **noise** is also a loud sound that annoys or disturbs you: *That machine makes a terrible noise.*

noisy *adjective*: **noisier, noisiest**
Someone or something that is **noisy** makes a lot of noise: *The traffic is very noisy at this time of night.*

the opposite is **quiet**

none *pronoun*
None means 'not any' or 'not one': *I'll have to get some more biscuits — there are none left.*

◻ *None of the people in the room spoke English.*

nonsense *noun*
Nonsense is stupid words or actions, or something which has no meaning: *His ideas are nonsense.* ◻ *She's talking nonsense.*

noodle *noun*: **noodles**
Noodles are long thin strips made from a mixture of flour, eggs, and water.

noon *noun*
Noon is twelve o'clock in the middle of the day: *Our train leaves at noon.*

no-one *pronoun*
No-one means 'not anybody': *I phoned you this morning, but no-one answered.*

nor *conjunction*
You use **nor** with 'neither' to mean 'and not': *Neither Robert nor George knew the answer.* ◻ *I didn't know where I was; nor did he.*

normal *adjective*
Something is **normal** if there isn't anything special or unusual about it: *It's normal to feel tired when you've been ill.* ◻ *We left at the normal time.*

the opposite is **abnormal**

north *noun*
North is the direction to your left when you face the rising sun: *The wind is blowing from the north.*

nose *noun*: **noses**
Your **nose** is the part of your face that you smell and breathe through: *She held the flowers to her nose.* [see picture at **face**]

nostril *noun*: **nostrils**
Your **nostrils** are the two
openings in your nose.

not *adverb*
You use **not** to make a negative
statement: *'Are you ready?' 'No,
not yet.'* ❑ *That's not a nice thing
to say.* ❑ *I haven't seen him today.*
❑ *He doesn't know.* ❑ *Not one leaf
was left on the plant.*

> ▸When **not** follows a verb it is
> often shortened to **n't**.

note *noun*: **notes**
1 A **note** is a short letter: *I sent
her a note about our plans for
Saturday.*
2 A **note** is also a printed piece
of paper used as money: *I've only
got a ten-dollar note — do you
have any change?*
3 In music, a **note** is a sound
that you sing or play, or a mark
which represents this sound: *He
learned to play a simple tune,
using only five notes.*

notebook *noun*: **notebooks**
A **notebook** is a small book that
you use to write in: *The
policeman wrote the information
in his notebook.*

nothing *pronoun*
Nothing means 'no thing' or 'not
anything': *There's nothing in the
cupboard.* ❑ *'What did you do
yesterday?' 'Oh, nothing much.'*

notice *noun*: **notices**
1 A **notice** is a sign which gives
information or instructions: *The
notice read 'Please do not walk on
the grass'.* ❑ *A notice on the wall
showed the times of the football
matches.*
2 Notice is also attention that
you pay to someone or

something: *He didn't take any
notice of me.*

notice *verb*: **notices, noticed,
noticing, has noticed**
You **notice** something when you
see it: *I didn't notice the time.*
❑ *Did you notice their new
curtains?*

November *noun*
November is the eleventh month
of the year, between October and
December: *His birthday is at the
beginning of November.*

now *adverb and conjunction*
1 Now means 'at the present
time': *He is living in Berlin now.*
❑ *I'm tired now.*
2 If you do something **now** you
do it immediately: *We have to
leave now.*
3 Now also means 'because of
what has happened': ❑ *Now that
Paul's got a job, we can start
saving for a car.*

nowhere *adverb*
Nowhere means 'not anywhere'
or 'no place': *'Where are you going
tonight?' 'Nowhere; I haven't got
any money.'*

numb *adjective*
A part of your body is **numb** if
you cannot feel it: *It's so cold my
fingers are numb.*

'num'

number *noun*: **numbers**
1 A **number** is a figure such as 1,
2 or 3: *Think of a number
between 1 and 10.*
2 A **number** is also a series of
figures: *What is Matt's telephone
number?*
3 A **number** is also a quantity of
something: *There was a large
number of children in the park.*

nurse *noun*: **nurses**
A **nurse** is a person who cares for people who are ill: *A nurse visits him at home every day.*

nursery *noun*: **nurseries**
1 A **nursery** is a place where young children are looked after while their parents are at work.
2 A **nursery** is also a bedroom for a baby or young child.

nut *noun*: **nuts**
1 A **nut** is a kind of fruit with a hard shell round it.
2 A **nut** is also a round piece of metal with a hole in the middle that you screw a bolt into: *The gate was held together with nuts and bolts.* [see picture at **bolt**]

Oo

oar *noun*: **oars**
An **oar** is a long piece of wood with a flat end, used to row a boat: *Jim let go of the oar and it fell in the water.*

obedient *adjective*
An **obedient** person or animal does what people tell it to do: *The obedient dog brought the stick back to its owner.* ❑ *His obedient children followed in silence.*

the opposite is **disobedient**

obey *verb*: **obeys, obeyed, obeying, has obeyed**
You **obey** someone when you do what they tell you to do: *The soldiers obeyed the order and began to fire.*

the opposite is **disobey**

object *noun*: **objects**
An **object** is a thing that you can see and touch: *There were lots of strange objects on the table.*

'**ob**-jekt'

object *verb*: **objects, objected, objecting, has objected**
You **object** to a person or thing when you say that you dislike them or don't agree with them: *I object to that sort of behaviour in public.* ❑ *I objected to Paul being there, so he left the room.*

'ob-**jekt**'

obvious *adjective*
Something that is **obvious** can be clearly seen or understood: *It was obvious that she was*

unhappy. ❑ *There is no obvious reason why this should happen.*

occasion *noun*: **occasions**
1 An **occasion** is a particular time when something happens: *I've met him on several occasions.*
2 An **occasion** is a special event: *It must be a special occasion — he's wearing a tie.*

occasional *adjective*
Occasional things don't happen regularly or often: *They made occasional trips to London.*

occasionally *adverb*
Occasionally means 'not regularly' or 'not often': *Occasionally, we go and stay with our friends in France.*

occupation *noun*: **occupations**
A person's **occupation** is their job: *'What is your occupation?' 'I'm a teacher.'*

occupy *verb*: **occupies, occupied, occupying, has occupied**
1 Something that **occupies** a space fills it: *The bookcase will occupy all of this wall.*
2 A seat in a cinema or a toilet **is occupied** when someone is using it: *Excuse me, is this seat occupied?*
3 People **occupy** a house or a building if they live or work there: *Our old house is now occupied by a young couple.* ❑ *Their office occupies the first floor of the building.*
4 You **occupy** yourself or your time when you keep busy: *After*

lunch, he occupied himself with the garden.

occur *verb*: **occurs, occurred, occurring, has occurred**
Something **occurs** when it happens: *The explosion occurred just after midnight.*

ocean *noun*: **oceans**
An **ocean** is one of the five large areas of sea in the world: *The west coast of the USA is on the Pacific Ocean and the east coast is on the Atlantic Ocean.*

❝o-shun❞

o'clock
You use **o'clock** after a number to give the hour: *The train leaves at ten o'clock.* □ *'What time did you get home?' 'After eight o'clock.'*

> ▸ You do not use **o'clock** when you are talking about a time that is a certain number of minutes before or after the hour.

October *noun*
October is the tenth month of the year, between September and November: *We had snow last October.*

odd *adjective*: meanings 1 and 2: **odder, oddest**
1 Something that is **odd** is strange: *His behaviour was rather odd today.*
2 Two things are **odd** if they do not make a pair: *He's wearing odd socks.*
3 Odd is also used to describe numbers that cannot be divided by 2, such as 3, 21 and 101.

meaning 3: the opposite is **even**

of *preposition*
1 You use **of** to show a connection between two things or groups: *I can't find the lid of this box.* □ *She's a good friend of mine.* □ *one of our greatest poets.*
2 Of also means 'showing': *This is a photograph of my husband.*
3a Of means 'containing' or 'made from': *He gave me a bunch of flowers.* □ *a bag of sweets* □ *a band of gold.* **b** You also use **of** to give an amount or measurement of something: *a kilo of tomatoes* □ *twenty litres of petrol.*
4a Of is used to show what something is about: *the story of his life.* **b** You also use **of** to show the cause of something: *He died of hunger and cold.*
5 Of is also used in descriptions: *A boy of twelve* □ *a man of great courage.*

off *adverb and preposition*
1a Off means away from a place or position: *She took off her jacket.* □ *Take your shoes off.* □ *He marched off down the road.* □ *Fiona took all the books off the shelf and put them in a box.* □ *The elephant had broken branches off the tree.* □ *My hat blew off.* **b** You are **off** somewhere when you are leaving to go there; you say someone is **off** somewhere when they are away at that place: *Where are you off to?* □ *I'm off to work now.* □ *He's off visiting friends in Canada.*
2 Off also means 'out of a vehicle': *The bus stopped and everyone got off.*
3 A light, machine or engine is **off** when the power that makes it work is not on: *Remember to switch off all the lights.* □ *Is the cooker off?* □ *He stopped the car and turned the engine off.*

4 Someone is **off** when they are not at work or school: *He's got a cold and will be off school today.* ❑ *I'm taking two weeks off.*

5 Food goes **off** when it goes bad: *I think this milk's gone off.*

6 An event is **off** if it has been cancelled: *The match is off because it's raining.*

7 **Off** is used to show that something is done completely: *Have you finished off your essay yet?* ❑ *We've paid off our loan.*

offend *verb*: **offends, offended, offending, has offended**
Someone **offends** you when they say or do something that upsets you: *The TV programme offended a lot of people.*

offer *verb*: **offers, offered, offering, has offered**
1 You **offer** someone something when you ask them if they would like it: *She offered me some more tea.*
2 You **offer** to do something when you say that you will do it: *He offered to help me carry the bags.*

office *noun*: **offices**
1 An **office** is a building or a set of rooms where people do work for a business: *We have modern new offices in the city centre.*
2 Someone's **office** is the room where they work: *I had to see my boss but she wasn't in her office.*

officer *noun*: **officers**
1 An **officer** in the army is a person who is in charge of ordinary soldiers.
2 A police **officer** is a policeman or policewoman: *A police officer arrived moments later.*

often *adverb*
1 **Often** means 'many times': *I often go to work by bike.*
2 You use **often** to ask questions about the number of times something happens: *How often do you go to the dentist?*

same as **frequently**

oh
People often say '**oh!**' when they are surprised or annoyed by something: *Oh look, there's Helen.* ❑ *Oh no, I've forgotten my keys.* ❑ *Oh, you frightened me!*

oil *noun*
1 **Oil** is a thick dark liquid that is found under the ground, and is used as a fuel.
2 **Oil** is also a kind of liquid fat that is used in cooking: *vegetable oil.*

OK or **okay**
1 You say **OK** when you agree, or you want to say yes: *'Do you want to meet me outside the restaurant?' 'OK, see you about 8 o'clock.'*
2 **OK** also means 'all right': *You don't look well — do you feel okay?* ❑ *Do I look OK in this dress?*

old *adjective*: **older, oldest**
1 An **old** person or animal has lived for a long time: *The old man walked slowly across the road.*
2 **Old** objects were made a long time ago: *He collects old books.*
3 You say something is **old** if it is not used any more: *I threw my old watch away and bought a new one.*
4 You use '**old**' when you are talking about someone's age: *How*

old is Emma? □ *I'm twenty years old.*

---

meaning 1: the opposite is
young
meanings 2 and 3: the opposite
is **new**

---

on *preposition and adverb*
1 On means 'supported by',
'covering', or 'attached to': *The
books are on the bottom shelf.*
□ *She has a scarf on her head.*
□ *Can you see that bird on the
fence?* □ *a cake with candles on it*
□ *There's a picture hanging on the
wall.* □ *Remember to stick a stamp
on the enevelope.*
2 On is also used to talk about
the place where a moving thing
stops: *I stepped on a pin.* □ *He
put the plates on the table.* □ *The
cups fell on the floor.* □ *The bird
landed on my finger.* □ *She
climbed on to the roof.*
3a You get **on** a bus or train when
you go inside it: *Paul and I get on
the train at the same station.*
b You are **on** a horse, bicycle or
motorbike when you are riding it.
4 You are **on** a part of your body
when your weight is supported by
that part: *The baby had turned on
to its side.* □ *She was on her
knees, praying.*
5 You put clothes **on** when you
cover your body with them; you
have something **on** when you are
wearing it: *He put his coat and
hat on.* □ *They had long white
dresses on.*
6a Something is **on** paper or
some other material when it is
printed, drawn or written there:
*The map of India is on the next
page.* □ *I can't see her name on
the list.* **b** Information is **on**

computer, or **on** file, when it is
stored in a computer or in a file.
7 A book or talk is **on** a certain
subject if it is about that subject:
*Do you think I'll find something on
fishing in the library?*
8 You are **on** a journey when you
are travelling somewhere: *Did
you stop anywhere on your way
home?*
9 You use **on** to describe the
position of a building in a road,
or to describe certain other
places: *The house is on the main
street.* □ *There are no people on
the island.* □ *He lives on a farm.*
10 A machine is **on** when it is
working; you switch it **on** when
you press the switch that makes it
start working: *The lights were all
on, but there was no-one at home.*
□ *Turn the oven on.*
11 A television programme is **on**
when it is being broadcast; a film,
play or other show is **on** when it
is being shown or performed:
What's on after the news? □ *There's
a new film on at the cinema.*
12 Something goes **on** when it
continues; you go or keep **on** with
something when you continue it:
*The bad weather went on for
months.* □ *Keep on studying and
you'll do well in your exams.*

▷ **and so on**
You use **and so on** at the end of
a list to show that there is more
of the same kind of thing: *He's
got a cold — a sore throat, a sore
head and so on.*

▷ **on and on**
Something goes **on and on**
when it continues for a very long
time: *His talk was interesting at
first, but it went on and on.*

once *adverb*
1 Something happens **once** when it happens one time: *We go to the theatre once a week.* ❑ *He did it only once.*
2 Once also means 'at some time in the past': *We once had a dog called Snowy.* ❑ *There were once three cinemas in the town; now there is only one.*

▷ **all at once**
1 All at once means 'all at the same time': *The snake swallowed the frog all at once.*
2 All at once also means 'suddenly': *All at once, there was a loud knock at the door.*

▷ **at once**
Something that happens **at once** happens immediately: *He did what she asked at once.* ❑ *Come here at once!*

once *conjunction*
Once means 'as soon as' or 'when': *Once John arrives, we can leave.*

one *noun and adjective*: **ones**
1 One is the number or figure 1: *Seven plus one is eight.*
2 One is the time of 1 o'clock: *The shop closes at one.*
3 One is also the age of one; someone who is **one** is one year old: *She's one tomorrow.*

▷ **one or two**
You use **one or two** to mean 'a few' or 'not many': *There are one or two words here that I don't understand.*

one *determiner*
One means one in number: *The chocolate cost one dollar.* ❑ *There was one big window and two smaller windows.*

one *pronoun*: **ones**
1 You use **one** to talk about a single person or thing, especially when it has already been mentioned: *I've found the history book, but I can't find the maths one.* ❑ *I like both dresses but I think I'll wear the black one.* ❑ *Which one is your brother?* ❑ *I prefer the red one.* ❑ *'I'm looking for two men.' 'We're not the ones you're looking for.'*
2 You also use **one** to talk about a single person or thing as a member of a group: *He's one of my friends.* ❑ *Can I have one of your chocolates?*
3 You can use **one** to talk about people in general, in a very formal way: *One must try not be rude to others.* ❑ *One can see the mountains from here.*

▷ **one another**
People and animals do something to **one another** when they do it to each other: *They talked to one another all through the film.*

▷ **one by one**
One by one means 'one after the other': *He ate all the sweets one by one.* ❑ *People were coming through the gates one by one.*

onion *noun*: **onions**
An **onion** is a round vegetable with a thin brown skin and a very strong taste and smell.

only *adjective*
Someone or something is the **only** one if there are no others of the same type: *He's the only person in the room with dark hair.*

only *adverb*
1 Only means 'not more than': *There are only three biscuits left.* ❑ *He only lives a mile away.*
2 Only also means 'just, and

nothing else': *I was only trying to help.*

open *adjective*
1 Something is **open** when it not closed: *The shop is open on Sundays.* □ *I'm cold; is the window open?*
2 Something is **open** when it is not covered: *an open car.*

open *verb*: **opens, opened, opening, has opened**
1 You **open** a door or a window when you move it into a position so that it is no longer closed: *Would you open the window, please?*
2 A shop or other business **opens** when it is ready for customers to come in and buy things: *What time does the shop open?*

the opposite is **close** or **shut**

operate *verb*: **operates, operated, operating, has operated**
1 You **operate** a machine when you make it work: *How do you operate this computer?*
2 A machine **operates** when it works: *This fridge isn't operating properly.*
3 Doctors **operate** when they cut into a patient's body and repair or remove a damaged part: *The doctor operated on the man's heart.*

opposite *preposition*
One thing is **opposite** another when it is facing it: *The bank is opposite the library.* □ *He is sitting opposite Howard.* □ *North is opposite south, and east is opposite west.*

opposite *adjective*
1 The **opposite** side of

something is the other side of it: *Jane was on the opposite side of the street.* □ *He was walking along the opposite bank of the river.*
2 Opposite also means 'completely different': *They walked off in opposite directions.*

opposite *noun*: **opposites**
One thing is the **opposite** of another if it is completely different from it: *Hot is the opposite of cold.*

or *conjunction*
1 You use **or** when you want to say that something else is possible: *We could go tonight or tomorrow.*
2 Or also means 'because if you don't': *You must get up now or you'll be late for work.*

orange *noun and adjective*: **oranges**
1 An **orange** is a fruit with a thick skin and a sweet taste.
2 Orange is also the colour of this fruit, between red and yellow: *Her dress is orange.* □ *an orange scarf.*

orchestra *noun*: **orchestras**
An **orchestra** is a large group of musicians who play instruments together: *Her brother plays the violin in the school orchestra.*

ʻor-kes-traʼ

order *noun*: **orders**
1 An **order** is an instruction to do something: *The soldier was given the order to shoot.*
2 An **order** is also a request for something to be sent to you: *The waiter came to take our order.*
3 The **order** of things is the arrangement that they are put in, one after the other: *Do you know*

the order of letters in the English alphabet?

▷ **in order to**
You use **in order to** when you are talking about why something is done: *He had to lie on his stomach in order to get through the narrow gap.*

▷ **out of order**
A machine that is **out of order** is not working: *The notice on the bathroom door read 'out of order'.*

order *verb*: **orders, ordered, ordering, has ordered**
1 You **order** someone to do something when you instruct them to do it: *The doctor ordered her patient to rest for a few days.*
2 You **order** food in a restaurant when you choose it and ask for it: *We both ordered fish.*
3 You **order** goods when you ask a company to send them to you: *I ordered some magazines from the newsagent.*

ordinary *adjective*
Something is **ordinary** when it is normal and not very special: *His parents are both famous actors, but mine are just ordinary.* ▫ *It was an ordinary Monday morning when he phoned with the good news.*

organ *noun*: **organs**
1 An **organ** is a part of your body that has a special purpose: *Eyes are the organs that we use to see.*
2 An **organ** is also a musical instrument with keys like a piano: *He plays the organ in the church.*

organization *noun*: **organizations**
An **organization** is a group of people who work together for a purpose: *He's the boss of a huge organization.*

organize *verb*: **organizes, organized, organizing, has organized**
1 You **organize** something when you arrange and prepare it: *We've organized a surprise party for his birthday.*
2 You also **organize** something when you put it into order: *He organized all the papers on his desk.*

orphan *noun*: **orphans**
An **orphan** is a child whose parents are both dead: *He's been an orphan since his parents died in a car crash.*

'or-fan **'**

other *determiner and pronoun*
1 Other people or **other** things are people or things that are not the ones you are talking about: *Apart from me, there were five other customers in the shop.*
2 You use **other** when you are talking about the second of two people or things: *Where's my other shoe?*
3 The **others** are the rest of the people or things in a group: *Michael and the others are going to be late.*

ouch
You say '**ouch!**' when someone or something has hurt you: *Ouch! That really hurt.*

ought *verb*
You say someone **ought** to do something if you think they should do it: *You ought to invite Mary to the party; she doesn't know many people.*

ounce *noun*: **ounces**
An **ounce** is a unit of measurement of weight, equal to about 28 grams: *You need five ounces of flour to make this cake.*

▸written **oz** for short

our *determiner*
Our means 'belonging to us': *Our dog is called Maya.*

▸This is **our** garden.
▸The car isn't really **ours**.

ours *pronoun*
Ours means 'belonging to us': *The house on the corner is ours.*

ourselves *pronoun*
1 You use **ourselves** to show that you and others are affected by your own actions: *We bought ourselves a new car.* ❑ *We really enjoyed ourselves at Dave's party.*
2 'We did it **ourselves**' means 'we did it without any help': *We painted the whole flat ourselves.*

out *adverb*
1 You go **out** when you leave a place so that you are no longer inside it: *He went out of the room.* ❑ *It was too hot inside the room and I had to get out.*
2 You are **out** when you are not at home or at your place of work: *I came to visit you last night but you were out.*
3 **Out** also means 'from inside': *I lifted the puppy out of his basket.* ❑ *She took her diary out of the drawer.*
4 A light is **out** if it is not shining: *All the lights were out, so I thought they were in bed.*
5 A book, newspaper or magazine comes **out** when you can buy it: *Is his new book out yet?*

6 The tide is **out** when the water in the sea is at its lowest level.
7 **Out** is also used with words like 'speak', 'call', and 'cry' to show that the sound can be heard clearly.
8 **Out** also means 'completely': *You look tired out.*

outdoor *adjective*
Outdoor describes things that are outside, or that happen outside: *an outdoor swimming pool.*

the opposite is **indoor**

outdoors *adverb*
Outdoors means 'outside': *We spent all of our holiday outdoors.*

the opposite is **indoors**

outer *adjective*
1 **Outer** means 'on the outside': *The outer walls of the building need to be painted.*
2 **Outer** also refers to the part that is furthest from the centre or the middle: *He lives in outer London.*

the opposite is **inner**

outfit *noun*: **outfits**
An **outfit** is a set of clothes: *She bought a new outfit for the wedding.*

outside *preposition and adverb*
a Someone or something goes **outside** when they go out of a room or a building: *We all went outside to look at the sunset.*
b Someone or something is **outside** when they are in the open: *Johnny is outside in the garden.* ❑ *He was standing outside the gate.*

the opposite is **inside**

outside *noun*
The **outside** of something is the outer surface of it: *The outside of the house is painted red.*

the opposite is **inside**

outside *adjective*
1 Outside is used to describe things that are on the outer surface, or that are not in the main part of a building: *an outside toilet.*
2 Outside is also used to describe people or things that are not part of your group: *We got outside help because we couldn't do the work ourselves.*

the opposite is **inside**

oval *adjective*
Oval objects are shaped like an egg, but flat: *an oval mirror.*

oven *noun*: **ovens**
An **oven** is the part of a cooker inside which food is cooked or baked: *The instructions said: 'Cook the bread in a hot oven for twenty-five minutes'.*

over *preposition and adverb*
1 One thing is **over** another if it is higher than it: *We hung the painting over the fire.* ❑ *The helicopter flew over our heads.*
2 One thing is **over** another thing if it covers it: *Nick fell asleep on the floor, so we put a blanket over him.*
3a One thing goes **over** another when it moves from one side of that thing to the other side of it: *He jumped over the stream.*
b Over also means 'across': *He came over to talk to me.*
4 Something is **over** an amount or number when it is more than it: *The whole thing cost over £10.*

❑ *He must be over eighty years old.*
5 Over also means 'during': *Over the years it's changed from a little village to a city.*
6 Something that is **over** is finished: *The match was over in a couple of hours.*

overflow *verb*: **overflows, overflowed, overflowing, has overflowed**
Liquid **overflows** when it has reached the top of a container, and it begins to spill over the sides: *We had so much rain last week that the river overflowed.*

overhead *adjective and adverb*
Overhead means above your head: *There are overhead wires along the street.* ❑ *A plane was flying overhead.*

overseas *adverb*
Overseas means 'abroad': *Mrs Smith has gone overseas on business.*

owe *verb*: **owes, owed, owing, has owed**
You **owe** someone money when you have borrowed it from them and you have not yet paid it back: *I owe my dad $5.*

rhymes with **no**

owl *noun*: **owls**
An **owl** is a bird that has a round flat face, a curved beak and large eyes, and usually hunts at night.

owl

own *determiner and pronoun*
Your **own** things are things that belong to you and to no-one else: *He has his own computer.* ❑ *I have my own car.* ❑ *My friend lent me his pen because I've lost my own.*

▷ **on your own**
1 You are **on your own** when you are alone: *I'll be on my own this evening — everyone is going out.*
2 You do something **on your own** when you do it without any help: *I had to move the furniture on my own.*

own *verb*: **owns, owned, owning, has owned**
You **own** something if it belongs to you: *They own their home but we rent ours.* ❑ *Who owns that dog?*

owner *noun*: **owners**
The **owner** of an animal or thing is the person who owns it: *Are you the owner of that flat?*

ox *noun*: **oxen**
An **ox** is a bull; oxen are often used to pull carts and ploughs.

Pp

pace *noun*
The **pace** of something is the speed at which it happens: *Machines often work at a faster pace than human beings.*

▷ **keep pace with**
You **keep pace with** someone when you move forward at the same rate as them: *He couldn't keep pace with the other children and got left behind.*

pack *noun*: **packs**
1 A **pack** is a bag that is carried on the back: *They had enough food in their packs for several days.* ❑ *Two ponies carried the packs up the mountain.*
2 A **pack** of cards is a set of playing cards: *How many tens are there in a pack of cards?*

pack *verb*: **packs, packed, packing, has packed**
1 You **pack**, or you **pack** a bag, when you put things in a bag before you go on a journey: *We spent the day packing.* ❑ *Did you pack this bag yourself, sir?*
2 People or things **are packed** into a place when there is very little space between them: *The shops were packed with people.* ❑ *The fish are packed tightly into tins.*

package *noun*: **packages**
A **package** is something that has been prepared for posting: *A man on a motorbike delivered a package to the office.*

packet *noun*: **packets**
A **packet** is small container

made of thin plastic or paper: *Are there any biscuits left in that packet?* ❑ *a packet of tea.*

pad *noun*: **pads**
A **pad** is a number of sheets of paper stuck together along one edge: *Can I have a sheet of paper from your drawing pad?*

paddle *noun*: **paddles**
A **paddle** is a short light oar, used to push a small open boat through the water.

paddle *verb*: **paddles, paddled, paddling, has paddled**
1 You **paddle** a boat when you use a paddle to make it move: *We had to paddle very fast to make the boat go forward.*
2 You **paddle** when you walk in shallow water, especially at the edge of a lake or the sea: *The smaller children were paddling in the sea.*

page *noun*: **pages**
A **page** is one side of a sheet of paper in a book, newspaper or magazine: *How many pages are there in this dictionary?* ❑ *The story was on the front page of today's newspaper.* ❑ *Open your books at page 123.*

paid *verb*
see **pay**: *I think you paid too much for that ticket.* ❑ *He paid the bill and left the restaurant.*

pain *noun*: **pains**
1 You feel **pain** when something hurts you, or you are injured: *He's broken his ankle and he's in a lot of pain.*

2 A **pain** is a unpleasant feeling that you get in part of your body when you have been hurt or are ill: *She had a pain in her stomach.* ❑ *The pains in his chest were getting worse.*

painful *adjective*
Something that is **painful** causes pain: *Is your back still painful?* ❑ *That cut on your finger looks very painful.*

painless *adjective*
Something that is **painless** does not cause pain: *If the dentist gives you an injection, having a tooth out should be painless.*

paint *noun*: **paints**
1 Paint is a liquid that you put on to surfaces to cover or colour them: *You can use this brush to paint the walls.* ❑ *What colour paint are you going to put on the front door?*
2 Paints are coloured materials that you use to colour pictures with: *We bought him a box of paints for his birthday.*

paint *verb*: **paints, painted, painting, has painted**
1 You **paint** a surface when you cover it or decorate it using paint: *I painted the garden gate.*
2 You **paint** when you make a picture using paints: *Most children like to draw and paint pictures.*

painter *noun*: **painters**
1 A **painter** is a person whose job is to paint the walls inside and outside buildings: *The house will look much better when the painters have finished.*
2 A **painter** is also an artist who paints pictures: *Her father was a successful painter.*

painting *noun*: **paintings**
A **painting** is a picture made using paints: *We went to look at the paintings in the Louvre.*

pair *noun*: **pairs**
1 A **pair** is two things of the same kind that are used together: *a pair of shoes* ❑ *I got three new pairs of socks for my birthday.* ❑ *a pair of earrings.*
2 A **pair** also refers to certain things that are made up of two parts: *a pair of scissors* ❑ *a pair of pants* ❑ *two pairs of trousers.*
3 A **pair** of people or animals is two people or animals that are together: *two pairs of dancers* ❑ *a pair of pigeons, one male and one female* ❑ *The children discussed the problem in pairs.*

palace *noun*: **palaces**
A **palace** is a large house where a king, queen or president lives: *The president of France lives in the Elysée Palace.*

pale *adjective*: **paler, palest**
1 Pale colours are not bright or dark: *a pale pink rose* ❑ *The walls were painted pale green.*
2 Your skin goes **pale** when it has less colour than usual, because you are ill or have had a shock: *You look pale. Are you feeling all right?* ❑ *His face went pale with fright when he saw the animal.*

meaning 1: the opposite is **dark**

painters

palm *noun*: **palms**
1 The **palm** of your hand is the inside surface of your hand between your wrist and your fingers: *I held the baby bird in the palm of my hand.* ❑ *Moira held out her palm.*
2 A **palm** is a tall tree that grows in warm countries; palms have long pointed leaves growing from the top of the trunk: *a coconut palm* ❑ *date palms.*

'pahm'

palm

palm

pan *noun*: **pans**
A **pan** is a round metal container with a handle, used for cooking food in: *Put the rice and water in a pan and cook it for fifteen minutes.*

pane *noun*: **panes**
A **pane** of glass is one of the flat sections of glass fitted into a window or door: *The windowpanes were covered with ice.*

pant *verb*: **pants, panted, panting, has panted**
A person or animal **pants** when they breathe very quickly through their mouth: *The dogs were panting in the heat of the sun.*

pants *noun*
1 Pants are a piece of clothing that you wear to cover your bottom, under your other clothes: *Don't forget to pack six pairs of socks and pants.*
2 In North America, people call

trousers **pants**: *He put his wallet in the back pocket of his pants.*

paper *noun*: **papers**
1 Paper is a material made in thin sheets, used for writing and drawing on, and wrapping things: *a sheet of paper* ❑ *a paper bag* ❑ *a paper handkerchief* ❑ *a parcel wrapped in brown paper.*
2 A **paper** is a newspaper: *He buys a paper every morning.* ❑ *The story was in the local paper.*

parade *noun*: **parades**
A **parade** is a large number of people or vehicles moving slowly along, usually to celebrate an event: *We watched the parade of athletes at the opening ceremony of the games.*

paragraph *noun*: **paragraphs**
A **paragraph** is a section of writing made up of several sentences, with the first sentence starting on a new line: *Begin a new paragraph when you start writing about another subject.*

parcel *noun*: **parcels**
A **parcel** is something that has been wrapped up so that it can be carried or posted: *The postman delivered a parcel this morning.* ❑ *What's in that big brown parcel?*

pardon *noun*
'**Pardon?**' is a word you use when you want to ask someone to repeat something.

▷ **I beg your pardon**
You say **I beg your pardon** to someone when you want to apologize politely for something you have done, or for not having heard what they said: *I beg your pardon. I didn't realize you were on the telephone.*

same as **excuse me**

parent *noun*: **parents**
Your **parents** are your mother and your father: *His parents died when he was a baby.* ❑ *Parents are welcome to come and meet the teachers.*

park *noun*: **parks**
A **park** is a large public piece of land in a town or city; people walk, sit and play in parks: *Dad takes the dog for a walk in the park every morning.*

park *verb*: **parks, parked, parking, has parked**
You **park** a vehicle when you stop it somewhere and leave it there: *You'll have to move your motorbike. You can't park it here.* ❑ *There were ten police cars parked outside the house.*

parrot *noun*: **parrots**
A **parrot** is a bird with a thick curved beak. Some parrots can learn to imitate human speech.

part *noun*: **parts**
1 The **parts** of something are the bits or pieces that it is made up of: *Your feet, hands and head are all parts of your body.*
❑ *Which part of the country do you come from?* ❑ *The second part of the exam was very difficult.*
2 A **part** is also one of the people that an actor plays in a play or film: *He's had parts in several successful films.*

▷ **play a part**
1 People **play a part** when they act one of the parts in a play or film: *Jack is playing the part of Macbeth in the school play.*
2 You **play a part** in a group activity when you do something

to make it happen: *This man didn't play any part in the robbery.*

▷ **take part**
You **take part** in an activity when you are involved in it: *Some of them refused to take part in the strike.*

part *verb*: **parts, parted, parting, has parted**
1 To **part** something is to divide it so that it forms two separate sections: *Her hair was parted in the middle.* ❑ *He parted his lips, but didn't speak.*
2 People or things **part**, or **are parted**, when they go away from each other: *We parted at the station.* ❑ *The puppies were parted from their mother after a month.*

▷ **part with**
You **part with** something when you give it away or sell it: *She doesn't want to part with the dog.*

particular *adjective*
A **particular** person or thing is one that you identify as different from people or things in general: *This particular washing machine uses less water than other models.* ❑ *Do you want to speak to any particular person in the office?*

particularly *adverb*
Particularly means 'especially' or 'more than usual': *It was particularly cold that morning.* ❑ *'Did you enjoy the party?' 'Not particularly. I didn't know anyone there.'*

partner *noun*: **partners**
1 Partners are two people who do something together: *Some people came to the dance without partners.*
2 In business, a **partner** may be

one of a group of more than two people or companies working together: *This is Peter, one of my business partners.*

3 Your **partner** is also your husband, wife, girlfriend or boyfriend.

party *noun*: **parties**
A **party** is an event where people meet to celebrate something, or to enjoy themselves together: *When I was a student I went to lots of parties.* ❑ *Are you having a birthday party this year?*

pass *noun*: **passes**
1 A **pass** is a successful result in an examination: *Did you get a pass in your English test?*
2 A **pass** is also a ticket that shows that you have permission to enter a building or to travel free: *The guard at the gate asked to see our passes.*

meaning 1: the opposite is a **fail**

pass *verb*: **passes, passed, passing, has passed**
1 Someone or something **passes** you when they go past you: *He passed me in the corridor.* ❑ *Do you pass the school when you're driving to work?* ❑ *If you're passing a letter box would you post this letter for me, please?*
2 Someone or something **passes** you when they come from behind you and move in front of you: *A lorry tried to pass me as I was driving round the corner.*
3 To **pass** also means to move along or through: *You have to pass along a dark corridor to get to the rooms at the other end of the building.* ❑ *We passed through several pretty little villages.*

4 You **pass** something to someone else when you hand it to them: *Could you pass me the butter, please?* ❑ *The boy passed the note to his friend at the desk behind him.*
5 You **pass** when you get a successful result in a test or an examination: *You're a good driver now. You'll pass your driving test easily.*
6 Time **passes** when it goes by; you do something to **pass** the time when you occupy yourself by doing that thing: *When you are young, time seems to pass very slowly.* ❑ *We played games to pass the time until lunch was ready.*

meaning 5: the opposite is **fail**

▷ **pass on**
You **pass** something **on** when you give it or teach it to other people.

passenger *noun*: **passengers**
A **passenger** is a person travelling in a vehicle who is not the driver or pilot: *This bus carries 50 passengers.*

passport *noun*: **passports**
A **passport** is a small book with a person's name, description and photograph; you need a passport for travelling to foreign countries: *We had to show our passports before we could cross the border into China.*

past *preposition and adverb*
1 You go **past** someone or something when you move towards them and go beyond them: *Children waved to us as we drove past.*
2 One place is **past** another when it is beyond that other

place: *Our house is just past the station.*

3 A number of minutes **past** the hour is that number of minutes after the hour: *It happened at five minutes past twelve.* ❑ *'What time is it?' 'It's past midnight.'*

past *noun*

The **past** is the time before the present: *In the past, more people lived in the countryside than in the city.*

the opposite is the **future**

past *adjective*

1 Past describes things that belong to the time before the present: *In times past, it took much longer to travel from one place to another.*

2 You also use **past** to talk about any period of time, such as a minute, an hour or a day, just before now: *I've been waiting here for the past two hours.*

pasta *noun*

Pasta is a food made from a mixture of flour, eggs and water, cut into various shapes.

paste *noun*

Paste is soft wet stuff of various kinds; paste is used for cleaning things or sticking paper: *Mix the flour and water until it forms a sticky paste.* ❑ *I need a new tube of toothpaste.*

pastime *noun*: **pastimes**

A **pastime** is an activity that you enjoy doing when you are not at work: *Reading is one of my favourite pastimes.*

pastry *noun*: **pastries**

1 Pastry is a food made from flour, fat and water; it is used to make pies and tarts: *Bake the*

pastry in a hot oven. ❑ *Put the meat and vegetables in a dish and cover them with a layer of pastry.*

2 A **pastry** is a cake made with sweet pastry: *This shop sells delicious cakes and pastries.*

pat *verb*: **pats, patted, patting, has patted**

You **pat** someone or something when you to hit them gently with your hand, in a friendly way: *The boy was patting the dog when it bit him.* ❑ *My mother patted me on the shoulder and I woke up.*

path *noun*: **paths**

A **path** is a narrow way that you can walk along: *When you walk through the forest, try to stay on the path.* ❑ *He was running down the garden path towards us.*

patience *noun*

Someone who has **patience** can wait for a long time, or can do something for a long time, without complaining: *You need to have a lot of patience to teach young children.* ❑ *After three hours he lost patience and went home.*

patient *adjective*

A **patient** person or animal has a lot of patience: *You won't have to wait much longer. Try to be patient.* ❑ *The old horse was very patient, letting the children climb on its back.*

patient *noun*: **patients**

A **patient** is a person who is being treated by a doctor or dentist: *Most of the doctor's patients are old people and children.*

pattern *noun*: **patterns**

A **pattern** is a design on cloth, paper or some other material: *I* *like the colour of this material, but I don't like the pattern.* ❑ *The curtains had a pattern of leaves and flowers.*

pause *verb*: **pauses, paused, pausing, has paused**
You **pause** when you stop doing something, or stop speaking, for a short time: *He had to pause several times during his speech.*

‘ **pawz** ’

pavement *noun*: **pavements**
A **pavement** is a path with a hard surface along the side of a road or street: *Please do not ride your bicycle on the pavement.*

paw *noun*: **paws**
The feet of certain animals, such as dogs, cats, lions and bears, are called **paws**: *The lion had a thorn in one of its paws.*

pay *verb*: **pays, paid, paying, has paid**
1 You **pay** for something when you give money for it: *How much did you pay for the meal?* ❑ *They pay all their bills at the end of each month.* ❑ *Will you be paying in cash or by cheque?* ❑ *He works very hard, but he isn't paid very much.*
2 You **pay** attention to someone or something when you give that person or thing your attention: *You should pay more attention when you're driving.*
3 You **pay** someone a visit when you visit them: *Mary paid me a visit last week.*

▷ **pay back**
You **pay back** money you have borrowed when you return it to the person who lent it to you: *Will you lend me $10? I'll pay you back on Friday.*

payment *noun*: **payments**
A **payment** is an amount of money that is paid: *He makes regular monthly payments.*

pea *noun*: **peas**
Peas are very small round green vegetables: *The rice is mixed with peas and mushrooms and then fried.*

peace *noun*
1 People or countries are at **peace** with each other when they are not at war: *There has been peace between the two countries for fifty years.*
2 Peace is also a period when nothing disturbs you and you feel quiet and calm: *They go away to the country every weekend to get some peace.* ❑ *He said that he wanted some peace to do some studying.*

meaning 1: the opposite is **war**

peaceful *adjective*
A place is **peaceful** when it is quiet and calm and there is no noise: *The house always seems very peaceful when the children have gone to school.*

peanut *noun*: **peanuts**
A **peanut** is a small brown nut that grows in a shell under the ground: *In winter, people often feed wild birds with peanuts.*

pear *noun*: **pears**
A **pear** is a sweet fruit that is round at the bottom and narrow at the top. It has green or yellow skin and juicy pale yellow flesh.

peck *verb*: **pecks, pecked, pecking, has pecked**
A bird **pecks** when it strikes something with its beak: *The chickens were pecking at the*

ground searching for insects and worms.

pedal *noun*: **pedals**
A **pedal** is the part on a bicycle or a piano that you press with your foot: *This bicycle is too big. His feet don't reach the pedals.* ❑ *You can make the piano sound louder by pressing this pedal.*

pedal *verb*: **pedals, pedalled, pedalling, has pedalled**
You **pedal** a bicycle when you make it move forwards by pressing down on the pedals: *I can't pedal very fast on this hill.*

pedestrian *noun*: **pedestrians**
A **pedestrian** is a person who is walking along a road or a street: *The lorry ran on to the pavement and knocked down three pedestrians.*

pedestrian crossing *noun*: **pedestrian crossings**
A **pedestrian crossing** is a place on a street marked with lines, where traffic must stop to allow pedestrians to cross.

peel *noun*
Peel is the skin that you take off certain fruits such as oranges, and certain vegetables such as potatoes.

peel *verb*: **peels, peeled, peeling, has peeled**
You **peel** fruit and vegetables, such as oranges, apples, potatoes and onions, when you pull or cut the skin off: *Nina was peeling the potatoes for the evening meal.*

peg *noun*: **pegs**
1a A **peg** is a short piece of wood or metal used to fasten one thing to another: *They used wooden pegs to fasten the tent to the ground.* **b** A **peg**, or a clothes **peg**, is a wooden or plastic object that you use to fasten wet clothes to a line.
2 A **peg** is also a hook on a wall or a door: *The children each had a peg to hang their coat on.*

pen *noun*: **pens**
A **pen** is a long thin object filled with ink; it is used to write with: *This pen has run out of ink. Can I borrow yours?*

pencil *noun*: **pencils**
A **pencil** is a long thin piece of wood with a hard black or coloured material running through the centre; you use a pencil for writing or drawing: *Write your essay in ink, not in pencil.* ❑ *You need a sharp point on your pencil for drawing the details.*

people *noun*
People are men, women and children: *How many people live in Singapore?* ❑ *He's one of those people who always arrive an hour late.*

pepper *noun*: **peppers**
1 Pepper is a spice made from the dried, hot-tasting berries of the pepper plant; pepper is used to season food: *Did you remember to put salt and pepper in the soup?*
2 A **pepper** is a shiny oval vegetable that is green, yellow, red or orange in colour: *For lunch we had peppers stuffed with rice.*

perfect *adjective*
1 Something that is **perfect** has no faults: *Don't worry if you make mistakes. Nobody's perfect.*
2 A **perfect** thing is just right, or the best of its kind: *It is a perfect day for lying on the beach.*

perform *verb*: **performs, performed, performing, has performed**
1 You **perform** when you entertain an audience by acting, dancing, singing or playing a musical instrument: *I don't like performing in public because I get too nervous.*
2 You **perform** something when you do it or carry it out: *Sometimes they perform fifteen operations in one day.*

performance *noun*: **performances**
A **performance** is the performing of something, especially for an audience: *This is the first performance of his new play.*

perfume *noun*: **perfumes**
1 Perfume is a liquid that people, especially women, put on their skin to make it smell nice: *What's that perfume you're wearing? It smells lovely.*
2 A **perfume** is a pleasant smell: *The garden was filled with the perfume of roses.*

perhaps *adverb*
Perhaps means 'maybe' or 'it is possible that': *Perhaps we should put on our coats.* ❑ *Mr Lee hasn't arrived yet. Perhaps his car's broken down again.*

period *noun*: **periods**
1 A **period** is a certain length of time: *a long period of hot weather* ❑ *It was during this period that he painted the famous 'Guernica'.*
2 In schools, a **period** is the time given to a lesson in a particular subject: *We have four periods of English each week.*

permission *noun*
Someone gives you **permission** for something when they say you are allowed to do it: *Ask your manager for permission before you take a day off.* ❑ *He borrowed my bike without my permission.*

permit *verb*: **permits, permitted, permitting, has permitted**
To **permit** something is to allow someone to do it: *Smoking is not permitted.* ❑ *The farmer doesn't permit camping on his land.*

same as **allow**
the opposite is **forbid**

person *noun*: **people**
A **person** is a man, woman or child: *He's the kindest person I have ever met.* ❑ *There's enough space for one more person.*

personal *adjective*
Personal means belonging to you, or about you and no-one else: *These are my personal things; please don't touch them.* ❑ *She asked me a lot of personal questions.*

personality *noun*: **personalities**
Your **personality** is the way you behave, and the sort of person you are: *She has a very cheerful personality.*

persuade *verb*: **persuades, persuaded, persuading, has persuaded**
You **persuade** someone to do something when you make them do it by arguing with them and advising them: *Her father tried to persuade her to stay at home for another year.*

'per-**swayd** '

pest *noun*: **pests**
A **pest** is a creature such as a rat

or a mosquito, that is harmful to people, animals, plants or things: *This beetle is a serious pest in areas where potatoes are grown.*

pet *noun*: **pets**
A **pet** is a tame animal that you keep in your home: *The children want a pet.* ❑ *We went to the pet shop to buy a kitten.*

petal *noun*: **petals**
The **petals** on a flower are the coloured parts that open out: *The colours of the petals attract insects.*

petrol *noun*
Petrol is a liquid fuel for cars and other vehicles: *The petrol tank is nearly empty.*

> ▸ In North America, **petrol** is called **gas**.

> ▸ Remember that the letters '**ph**' at the beginning of the following words are pronounced '**f**'.

phone *noun*: **phones**
A **phone** is a telephone: *Is that the phone ringing?*

‘**fone** ’

phone *verb*: **phones, phoned, phoning, has phoned**
You **phone** someone when you dial their telephone number so that you can talk to them: *Remember to phone your mother on Saturday.*

phone

photo or **photograph** *noun*: **photos** or **photographs**
A **photo**, or a **photograph** is a picture taken with a camera: *Do you have any photos of yourself as a child?* ❑ *We took a lot of photographs when we were in Bali.*

‘**foe**-toe ’, ‘ **foe**-te-graf ’

phrase *noun*: **phrases**
A **phrase** is a group of words, which together have a meaning; a phrase can be used on its own or as part of a sentence.

‘ **fraze** ’

piano *noun*: **pianos**
A **piano** is a large musical instrument with a row of white keys and a row of black keys; you press the keys down with your fingers: *Can you play the piano?* ❑ *He started taking piano lessons when he was five.*

piano

pick *verb*: **picks, picked, picking, has picked**
1 You **pick** someone or something when you choose them: *She always picks the chocolates with the soft centres.* ❑ *They never pick him to play in the football team.* ❑ *We were told to pick a book from the school library.*
2 You **pick** fruit or flowers when you take them from the plant they are growing on: *She picked flowers from the garden to decorate the house.* ❑ *The fruit isn't ready for picking yet.*

▷ **pick up**
1 You **pick** something **up** when you lift it: *The children had to pick up their toys.* ❑ *We picked up the boxes and carried them outside.*
2 You **pick** someone or something **up** when you go and collect them from somewhere: *Will you pick me up from the station at five o'clock, please?* ❑ *He's gone to the post office to pick up his mail.*
3 You **pick** something **up** when you learn it without being taught: *She just picked it up, watching other people do it.*
4 You **pick** yourself **up** when you stand up again after you have fallen: *At first he fell off his horse quite often, but he always picked himself up and got on again.*

picnic *noun*: **picnics**
A **picnic** is a meal that you take with you and eat outside: *It's a beautiful day. Let's have a picnic on the beach.* ❑ *We filled the picnic basket with sandwiches and fruit.*

picture *noun*: **pictures**
1 A **picture** is a drawing or painting: *This picture was painted by a French artist called Degas.*
2 A **picture** is also a photograph: *Will you take a picture of me in the garden?* ❑ *That's a good picture of you.*

pie *noun*: **pies**
A **pie** is a kind of food made with pastry, with meat, vegetables or fruit inside: *My mother bakes delicious apple pies.* ❑ *He made a pie with the meat from yesterday's dinner.*

piece *noun*: **pieces**
1 A **piece** is a part of something:
It looks like a piece from a car's engine. ❑ *Jill was doing a jigsaw with 2000 pieces.*
2 A **piece** is also a bit of something: *I'd like another piece of apple pie, please.* ❑ *She wrote my address on a piece of paper.* ❑ *Be sure to pick up all the pieces of broken glass.* ❑ *a piece of clothing.*
3 A **piece** is also one of the objects that you move around the board in games such as chess.

pier *noun*: **piers**
A **pier** is a long platform made of stone, metal or wood; it is built from the shore into the water on a lake or by the sea: *There were a few people fishing from the end of the pier.*

rhymes with **ear**

pig *noun*: **pigs**
A **pig** is an animal with a fat body, short legs, a short curly tail, and a large nose which is round and flat at the end. People keep pigs for their meat which is called pork, ham or bacon.

pig

pile *noun*: **piles**
A **pile** is a number of things lying on top of each another, or a heap of stuff such as earth or sand; you put things in a **pile** when you place them one on top of the other: *Vic cut up the wood and put it in a pile by the back door.* ❑ *There were piles of books lying all over the floor.*

pile *verb*: **piles, piled, piling, has piled**
You **pile** things somewhere when you put them one on top of the other to form a pile, you **pile** something **up** when you make a heap with it: *Jenny took the books off the shelves and piled them in a corner.* ❑ *The men were piling the earth up around the edge of the hole.*

pill *noun*: **pills**
A **pill** is medicine in a hard, round form that you swallow: *These pills will make your headache go away.* ❑ *He has to take three different kinds of pills every day.*

pillow *noun*: **pillows**
A **pillow** is a soft cushion that you rest your head on, especially when you are in bed: *These pillows are filled with feathers.* ❑ *A pillowcase or pillowslip is a cover that you put on a pillow.*

pilot *noun*: **pilots**
A **pilot** is a person who flies an aircraft: *a helicopter pilot* ❑ *The pilot sits in a compartment at the front of the aeroplane.*

pin *noun*: **pins**
A **pin** is a short thin piece of metal with a sharp point at one end; pins are used for holding pieces of cloth or paper together: *The hem was held up with pins.* ❑ *Put a pin in each corner of the poster.*

pin *verb*: **pins, pinned, pinning, has pinned**
You **pin** something, or you **pin** it **up**, when you fasten or fix it to something using pins: *He pinned a notice to the door.* ❑ *Before you sew the hem, pin it up.*

pinch *verb*: **pinches, pinched, pinching, has pinched**
1 Someone **pinches** you when they squeeze your flesh between their thumb and first finger: *He smiled at me and pinched my cheek in a playful way.*
2 '**Pinch**' sometimes means 'steal': *Someone's pinched my ruler again!*

pineapple *noun*: **pineapples**
A **pineapple** is a large fruit with rough brown skin and juicy yellow flesh. Pineapples grow on low plants, in hot countries.

pineapple

pink *noun and adjective*: **pinks**
Pink is a colour between red and white: *The little girl wore a pretty pink dress.* ❑ *As the sun went down the clouds turned pink.* ❑ *She had been running, and her cheeks were a bright pink.*

pint *noun*: **pints**
A **pint** is a unit for measuring liquids, equal to about half a litre: *Two pints of milk, please.*

pipe *noun*: **pipes**
1 A **pipe** is a long metal or plastic tube through which water, oil or gas is carried: *There's a leak in this pipe.*
2 A **pipe** is also a narrow tube with a small bowl at the end, used for smoking tobacco: *The old men were sitting in the shade smoking their pipes.*

pitch *noun*: **pitches**
A **pitch** is a large field with lines marked on it, used for playing

games such as football and hockey: *The crowd cheered when the teams came on to the pitch.*

pity *noun*

1 You feel **pity** for someone when you have a feeling of sadness because they are suffering: *When he saw the starving people he was filled with pity.*

2 You say 'it's a **pity**' or 'what a **pity**' when something makes you a little sad: *It's a pity the sun isn't shining — we wanted to sit in the garden today.* ❑ *'I've broken my favourite vase!' 'Oh, what a pity!'*

place *noun*: **places**

1 A **place** is a certain spot or area, or a certain town or city: *Is this the place where the accident happened?* ❑ *It's one of those places where there are a lot of mosquitoes.* ❑ *Salesmen often have to travel from place to place.* ❑ *This is one of the coldest places on Earth.*

2 A person's or a thing's **place** is the space where they belong: *I'll have to find another place for this book.* ❑ *We all took our places and the parade started moving down the street.*

3 A **place** is also a seat for one person: *Are there any places left on the 6 o'clock train?*

4 Your **place** in a race or competition is your position in it: *The German athlete finished the race in second place.* ❑ *He was in last place until the end of the race.*

▷ **all over the place**
Things are **all over the place** when they are scattered across a certain area: *The beach was very dirty, with rubbish all over the place.*

▷ **in place**
Something is **in place** when it is where it fits or belongs: *All the furniture is back in place and we can use the room again.*

▷ **out of place**
Someone or something is **out of place** when they do not fit or belong somewhere: *He felt out of place in jeans, when everyone was wearing suits.* ❑ *Someone has moved the books; they're all out of place.*

▷ **take place**
Something **takes place** when it happens: *When did the first robbery take place?*

place *verb*: **places, placed, placing, has placed**
You **place** something somewhere when you put it there: *Vases of flowers were placed in all the bedrooms.* ❑ *She placed her hand on his shoulder.*

plain *adjective*: **plainer, plainest**

1 Plain things have no pattern on them, or are simple in shape and design: *She was wearing a plain black skirt.* ❑ *This wallpaper is too plain — I'd prefer one with a pattern on it.* ❑ *Her wedding ring was a plain gold band.*

2 Plain also means ordinary and not special in any way: *I like plain food without too many spices.*

3 Something that is **plain** is easy to understand or see: *She made it quite plain that she didn't like the new house.* ❑ *It was plain that he wasn't happy.*

plan *noun*: **plans**

1 A **plan** is an idea about how to do something, or a drawing showing how something will be

done: *If my plan works, we will be rich.* ❑ *I think it would be a better plan to go home by train.* ❑ *He's made a plan of the new garden.*
2 Plans are arrangements to do something: *We don't have any holiday plans this year.* ❑ *They were going to the beach but the rain spoiled their plans.*

plan *verb*: **plans, planned, planning, has planned**
1 You **plan** something when you decide how you will do it: *They've been planning the trip for three months.*
2 You **plan** to do something when you think about how or when you will do it: *When do you plan to visit Hong Kong again?* ❑ *I'm planning to tell him the news tomorrow night.*

plane *noun*: **planes**
A **plane** is an aeroplane: *In Australia, some doctors visit their patients by plane.* ❑ *The plane crashed, killing everyone on board.*

planet *noun*: **planets**
A **planet** is a huge round object in space that moves round the sun or another star: *Which two planets are closest to the Earth?* ❑ *The planet Pluto was discovered in 1930.*

plank *noun*: **planks**
A **plank** is a long flat piece of wood: *These planks are five centimetres thick and two metres long.* ❑ *They made a bridge over the stream using a plank of wood.*

plant *noun*: **plants**
A **plant** grows in the ground and has roots, a stem and leaves: *flowering plants* ❑ *These plants grow well in strong sunlight.*

plant *verb*: **plants, planted, planting, has planted**
You **plant** a seed or a young plant when you put it in the ground so that it will grow: *I'm going to plant some potatoes.* ❑ *Plant the seeds about five centimetres apart.*

plastic *noun*
Plastic is a light strong material that is made from oil; it is used for making many different objects: *This window isn't glass — it's made of clear plastic.* ❑ *When we go camping we use plastic cups and plates.* ❑ *Are these pipes made of plastic or metal?*

plate *noun*: **plates**
A **plate** is a flat dish used for serving food: *Mary laid the table with plates, cups, glasses and knives and forks.* ❑ *The waiter dropped a plate of vegetables on the floor.* ❑ *The hole was the size of a large dinner plate.*

platform *noun*: **platforms**
1 A **platform** is a raised area from where people can be seen by an audience: *When the president got on to the platform the crowd cheered.*
2 A **platform** is also a raised area beside the railway line at a railway station where passengers get on and off trains: *The train to London will be leaving from Platform 6.* ❑ *The platform was crowded with people waiting for the next train into Tokyo.*

play *verb*: **plays, played, playing, has played**
1 You **play** a game when you take part in it: *He plays golf every Sunday.* ❑ *Do you play chess?* ❑ *The boys were playing football*

in the street.
2 Children **play** when they have fun with toys or when they enjoy themselves by running, climbing, or pretending to be different people: *The baby was playing with his toes.* ❑ *He likes playing with his toy cars.* ❑ *Let's play soldiers.*
3 You **play** a musical instrument when you make music with it: *I'm learning to play the guitar.* ❑ *Kurt was playing a tune on the piano.*
4 You **play** records, tapes or CDs when you listen to them: *They always play my favourite tunes on that radio programme.*
5 An actor **plays** a part when he or she acts in a play or film: *Who would like to play the part of the king?*

play *noun*: **plays**
A **play** is a story written for acting and performing in a theatre, or on television, or on the radio: *William Shakespeare wrote more than thirty plays.* ❑ *There's a new play on television tonight.*

player *noun*: **players**
A **player** is a person who takes part in a game: *Pelé was one of the world's greatest football players.* ❑ *Tennis is a game for two or four players.*

playful *adjective*
Playful means 'liking to play' or 'having fun': *The baby monkeys are very playful and spend a lot of time swinging from branches.* ❑ *He jumped round me like a playful puppy.*

playing card *noun*: **playing cards**
Playing cards are cards with pictures and numbers on them used for playing various games.

There are usually 52 cards in a pack.

pleasant *adjective*
Someone or something that is **pleasant** is nice: *He's a very pleasant young man.* ❑ *On a hot day like this, it's pleasant to sit in the shade.* ❑ *There was a pleasant breeze blowing from the sea.*

the opposite is **nasty** or **unpleasant**

please *adverb*
1 You say **please** when you are asking politely for something: *Please may I have some more cake?* ❑ *Would you close the door when you go out, please?* ❑ *Please take a seat.* ❑ *May I speak to the manager, please?*
2 You also use **please** when you are accepting something that someone has offered to you: *'Would you like some more coffee?' 'Yes, please.'*

▸When you want to show that you do not want something that someone has offered you, you say 'No, **thank you**.'

please *verb*: **pleases, pleased, pleasing, has pleased**
1 Something **pleases** you when it makes you happy or satisfied: *Andrew worked very hard at college to please his parents.* ❑ *She's one of these people who is very difficult to please.*
2 You do what you **please**, or you **please** yourself, when you do what you want to do, even though other people want something different: *He always does what he pleases and doesn't care if he hurts my feelings.* ❑ *'I don't want to go for a walk.'*

'Please yourself, but we are all going.'

pleased *adjective*
Someone is **pleased** when they are happy or satisfied: *'I got the job.' 'I'm so pleased.'* ◻ *His teachers are very pleased with his progress.* ◻ *I'm pleased to welcome you all to Scotland.*

pleasure *noun*
You feel **pleasure** when you have a feeling of happiness or satisfaction: *'Thank you very much for helping me.' 'It was my pleasure.'* ◻ *Gardening gives them a lot of pleasure.*

plenty *noun*
When there is **plenty** of something there is enough of it, or more of it than is needed: *You've still got plenty of time to decide.* ◻ *There's plenty of food for everyone.* ◻ *'Do you need some more money?' 'No thanks, I've got plenty.'*

plough *noun*: **ploughs**
A **plough** is a tool with a large heavy metal or wooden blade that is used on farms to break up the soil: *On modern farms, ploughs are usually pulled by a tractor.*

rhymes with **cow**

plough *verb*: **ploughs, ploughed, ploughing, has ploughed**
Farmers **plough** when they break up the soil using a plough: *We ploughed these fields in spring.*

plug *noun*: **plugs**
1 A **plug** is a small plastic box at the end of an electric wire. It has two or three metal pins that connect it to the electricity supply: *You'll have to change the plug on your hairdryer before you*

go abroad.
2 A **plug** is also a small round piece of rubber that you put over the hole in a washbasin, sink or bath to keep the water in.

plum *noun*: **plums**
A **plum** is a small oval fruit with dark red or yellow skin, and a stone in the middle: *There are lots of plums on the tree in our garden.* ◻ *plum jam.*

plumber *noun*: **plumbers**
A **plumber** is a person whose job is to fit and mend pipes in houses and other buildings: *One of the water pipes was leaking and we had to call a plumber.*

'**plum**-er'

plural *noun*: **plurals**
The **plural** of a word is the form you use to talk about more than one: *The plural of 'mouse' is 'mice', but the plural of 'house' is 'houses'.* ◻ *The words 'men', 'women' and 'children' are all plurals.*

plus *preposition and adjective*
1 You use **plus** when you are adding one number to another: *Two plus two equals four.*
2 **Plus** is also used to describe a number or a grade that is slightly higher than the figure or letter given with it: *Jason got a B plus for his English essay and Marjorie got a B.*

pocket *noun*: **pockets**
A **pocket** is an extra piece sewn on to a piece of clothing with an opening along one edge; you can put things in it: *He was leaning against the wall with his hands in his pockets.* ◻ *This jacket doesn't have any pockets.* ◻ *He put the letter in his pocket and forgot about it.*

poem *noun*: **poems**
A **poem** is a piece of writing arranged in lines, often with words that rhyme at the end of each line: *We had to learn a poem every week.* ❏ *He sent her a card with a love poem written in it.*

poet *noun*: **poets**
A **poet** is a person who writes poems: *Keats and Shelley are two of the most famous English poets.*

poetry *noun*
Poetry is poems in general: *My sister writes poetry.* ❏ *Do you like modern poetry?*

point *verb*: **points, pointed, pointing, has pointed**
1 You **point** at or to something when you show something by stretching your first finger in that direction: *The little girl pointed at the doll she wanted.* ❏ *Point to the place that hurts.*
2 You **point** a weapon when you aim it in a certain direction: *You shouldn't point a gun at anyone — it's dangerous.*
3 Something **points** in a certain direction when that is the direction it goes in: *The needle points north.* ❏ *Plant the bulbs with the narrow end pointing down.*

▷ **point out**
You **point** something **out** when you show it to people, or bring it to their attention: *Can you point him out in this photo?* ❏ *She pointed out that she was not a child any more.*

point *noun*: **points**
1 A **point** is the sharp end of something such as a pin or a knife: *Make sure you've got a good point on your pencil.* ❏ *He*
was cleaning his fingernails with the point of his knife.
2 A **point** is also a particular place or spot, or a particular time: *Standing at this point, you can see the whole town below you.* ❏ *From that point we were friends again.*
3 A **point** is also one mark that is scored in a game, test or examination: *The German tennis player won the next six points.* ❏ *You get two points for each correct answer.*
4 Something has a **point** when there is a purpose or reason for doing it: *Is there any point in waiting here?*

pointed *adjective*
A **pointed** object has a sharp end: *He was wearing a funny pointed hat.* ❏ *A pointed piece of metal tore a hole in my sleeve.*

poison *noun*: **poisons**
Poison is anything that can kill or harm people or animals if it gets into their bodies: *They used arrows with poison on the tips.*

poisonous *adjective*
Something that is **poisonous** contains poison: *The leaves of this tree are very poisonous.*

poke *verb*: **pokes, poked, poking, has poked**
You **poke** something when you press your finger into it, or you push a sharp object into it: *He poked himself in the eye by accident.* ❏ *Dad poked a stick down the blocked pipe.*

pole *noun*: **poles**
A **pole** is a long thin piece of wood or metal: *The flag was tied to a pole at the back of the boat.*

❏ *The athletes use a long pole to push themselves off the ground.*

police *noun*: **police**
The **police** are the men and women whose job it is to make sure that people are protected from crime, and that people obey the law: *Call the police — I've been robbed!* ❏ *He wants to join the police when he leaves school.*

policeman or **policewoman** *noun*: **policemen** or **policewomen**
A **policeman** or **policewoman** is a member of the police: *My dad is a policeman.*

police station *noun*: **police stations**
A **police station** is a building where the police work and where they take people they have arrested.

polish *noun*
Polish is stuff that you rub on to things to make them shine: *This isn't furniture polish — it's shoe polish.*

polish *verb*: **polishes, polished, polishing, has polished**
You **polish** something when you rub it to make it shine: *These are the brushes we use to polish our shoes.* ❏ *He washes and polishes his car once a week.*

polite *adjective*
People who are **polite** have good manners and are not rude: *It's polite to wait until everyone's finished before you leave the table.* ❏ *He's a very polite young man.*

the opposite is **impolite** or **rude**

politely *adverb*
Politely means 'in a polite way'.

pond *noun*: **ponds**
A **pond** is a small area of still water: *There was a pond in the middle of the village where the animals went to drink.*

pony *noun*: **ponies**
A **pony** is a kind of small horse.

pool *noun*: **pools**
1 A **pool** is an area of still or slow-moving water: *When the tide went out, pools were left amongst the rocks.*
2 A small area of liquid lying on a surface is also called a **pool**: *There was a pool of blood on the floor where he had cut his foot.*
3 A **pool** is also a swimming pool: *The children spent all day playing in the pool.*

poor *adjective*: **poorer, poorest**
1 Poor people or countries have very little money: *Rich countries should do more to help poorer countries.* ❏ *They were so poor they couldn't afford shoes.*
2 You also use **poor** to describe someone or something that you feel pity for: *That poor dog is tied up all day long.* ❏ *He's lost his mother, the poor little thing.*
3 Something that is **poor** is not good: *Bats have poor sight but very good hearing.* ❏ *That was a very poor result for our team.*

meaning 1: the opposite is **rich** or **wealthy**

pop or **pop music** *noun*
Pop or **pop music** is modern music that is liked by a lot of people, especially young people: *We went to a pop concert in the park.*

popular *adjective*
Popular people or things are

liked by a lot of people: *He was very popular at school.* ❑ *This island is a popular place to come on holiday.*

pork *noun*
Pork is the meat of a pig: *We had roast pork for dinner.*

port *noun*: **ports**
A **port** is a place beside the sea where ships can stop; goods are loaded and unloaded, and passengers get on and off boats at a port: *The ship sailed into port.* ❑ *The ferry sails to a port on the west coast of Denmark.*

same as **harbour**

position *noun*: **positions**
1 The **position** of something is the place where it is: *From the sun's position in the sky we knew it was about midday.* ❑ *Is this piece of furniture in the best position?*
2 You are sitting, standing, or lying in a certain **position** when you have put your body that way: *He was lying in a very uncomfortable position.*

possible *adjective*
1 Something that is **possible** can be done: *Is it possible to fly from Singapore to Los Angeles?* ❑ *It won't be possible to get back home in time for dinner.*
2 Something is **possible** when it may be so or may happen: *It's possible that he didn't get your letter.*

meaning 1: the opposite is **impossible**

post *noun*: **posts**
1 The **post** is the system of collecting, carrying and delivering letters and parcels; the **post** is also the letters and parcels that are sent by this system: *The books I ordered will be delivered by post.* ❑ *Has the morning post come yet?* ❑ *He always gets a lot of post.*
2 A **post** is a pole fixed in the ground: *He kicked the ball between the posts.* ❑ *She was looking at the sky when she walked into a lamp-post.*

meaning 1: same as **mail**

post *verb*: **posts, posted, posting, has posted**
You **post** a letter or parcel when you send it by post: *I asked Elizabeth to post some letters for me.* ❑ *The letter was posted in Cairo ten days ago.*

postage *noun*
Postage is the money you pay for sending a letter or parcel by post: *Is the postage the same for Switzerland as it is for France?*

postcard *noun*: **postcards**
A **postcard** is a small piece of card, often with a picture on one side, that you sent by post: *Write your answer on a postcard and send it to the BBC.* ❑ *When we were on holiday we sent postcards to all our friends at home.*

poster *noun*: **posters**
A **poster** is a large notice that you can stick on a wall: *There were posters all over the town advertising the pop concert.*

postman *noun*: **postmen**
A **postman** is a person whose job it is to deliver letters and parcels: *Our postman usually delivers our mail at about eight o'clock in the morning.*

pot *noun*: **pots**
1 A **pot** is a deep container used

for cooking things in: *The stew was cooked in a pot over the fire.*
2 A **pot** is also a container with a handle, a lid and a part shaped for pouring, for holding tea or coffee: *Is there any more tea in the pot?*
3 A **pot** is also a container that a plant is grown in: *flower pots.*

potato *noun*: **potatoes**
A **potato** is a round or oval vegetable that grows in the ground. It has thin brown skin and white flesh. Potatoes can be boiled, roasted, baked or fried: *I had a baked potato with cheese for lunch.* ❑ *They eat potatoes nearly every day.*

pound *noun*: **pounds**
1 The **pound** is the main unit of money used in Britain: *How many dollars are there to a pound?* ❑ *This ring cost hundreds of pounds.*
2 A **pound** is also a unit of weight that is equal to 0.454 of a kilogramme: *'How much weight have you lost?' 'About ten pounds.'*

> ▸ meaning 1: The sign **£** is used to represent the unit of money; it is written before the number: *£100.*
> ▸ meaning 2: **pound** is often written **lb**.

pour *verb*: **pours, poured, pouring, has poured**
1 You **pour** a liquid when you make it flow out of a container: *Would you like me to pour the tea?*

pour

2 Liquid **pours** when it flows downwards in a stream: *Tears poured down her cheeks.*
3 You can say it **is pouring** when rain is falling very heavily: *We can't go out now; it's pouring.*

powder *noun*
Powder is stuff that is made up of very fine bits, like dust: *The spices are in the form of a very fine powder.*

power *noun*
1 Power is strength: *You need a lot of power in your muscles to lift heavy weights like these.*
2 Power is the energy that makes a machine or engine work: *electric power.*
3 Someone in a position of control has the **power** to do something when they are allowed by law to do it: *The police have the power to arrest you if you break the law.*

powerful *adjective*
Something that is **powerful** has a lot of strength or power: *He has powerful leg muscles.* ❑ *a powerful country.*

practice *noun*: **practices**
1 Practice is the act of doing something often so that you can do it better: *You need to do a lot of practice when you are learning to play the violin.*
2 A **practice** is a period spent practising: *We'll have one more practice on the afternoon before the show.*

practise *verb*: **practises, practised, practising, has practised**
You **practise** something when you do it again and again so that you get better at it: *Practise speaking English regularly.*

praise *verb*: **praises, praised, praising, has praised**
You **praise** someone or something when you say how good they are and how much you admire them: *Everyone praises her cooking.*

prawn *noun*: **prawns**
Prawns are small sea creatures with shells, long tails and lots of legs; you can cook them and eat them: *He made a prawn curry.*

prawn

pray *verb*: **prays, prayed, praying, has prayed**
People **pray** when they speak to God or a god, to ask for something, to show thanks or to ask to be forgiven: *She prayed every night, asking God to send her husband home safely from the war.*

prayer *noun*: **prayers**
A **prayer** is the words a person says when they pray: *The children said a prayer every night before they went to bed.*

precious *adjective*
Something that is **precious** is very valuable: *Gold and silver are precious metals.*

prefer *verb*: **prefers, preferred, preferring, has preferred**
You **prefer** something when you like it better, or want it more, than others: *Would you prefer coffee or tea?* ❑ *Which do you prefer — the red dress or the green one?* ❑ *He prefers to cook his own meals.*

prepare *verb*: **prepares, prepared, preparing, has prepared**

1 You **prepare** something when you make it ready: *Patsy was in the kitchen preparing supper.*
2 You **prepare** for something when you get ready for it: *He's preparing for his exams*

present *adjective*
1 Someone or something is **present** when it is in the place being talked about: *The poisonous gas is still present in the air.* ❑ *Were you present at this morning's lesson?*
2 Present is used to describe things that belong to the time that we are living in now: *The present arrangement suits us all very well.*

present *noun*: **presents**
1 A **present** is gift that you receive from someone, or give to someone: *Did John remember to buy you a birthday present?* ❑ *The money was a present from my father.*
2 The **present** is the time now, or the things that are happening now: *The story starts in the present, and ends five hundred years in the future.* ❑ *We are living in the present, not in the past, and not in the future.*

president *noun*: **presidents**
1 President is a title used for the leader of some countries: *Who is the president of Russia?* ❑ *President Clinton.*
2 A **president** is also the leader of a club or the head of a business: *My uncle is president of the local cricket club.*

press *verb*: **presses, pressed, pressing, has pressed**
1 You **press** something when you

push it: *Gerry pressed the bell several times.* ❑ *Something hard was pressing against my back.* ❑ *If you press this button the computer saves your work.*

2 You **press** clothes or material when you make them smooth using an iron: *I'll press these trousers for you.*

press *noun*
The **press** is the people who work for newspapers and other organizations that report news: *The press are outside, waiting for a statement.*

pretend *verb*: **pretends, pretended, pretending, has pretended**
1 You **pretend** to do something when you try to make people believe that you are doing it: *He was just pretending to be angry.* ❑ *She pretended to be asleep when her mother came into her bedroom.*

2 You **pretend** when you imagine to yourself that something is true for fun: *The little girl pretended the bath was a ship sailing on the sea.*

pretty *adjective*: meaning 1: **prettier, prettiest**
1 A **pretty** person or thing is attractive or nice to look at: *My sister was always much prettier than me.* ❑ *a pretty summer dress.*

2 You can use **pretty** in the same way as 'rather' or 'very': *It was pretty silly to take your hat and gloves off when it is so cold.* ❑ *It's a pretty good film.*

'prit-*ee* **'**

prevent *verb*: **prevents, prevented, preventing, has prevented**

To **prevent** something is to stop it happening: *Eat plenty of fruit to prevent colds.* ❑ *I tried to prevent him from going, but he went anyway.*

previous *adjective*
The **previous** thing is the one just before this one, or just before the one you have been talking about: *What did you do in your previous job?* ❑ *I'd met him the previous day.*

price *noun*: **prices**
The **price** of something is the amount of money it costs: *The farmers got high prices for their corn.* ❑ *What's the price of petrol here?*

prick *verb*: **pricks, pricked, pricking, has pricked**
Something with a sharp point **pricks** you when its point goes into your flesh: *She pricked her finger with a needle.*

pride *noun*
Pride is the feeling of being pleased with something you have done, or with the things that belong to you: *He spoke of his successes with pride.* ❑ *Lily thought with pride of her beautiful new flat.*

priest *noun*: **priests**
A **priest** is a man who teaches a certain religion and works in a church or temple.

print *verb*: **prints, printed, printing, has printed**
1 A book or paper **is printed** when its words are put on paper by a machine: *This book was printed in Singapore.*

2 You **print** words when you write them without joining each letter to the next one: *Print your name in ink at the top of the form.*

printer *noun*: **printers**
1 A **printer** is a machine that prints words: *The printer is linked to all the computers in the office.*
2 A **printer** is also a person or company that prints books or papers: *Is that book ready for the printer's yet?*

prison *noun*: **prisons**
A **prison** is a building where criminals have to live, locked in small rooms: *The robbers were sent to prison for ten years.* ❑ *Two dangerous criminals have escaped from the prison.* ❑ *Their father is in prison.*

prisoner *noun*: **prisoners**
1 A **prisoner** is someone who is in prison: *The prisoners were allowed to exercise in a small yard.*
2 An enemy in a war takes people **prisoner** when they catch them and don't allow them to return to their own side.

private *adjective*
Private things and places are for one person only, or for a small group of people: *The sign on the gate read 'Private. Keep Out.'* ❑ *The two men went into another room for a private conversation.*

the opposite is **public**

prize *noun*: **prizes**
A **prize** is a gift that you win in a competition or as a reward for good work: *Peter won second prize in the singing competition.*

probably *adverb*
You use **probably** when you think that something may happen, or has happened, or may

be true: *I'll probably finish work at about eight o'clock.* ❑ *'Are you going to the party?' 'Probably, but I'm not sure.'* ❑ *'Do you believe his story?' 'Well, it's probably true.'*

problem *noun*: **problems**
A **problem** is something that has gone wrong, or a difficult question that has to be solved: *There seems to be a problem with my computer — it isn't working properly.* ❑ *He loves solving problems.*

process *noun*: **processes**
A **process** is a series of stages that something passes through before it becomes something else: *The caterpillar goes through a long process before it becomes a butterfly.* ❑ *We studied the process for making a car.*

produce *verb*: **produces, produced, producing, has produced**
1 Things **are produced** when they are made in large numbers or amounts: *This factory produces television sets and computer screens.* ❑ *This part of the United States produces most of the grain in the country.*
2 You **produce** something when you take it out: *He produced a piece of paper from his pocket and started to read from it.*
 ❝pro-**djoos**❞

product *noun*: **products**
Products are things that are made or produced: *Japan sends products to all parts of the world.* ❑ *Gold is one of South Africa's most important products.*

profit *noun*: **profits**
A **profit** is the money you get when you sell something for

more than you paid for it: *If you buy something for $40, and you sell it for $50, the profit is $10.*

the opposite is **loss**

program *noun*: **programs**
A **program** is a set of instructions that a computer uses: *This program is used to design buildings and machines.*

programme *noun*: **programmes**
1 A **programme** is a show on television or on the radio: *There are some very good children's programmes on TV.*
2 A **programme** is also a printed piece of paper that gives you information about an event such as a concert: *There was a girl standing by the theatre door selling programmes.*

progress *noun*
You make **progress** when you go forward, or when you succeed in moving from one stage to the next: *There was a strong wind and the yachts made a lot of progress.* ❏ *All the children are making excellent progress at school.*

promise *verb*: **promises, promised, promising, has promised**
1 You **promise** to do, or not to do something when you say that you will, or will not do it: *I promised to be at their wedding.* ❏ *Do you promise not to tell anyone my secret?*
2 You **promise** something to someone when you say that you will give it to them: *He promised me a good meal in an expensive restaurant.*

promise *noun*: **promises**
You make a **promise** when you

promise to do, or not to do something: *He made a promise that he would never tell anyone about it.*

pronounce *verb*: **pronounces, pronounced, pronouncing, has pronounced**
The way you **pronounce** a word is the way you say it: *You pronounce 'threw' and 'through' in the same way.* ❏ *British and American people pronounce 'tomato' in different ways.*

pronunciation *noun*: **pronunciations**
The **pronunciation** of a word is the way people say it: *I don't know the pronunciation of this word.*

proof *noun*
Proof is information that shows that something is true: *We have no proof that there is life on other planets.* ❏ *The police didn't have enough proof to arrest the men.*

proper *adjective*
The **proper** way to do something is the right or correct way to do it; the **proper** place for something is the correct place for it: *Is this the proper way to hold chopsticks?* ❏ *Please put the books back in their proper place.*

properly *adverb*
Properly means 'in the right or correct way': *My hand hurts; I can't write properly.* ❏ *She didn't do the work properly.*

protect *verb*: **protects, protected, protecting, has protected**
To **protect** someone or something is to keep it safe from harm or danger: *You'll need sunglasses to protect your eyes.*

◻ *They are paid a lot of money to protect the president.*

same as **guard**

protest *verb*: **protests, protested, protesting, has protested**
You **protest**, or you **protest** against something, when you tell people that you do not like it or want it: *I didn't think it was right, so I protested.* ◻ *People gathered in the village to protest against the plans for a new road.*

proud *adjective*: **prouder, proudest**
1 You are **proud** of something you have done, or of things that belong to you, when you are pleased with them: *He's very proud of his new car.* ◻ *That was an excellent mark. You should be proud of yourself.* ◻ *If you win the competition, your family will be very proud.*
2 A **proud** person thinks they are better or more important than other people: *She's too proud to talk to us.*

prove *verb*: **proves, proved, proving, has proved**
You **prove** something when you show that it is true: *Can you prove that this man stole your wallet?* ◻ *It was proved that the disease was carried by insects.*

provide *verb*: **provides, provided, providing, has provided**
Someone or something **provides** you with what you need when they give it to you: *Cows provide us with milk.* ◻ *Books are not provided by the college.* ◻ *People work to provide themselves with the things they need.*

public *noun*
'The **public**' refers to people in general, rather than any group of people in particular: *The new library will be open to the public on Wednesday.* ◻ *The president spoke to the public in ten different cities this month.*

▷ **in public**
You do something **in public** when you do it in front of people, or in front of an audience: *She was never seen in public again.* ◻ *He's very shy and doesn't like speaking in public.*

public *adjective*
Public refers to things that can be used by all people: *You'll be able to get that information at the public library.* ◻ *He made the call from a public telephone in the street.*

the opposite is **private**

pudding *noun*: **puddings**
A **pudding** is a sweet food that you eat the end of a meal: *What's for pudding, Mum?* ◻ *She made a rice pudding.*

puddle *noun*: **puddles**
A **puddle** is a shallow pool of water lying on the surface of something: *The children enjoyed playing in the puddles.*

pull *verb*: **pulls, pulled, pulling, has pulled**
To **pull** something is to make it move by holding it and leaning away from it: *She pulled the door shut and locked it.* ◻ *An old donkey pulled the cart.*

the opposite is **push**

pump *noun*: **pumps**
A **pump** is a machine that forces air or liquid into, or out of something: *They used a pump to force water through the pipes.*

❏ *There's a pump at the garage for putting air into your tyres.*

pump *verb*: **pumps, pumped, pumping, has pumped**
Air or a liquid **is pumped** when it is forced somewhere by a pump: *Oil was pumped up from the bottom of the sea.* ❏ *The tyre was nearly flat and we had to pump some air into it.*

punch *verb*: **punches, punched, punching, has punched**
One person **punches** another when they hit them hard with their fist: *They punched him in the face and ran off with his money.*

punctuation *noun*
Punctuation is the name for marks such as full stops and question marks; you use punctuation when you are writing, to separate different parts of a sentence, or to show where a sentence ends.

punish *verb*: **punishes, punished, punishing, has punished**
You are **punished** when someone makes you suffer because you have done something wrong: *He was never punished for the crime.* ❏ *The teacher punished the boy for talking.*

punishment *noun*: **punishments**
A **punishment** is something done to punish someone: *Is prison the best punishment for this man?* ❏ *She had to stay at home all weekend as a punishment for lying.*

the opposite is **reward**

pupil *noun*: **pupils**
A **pupil** is a child or young person who learns from

someone: *Their school has more than 800 pupils.* ❏ *When he was a young man he became a pupil of Leonardo da Vinci.*

puppet *noun*: **puppets**
1 A **puppet** is a doll that can be moved by strings attached to parts of its body.
2 A **puppet** is also also a soft doll that fits over your hand.

puppy *noun*: **puppies**
A **puppy** is a baby dog: *Our dog has had puppies.*

pure *adjective*: **purer, purest**
1 Something that is **pure** is not mixed with anything else: *The walls in the temple were covered with pure gold.*
2 Something that is **pure** is clean and is not harmful: *Don't drink the water unless you are sure that it is pure.*

purple *noun and adjective*: **purples**
Purple is a dark colour between red and blue: *This plant has purple berries.* ❏ *The sky went a deep purple just before night fell.*

purpose *noun*: **purposes**
The **purpose** of something is the reason for doing it: *What's the purpose of this meeting?*

▷ **on purpose**
You do something **on purpose** when you mean to do it, rather than doing it by accident: *She broke that glass on purpose; it wasn't an accident.*

purse *noun*: **purses**
1 A **purse** is a small bag for holding money: *Someone stole her purse out of her handbag.*
2 In North America, a woman's handbag is called a **purse**: *She*

opened her purse and took out a notebook and pen.

push *verb*: **pushes, pushed, pushing, has pushed**
You **push** someone or something when you lean against them to make them move: *The car broke down and we had to push it.* ❑ *I was pushed forward by the crowd.* ❑ *He pushed the book across the table towards me.* ❑ *The doctor pushed the wheelchair along the corridor.*

push

the opposite is **pull**

put *verb*: **puts, put, putting, has put**
1 You **put** something somewhere when you place it there: *Where did you put my dictionary?* ❑ *I put it on the top shelf.* ❑ *You've put too much salt in this soup.* ❑ *Don't put that pencil in your mouth.* ❑ *He put his hand on my arm.* ❑ *She put the flowers in water.*
2a You **put** words on a page when you write them down: *Put your signature on this line.* **b** You **put** something in a certain way when that is how you say it: *I thought she put it very well; funny but not rude.*
3 You **put** a question or suggestion to someone when you ask or suggest it: *He said he would put my suggestions to the headteacher.*
4 You **put** time, money or energy into something when you spend

it doing that thing: *He puts most of his time into studying for his exams.*
5 Someone or something **puts** you into a good or bad mood when they make you feel that way: *Getting stuck in traffic always puts him into a bad mood.*

▷ **put away**
You **put** something **away** when you put it back in the place where it is usually kept: *They washed all the dishes and put them away in the cupboards.*

▷ **put down**
1 You **put** something **down** when you lay it somewhere: *Put that knife down — you might cut yourself!* ❑ *He put his suitcase down on the floor.*
2 You **put** something such as an idea **down** when you write it: *She put all her thoughts down in her diary.*
3 You **put** something **down** when you lower it: *When it stopped raining, they put their umbrellas down.*

▷ **put off**
1 You **put** something **off** when you delay doing it: *Several people couldn't come to the meeting so we had to put it off.*
2 You **put off** a light or machine when you switch it off so that it stops working: *Remember to put off all the lights when you go to bed.*

meaning 2: the opposite is **on** or **switch on**

▷ **put on**
1 You **put on** clothes when you dress yourself: *Are you going to put on that nice new dress you*

bought? □ *He's too young to put his shoes on by himself.*
2 You **put on** a light or a machine when you switch it on so that it begins to work: *He put on the TV to watch the football match.*

meaning 1: the opposite is **take off**
meaning 2: the opposite is **put off** or **switch off**

▷ **put up**
1 You **put up** something when you raise it: *The little boy put up his hand to get the teacher's attention.*
2 You **put** something **up** on a wall when you fix it to the wall: *They put our names and grades up on the wall.*
3 The cost of something **is put up** when it is increased: *The government promised that it would not put up taxes.*

puzzle *noun*: **puzzles**
1 A **puzzle** is a problem that makes you think very hard: *Trying to work out what had happened was a bit of a puzzle.*
2 A **puzzle** is also a game in which you have to fit a lot of pieces together: *One of his hobbies is doing puzzles.*

puzzle *verb*: **puzzles, puzzled, puzzling, has puzzled**
Something **puzzles** you when you find it difficult to understand: *His answer puzzled me.* □ *I was puzzled by the fact that there was no-one in the house.*

pyjamas *noun*
Pyjamas are a set of clothing made up of a shirt and trousers which you wear in bed: *a pair of striped pyjamas.*

'pa-**ja**-mas'

Qq

qualification *noun*: **qualifications**
A **qualification** is an exam you have passed or a skill that you have, that makes you suitable for a particular type of work: *My qualifications are not suitable for that job.* ❑ *It's difficult to get work without any qualifications.*

qualify *verb*: **qualifies, qualified, qualifying, has qualified**
1a You **qualify** as a doctor or a lawyer when you pass all the exams that are needed to do the job: *I qualified as a doctor on my thirtieth birthday.* **b** A person or team that **qualifies** for a competition reaches the standard necessary to take part in it: *We didn't qualify for the final.*
2 A skill or a test that you have passed **qualifies** you to do something when it allows you to do it: *This test qualifies you to drive a car, but not a lorry.*

quality *noun*: **qualities**
1 The **quality** of something is how good or bad it is: *The quality of her work is very high.*
2 Someone's **qualities** are the parts of their character that make them behave in a particular way: *Her best qualities are her kindness and honesty.* ❑ *What qualities make someone a good nurse?*

quantity *noun*: **quantities**
A **quantity** is an amount or number: *I've ordered a small quantity of paper.* ❑ *Elephants eat large quantities of grass and leaves.*

quarrel *noun*: **quarrels**
A **quarrel** is an argument: *They've had a quarrel and they're refusing to speak to each other.*

quarrel *verb*: **quarrels, quarrelled, quarrelling, has quarrelled**
You **quarrel** when you disagree with someone in an angry way: *We often hear them quarrelling next door.*

quarter *noun*: **quarters**
A **quarter** is one of four equal parts of something: *We cut the cake into quarters.*

▷ **quarter past**
The time is **quarter past** a particular hour when it is fifteen minutes after it: *Tell me when it's quarter past four.*

 quarter past four

▷ **quarter to**
The time is **quarter to** a particular hour when it is fifteen minutes before it: *We left at quarter to twelve.*

 quarter to twelve

quay *noun*: **quays**
A **quay** is the edge of a harbour, where ships are loaded or unloaded.

'key'

queen *noun*: **queens**
1 A **queen** is a woman who rules

a country: *The queen ruled the country for over 60 years.*
2 A **queen** is also the wife of a king: *The king and queen waved at the crowds.*

question *noun*: **questions**
1 You ask a **question** when you want to know something: *After the talk, some people asked questions.*
2 A **question** is a problem in an exam that you have to find the answer to: *I didn't have enough time to answer all the questions.*

question mark *noun*: **question marks**
A **question mark** is the mark (?) that you write after a sentence which is a question.

queue *noun*: **queues**
A **queue** is a line of people waiting for something: *There was a very long queue outside the cinema.*

'kjoo'

queue *verb*: **queues, queued, queuing, has queued**
People **queue** when they stand in a line waiting for something: *We had to queue for three hours to get the tickets.*

queue

quick *adjective*: **quicker, quickest**
1 Something is **quick** when it is fast: *He's the quickest worker in the factory.* □ *He gave her a quick*

smile. □ *We'll have to be quick — it's getting late.*
2 An activity is **quick** when it doesn't take a very long time: *What's the quickest way to get home?* □ *This recipe's quite quick to make.*

quickly *adverb*
Something happens **quickly** if it happens at great speed: *She drives too quickly for me.* □ *Come quickly! Someone's fallen in the river!*

quiet *adjective*: **quieter, quietest**
1a A place is **quiet** when there is no noise there: *It's very quiet in the library.* □ *He lives in a quiet little town on the coast.* **b** A machine is **quiet** when it does not make much noise: *I want a car with a quieter engine.*
2a People who are **quiet** don't talk much: *She's a shy quiet little girl.* **b** People become **quiet** when they stop talking or making a noise: *Please be quiet and listen to me.*

quilt *noun*: **quilts**
A **quilt** is a warm cover for a bed, filled with feathers or some other material.

quite *adverb*
1 Quite means 'rather': *It was quite windy last night.* □ *I'm quite hungry but I don't mind waiting.*
2 Quite also means 'completely': *I'm afraid I'm not quite ready.*

rhymes with **right**

quiz *noun*: **quizzes**
A **quiz** is a competition in which you have to answer questions on different subjects: *He took part in a quiz show on television.*

Rr

rabbit *noun*: **rabbits**
A **rabbit** is a small animal with soft fur and long ears: *He has two black and white rabbits which he keeps as pets.*

race *noun*: **races**
1 A **race** is a competition to find out which person, animal or vehicle is the fastest: *Who won the race?* ❑ *a horse race.*
2 A **race** of people is a particular group of people from a certain part of the world who have the same skin colour and features: *the African races.*

race *verb*: **races, raced, racing, has raced**
People, animals or vehicles **race** when they compete against each other to find out which is the fastest: *Come on, I'll race you to the door.* ❑ *The two cars were racing on the old road.*

racket or **racquet** *noun*: **rackets** or **racquets**
A **racket** is a type of bat. It has an oval-shaped head with strings across it, and a handle. Rackets are used to hit the ball in various sports: *a tennis racket.*

radio *noun*: **radios**
A **radio** is a device for listening to programmes which are being broadcast: *The whole family sat listening to the news on the radio.*

rag *noun*: **rags**
1 A **rag** is a piece of old cloth, especially one used for cleaning: *He cleaned his tools with an old rag.*

2 Rags are old torn clothes: *The children were dressed in rags.*

rage *noun*
You are in a **rage** when you are very angry: *He was in a terrible rage; shouting and asking for his money.*

rail *noun*: **rails**
1 The long steel bars which trains run on are called **rails**.
2 You travel by **rail** when you travel on a train: *He doesn't like flying, so he's going to London by rail.*
3 A **rail** is a bar that you can hold: *The old man held the rail as he walked down the steps.*
4 A **rail** is also a bar which you can hang things on: *a towel rail.*

railings *noun*
Railings are upright metal bars, used to make a fence: *The park was surrounded by railings.*

railway *noun*: **railways**
1 The **railway** is the business of running trains and carrying goods and passengers by rail: *My grandfather worked on the railway.*
2 A **railway** is the tracks on which trains run: *Their house looks on to the railway.*

railway station *noun*: **railway stations**
A **railway station** is a place where trains stop and where passengers get on and off.

rain *noun*
Rain is water which comes from clouds and falls on the ground in

drops: *We have had a lot of rain recently.*

rain *verb*: **rains, rained, raining, has rained**
It **rains** when drops of water fall from the clouds: *I think it's going to rain later.* ❑ *It rained all day.* ❑ *Look! It's raining again!*

rainbow *noun*: **rainbows**
A **rainbow** is the curved shape that you sometimes see in the sky when the sun comes out after a rain shower. Rainbows are made up of seven colours.

raincoat *noun*: **raincoats**
A **raincoat** is a waterproof coat which you wear to keep dry when it is raining.

raise *verb*: **raises, raised, raising, has raised**
1 You **raise** something when you lift it to a higher position: *If you agree, raise your hand.* ❑ *They used a special crane to raise the old boat out of the water.*
2 You **raise** something when you increase it: *The company promised not to raise its prices again.*

rake *noun*: **rakes**
A **rake** is a garden tool that is like a big comb with a long handle; it is used to gather leaves and make soil smooth.

ran *verb*
see **run**: *He ran all the way so he wouldn't be late.*

rang *verb*
see **ring**: *The telephone rang for a long time before anyone answered it.*

rare *adjective*: **rarer, rarest**
Something that is **rare** is very unusual: *There is a rare flower growing in the park.* ❑ *It's rare to*
find this type of butterfly in Britain.* ❑ *His visits are becoming rarer.*

the opposite is **common**

raspberry *noun*: **raspberries**
A **raspberry** is a small soft red fruit that grows on a bush: *We used the raspberries to make jam.* ❑ *a raspberry tart.*

rat *noun*: **rats**
A **rat** is an animal that looks like a large mouse, with a long tail and sharp teeth.

rate *noun*: **rates**
1 The **rate** at which something happens is the speed at which it happens: *We'll all have to work at a faster rate or we won't finish on time.*
2 The **rate** that you are paid is the amount of money you earn for a particular amount of work that you do.

rather *adverb*
1 Rather means 'quite' or 'a bit': *I'm rather tired.* ❑ *It was rather a long book.*
2 You use **rather** to say that you would prefer to do something: *I would rather have a cup of tea than a glass of wine.*
3 Rather also means 'instead of': *Would you like to go to the theatre rather than the cinema?*

rattle *verb*: **rattles, rattled, rattling, has rattled**
1 Something **rattles** when it makes a hard knocking sound: *The gate rattled in the wind.*
2 You **rattle** something when you shake it and produce a hard knocking sound: *He rattled the money box to find out if it was full.*

raw *adjective*
Food is **raw** when it hasn't been cooked: *You can eat most vegetables raw.*

ray *noun*: **rays**
Rays are bands of light or heat: *The rays of the sun shone through the window.*

razor *noun*: **razors**
A **razor** is a tool with a very sharp blade, used for shaving hair: *Andrew cut himself with his razor.*

reach *verb*: **reaches, reached, reaching, has reached**
1 You **reach** a place when you arrive there: *We reached Manchester by early morning.*
2 You can **reach** something if you can touch it: *I'm not tall enough to reach the top shelf.*
3 You **reach**, or **reach out** when you stretch out your arm to try and get something: *She reached out for a biscuit.*

react *verb*: **reacts, reacted, reacting, has reacted**
A person or thing **reacts** when they move or change because of something that has happened: *These sunglasses react to strong sunlight by getting darker.* □ *I knew he was unconscious because he didn't react when I pinched his arm.*

read *verb*: **reads, read, reading, has read**
1 You **read** when you look at printed words and you understand them: *He hasn't learnt to read yet.*
2 You also **read** when you look at printed words and say them aloud: *Everyone listened as the young boy began to read.*

3 A sign or a notice **reads** a particular piece of information when that is what is written on it: *The sign read 'No Smoking'.*

▸Note that in the present tense, **read** rhymes with 'seed'. In the past, **read** rhymes with 'head'.

reader *noun*: **readers**
A **reader** is someone who reads a lot, or someone who reads a particular newspaper: *He's not a keen reader — he prefers to watch television.* □ *This page is for readers' letters.*

ready *adjective*
1 You are **ready** to do something when you are prepared and can do it immediately: *Are we all ready to leave now?*
2 Something is **ready** when it can be used immediately: *When will dinner be ready?*
3 Someone is **ready** to do something when they are willing to do it: *I'm ready to help if you need me.*

real *adjective*
1 Someone or something is **real** if it exists: *Was he a real person, or just someone in a story?*
2 Something is **real** if it is natural: *This coat is made from real leather.*
3 **Real** also describes what is correct and true: *What's his real name?*

realize *verb*: **realizes, realized, realizing, has realized**
You **realize** something when you understand it: *I realized my mistake before it was too late.*

really *adverb*
1 **Really** means 'very': *I'm really tired; I think I'll go to bed.* □ *He*

got a really good mark in the exam.

2 Really also means 'in fact': *I know his story, but what really happened?* ❏ *Have you really met the president?*

3 You use '**really?**' to show surprise or shock: *'He's arriving this afternoon.' 'Really?'*

rear *noun*
The **rear** of something is the back part of it: *He entered by the door at the rear of the building.*

reason *noun*: **reasons**
The **reason** for something is the thing that made it happen: *What was her reason for being late?* ❏ *He gave no reason for his bad behaviour.*

receive *verb*: **receives, received, receiving, has received**
You **receive** something when you get it or you are given it: *Did you receive my letter?*

'ri-**seev** '

recent *adjective*
Recent describes things that happened a short time ago: *My job has changed a lot in recent months.*

recently *adverb*
Something that happened **recently** happened a short time ago: *Mark came to see me recently.*

recipe *noun*: **recipes**
A **recipe** is a set of instructions that you follow when you are cooking something: *Could you give me the recipe for your chocolate cake?*

'**res**-i-pi '

recite *verb*: **recites, recited, reciting, has recited**

You **recite** something when you say it aloud from memory: *He could recite the complete play.*

recognize *verb*: **recognizes, recognized, recognizing, has recognized**
You **recognize** a person or thing when you know them because you have seen or heard them before: *I thought I recognized your voice.* ❏ *Would you recognize the burglar if you saw him again?*

record *noun*: **records**
1 A **record** is a round, flat piece of black plastic that has sound recorded on it, especially music: *We spent the evening listening to old records.*

2 A **record** is also a high score or a fast time in sport that no-one has managed to beat: *She holds the world record for running 400 metres.*

3 A **record** is a written report giving information about something: *We kept a record of everything that was said at the meeting.*

'**rek**-ord '

record *verb*: **records, recorded, recording, has recorded**
You **record** sound or a television programme when you copy it on to special tape so that you can listen to it later: *We recorded the film that was on television last night.*

'ri-**kord** '

record player *noun*: **record players**
A **record player** is a machine for playing records on.

recover *verb*: **recovers, recovered, recovering, has**

recovered
1 You **recover** from an illness or injury when you get better: *Have you recovered from the flu now?*
2 Something that has been in a bad situation **recovers** when it improves: *It will take many years for the country to recover from the war.*

rectangle *noun*: **rectangles**
A **rectangle** is a flat shape with two long sides and two shorter sides.

red *noun* and *adjective*
Red is the colour of blood: *The curtains in the bedroom are red.* ❑ *She's wearing a red dress.*

reduce *verb*: **reduces, reduced, reducing, has reduced**
Something **reduces** when it gets smaller in size or amount; you **reduce** something when you make it smaller in size or amount: *As it boils, the liquid reduces to a thick sauce.* ❑ *We must reduce the amount of money we spend on food.*

'ri-djoos'

refer *verb*: **refers, referred, referring, has referred**
You **refer** to someone or something when you mention that person or thing: *In his letter, he doesn't refer to his wife and children.* ❑ *Who are you referring to?*

referee *noun*: **referees**
A **referee** is the person in charge of a sports match or a game; the referee has to make sure that the players do not break the rules: *The referee blew his whistle at the end of the football match.*

refrigerator *noun*: **refrigerators**
A **refrigerator** is an electric machine for keeping food cool, so that it doesn't go bad: *The milk is in the refrigerator.*

refuse *verb*: **refuses, refused, refusing, has refused**
1 You **refuse** to do something when you say that you do not want to do it, and that you will not do it: *She refused to help him.* ❑ *He refused to let me borrow his car.*
2 You **refuse** an invitation when you say 'no' to it: *They asked us to their wedding but we had to refuse.*

'ri-fyooz'

meaning 2: the opposite is **accept**

region *noun*: **regions**
A **region** is a part of a country, a continent or the sea: *For people who live in desert regions, water is very precious.* ❑ *Which region of China does this dish come from?*

regular *adjective*
1 Things that are **regular** always happen at the same time: *It is important to eat regular meals.*
2 Regular means 'frequent': *She's a regular visitor to this museum.*
3 Regular also means 'usual': *My regular day for shopping is Saturday.*

regularly *adverb*
1 Things that happen **regularly** happen often: *They play football regularly.*
2 Things also happen **regularly** if they happen at the same time each day, each week or each year: *Take this medicine regularly, three times a day.*

rehearse verb: **rehearses, rehearsed, rehearsing, has rehearsed**
Actors or singers **rehearse** when they practise before they perform in front of an audience: *Let's rehearse our lines again.*

related adjective
Two people are **related** when they belong to the same family: *They look so similar; are they related?*

relation noun: **relations**
Your **relations** are your relatives.

relative noun: **relatives**
Your **relatives** are the people who belong to your family: *All our friends and relatives are coming to the party.*

relax verb: **relaxes, relaxed, relaxing, has relaxed**
You **relax** when you rest: *After work, she likes to relax.*

release verb: **releases, released, releasing, has released**
1 Someone **is released** from a prison when they are allowed to leave it: *He was released from prison last week.*
2 You **release** something when you stop holding it: *He released her arm and ran away.*

religion noun: **religions**
1 **Religion** is belief in a god or gods.
2 A **religion** is a system of beliefs held by a group of people; they believe in one god or in several gods, and usually follow certain rules in the way they live their lives: *Eating pork is against his religion.*

remain verb: **remains, remaining, has remained**
1 A person or thing **remains** in a place when they stay there: *I'll remain here while you make the arrangements.*
2 A part of something **remains** when it is still there after the main part has gone: *All that remained were a few crumbs.*
3 You **remain** in a particular state when you continue to be in it: *Everyone remained silent as the teacher spoke.*

remark noun: **remarks**
A **remark** is something that you say: *Joe made a cheeky remark about James's parents.*

remark verb: **remarks, remarked, remarking, has remarked**
You **remark** when you say something: *He remarked that the weather was beautiful.* ❑ '*We've had a lovely time,*' *remarked Peter.*

remember verb: **remembers, remembered, remembering, has remembered**
1 You **remember** something when you keep it in your mind: *I must remember to phone Rosemary.*
2 You also **remember** something when it comes back into your mind: *Do you remember our first holiday in Greece?.*

the opposite is **forget**

remind verb: **reminds, reminded, reminding, has reminded**
1 You **remind** someone of something when you make them remember it: *Remind me to go to the bank tomorrow.*
2 One thing **reminds** you of another when it makes you think of that thing: *That smell reminds me of home.*

remove verb: **removes, removed, removing, has removed**
You **remove** something when you take it away: *We removed all the rubbish from the floor.* ❏ *The dentist removed the painful tooth.*

rent noun: **rent**
Rent is money that you pay to the owner of a house so that you can live there: *The rent on our flat is £400 per month.*

rent verb: **rents, rented, renting, has rented**
1 You **rent** a flat or a house when you pay money to the owner so that you can live there: *We rent our flat, but they own theirs.*
2 You **rent**, or **rent out** your flat or house when you let people live there in return for money: *Mr Alexander has three flats which he rents out.*

repair verb: **repairs, repaired, repairing, has repaired**
You **repair** something that is broken when you make it work again: *How much will it cost to repair the car?* ❏ *He repairs musical instruments.*

same as **mend**

repeat verb: **repeats, repeated, repeating, has repeated**
You **repeat** something you have just said when you say it again: *Sorry, I didn't hear you. Could you repeat that?*

replace verb: **replaces, replaced, replacing, has replaced**
1 You **replace** a part when you provide a new part to take its place: *They replaced all the broken windows.* ❏ *The workmen were replacing broken roof tiles.*
2 You also **replace** something

when you put it back in the place where it belongs: *She replaced the book on the shelf.*

reply verb: **replies, replied, replying, has replied**
You **reply** to someone who has spoken or written to you when you answer them: *He asked how old I was, and I replied that I was seventeen.* ❏ *'How are you?' 'Fine,' he replied.* ❏ *When are you going to reply to that letter?*

reply noun: **replies**
A **reply** is an answer, either spoken or written: *I said 'good morning' to him, but there was no reply.* ❏ *Have you had a reply to your letter yet?*

report noun: **reports**
1 A **report** is a description of something that has taken place: *He had to write a report after the meeting.*
2 A **report** is also a list of a student's grades with remarks: *Andy didn't get a very good report this year.*

report verb: **reports, reported, reporting, has reported**
1 You **report** something that has happened when you tell people about it: *He reported the accident to the police.*
2 You **report** someone who has done something wrong when you complain about them to a person in charge: *I reported him to the boss.*

reporter noun: **reporters**
A **reporter** is someone whose job is to get information about people or events and write stories for newspapers, television or radio.

represent *verb*: **represents, represented, representing, has represented**
One thing **represents** another when it acts as a sign for it: *This flag represents France.*

reptile *noun*: **reptiles**
A **reptile** is a type of animal, such as a crocodile or snake, which has skin made up of many scales.

request *verb*: **requests, requested, requesting, has requested**
You **request** something when you ask for it politely: *I requested a meeting with my boss.*

require *verb*: **requires, required, requiring, has required**
You **require** something when you need it: *If you require more paper, there's plenty here.* ❑ *The sign read 'Shop assistant required'.*

rescue *verb*: **rescues, rescued, rescuing, has rescued**
You **rescue** someone when you save them from danger: *The firefighters rescued the family from the burning house.*

respect *noun*
You have **respect** for someone when you admire them because they have good qualities: *I have no respect for cheats.*

respect *verb*: **respects, respected, respecting, has respected**
You **respect** someone when you admire them because they have good qualities such as honesty or strength: *I respect him because he works so hard.*

rest *noun*: **rests**
1 You have a **rest** when you stop working or exercising and spend

some time doing nothing: *I've worked hard all day, so I need a rest.* ❑ *We stopped for a rest and admired the view.*
2 When only part of something has gone, the part that is still there is the **rest**: *I couldn't eat the rest of my dinner.* ❑ *Don't stop there — tell us the rest of the story.*

rest *verb*: **rests, rested, resting, has rested**
1 You **rest** when you spend some time doing nothing: *She's resting in bed.*
2 One thing **rests** against another when it leans against it: *The ladder was resting against the wall.*

meaning 1: the opposite is **work**

restaurant *noun*: **restaurants**
A **restaurant** is a place where you can buy and eat a meal: *an Italian restaurant.*

❛ **rest**-ront ❜

result *noun*: **results**
1 One thing happens as a **result** of another when it is caused by that other thing: *He lost his arm as a result of an accident.*
2 Results are the marks that you get in an exam or a test: *I got much better results in my exams this time.*
3 The **result** of a match is the final score: *What was the result of the football match?*

return *verb*: **returns, returned, returning, has returned**
1 You **return** somewhere when you go back there after having been away: *She returned from her holiday on a cold wet day.* ❑ *He's returning to work in two weeks.*

2 You **return** something when you give it back: *I forgot to return my library books.*

return ticket *noun*: **return tickets**
A **return ticket** is a ticket that allows you to travel to a place and then back home again: *Buy a return ticket — it's cheaper than two singles.*

reward *noun*: **rewards**
1 A **reward** is a gift that you receive because you have behaved well or worked hard: *When your dog obeys, give it a reward .*
2 A **reward** is also a sum of money offered for information about something that is lost: *They offered a reward of £50 for the return of their cat.*

meaning 1: the opposite is **punishment**

rhyme *verb*: **rhymes, rhymed, rhyming, has rhymed**
Words **rhyme** when they sound the same, except for the first letter: *'Tame' rhymes with 'same'.* ❑ *Can you think of a word that rhymes with 'orange'?*

rhymes with **time**

ribbon *noun*: **ribbons**
A **ribbon** is a long strip of coloured material: *She tied her hair with a ribbon.*

rice *noun*
Rice is a kind of food made up of small thin seeds; you boil rice in water until it is soft enough to eat: *a bowl of boiled rice.*

rich *adjective*: **richer, richest**
A **rich** person is someone who has a lot of money: *He comes from a rich family, and doesn't need to work.*

same as **wealthy**
the opposite is **poor**

rid *verb*
▷ **get rid of**
1 You get **rid** of something when you throw it away, sell it, give it away or remove it: *Why don't you get rid of that old car and buy a new one?* ❑ *You've got rid of your beard!*
2 You get **rid** of an illness when it goes away, or when you do something to make it go away: *I just can't get rid of this cold.*

ride *verb*: **rides, rode, riding, has ridden**
1 You **ride** a horse or a bicycle when you travel on it: *We rode the horses through the forest.*
2 You **ride** in a car or in some other vehicle when you travel in it: *I prefer to ride in a train than in a car.*

ride is also a noun: *It's a beautiful day; lets go for a bike ride.*

rider *noun*: **riders**
A **rider** is a person who rides a horse or some kind of vehicle: *a motorbike rider.*

right *adjective*
1 The **right** side is the side with the hand that most people write with: *I wear my watch on my right hand.*
2 Someone or something that is **right** is correct: *That's the right answer.* ❑ *I hope I've made the right decision.*

meaning 1: the opposite is **left**
meaning 2: the opposite is **wrong**

▷ **right away**

You do something **right away** when you do it immediately: *'He's very ill.' 'I'll come right away.'*

▷ **right now**

You do something **right now** when you do it immediately: *Shall I type this letter right now?*

right *adverb*

1 Right means 'all the way': *He stayed right till the end.* □ *Carry on right to the end of the road and then turn left.*

2 Right also means 'close': *He was standing right beside me.*

3 You turn **right** when you turn towards your right side: *Turn right and walk down the lane until you come to the church.*

---

meaning 3: the opposite is **left**

---

right *noun*

Something is on, or to the **right** when it is on, or to the right side: *The museum is on the right, just past the post office.* □ *He pointed to the right.*

ring *noun*: **rings**

1 A **ring** is a small circle of metal that you wear on your finger: *She bought a beautiful silver ring.* □ *a wedding ring.*

2 A **ring** is also a circle: *Everyone sat in a ring round the fire.*

3 A **ring** is the sound a bell makes: *I need an alarm clock with a loud ring.*

4 You give someone a **ring** when you telephone them: *I'll give you a ring before the weekend.*

ring *verb*: **rings, rang, ringing, has rung**

1 Something **rings** when it makes the sound of a bell: *The telephone rang but no-one answered.*

2 You **ring** someone when you telephone them: *I'll ring you later.*

rip *verb*: **rips, ripped, ripping, has ripped**

A piece of material **rips** when someone or something tears it: *He ripped the sheets into strips to make bandages.*

ripe *adjective*: **riper, ripest**

Fruit is **ripe** when it is ready to be eaten: *I've got some bananas, but they aren't very ripe.*

rise *verb*: **rises, rose, rising, has risen**

1 Something **rises** when it moves upwards: *Steam rose from the boiling water.*

2 You **rise** when you get out of bed in the morning: *He rises at 7 o'clock every morning.*

3 People **rise** when they stand up: *Everyone rose when she entered the room.* □ *He rose from his chair and stood behind his desk.*

4 The sun **rises** when it appears in the morning and slowly gets higher in the sky.

5 An amount **rises** when it increases: *Bus fares will rise on the first of March.*

6 A level **rises** when it increases: *The temperature rose to 80°.* □ *With all the recent rain, the river is rising.*

---

meanings 5 and 6: the opposite is **fall**

---

river *noun*: **rivers**

A **river** is a large stream of water that flows across land: *They live in a cottage by the river.* □ *The River Tay flows through Perth.*

road *noun*: **roads**
A **road** is a wide path with a hard surface, which vehicles can travel on: *You have to cross the road to get to the shops.*

roar *noun*: **roars**
A **roar** is a loud deep noise: *The lion gave a loud roar.* ❑ *The roar of the traffic kept us awake.*

roast *verb*: **roasts, roasted, roasting, has roasted**
You **roast** meat when you cook it in an oven or over a fire.

rob *verb*: **robs, robbed, robbing, has robbed**
Someone **robs** a place or another person when they steal from them: *They got ten years in jail for robbing a bank.*

robber *noun*: **robbers**
A **robber** is a person who steals things, especially from a bank or a shop.

robbery *noun*: **robberies**
Robbery is the stealing of things, especially from a bank or a shop: *He's been in jail for robbery.*

rock *noun*: **rocks**
Rock is a hard material that the Earth is made of; a rock is a piece of this: *He built his house on solid rock.* ❑ *He used a rock to break the window.*

rock *verb*: **rocks, rocked, rocking, has rocked**
Someone or something **rocks** when it swings gently from side to side, or backwards and forwards: *The boat rocked in the wind.*

rocket *noun*: **rockets**
1 A **rocket** is a large cylinder with a pointed end, that is used to send people into space: *A rocket was first sent to the moon in the 1960s.*

2 A **rocket** is also a kind of firework that goes high into the air.

rod *noun*: **rods**
A **rod** is a long thin pole: *a fishing rod.*

rode *verb*
see **ride**: *He rode there on his bike.*

roll *noun*: **rolls**
1 A **roll** of paper or film is a long piece of it wrapped round a tube: *We bought ten rolls of wallpaper.* ❑ *a roll of film.*

2 A **roll** is a small round piece of bread, which you can cut in half and fill with food such as cheese: *We bought ham and tomato rolls for our lunch.*

roll *verb*: **rolls, rolled, rolling, has rolled**
1 Something **rolls** when it moves by turning over: *The ball rolled down the hill.*

2 You **roll** something up when you turn it over to form a tube: *She rolled up the old map and put it away.*

roller skate *noun*: **roller skates**
Roller skates are boots with small wheels on the bottom, used for skating.

roller skate

roof *noun*: **roofs**
1 A **roof** is a covering for a building: *Their house has a flat roof.*

2 A **roof** is also a covering for a car.

room *noun*: **rooms**
1 A **room** is a separate area with walls and a ceiling inside a building: *How many rooms are there in your house?* ❑ *Where is*

the bathroom? ❏ *Can I book a room for Saturday night?*
2 There is **room** for something if there is enough space for it: *There's plenty of room for the children to play.* ❏ *We don't have enough room for a dog.* ❏ *There's room for one more person here.*

root *noun*: **roots**
The **roots** of a plant are the parts of it that grow underground.

rope *noun*: **ropes**
1 Rope is a kind of very thick string, made from long pieces of material twisted together. It is used to tie large things together or to lift heavy weights: *They tied the boat to the shore with rope.*
2 A **rope** is a piece of this: *They needed ropes to climb the mountain.* ❏ *If you pull this rope a bell will ring.*

rose *noun*: **roses**
A **rose** is a flower with broad petals and thorns on its stem: *We bought her a bunch of roses for her birthday.*

rose *verb*
see **rise**: *We rose at four this morning.* ❏ *The sun rose and the birds began to sing.*

rot *verb*: **rots, rotted, rotting, has rotted**
Something **rots** when it gets old and begins to go soft or break into small pieces: *The wooden steps soon rotted in the rain.* ❏ *We found some potatoes rotting at the back of the cupboard.*

rotten *adjective*
1 Food is **rotten** if it is old and has gone bad: *I can smell rotten eggs.*
2 Wood is **rotten** if it is old and has begun to go soft: *Be careful. Some of these stairs are rotten.*

rough *adjective*: **rougher, roughest**
1 A surface is **rough** if it is not smooth, and feels uneven when you touch it: *She has very rough hands.*
2 Rough means 'not gentle': *He has a rough, loud voice.*
3 Rough weather is stormy and windy: *It was rough out on the sea last night.*

'ruf '

meaning 1: the opposite is **smooth**

route *noun*: **routes**
A **route** is a way that people or vehicles use to get to a place: *He usually walks home by a shorter route.*

round *adjective*: **rounder, roundest**
1 Something that is **round** is shaped like a circle: *We all sat at the round table.*
2 You also say that something is **round** if it is shaped like a ball: *The Earth is round.*

round *preposition*
1 One thing is **round** another if it is on all sides of it: *The bees were all round us.*
2 You look **round** a place when you look at different parts of it: *In the afternoon we looked around the old town.*

round *adverb*
1 Something goes **round** when it turns like a wheel: *The wheels went round very fast.*
2 You turn **round** when you turn to face in the opposite direction: *He turned round and saw Samuel standing behind him.*
3 You go **round** to someone's house when you visit them: *Shall*

we go round to Patricia's tonight?
❑ *Would you like to come round for dinner on Saturday?*

row *noun*: **rows**
A **row** of people or things is a line of them: *We sat in the front row of the theatre.*

rhymes with **toe**

a row of people

row *verb*: **rows, rowed, rowing, has rowed**
You **row** a boat when you make it move using oars: *We rowed across the lake.*

rhymes with **toe**

to row

row *noun*: **rows**
A **row** is a noisy argument: *We heard our neighbours having a row last night.*

rhymes with **now**

royal *adjective*
A **royal** person or thing is connected with a king or a queen: *the royal family.*

rub *verb*: **rubs, rubbed, rubbing, has rubbed**
1 You **rub** something when you move your hand backwards and forwards over it: *He rubbed his eyes.*
2 One thing **rubs** another when it moves backwards and forwards

while pressing against it: *These shoes are rubbing my heels.*

▷**rub out**
You **rub out** pencil marks when you remove them using a rubber: *I'll have to rub this out and start again; it's all wrong*

rubber *noun*: **rubbers**
1 Rubber is a strong material that bends easily; it is used to make tyres: *rubber tyres.* ❑ *rubber gloves.*
2 A **rubber** is a piece of this material which can be used to remove pencil marks: *Can I borrow your rubber?*

meaning 2: same as **eraser**

rubbish *noun*
1 Rubbish is paper and other things that you throw away: *Please put all your rubbish in the bin.*
2 People talk **rubbish** when they say silly things: *Don't listen to him — he's talking rubbish.*

rucksack *noun*: **rucksacks**
A **rucksack** is a bag with straps that you carry on your back: *He carried the tent in his rucksack.*

rude *adjective*: **ruder, rudest**
A **rude** person is someone who is not polite; **rude** behaviour is bad behaviour: *It's rude to interrupt when someone is speaking.*

❛**rood**❜

rug *noun*: **rugs**
A **rug** is a small carpet: *We've got a new rug for the living room.*

rugby *noun*
Rugby is a game played by two teams of thirteen or fifteen players with an oval ball. The players can kick or carry the ball.

ruin *verb*: **ruins, ruined, ruining, has ruined**
Something **is ruined** when it is damaged or spoiled: *The paintings were all ruined by the rain.* ❑ *You'll ruin your shoes if you play football in them.*

rule *noun*: **rules**
A **rule** is a law which tells you what you are allowed to do in a game or at school: *Do you know the rules of rugby?*

rule *verb*: **rules, ruled, ruling, has ruled**
Someone **rules** a country when they control it, and sometimes make its laws: *This country is ruled by a king.*

ruler *noun*: **rulers**
1 A **ruler** is a person who controls a country.
2 A **ruler** is a straight piece of wood or plastic which you use to draw straight lines and to measure things: *Have you got a ruler I could borrow, please?*

run *verb*: **runs, ran, running, has run**
1 You **run** when you use your legs to move very fast: *We were late so we had to run all the way to the station.*
2 Vehicles **run** when they move along: *Trains run on rails but cars run on the roads.*
3 Liquids **run** when they flow: *Water was running down the walls.*
4 You **run** an organization when you are in charge of it: *He runs a large oil company.*
5 Trains and buses **run** when they take passengers to places: *This bus doesn't run on Sundays.*

▷ **run after**
You **run after** someone when you run and try to reach them:

Tim ran after the man but he couldn't catch him.

▷ **run away**
1 You **run away** from a place when you escape quickly by running: *He rang the bell on the door, and then ran away.*
2 People **run away** from home when they leave home without telling anyone: *When Jim ran away, his parents were very worried.*

▷ **run into**
1 You **run into** someone when you meet them by chance: *I ran into Melanie yesterday.*
2 One vehicle **runs into** another object, when it hits it: *He lost control of the car and ran into a wall.*

▷ **run on**
A vehicle **runs on** a certain type of fuel when it uses that fuel to make it move: *They have designed a car that runs on electricity.*

▷ **run out**
Something **runs out** when there is none remaining; you **run out** of something when you have used it all: *The milk's run out. Could you get some more, please?* ❑ *We ran out of petrol ten miles from home.*

runner *noun*: **runners**
A **runner** is a person who runs: *He's a fast runner.*

rung *verb*
see **ring**: *The telephone has rung five times today.*

rush *verb*: **rushes, rushed, rushing, has rushed**
You **rush** when you do something very fast because you are late: *If you rush, you'll make mistakes.*

rush *noun*
You are in a **rush** if you are in a hurry: *He's always in a rush so we never speak to him*

Ss

sack *noun*: **sacks**
A **sack** is a large bag made of cloth, plastic or paper; sacks are used to store things such as grain, coal or potatoes: *Two sacks of potatoes.*

sad *adjective*: **sadder, saddest**
1 A person is **sad** when they are unhappy: *They were very sad when they had to leave their home.*
2 A **sad** story makes you feel unhappy: *The film had a sad ending.* ❑ *That's one of the saddest things I have ever heard.*

the opposite is **happy**

saddle *noun*: **saddles**
A **saddle** is a seat on a horse, a bicycle or a motorcycle: *He jumped on to the saddle and rode away.* ❑ *You need to raise the saddle on your bike.*

safe *adjective*: **safer, safest**
1 Safe things do not cause harm, or do not involve danger: *That ladder isn't very safe.* ❑ *Adele's a safe driver. She's never had an accident.* ❑ *Is it safe to walk at night here?*
2 People or things are **safe** when they are protected from harm, or when they are not in danger: *Will you be safe in this old car?* ❑ *You should keep your money in a safe place.* ❑ *She phoned to say that she was safe and well.*

the opposite is **dangerous**

safe *noun*: **safes**
A **safe** is a strong metal box in which you can lock away money and valuable things like jewellery: *They broke into the bank's safe and stole all the money.* ❑ *The diamonds were in a small safe behind a mirror.*

safely *adverb*
You do something **safely** when you do it in a way that does not involve harm or danger: *Dad told me to drive safely.* ❑ *They arrived at the top of the mountain safely.*

safety *noun*
Safety is the fact of being safe: *Children can play in safety here.* ❑ *In bad weather, we worry about his safety.*

the opposite is **danger**

safety belt *noun*: **safety belts**
A **safety belt** is a strong strap that you wear across your body to protect you from being injured in a car or aeroplane if it stops suddenly or crashes.

said *verb*
see **say** : *They said it's going to be cold today.* ❑ *Can you tell me what she said?*

sail *noun*: **sails**
1 A **sail** is a large sheet of strong cloth that is attached to the mast of a boat; the sail catches the wind and makes the boat move forwards: *A light breeze filled the sails and the yacht moved slowly out of the harbour.*
2 A **sail** is a journey by boat or ship: *It was a ten hour sail to the next island.*

sail *verb*: **sails, sailed, sailing, has sailed**
1 A boat **sails** to a place when it moves across water towards that place: *They sailed to New York in a week.* ❑ *The ferry sails from Dover to Calais six times a day.*
2 You **sail** a boat when you make it move across water using a sail: *We're learning how to sail.* ❑ *This big yacht needs fifteen people to sail it.*

sailing *noun*
1 Sailing is the activity or sport of sailing boats: *We used to go sailing every weekend.* ❑ *a sailing boat.*
2 A **sailing** is a regular voyage made by a ship or ferry: *There are sailings between the islands every day.*

sailor *noun*: **sailors**
A **sailor** is a member of a ship's crew who helps to sail the ship.

salad *noun*: **salads**
Salad, or a **salad**, is a mixture of vegetables served cold: *Do you want salad with your steak?* ❑ *We made a salad with lettuce, tomatoes and onions.* ❑ *potato salad.*

salary *noun*: **salaries**
A person's **salary** is the money they earn each month or each year for the work they do: *It's a good job, but the salary's terrible.* ❑ *His yearly salary is $40 000.*

sale *noun*: **sales**
1 The **sale** of something is the act of selling it; something that is for **sale** can be bought: *The sale of their house took 3 months.* ❑ *Sales of computers have increased a lot recently.* ❑ *Is this car for sale?*

2 A shop has a **sale** when it sells goods for prices that are cheaper than usual: *I bought this dress in a sale.* ❑ *Did you buy anything in the summer sales?*

salesman *noun*: **salesmen**
A **salesman** is a man whose job is to sell goods to shops or to the public: *a car salesman.* ❑ *He's working as a salesman for a large company in Japan.*

saleswoman *noun*: **saleswomen**
A **saleswoman** is a woman whose job is to sell goods to shops or to the public: *The saleswoman helped us choose a new washing machine.*

salt *noun*
Salt is a white powder that you put on food to improve its taste: *These potatoes need more salt.*

salty *adjective*: **saltier, saltiest**
Something that is **salty** tastes of salt, or has too much salt in it: *Sea water is salty.* ❑ *This soup tastes salty.*

same *adjective, pronoun and adverb*
People or things are the **same** when they are not different in any way; people feel the **same** when they feel as they did before, or as another person does: *Our children are the same age.* ❑ *He travels the same way to work every day.* ❑ *All the shop assistants were dressed the same.* ❑ *They have the same name.* ❑ *Does 'quick' mean the same as 'fast'?* ❑ *She loved him, and he felt the same about her.*

the opposite is **different**

sand *noun*
Sand is the pale brown or yellow

material that covers beaches and some deserts.

sandal *noun*: **sandals**
Sandals are light shoes with straps. People wear them when the weather is warm.

sandal

sandwich *noun*: **sandwiches**
A **sandwich** is a snack made of two slices of bread with meat, cheese or some other food in between: *Do you want a bacon sandwich for lunch?*

sang *verb*
see **sing**: *We sang the song in French.*

sank *verb*
see **sink**: *The ship sank to the bottom of the sea.* ❏ *She sank to her knees.*

sat *verb*
see **sit**: *The cat sat by the fire.* ❏ *She fell asleep as soon as she sat down.*

satisfactory *adjective*
You say that something is **satisfactory** when it is good enough to satisfy you: *Her work is quite satisfactory.* ❏ *He didn't give a satisfactory excuse for his behaviour.*

satisfy *verb*: **satisfies, satisfied, satisfying, has satisfied**
Something **satisfies** you when you get what you want or need from it: *It's sometimes difficult to satisfy all our customers.*

satisfied *adjective*
You are **satisfied** when you are happy with what you have: *He was quite satisfied with the money he was earning.*

Saturday *noun*: **Saturdays**
Saturday is the sixth day of the week, the day after Friday: *Are you coming to visit us next Saturday?* ❏ *I always go skating on Saturdays.*

sauce *noun*: **sauces**
Sauce, or a **sauce**, is a liquid that you pour over food to make it taste better: *ice cream with chocolate sauce.* ❏ *The chicken is served with a mushroom and cream sauce.* ❏ *tomato sauce.*

saucepan *noun*: **saucepans**
A **saucepan** is a deep round cooking pot with a handle, and often a lid.

saucer *noun*: **saucers**
A **saucer** is a small round dish that you put under a cup.

sausage *noun*: **sausages**
Sausages are a food made of chopped meat and spices in a thin tube-shaped covering: *Would you like your sausages grilled or fried?*

save *verb*: **saves, saved, saving, has saved**
1 You **save** someone when you bring them out of danger: *The two firefighters saved the children from the burning building.* ❏ *They tried everything, but they couldn't save the man's life.*
2 You **save** something when you keep it instead of throwing it away: *We always save these plastic yoghurt pots.*
3 You **save**, or you **save up**, when you keep money instead of spending it: *We've started saving for our holiday.* ❏ *Bob is saving up for a new car.*

4 You **save** money, water or fuel when you use less than before, or less than expected: *I bought the dress in a sale and saved $30.* ❑ *We can save water if we have showers instead of baths.*

5 You **save** new information on a computer when you store it in its memory.

saving *noun*: **savings**
1 You make a **saving** on something when you spend less than usual on it: *You can make a saving of $5 if you buy two jars of coffee instead of one.*
2 Your **savings** are money that you have saved and not spent: *You should put your savings in the bank.*

saw *verb*
see **see**: *I saw Helen in the library last Saturday.* ❑ *When he saw the price he decided not to buy it.*

saw *noun*: **saws**
A **saw** is a tool that has a long blade with an edge like a row of sharp teeth; a saw is used for cutting wood: *an electric saw* ❑ *The men used saws and axes to cut down the trees.*

saw

saw *verb*: **saws, sawed, sawing, has sawn**
You **saw** wood when you cut it using a saw: *This machine saws the trees into planks.* ❑ *Dad's outside sawing wood for the fire.*

say *verb*: **says, said, saying, has said**
1a You **say** something when you speak words: *What did you say?* ❑ *He said he wanted to meet me later, and I said 'OK'.* ❑ *Why don't you say sorry to her?* **b** You **say** something to other people when you tell them facts or give them information: *Did he say what time he was leaving?* ❑ *Mr Henry says there's going to be a storm.* ❑ *They say that strange things happen in that old house.*
2 A letter, a book or a notice **says** something when that is what is written there: *What does the letter say?* ❑ *It says in this book that he was born in 1956.* ❑ *The notice said 'No smoking'.*
3 You **say** something to yourself when you think it, or whisper it: *'I'm not afraid,' he said to himself.*
4 You **say** something that you have learnt when you repeat it: *My friend can say the alphabet backwards.*

scale *noun*: **scales**
1 In music, a **scale** is a certain group of notes going up and down in order: *Sam was practising scales on the piano.* ❑ *Do you know the scale of C?*
2 A **scale** is also a series of numbers or marks used for measuring things: *This scale is for measuring very small differences in heat.*
3 The tiny thin flat pieces that cover the skin of fishes and reptiles are called **scales**.

scales *noun*
A set of **scales** is a machine used for weighing: *a set of kitchen scales* ❑ *You can weigh*

yourself on the scales in the bathroom.

kitchen scales   bathroom scales

   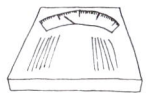

scalp *noun*: **scalps**
Your **scalp** is the skin on your head under your hair: *This shampoo is good for an itchy scalp.*

scar *noun*: **scars**
A **scar** is a mark on the skin which remains after an injury has healed: *He's got a scar on his face where the dog bit him.*

scare *verb*: **scares, scared, scaring, has scared**
Something **scares** you when it makes you feel frightened: *You're scaring the children with your stories.* ❑ *The dog jumped into the lake and scared the ducks.*

scared *adjective*
Scared means 'frightened': *She had a scared look on her face.*

scarf *noun*: **scarfs** or **scarves**
1 A **scarf** is a long narrow piece of clothing that you wear round your neck in cold weather.
2 A **scarf** is also a square piece of cloth that a woman wears over her head or round her shoulders: *She was wearing a silk scarf on her head.*

scatter *verb*: **scatters, scattered, scattering, has scattered**
You **scatter** things when you throw them or leave them in a lot of different places: *The children had scattered their toys all over the kitchen floor.*

scene *noun*: **scenes**
1 A **scene** is a view of a place that you see in front of you: *The hills covered in snow made a beautiful winter scene.*
2 The **scene** of an event or a crime is the place where it happened: *The police were looking for clues at the scene of the crime.*
3 A **scene** is one of the sections of a play or film: *These words are from a famous scene in Romeo and Juliet.*

scent *noun*: **scents**
A **scent** is a smell, usually a pleasant one: *This is a beautiful rose, but it has no scent.*

same as **smell**

school *noun*: **schools**
A **school** is a place where children go to learn: *Children here usually start school when they are five years old.* ❑ *What do you want to do when you leave school?* ❑ *All the schools were closed because of the bad weather.*

schoolteacher *noun*: **schoolteachers**
A **schoolteacher** is a person who teaches children in school.

science *noun*
Science is the study of natural things such as animals, plants, rocks, metals, water, air and heat: *Did you get a good mark in your science test?* ❑ *He's better at science than at languages.*

scissors *noun*
Scissors are a tool with two blades that cross over each other. You use them to cut paper, hair or cloth: *You need scissors and*

glue to make this model. ❑ Do you have a pair of kitchen scissors?

scooter noun: **scooters**
1 A **scooter** is a vehicle similar to a motorcycle but with a less powerful engine.
2 A **scooter** is also a a flat board with two wheels and an upright bar at the front. You move along on it by pushing one foot against the ground.

score verb: **scores, scored, scoring, has scored**
You **score**, or your team **scores**, when you get a point in a game: They scored in the last minute of the game. ❑ He scored some excellent points in the tennis match.

▷ **score out**
You **score out** a mistake in writing when you draw a line through it: 'I've signed my name in the wrong place.' 'Don't worry, just score it out.'

score noun: **scores**
A **score** is the number of points that a team or a player wins in a game: What's the score? ❑ The score is three goals to two.

scrap noun: **scraps**
1 A **scrap** is a small piece that has been cut from a larger piece: The dogs sat under the table waiting for scraps of meat. ❑ He wrote something on a scrap of paper.
2 Scrap is waste material, especially metal: The old car was sold for scrap.

scrape verb: **scrapes, scraped, scraping, has scraped**
1 You **scrape** something when you damage it by moving it against something hard: She fell and scraped her knees on the rocks. ❑ The lorry drove too close and scraped the side of our car.
2 You **scrape** one thing off another when you remove it using a sharp object: Harry scraped the old paint off the door with a knife. ❑ I had to scrape the ice off the car's windows.

scratch verb: **scratches, scratched, scratching, has scratched**
1a Something sharp **scratches** you when it makes a long narrow cut on your skin: The cat scratched my face with its claws.
b You **scratch** yourself when you rub your skin with your fingernails, to stop it itching: Try not to scratch those spots; they may leave scars.
2 Something sharp **scratches** glass, paint or metal when it damages the surface by making a long narrow mark in it: Somebody's scratched the car with a key.

scratch noun: **scratches**
A **scratch** is a mark made by scratching: Did the cat make those scratches on your hand?

scream verb: **screams, screamed, screaming, has screamed**
Someone **screams** when they give a very loud, high cry, usually because they are frightened, angry or in pain: The child screamed with pain when we tried to move him. ❑ 'Help!' she screamed.

screen noun: **screens**
1 A **screen** is the surface on which words and pictures appear on a television set, on a computer or in the cinema: The picture isn't

very clear; is the screen clean?
[see picture at **computer**]
2 A **screen** is also a flat, upright
piece of furniture used for
dividing a room: *The nurse pulled
a screen around his bed so that
the doctor could examine him.*

screw *noun*: **screws**
A **screw** is a thin piece of metal
with a sharp end that you put
into a surface by twisting. Screws
are used to fasten things together

screw *verb*: **screws, screwed,
screwing, has screwed**
1 You **screw** things together
when you fasten them together
using screws; you **screw**
something on when you fasten it
to a surface using screws: *They
screwed the two pieces of wood
together to form a cross.* ❑ *The
picture was screwed on to the
wall.*

screw   screwdriver

2 You **screw** a lid on when you
attach it with a twisting
movement: *He always forgets to
screw the lid on the toothpaste.*

screwdriver *noun*: **screwdrivers**
A **screwdriver** is a tool for
turning screws into a surface. It
has a tip shaped to fit into the
end of the screw.

scrub *verb*: **scrubs, scrubbed,
scrubbing, has scrubbed**
You **scrub** something when you
rub it hard with a cloth or a brush
and water: *You'll have to scrub
hard to remove these stains.* ❑ *She
was scrubbing the floor with a
brush and soapy water.*

sea *noun*: **seas**
1 The **sea** is the salt water that
surrounds the areas of land on
the Earth's surface: *We could see
the sea from the window of the
cottage.* ❑ *It's dangerous to swim
in the sea here.* ❑ *The sea's very
calm this morning.*
2 A **sea** is a certain piece of sea:
*They fish in the Baltic Sea and the
North Sea.* ❑ *The seas here are
covered with ice at this time of year.*

meaning 1: same as **ocean**

seafood *noun*
Seafood is fish and shellfish
from the sea, which you can eat:
a seafood restaurant.

seal *verb*: **seals, sealed, sealing,
has sealed**
1 An opening **is sealed** when it
is closed so that air or water
cannot enter it: *Every bottle is
carefully sealed for your safety.*
2 You **seal** an envelope when
you close it by sticking the open
edges together.

seam *noun*: **seams**
A **seam** is the join between two
edges of material that are sewn
together: *This old jacket is coming
apart at the seams.*

search *verb*: **searches, searched,
searching, has searched**
1 You **search** for something
when you look for it carefully in
several different places: *She spent
all day searching for her keys.*
2 You **search** a place for
something when you look
carefully in every part of it: *The
police searched the house for the
stolen money.*

seashell *noun*: **seashells**
Seashells are the shells of sea

creatures; they are often found on beaches or in the sea.

seaside noun
The **seaside** is a place beside the sea: Let's go to the seaside this weekend.

season noun: **seasons**
1 The **seasons** are the four main divisions of the year; they are spring, summer, autumn and winter: Which is the best season to vist New York?
2 A **season** is also a period of time in the year when something particular happens: We went to China during the wet season. □ There's a lot to do on a farm during the growing season.

season verb: **seasons, seasoned, seasoning, has seasoned**
You **season** food when you put salt or spices on it to make it taste better: Season the stew with salt and pepper.

seat noun: **seats**
A **seat** is something that you sit on; you take a **seat** when you sit down: Are there enough seats for everyone? □ There were no seats so we had to stand. □ a garden seat □ Please take a seat, everyone.

seat belt noun: **seat belts**
A **seat belt** is a strong strap that you wear across your body to protect you from being injured in a car or aeroplane if it stops suddenly or crashes.

seaweed noun
Seaweed is a plant that grows in the sea: Can you eat this kind of seaweed?

second noun: **seconds**
1 A **second** is one of the sixty parts of a minute: He ran 100

metres in less than ten seconds.
2 A **second** is also any short amount of time: Could you wait a second, please?

meaning 2: same as **moment**

second adjective and adverb
A **second** person or thing comes next after the first: Would you like a second cup of tea? □ She's in her second year at college. □ They meet on the second Friday in every month. □ Chris came second in the race.

secret noun: **secrets**
A **secret** is a piece of information that you keep hidden from other people: 'When are they getting married?' 'I can't tell you; it's a secret.'

secret adjective
Secret information or places are kept hidden from most people: The children found a secret room behind the fireplace. □ He went to prison for passing on secret information.

secretary noun: **secretaries**
A **secretary** is a person whose job is to type letters, answer the telephone and make arrangements for someone: The secretary answered the phone, and said that Katherine was in a meeting.

section noun: **sections**
A **section** of something is a part of it: Divide the orange into sections. □ Dictionaries are in this section of the library.

see verb: **sees, saw, seeing, has seen**
1a You **see** something when you notice it with your eyes, or when you look at it: Can you see that

little house in the distance?
□ *He looked at her and saw that
she was crying.* □ *Are your hands
clean? Let me see them.* **b** You
can **see** when you have the
power of sight: *He can't see very
well without his glasses.*
2 You **see** a play, a film or a
television programme when you
watch it: *This is my favourite film.
I've seen it five times.* □ *Did you
see the president on TV last night?*
3 You **see** someone when you
meet or visit them: *I'm seeing my
sister this afternoon.* □ *Some
students go home to see their
parents at weekends.* □ *Have you
seen a doctor about this problem?*
4 You **see** something when you
understand it: *I don't see what
you mean.* □ *'You have to put this
piece here like this.' 'I see.'*
5 You **see** what is happening
when you find out about it: *See if
John can come and help us.*
□ *Let's wait and see what happens.*

▷ **see about**
You **see about** something that
needs to be done when you deal
with it: *I'll see about getting a new
lock for this door.*

▷ **see someone off**
You **see someone off** when you
go with them to the station or the
airport to say goodbye to them:
*The whole family came to see me
off at the airport.*

▷ **see to**
You **see to** someone or
something when you deal with
them: *Is anyone seeing to this
customer?* □ *I've got a big pile of
papers to see to before I can go
home.*

seed *noun*: **seeds**
A **seed** is the small object that is
produced by a plant, from which
a new plant will grow: *grass seed.*
□ *Sow the seeds in small pots and
cover them with a plastic bag.*

seem *verb*: **seems, seemed,
seeming, has seemed**
1a A person or thing **seems** a
certain way when that is how
they appear to be: *She seems a
very nice girl.* □ *He seemed to be a
bit happier than before.* □ *These
rooms seem bigger without
furniture.* **b** Something **seems** to
be a certain way to you when that
is how you feel about it: *It seems
strange that he hasn't phoned.*
□ *'How long have you lived here?'
'Two months, but it seems much
longer.'*
2 You use **seem** to talk about
information that you think is true:
*There seems to be a problem at
the factory.*

seen *verb*
see **see**: *The president hasn't been
seen in public for a week.* □ *Have
you seen my umbrella?*

select *verb*: **selects, selected,
selecting, has selected**
You **select** a person or thing
from a group when you carefully
choose them: *We will select three
students from each university.*

same as **choose** or **pick**

self *noun*: **selves**
The **self** is the whole of a person
— their body, their personality
and the way they behave: *She
was quite ill, but now she's her old
self again.*

selfish *adjective*
A **selfish** person doesn't like

sharing things with other people: *She taught her children not to be selfish.* □ *He's so selfish; he hasn't offered his friends any of the money.*

the opposite is **generous**

sell *verb*: **sells, sold, selling, has sold**
You **sell** something when you give it to someone and they give you money for it: *This shop sells children's clothes and shoes.* □ *They are selling their house.* □ *She sold her old car for $550.*

the opposite is **buy**

selves *noun*
see **self**: *The experience taught us to understand our true selves.*

send *verb*: **sends, sent, sending, has sent**
1a You **send** a letter or parcel, when you post it: *She always sends me a birthday present.* □ *They sent the parcel to the wrong address.* **b** You **send** a fax or an e-mail when you instruct the fax machine or computer to deliver it to someone.
2 You **send** someone to a place when you make them go there: *We sent the children to their aunt's for the holidays.* □ *The manager sent his assistant to talk to us.*
3 An object **is sent** through the air when it is thrown or pushed so that it travels quickly through the air: *Gavin kicked the ball and sent it high into the air.* □ *The bomb sent pieces of metal flying everywhere.*

▷ **send for**
1 You **send for** someone when you tell them to come to you: *The headteacher sent for the three*

boys. □ *He's very ill — we'll have to send for the doctor.* **2** You **send for** something when you ask someone to bring it to you: *We sent for a taxi to take us to the airport.*

▷ **send off**
You **send** a letter or parcel **off** when you post it: *When did you send off the form?*

▷ **send out**
1 You **send out** letters when you write to various people; a machine **sends out** a signal when it gives a signal: *Have you sent those letters out yet?* □ *This machine sends out a signal so that other people know where our boat is.* **2** Someone **sends** you **out** of a place when they tell you to leave it: *The teacher sent the child out of the room.*

sense *noun*: **senses**
1 Your **senses** are the five powers that you have which make you notice things; these are the powers of seeing, hearing, touching, smelling and tasting: *Dogs have a very good sense of smell.* □ *He uses his senses of hearing and touch to help him move around.*
2 Someone who has **sense** has the ability to make good decisions: *Will he have the sense to come down from the mountain before dark?*

▷ **make sense**
1 Something **makes sense** to you when you can understand it: *I couldn't make sense of the figures he had given me.*
2 Something also **makes sense** when it is the sensible thing to do: *It makes sense to have some*

extra money in case something goes wrong.

sensible *adjective*
A **sensible** person is able to make good decisions: *It wasn't very sensible to leave your books outside.*

same as **wise**

sent *verb*
see **send**: *I sent him the magazine last week.* ❑ *Has the letter been sent yet?* ❑ *Kate was sent to school in France.*

sentence *noun*: **sentences**
A **sentence** is a group of words that make a statement or ask a question. A written sentence starts with a capital letter and ends with a full stop: *He wrote two sentences and then fell asleep.*

separate *adjective*
1 Separate things are not joined to each other or linked in any way: *They divided the house into three separate flats.* ❑ *The library building is separate from the rest of the college.*
2 Separate also means 'different': *They sleep in separate bedrooms.* ❑ *The lists were on three separate pieces of paper.*

separate *verb*: **separates, separated, separating, has separated**
You **separate** two people or things when you move them away from each other; people and things **separate** when they move away from each other: *The teacher separated the two boys because they were talking.* ❑ *A big piece of ice separated from the rest and fell into the sea.*

the opposite is **join**

September *noun*
September is the ninth month of the year, between August and October: *He was born in September in 1972.* ❑ *The weather has been very warm for September.*

series *noun*: **series**
1 A **series** is a number of things or events that are connected, and that happen one after the other: *Last year, there was a series of burglaries in our street.* ❑ *He's also written a series of books for younger children.*
2 A **series** is also a number of television or radio programmes which deal with the same subject: *There's a new series on television about famous presidents.*

serious *adjective*
1 A **serious** situation is a very bad one: *His injuries are very serious, and he may die.* ❑ *Murder is a very serious crime.*
2a A **serious** person does not smile or laugh very much: *Why are you looking so serious? There's nothing to worry about.*
b Serious work takes a lot of effort: *I need to do some serious studying before this exam.*
3 You are **serious** about something when you are not joking about it: *He said he was very angry, but he wasn't serious.*

serve *verb*: **serves, served, serving, has served**
1 You **serve** food when you put it on plates so that people can eat it; you **serve** drinks when you put them in glasses for people to drink: *Come to the table now — I'm serving the soup.* ❑ *The wine*

was served by a wine waiter.
2 A shop assistant **serves**
customers by helping them and
and selling goods to them: *They*
serve about 200 customers every
day.
3 You **serve** an organization or
your country when you do
something for it: *He served the*
company for forty years. ❑ *Young*
men have to serve in the army for
18 months.
4 In tennis, you **serve** when you
throw the ball in the air and hit it
over the net: *It's your turn to*
serve.

session *noun*: **sessions**
1 A **session** is a period of time
when a particular activity takes
place: *He needed ten sessions of*
treatment to help him to walk
again.
2 A **session** is also a term or a
year in a school or college: *The*
children will begin to learn English
next session.

set *noun*: **sets**
1 A **set** of things is a group of
things that belong together: *a tea*
set made up of six cups and six
saucers ❑ *a set of golf clubs*
❑ *They bought a set of saucepans*
for the new kitchen.
2 A **set** is also a television or a
radio: *The TV isn't working*
properly — I think we need a new
set. ❑ *He has a powerful set that*
can receive radio signals from all
over the world.

set *verb*: **sets, set, setting, has**
set
1 You **set** something down
somewhere when you place it
there: *Jilly set her books down on*
the table and began to do her

homework.
2 You **set** a table for a meal when
you put all the plates, glasses and
cutlery on the table: *Harry set the*
table for dinner.
3 The sun **sets** when it sinks
down in the sky in the evening:
We watched the sun setting in the
west.
4 Someone **sets** you a task when
they give you a task to do: *Every*
week, our teacher sets us a
spelling test.
5 You **set** an alarm when you
prepare it so that it will ring at a
certain time: *Did you remember*
to set the burglar alarm? ❑ *He set*
his alarm clock for six o'clock.

▷ **all set**
You are **all set** to do something
when you are ready to do it: *We*
were all set to go on holiday when
Tina fell and broke her leg.

▷ **set in**
Something unpleasant **sets in**
when it starts: *We were already*
hungry and tired when the rain set
in.

▷ **set off** or **set out**
Someone **sets off** or **sets out**
on a journey when they start it:
We set off at nine o'clock. ❑ *They*
seemed bright and cheerful when
they set out that morning.

▷ **set up**
1 You **set up** an event when you
make all the arrangements for it:
Will it be possible to set up a
meeting between the two
presidents?
2 You **set up** a new business
when you start it: *He set up a*
training school for secretaries.
3 You **set up** a tent or some
other structure when you put its

parts together so that it stands up: *They set their camp up at the bottom of the mountain.*

settle *verb*: **settles, settled, settling, has settled**
1 Someone who **settles** somewhere goes to live there: *Her family settled in Canada in 1947.*
2 Something **settles** on a surface when it lands there: *The butterfly settled on a flower.* ❑ *White dust settled on all the furniture.*
3 You **settle** yourself somewhere when you make yourself comfortable there: *He settled himself in a chair by the fire and started to tell us a story.*

▷ **settle down**
1 You **settle down** when your life becomes more stable than before: *One day, he'll settle down and get married.*
2 Excited children **settle down** when they become quiet and calm: *Settle down, children, and open your books.*

seven *noun and adjective*: **sevens**
1 Seven is the number or figure 7: *Eleven minus four is seven.* ❑ *Five sevens are thirty-five.* ❑ *Is this a seven or a two?*
2 Seven is the time of seven o'clock: *She gets up at seven every morning.*
3 Seven is also the age of seven; someone who is **seven** is seven years old: *At seven, he was much taller than the other children.* ❑ *My grandson was seven in January.*

seven *determiner and pronoun*
Seven means seven in number: *There were seven boys and fifteen girls in my class.* ❑ *There are seven days in a week.* ❑ 'There are six fish in the tank.' 'No, there are seven.'

seventeen *noun and adjective*: **seventeens**
1 Seventeen is the number 17: *Twelve and five is seventeen.* ❑ *Two seventeens are 34.*
2 Seventeen is the age of 17; someone who is **seventeen** is 17 years old: *From seventeen, you are allowed to drive a car.* ❑ *She's not sixteen, she's seventeen.*

seventeen *determiner and pronoun*
Seventeen means seventeen in number: *There were seventeen people in the room.* ❑ *I have twenty copies of the book, but I need another seventeen.*

seventh *determiner and adjective*
The **seventh** person or thing is the one that comes after sixth.

seventy *noun and adjective*: **seventies**
1 Seventy is the number or figure 70: *Ten multiplied by seven is seventy.*
2a Seventy is the age of 70; someone who is **seventy** is 70 years old: *He's nearly seventy but he's still working.* **b** A person in their **seventies** is between 70 and 79 years old: *My mother is in her seventies.*
3 The years in any century between 70 and 79 are often called 'the **seventies**': *My parents got married in the seventies.*

seventy *determiner and pronoun*
Seventy means seventy in number: *It's been seventy years since anyone lived in the old house.* ❑ 'How many people were at the wedding?' 'There were more than seventy.'

several *determiner and pronoun*
Several means more than two,

but not a lot: *Kenneth has been ill for several weeks.* ❏ *There are several books here about the war.* ❏ *'Are there any trees in your garden.' 'Yes, there are several.'*

sew *verb*: **sews, sewed, sewing, has sewn**
You **sew** when you attach one piece of material to another using a needle and thread: *My mother taught me how to sew.* ❏ *Gina cut out two pieces of material and sewed them together.* ❏ *I've sewn the button on your jacket.*

rhymes with **go**

sew

sewing machine *noun*: **sewing machines**
A **sewing machine** is a machine that is used to sew things.

sewn *verb*
see **sew**: *She's sewn the ribbons on the dresses.*

shade *noun*: **shades**
1 A **shade** is any of the varieties of a single colour: *This wallpaper is in shades of green, grey and blue.* ❏ *Do you prefer a darker or a lighter shade of blue?*
2 Shade is an area where there is no sunlight because a building or a plant is blocking it: *Let's sit in the shade — it's too hot in the sun.* ❏ *The lions were lying in the shade of a big tree.*

shadow *noun*: **shadows**
A **shadow** is a dark shape on a surface caused by an object

blocking the light: *The shadow of a man moved across the wall.* ❏ *Towards the evening our shadows began to get longer and we started to feel colder.*

shake *verb*: **shakes, shook, shaking, has shaken**
1 Something **shakes** when it moves quickly from side to side, or up and down: *The house shakes when big lorries go past.*
2 You **shake** your head when you move it from side to side to show that you mean 'no': *I asked her if she was feeling better and she shook her head.*
3 Your body **shakes** when it makes quick movements that you can't control, usually because you are frightened or shocked: *Her face was white and her hands were shaking.*

shall *verb*
1 You use **I**, or **we shall** with another verb, to say what you are going to do: *I shall be arriving home at five o'clock tomorrow.* ❏ *We shall not be coming to the party.*
2 You ask '**shall I...?**' or '**shall we...?**' when you are making a suggestion or asking someone's advice: *Shall I serve lunch now?* ❏ *Shall we go into the garden to have our coffee?* ❏ *What shall we do tomorrow?* ❏ *Shall I wear this dress tonight?*

▸You can shorten: **I shall** to **I'll**, **we shall** to **we'll**, and **shall not** to **shan't**.

shallow *adjective*: **shallower, shallowest**
A **shallow** container, or **shallow** water, is not deep: *Place the*

chicken in a shallow dish and cook it in the oven for 1 hour. ❑ *The children can play here where the water is shallow.*

---

the opposite is **deep**

---

shame *noun*
1 You feel **shame** when you have an unpleasant feeling because you have done something wrong: *He doesn't feel any shame for the terrible things he has done.*
2 You say 'it's a **shame**' or 'what a **shame**' when you feel a little sad about something: *It's a shame that they couldn't come to the wedding*

shampoo *noun*
Shampoo is a liquid containing soap that you use to wash your hair: *a bottle of shampoo.*

shan't *verb*
Shan't is short for **shall not**: *I shan't be going to work this morning — I've got a cold.*

shape *noun*: **shapes**
The **shape** of an object is the form it has: *You can buy pasta in many different shapes and sizes.* ❑ *Jane rolled the piece of paper into a long thin shape.*

shaped *adjective*
You use **shaped** to describe something that has a certain shape: *He had a square-shaped chin.*

share *verb*: **shares, shared, sharing, has shared**
1 You **share** something with other people when you all use it: *Everyone shares the garden behind the flats.* ❑ *She didn't want to share a bedroom with her little sister.*
2 People **share** things between them when they each have some: *We shared the money, giving everyone $50 each.* ❑ *Tim never shares his toys with his sister.*

shark *noun*: **sharks**
A **shark** is a large sea fish with a lot of sharp teeth: *The notice read 'No swimming. Sharks'.*

sharp *adjective*: **sharper, sharpest**
1 A **sharp** knife or pair of scissors has a very thin edge which can cut well: *Use a sharp knife to cut the meat.* ❑ *You need very sharp scissors to cut hair.*
2 A **sharp** needle or a **sharp** pencil has a very thin pointed end: *Make sure your pencil has a sharp point before you start drawing.*
3 A person or animal that has **sharp** eyes or ears can see or hear very well.
4 A **sharp** turn or bend changes direction very suddenly: *Slow down. There's a sharp bend in the road here.*

---

meanings 1 and 2: the opposite is **blunt**

---

shave *verb*: **shaves, shaved, shaving, has shaved**
People **shave** when they use a razor to cut hair from their body: *He cut himself while he was shaving.* ❑ *He shaved off his beard and nobody recognized him.*

shave

she *pronoun*
You use **she** when you are talking about a woman, a girl or a female animal that has already been mentioned: *'How's your mother?' 'She's very well, thank you.'* ❑ *Who's that girl? She looks like Helen.*

shed *noun*: **sheds**
A **shed** is a small building made from wood, which is used for storing things in: *We keep all the tools in the shed in the garden.*

she'd
She'd is short for **she had** or **she would**: *Louise said she'd received a letter from her son.* ❑ *She'd be very happy if you phoned her.*

sheep *noun*: **sheep**
A **sheep** is an animal that is often kept on farms for its wool and meat: *The sheep stood and watched us as we walked through the field.*

sheet *noun*: **sheets**
1 A **sheet** is a large piece of thin cloth that you put on a bed.
2 A **sheet** of paper or glass is a thin flat piece of it: *The men were carrying a large sheet of glass.*

shelf *noun*: **shelves**
A **shelf** is a long flat piece of wood, glass or metal that is fixed to a wall or in a cupboard; you store things such as books on shelves: *There's a jar of coffee on the top shelf of that cupboard.* ❑ *The shelves fell down when we put the books on them.*

shell *noun*: **shells**
1 A **shell** is the hard outer covering of an egg or a nut: *The baby birds use their beaks to break their shells.* ❑ *We used a hammer to break the coconut shell.*
2 The hard outer covering of certain sea creatures and of certain other animals is also called a **shell**: *The snail pulled its body inside its shell.* ❑ *The prawns were served in their shells.*

shellfish *noun*: **shellfish**
Shellfish is the name given to creatures that live in water and have hard coverings on the outside of their bodies: *Prawns are shellfish.*

she'll
She'll is short for **she will**: *We must phone her soon or she'll start to worry.*

shelter *noun*: **shelters**
Shelter, or a **shelter**, is a place that protects you from rain or stormy weather: *When it started to rain everyone took shelter under the trees.* ❑ *The boys built a shelter out of branches and leaves.*

shelter *verb*: **shelters, sheltered, sheltering, has sheltered**
1 A person or thing **shelters** in a place when they use that place as a shelter: *The boats were sheltering in the harbour until the storm was over.*
2 Something **shelters** you from the rain, the wind or the sun when it protects you from it: *A big hat will shelter your eyes from strong sun.*

shepherd *noun*: **shepherds**
A **shepherd** is a person whose job is to look after sheep: *The shepherd was bringing his flock down from the hills.*

‘**shep**-erd ’

she's
She's is short for **she is** or **she has**: *Do you know Kay? She's an old friend of mine.* ◻ *She's never met my parents before.*

shift *verb*: **shifts, shifted, shifting, has shifted**
You **shift** something when you move it to another position: *Could someone please help me shift this furniture?*

shine *verb*: **shines, shone, shining, has shone**
1 Something **shines** when it gives out light: *The sun's shining — let's go for a walk.* ◻ *The warning light shone brightly across the sea.*
2 You **shine** a light on something when you point the light in its direction: *He shone the light into the hole, but we couldn't see anything in there.*
3 Something that **shines** has a bright surface: *We had to polish our shoes until they shone.*

ship *noun*: **ships**
A **ship** is a large boat that sails on the sea: *You can only reach the island by ship.* ◻ *The soldiers got on board the ships at Southampton.*

shirt *noun*: **shirts**
A **shirt** is a piece of clothing that you wear on the top half of your body. A shirt usually has a collar, sleeves and buttons down the front: *She was wearing a loose shirt and jeans.* ◻ *He always wears a shirt and tie when he's working at the office.*

shiver *verb*: **shivers, shivered, shivering, has shivered**
You **shiver** when your whole body shakes because you are cold

or frightened: *They were standing outside, shivering in the cold.*

shock *noun*: **shocks**
1 You have a **shock** when you have a sudden unpleasant surprise which upsets you: *I had a terrible shock when I heard the news.*
2 Electricity gives you a **shock** when it gives you a sudden pain when you touch it: *I got a shock when I touched the cooker.*

shock *verb*: **shocks, shocked, shocking, has shocked**
Something bad or unpleasant **shocks** you when it upsets you a lot: *He was shocked at the boy's bad behaviour.*

shoe *noun*: **shoes**
You wear **shoes** to cover and protect your feet when you go outside. Shoes are usually made of leather or some other strong material: *I bought a new pair of shoes in the sale.* ◻ *He took his shoes and socks off and walked into the water.* ◻ *tennis shoes.*

shoelace
shoe

shoelace *noun*: **shoelaces**
Shoelaces are strings that are used to tie shoes: *My shoelace has broken.* ◻ *He never does his shoelaces up.*

shone *verb*
see **shine**: *The sun shone and the birds were singing.* ◻ *He shone the light in my face.* ◻ *Her eyes shone with pleasure.*

shook *verb*
see **shake**: *She shook the rug to remove the dust.* ◻ *He didn't say no; he just shook his head.*

shoot *verb*: **shoots, shot, shooting, has shot**
1 A person with a gun **shoots** when they fire the gun: *He shot at the target but he missed.* ❑ *How do you shoot this gun?*
2 A person with a gun **shoots** someone when they injure or kill them by hitting them with a bullet: *The policeman shot the man in the arm.*
3 A football or hockey player **shoots** when they send the ball very fast towards the goal: *Ollie tried to shoot from the centre of the pitch.*

shoot *noun*: **shoots**
A **shoot** is a very young plant that has just begun to grow from a seed, or a new part that has grown on a plant: *When the shoots appear, put the plants into pots.* ❑ *In spring, new young shoots appear all over this plant.*

shop *noun*: **shops**
A **shop** is a place where you can buy things: *There's a small shop in the village where you can buy fruit and vegetables.* ❑ *a shoe shop* ❑ *a toy shop.*

shop *verb*: **shops, shopped, shopping, has shopped**
You **shop** when you go to the shops and buy things: *The people here shop for fresh meat and vegetables every day.*

shop assistant *noun*: **shop assistants**
A **shop assistant** is a person whose job is to serve customers in a shop: *I asked the shop assistant if I could try the dress on.*

shopkeeper *noun*: **shopkeepers**
A **shopkeeper** is a person who owns a shop: *The shopkeepers here are not happy about the new supermarket.*

shopping *noun*
1 You go **shopping** when you go to the shops and buy things: *Let's go shopping for new clothes this weekend.*
2 Your **shopping** is the things you have bought: *She was carrying two heavy bags of shopping.*

shore *noun*
The **shore** is the land along the edge of a lake or the sea: *They swam to the opposite shore of the lake.* ❑ *We found some interesting things on the shore after the storm.*

short *adjective*: **shorter, shortest**
1 A **short** period of time or activity does not last for a great amount of time: *The days get shorter as winter gets nearer.* ❑ *He stayed for a short time in Los Angeles before moving to New York.* ❑ *We had a short discussion about work.*
2 Something that is **short** is not a great distance from one end to the other: *He wears shirts with short sleeves in the summer.* ❑ *a book of short stories* ❑ *The taxi driver knew the shortest way home.*
3 A **short** person is smaller than people who are of average height: *He's shorter than his brother, but much stronger.*

meaning 1: same as **brief**
meaning 1 and 2: the opposite is **long**
meaning 3: the opposite is **tall**

▷ **short for**
A word is **short for** another when it is a shorter way of saying it: *'Ray' is short for 'Raymond'.* ❑ *'I'll' is short for 'I will' or 'I shall'.*

▷ **short of**
You are **short of** something when you don't have enough of it: *We're a bit short of money at the moment.*

shortage *noun*: **shortages**
There is a **shortage** of something when there is not enough of it: *There's a shortage of teachers in science subjects.* ❑ *There was a shortage of water during the long hot summer.*

shorten *verb*: **shortens, shortened, shortening, has shortened**
You **shorten** something when you make it shorter: *I always have to shorten the legs on new trousers.* ❑ *You can shorten 'I will' to 'I'll'.*

shorts *noun*
Short trousers that do not cover your knees are called **shorts**: *Tennis shorts* ❑ *I packed three pairs of shorts for the beach.*

shot *noun*: **shots**
1 A **shot** is the firing of a bullet from a gun: *He fired three shots at the target.* ❑ *Was that a gunshot I heard?*
2 A **shot** is also the action of throwing, kicking or hitting a ball at a goal: *She took a shot at the goal.* ❑ *He reached the hole with his second shot.*
3 A photograph is also sometimes called a **shot**: *I got a really good shot of the bear fishing in the river.*

shot *verb*
see **shoot**: *Bob shot a rabbit for dinner.* ❑ *This animal has been shot with an arrow.*

should *verb*
1 You use **should** when you are talking about the right thing to do: *You should be more careful when you are crossing the road.* ❑ *You should lock all the windows and doors when you go out.* ❑ *What should I do?* ❑ *Shouldn't we tell him the truth?*
2 You use **should** when you are talking about what will probably happen: *It should take about three hours to get there.*
3 You also use '**I should**…' and '**we should**…' when you are talking about what you want to do: *We should like it very much if you came to visit us in February.*

▸ You can shorten:
I should to **I'd**: *I'd love to come with you to the dance.*
we should to **we'd**: *We'd be very pleased to accept your invitation.*
should not to **shouldn't**.

---

shoulder *noun*: **shoulders**
Your **shoulders** are the parts of your body at the top of your arms: *He lifted the sack on to his shoulders.* ❑ *You can carry this bag over your shoulder.* [see picture at **arm**]

shouldn't
Shouldn't is short for **should not**: *Shouldn't we be there now?* ❑ *You shouldn't go out alone after dark.*

should've
Should've is short for **should have**: *I think you're right. We*

should've turned left five minutes ago.

shout *verb*: **shouts, shouted, shouting, has shouted**
Someone **shouts** when they say something in a very loud voice: *I can't hear you; you'll have to shout.* ❑ *The two men were shouting at each other in angry voices.* ❑ *She was shouting, 'Help me!'*

shout *noun*: **shouts**
A **shout** is a loud cry that someone makes: *We heard their shouts of laughter as they walked past the house.*

shovel *noun*: **shovels**
A **shovel** is a large metal blade with a long handle; it is used for lifting and moving earth or sand.

show *verb*: **shows, showed, showing, has shown** or **has showed**
1 You **show** something to someone when you let them see it: *Show me your finger.* ❑ *He showed me his new camera.*
2 You **show** someone how to do something when you let them watch you doing it, so that they can learn how to do it: *Jane showed me how to make curtains.* ❑ *I'll show you how to send a fax.*
3 You **show** someone to a place when you guide them there: *A girl with a torch showed us to our seats in the cinema.*

▷ **show off**
1 You **show** something **off** when you let other people see and admire it: *David was showing off his new car to the neighbour.*
2 A person **shows off** when they try to make people admire them:

'I've read all of Shakespeare's plays,' he said, showing off.

▷ **show up**
Someone **shows up** when they arrive, especially after people have been waiting for them: *He said he would meet me at eight o'clock, but he didn't show up.*

show *noun*: **shows**
1 A **show** is a play or some other performance, either in the theatre or on television: *They won two tickets to see a show in London.* ❑ *Did you watch his show on TV last night? It was really funny.*
2 A **show** is also an event where people go to look at things: *We go to the flower show every year.*

shower *noun*: **showers**
1a A **shower** is a device that sprays water on you; you use it to wash yourself: *I suggest that you use the shower to wash your hair.*
b A **shower** is also a place where this device is fitted, usually in a bathroom: *We'd like a room with a shower and a bath, please.* **c** You are in the **shower**, or you are taking or having a **shower**, when you are standing under a shower, washing your body: *She was in the shower when the phone rang.*
2 A **shower** of rain is a short period of time when rain falls: *There will be some showers in the north today, but most other areas will enjoy some sun.*

shown *verb*
see **show**: *Has he shown you his new computer game yet?* ❑ *We were shown some photographs of the house.*

shrank *verb*
see **shrink**: *I washed this jumper in hot water and it shrank.*

shred *noun*: **shreds**
A **shred** of paper or cloth is a thin strip of it that has been torn from a larger piece: *He tore her letter into shreds and threw it in the bin.* ❑ *These shreds of cloth will be used to make paper.*

shrink *verb*: **shrinks, shrank, shrinking, has shrunk**
Something **shrinks** when it gets smaller: *This jumper will shrink if you wash it in hot water.* ❑ *Have I shrunk, or have you grown taller?*

shrug *verb*: **shrugs, shrugged, shrugging, has shrugged**
You **shrug** when you lift your shoulders quickly to show that you don't know or that you don't care: *I asked him if he was happy, and he just shrugged.*

shrunk *verb*
see **shrink**: *This jumper feels tight. Has it shrunk?*

shut *verb*: **shuts, shut, shutting, has shut**
1a You **shut** an open window, door or lid when you move it so that the opening is covered: *Could you shut that window, please? It's cold in here.* ❑ *She put the blankets in the box and shut the lid.* **b** You **shut** a drawer when you push it in so that it is closed; you **shut** a book when you move the two sides of it together so that the pages are covered: *I can't shut this drawer; there's too much in it.* ❑ *At 11.30, I shut my book and went to sleep.*
2 Someone **shuts** a shop or other public building when they close and lock it, often at the end of the day: *What time do you shut the shop on Saturdays?*
3 A factory or other business **is**

shut, or **is shut down**, when it stops producing things and people no longer work there: *The factory was shut down and thousands of workers lost their jobs.*

same as **close**
the opposite is **open**

▷ **shut off**
1 You **shut off** a machine or a tap when you stop it working: *The plumber shut off the water while he was repairing the pipes.*
2 Someone **shuts** themselves **off** from other people when they do not meet or talk to others.

▷ **shut up**
1 A place **is shut up** when it is closed and locked so that no-one can enter: *The butcher shut up his shop and went home.*
2 '**Shut up!**' is a very rude way of telling someone to be quiet.

shut *adjective*
Something is **shut** when it is not open: *Make sure all the windows are shut and the door is locked.*

shy *adjective:* **shyer** or **shier, shyest** or **shiest**
1 A **shy** person feels nervous when they have to talk to other people, especially people they don't know: *He was too shy to invite her to the party.* ❑ *She was very shy at first, but now she's enjoying her new school.*
2 A **shy** animal is easily frightened: *This small forest deer is a shy animal which you will rarely see.*

meaning 2: same as **timid**

sick *adjective:* **sicker, sickest**
1 A person or animal is **sick** when they are ill: *'Where's Kim?' 'She's sick today.'* ❑ *a hospital for sick and injured animals.*

2 A person or animal is **sick** when they bring food up from their stomach and it comes out of their mouth: *I think I'm going to be sick.* ❑ *The cat was sick on the kitchen floor.*

sickness *noun*
Sickness is the fact of being sick or feeling ill: *This medicine can cause sickness.*

side *noun*: **sides**
1 a One of the **sides** of a solid shape is one of its surfaces: *A cube has six sides.* **b** One of the sides of a flat shape is one of the lines that make up its outside edges: *A triangle has three sides, and a square has four sides.*
2 The **side** of a road is one of its two edges that are opposite each other: *The two men were sitting on the side of the road.* ❑ *Jim lives on the opposite side of the street.*
3 The **sides** of something are the surfaces that are not the top, bottom, front or back: *The lorry hit the left side of the car.* ❑ *The vase was lying on its side.* ❑ *The switch is on the side of the lamp.* ❑ *She stuck the label on the side of the jar.*
4 The **side** of something thin and flat, such as a piece of paper or cloth, is either of its two surfaces: *He wrote the letter on both sides of the paper.* ❑ *The bed cover has a pattern on one side.*
5 Your **sides** are the right and left parts of your body: *He said he couldn't feel anything on his left side.* ❑ *The baby was lying on its side.*
6 A **side** is one of the teams in a game or competition: *Which side won?*

sideways *adverb*
To move **sideways** is to move towards one side, not forwards or backwards: *The dancers moved sideways round the room.* ❑ *He stepped sideways to let us pass.*

sieve *noun*: **sieves**
A **sieve** is a piece of kitchen equipment that has lots of tiny holes in it; it is used to separate solid things from a liquid, or smaller pieces from larger ones. *If lumps form in the sauce, you can pour it through a sieve to remove them.*

‘siv ’

sigh *verb*: **sighs, sighed, sighing, has sighed**
A person **sighs** when they take a long deep breath and breathe out again loudly, because they are bored, tired or unhappy about something: *She sighed. 'What are we going to do now?' she said.* ❑ *He looked at the piles of dirty dishes and sighed.*

sight *noun*: **sights**
1 Sight is the ability to see: *He lost his sight during the war.* ❑ *Reading without enough light is very bad for your sight.*
2 A **sight** is something that you see: *He can't stand the sight of blood.*
3 Something is in **sight** when you can see it; something comes into **sight** when you begin to see it: *They looked down the road but there was nobody in sight.* ❑ *The clouds moved away and the moon came into sight again.*
4 Famous places that a lot of people visit are called **sights**: *They're not in Venice on business. They've come to see the sights.*

sign *noun*: **signs**
1 A **sign** is a mark that has a meaning: [=] *is the sign for 'is equal to'.*
2 You make a **sign** when you make a movement which tells other people something: *He made a sign for us to keep quiet.*
3 A **sign** is a board or notice with writing or a picture on it which gives you information: *The sign in the window said 'Rooms to Let'. □ That road sign means that you can't turn left.*
4 There is a **sign** of a person or thing when there is something that tells you that they are, or will be, present: *There was no sign of him in the garden. □ The black clouds were the first sign of the storm.*

sign *verb*: **signs, signed, signing, has signed**
You **sign** your name when you write your signature; you **sign** a letter, a form or a cheque when you write your signature on it: *Sign your name here, please. □ Don't forget to sign your cheque!*

signal *noun*: **signals**
1 A **signal** is a light, a sound or the movement of a hand, that gives a certain message: *The policeman gave us the signal to move forwards.*
2 A railway or traffic **signal** is a set of coloured lights which tell drivers when to stop and go: *Finally, the signal showed green and the train began to move forwards.*

signature *noun*: **signatures**
Your **signature** is the particular way that you write your name on cheques, letters and forms: *Could you read this and put your signature at the bottom, please?*

signpost *noun*: **signposts**
A **signpost** is a sign on a pole at the side of a road or path; it shows the direction or distance to places: *The last signpost read 'Paris 50 kilometres'.*

silence *noun*: **silences**
There is **silence** when there is no sound: *The crowd stood in silence watching the funeral car pass. □ There was a short silence before anyone spoke.*

silent *adjective*
1 A place is **silent** when there is no sound in it: *The forest was silent and we could hear our hearts beating.*
2 A person, animal or machine is **silent** when they do not make a sound: *We had to remain silent for half an hour.*

same as **quiet**

silk *noun*
Silk is a kind of cloth made of fine soft threads: *She was wearing a beautiful silk blouse.*

silly *adjective*: **sillier, silliest**
A person or their behaviour is **silly** when they don't behave in a sensible way: *That was a very silly thing to do. □ She knew that she was behaving like a silly child.*

same as **foolish**

silver *noun*
1 Silver is a pale grey precious metal used to make such things as jewellery, plates and spoons: *These spoons are made of silver.*
2 Something that is **silver** is made of this metal or is the pale grey colour of this metal: *The*

winner of the match gets a big silver cup. □ the silver moon.

similar *adjective*
Things that are **similar** are like each other in some way, but not exactly the same: *The two plates are similar, but they were made by different companies.* □ *Alice and I wore very similar dresses to the wedding.*

same as **like** or **alike**

simple *adjective*: **simpler, simplest**
1 Something that is **simple** is not difficult to do: *You should do a few simple exercises every day.* □ *The sum wasn't as simple as it looked.*
2 Simple things are plain and have not been decorated in any way: *She wore a simple black dress with no jewellery.*
3 People who live a **simple** life have only the most basic things they need to live: *The people here lead a very simple life without any modern machines.*

meaning 1: same as **easy**

since *conjunction, adverb and preposition*
1 Since means 'from the time that' or 'from that time until now': *Since her accident, she's had to use a wheelchair.* □ *He has been in prison since his arrest three months ago.* □ *He hasn't spoken to me since last week.*
2 You use **since** when you are talking about something that has happened after a particular time in the past: *A lot of things have happened since our last meeting.* □ *He's grown a lot since we saw him last year.*

3 You also use **since** in the same way as 'because': *Since we're all ready, we can leave early.*

sing *verb*: **sings, sang, singing, has sung**
1 People **sing** when they make musical sounds with their voices: *The men were singing as they worked.* □ *Sing us a song.* □ *We sang songs in the bus on the way home.*
2 Birds **sing** when they make various musical cries: *The birds were singing at five o'clock this morning.*

singer *noun*: **singers**
A **singer** is a person who sings: *Are you a good singer?* □ *Who's your favourite singer?*

single *adjective*
1 A **single** thing is only one: *She doesn't have a single grey hair.* □ *What's the single most important thing in life for you?*
2 Single beds or rooms are for one person only: *I'd like a single room with a bathroom for one night, please.*
3 A person who is **single** is not married: *Is your son still single?* □ *There were only one or two single women in the village.*
4 A **single** ticket is a ticket that allows you to travel to a place, but not back again: *Is it more expensive to buy two single tickets than a return?*

sink *verb*: **sinks, sank, sinking, has sunk**
1 Something **sinks** when it drops below the surface of a liquid and does not float on the top: *The ship hit a rock and started to sink.* □ *His feet were slowly sinking into the deep mud.*

2 Something **sinks** when it goes down to a lower level: *The sun was sinking in the sky and it was nearly time to go home.* ❑ *He sank to his knees and prayed.*

meaning 1: the opposite is **float**

sink *noun*: **sinks**
A **sink** is a deep bowl attached to a wall, which is used to wash things in. It has a hole in the bottom to let water out: *He piled up the dishes in the sink.*

sip *verb*: **sips, sipped, sipping, has sipped**
You **sip** a liquid when you drink it, taking very small amounts at a time: *She sat opposite him, sipping her hot coffee.*

sir *noun*
Sir is a polite form that people such as shop assistants or waiters use when they are speaking to a man; children also sometimes call their teachers **sir**: *Can I help you, sir?* ❑ *Sorry I'm late, sir.*

sister *noun*: **sisters**
Your **sister** is a woman or girl who has the same mother and father as you do: *My father has two sisters, but no brothers.*

sit *verb*: **sits, sat, sitting, has sat**
1 You **sit** when you rest your bottom on a chair; you **are sitting** when you are in a position with your bottom resting on a chair: *Come and sit next to me.* ❑ *Margaret was sitting on the edge of the bed.*
2 An object **is sitting** on a surface when it is on it: *The vase sits here on the top shelf.*
3 You **sit** an exam or test when you take an exam or test: *He's studying a lot at the moment*

because he's sitting his exams next month.

▷ **sit back**
1 You **sit back** when you rest your back while you are sitting, so that you are comfortable: *He sat back against the pillows.*
2 Someone **sits back** when they rest or do nothing: *There's no time to sit back; we've got another job starting next week.*

▷ **sit down**
You **sit down** when you move into a position of rest in a chair: *The students came in and sat down at their desks.*

▷ **sit up**
You **sit up** when you move yourself into a sitting position after you have been lying down or leaning back: *He sat up in bed to eat his lunch.*

sitting room *noun*: **sitting rooms**
A **sitting room** is a room in a house where you can sit and relax.

situation *noun*: **situations**
1 The **situation** that a person is in is the state that they are in: *They were in a difficult situation, with no food and no money.*
2 The **situation** that something is in is the position that it is in: *The situation of the land was perfect for growing grapes.*

six *noun and adjective*: **sixes**
1 **Six** is the number or figure 6: *Five plus one is six.* ❑ *Three sixes are eighteen.* ❑ *I wrote a six instead of a seven by mistake.*
2 **Six** is the time of six o'clock: *They usually finish work at about six in the evening.*
3 **Six** is also the age of six;

someone who is **six** is six years old: *Most children can read and write at six.* ❑ *He started school when he was six.*

six *determiner and pronoun*
Six means six in number: *He got six points for his team.* ❑ *There were twelve eggs in the box and six were broken.*

sixteen *noun and adjective*: **sixteens**
1 Sixteen is the number 16: *Ten and six is sixteen.* ❑ *Two sixteens are 32.*
2 Sixteen is the age of 16; someone who is **sixteen** is 16 years old: *He left school at sixteen.* ❑ *She's sixteen next Tuesday.*

sixteen *determiner and pronoun*
Sixteen means sixteen in number: *He was away from work for sixteen days.* ❑ *They ate all the cakes so I made another sixteen.*

sixth *determiner and adjective*
The **sixth** person or thing is the one that comes after fifth.

sixty *noun and adjective*: **sixties**
1 Sixty is the number or figure 60: *Fifty plus ten is sixty.*
2a Sixty is the age of 60; someone who is **sixty** is 60 years old: *She'll stop working when she's sixty.* **b** A person in their **sixties** is between 60 and 69 years old.
3 The years in any century between 60 and 69 are often called 'the **sixties**': *He was a child in the sixties.*

sixty *determiner and pronoun*
Sixty means sixty in number: *He went to jail for sixty days.* ❑ *We counted the letters; there were more than sixty.*

size *noun*: **sizes**
The **size** of something is how big it is: *What size shoes do you take?* ❑ *These potatoes are all different sizes.*

skate *noun*: **skates**
Skates are special boots with blades on the bottom that you wear to skate on ice.

skate *verb*: **skates, skated, skating, has skated**
People **skate** when they move on ice wearing special boots with blades on the bottom: *We skated on the frozen river in the winter time.*

skating *noun*
Skating is the sport or activity of moving on ice wearing skates: *We watched the skating on television.*

skeleton *noun*: **skeletons**
A person's or animal's **skeleton** is the structure of all the bones inside their body.

sketch *noun*: **sketches**
A **sketch** is a quick drawing without exact details: *He did a sketch of me while we were sitting in the garden.*

ski *noun*: **skis**
Skis are long narrow strips of metal that you attach to your feet, in order to move smoothly on snow.

ski *verb*: **skies, skied** or **ski'd, skiing, has skied** or **has ski'd**
People **ski** when they move smoothly on snow, using skis: *We skied down the mountain.*

skid *verb*: **skids, skidded, skidding, has skidded**
A vehicle **skids** when it slides sideways suddenly when the road is wet, or when the driver has put on the brakes too quickly: *Cars*

and lorries were skidding on the ice.

skill *noun*: **skills**
1 Someone has **skill** when they have the ability to do something well: *You need a lot of skill to play the piano like that.*
2 A **skill** is an ability that you have to do something well: *He took some lessons to improve his driving skills.*

skin *noun*: **skins**
1 Skin is the thin layer that covers the body: *Babies' skin is very soft.* ❑ *A snake loses its skin and then grows a new one.* ❑ *People with pale skins should not sit for long periods in the sun.*
2 The **skin** of a fruit or vegetable is the thin covering all round it: *Remove the skins from the tomatoes by putting them in hot water.*

skip *verb*: **skips, skipped, skipping, has skipped**
1 You **skip** when you move along jumping from one foot to the other: *Vicky skipped along, singing a happy song.*
2 You **skip** when you jump over a length of rope that you hold in both hands and turn over your head and under your feet: *Try skipping for ten minutes every day.*

skirt *noun*: **skirts**
A **skirt** is a piece of clothing that hangs down from the waist; it is worn by girls and women: *She was wearing a black skirt and a red jumper.* ❑ *Short skirts are in fashion at the moment.*

skull *noun*: **skulls**
Your **skull** is the hollow bone of your head that covers your brain:

They found the skull of a creature that looked like a huge rat.

sky *noun*
The **sky** is the area above the Earth where you can see clouds, the sun and the moon: *There were dark clouds in the sky.* ❑ *The whole sky became pink as the sun went down.*

skyscraper *noun*: **skyscrapers**
A **skyscraper** is a very tall building: *Which is the highest skyscraper in New York?*

slack *adjective*: **slacker, slackest**
Something that is **slack** is loose or not tight: *Keep the fishing line slack until the fish bites the hook.*

slam *verb*: **slams, slammed, slamming, has slammed**
You **slam** a door or a window when you push it hard so that it shuts with a loud bang: *I woke up when I heard the car door slamming.*

slang *noun*
Slang refers to certain words that people use when they are talking in an informal way, or to people who are part of the group they belong to.

slap *verb*: **slaps, slapped, slapping, has slapped**
One person **slaps** another when they hit them with the palm of their hand: *One of the children slapped her on the face and made her cry.*

sleep *verb*: **sleeps, slept, sleeping, has slept**
You **sleep** when you rest by closing your eyes and going into a state in which you do not know what is happening around you: *He slept through the whole film.* ❑ *'Good night. Sleep well.'*

▷ **sleep in**
You **sleep in** when you sleep for longer than you meant to and you get out of bed late.

sleep *noun*
A **sleep** is a period of time that you spend sleeping, or the rest you get when you are sleeping: *Did you have a good sleep?* ❑ *She always has a little sleep in the afternoons.*

▷ **go to sleep**
You **go to sleep** when you pass into a state of rest with your eyes closed: *He went to sleep in front of the fire, and woke up at 3am.*

sleepy *adjective*: **sleepier, sleepiest**
You are **sleepy** when you are tired and feel that you want to sleep: *It was nearly midnight and everyone was sleepy.*

sleeve *noun*: **sleeves**
The **sleeves** of a piece of clothing are the parts which cover your arms: *He wore a shirt with short sleeves.* ❑ *Mum was knitting one of the sleeves of the jumper.*

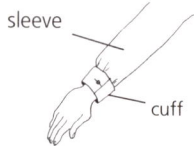
sleeve
cuff

slept *verb*
see **sleep**: *When we were on holiday we slept in a tent.* ❑ *I haven't slept for two nights.*

slice *noun*: **slices**
A **slice** is a thin flat piece that has been cut from something: *He cut two slices of bread to make a sandwich.* ❑ *Would you like another slice of cake?*

slice *verb*: **slices, sliced, slicing, has sliced**
You **slice** something when you cut thin flat pieces from it: *The shop has a special machine for slicing bread.*

slid *verb*
see **slide**: *The snake has slid away into the bushes.* ❑ *Jackie slid on the ice and hurt her back.*

slide *verb*: **slides, slid, sliding, has slid**
Someone or something **slides** when they move smoothly over a surface: *The children were sliding on the ice.* ❑ *The snake slid into a hole in the wall.*

slight *adjective*: **slighter, slightest**
A **slight** mistake or problem is not very great or not very serious: *There's a slight problem with this bill.* ❑ *He has a slight injury to one of his hands.* ❑ *I've got a slight headache.*

slim *adjective*: **slimmer, slimmest**
A **slim** person is thin in an attractive way: *You're looking very slim. Have you lost weight?*

slip *verb*: **slips, slipped, slipping, has slipped**
1 You **slip** when your feet slide by accident and you lose your balance: *The old lady slipped on the ice.* ❑ *Be careful not to slip on the wet floor.*
2a Something **slips** when it moves down from a higher position: *A large amount of earth has slipped down the mountain into the river.* **b** Something that you are holding **slips** when it suddenly moves out of the correct position, or you drop it by accident: *The razor slipped and he*

cut his face. ❏ *The plate slipped out of my hand and broke on the floor.*
3a You **slip** somewhere when you go there quietly, especially without being noticed: *She slipped out of the room when no-one was looking.* **b** You **slip** something into a place when you put it there quickly and quietly: *The man slipped a $50 bill into the waiter's hand.*

slipper *noun*: **slippers**
Slippers are soft, comfortable shoes that you wear in the home: *He got out of bed and put on his slippers.*

slippery *adjective*
1 A **slippery** surface may cause you to slip when you walk or drive on it, because it is wet or covered in ice: *Be careful; the roads are very slippery.*
2 A **slippery** object is difficult to hold on to, because it is wet or very smooth: *Fish are slippery things to hold.*

slope *verb*: **slopes, sloped, sloping, has sloped**
A line or surface **slopes** when it gradually rises upwards or goes downwards: *The garden slopes down to the sea.*

slope *noun*: **slopes**
A **slope** is the side of a hill: *There were lots of people skiing on the slopes.* ❏ *We had to climb up a slope to get to the house.*

slow *adjective and adverb*: **slower, slowest**
1 Something that is **slow** happens or moves at a low speed: *A bicycle is slower than a car.* ❏ *I can't work with him — he's too slow.*

2 A watch or clock is **slow** when it shows a time that is earlier than the correct time: *My watch is ten minutes slow.*
3 A person who is **slow** is not very clever, and finds it difficult to learn things: *He was too slow to keep up with the other pupils in the class.*

meaning 1: the opposite is **fast** or **quick**
meaning 2: the opposite is **fast**

▷ **slow down**
1 Someone or something **slows down** when they reduce their speed: *Slow down. You're talking too quickly.* ❏ *The lorry slowed down and stopped outside our house.*
2 Someone or something **slows** you **down** when they make you reduce your speed: *All that heavy luggage will slow us down.*

small *adjective*: **smaller, smallest**
A **small** person or thing is not big in size: *She's too small to reach that high shelf.* ❏ *These shoes are too big — you need a smaller pair.* ❏ *They live in the smallest house in the village.* ❏ *Some small boys were playing in the street.*
2a A **small** amount is very little of something: *I suggest you save a small amount of money each week.* **b** A **small** number is only a few: *We gave a party for a small number of close friends.*

same as **little**
the opposite is **big** or **large**

smart *adjective*: **smarter, smartest**
1a People who are **smart** are well-dressed and tidy: *You look*

smart today! What's the special occasion? **b Smart** clothes are neat and well-made: She was wearing a smart grey suit.
2 A **smart** person is clever. My brother is smarter than me.

meaning 2: the opposite is **stupid** or **foolish**

smash verb: **smashes, smashed, smashing, has smashed**
1 You **smash** something when you break it into small pieces: He dropped the box and smashed all the glasses.
2 One thing **smashes** into another when it hits it very hard causing a lot of damage: The lorry smashed into the wall at the side of the road.

smell noun: **smells**
1 Smell is the sense with which you notice things through your nose: Most animals have a better sense of smell than humans.
2 A **smell** is something that you notice using this sense: There's a smell of smoke in here.

smell verb: **smells, smelt** or **smelled, smelling, has smelt** or **has smelled**
1 You **smell** something when you notice it through your nose: Can you smell something strange? ❑ Smell this perfume — isn't it lovely?
2 Something **smells**, when it has a smell, often an unpleasant one; something **smells** of a particular thing when it has that smell: 'Do you like this cheese?' 'Not much — it smells. ❑ The kitchen smelt of frying bacon.

smile verb: **smiles, smiled, smiling, has smiled**

You **smile** when you turn the corners of your mouth upwards to show that you are happy, or that you think something is funny: The shop assistant smiled and asked if she could help me. ❑ When I told him the joke he smiled, but he didn't laugh. ❑ She smiled at everyone as she entered the room.

smile noun: **smiles**
A **smile** is an act of smiling: The baby stopped crying and gave us a big smile. ❑ He has a very nice smile.

smile

smoke noun
Smoke is the grey or black stuff that rises into the air when something is burning: They couldn't see anything because there was so much smoke. ❑ Smoke is bad for babies and young children.

smoke verb: **smokes, smoked, smoking, has smoked**
1 Something such as a fire or an engine **smokes** when smoke rises from it.
2 A person **smokes** when they breathe in the smoke from burning tobacco in a cigarette or pipe.

smooth adjective: **smoother, smoothest**
Something that is **smooth** has a polished or even surface with no lumps or holes in it: We walked on the smooth round stones on the beach. ❑ She has beautiful smooth skin.

the opposite is **rough**

snack *noun*: **snacks**
A **snack** is a small quick meal, often eaten between other meals: *We often have a cup of tea and a snack in the middle of the morning.*

snail *noun*: **snails**
A **snail** is a creature with a soft body protected by a shell; it moves very slowly: *Have you ever eaten snails?*

snake *noun*: **snakes**
A **snake** is an animal with no legs and a long narrow body covered with scales; it moves along the ground by twisting its body from side to side: *You can find only one kind of poisonous snake in Britain.*

snake

snap *verb*: **snaps, snapped, snapping, has snapped**
1 Something **snaps** when it breaks making a loud noise: *My pencil snapped in two.*
2 You **snap** your fingers when you make a sudden noise by pressing your middle finger across your thumb and then releasing it: *He snapped his fingers to get the waiter's attention.*
3 Something **snaps** shut when it closes suddenly making a loud noise: *The lid of the box snapped shut.*
4 A dog or other animal with sharp teeth **snaps** when it tries to bite someone or something: *The dogs ran after him snapping at his legs.*

snarl *verb*: **snarls, snarled, snarling, has snarled**
An animal such as a dog **snarls** when it shows its teeth and makes a deep noise in its throat to show that it is angry: *Our dog always snarls at the postman.*

snatch *verb*: **snatches, snatched, snatching, has snatched**
You **snatch** something when you grab it quickly: *One of the boys snatched the ball and ran away with it.*

sneak *verb*: **sneaks, sneaked, sneaking, has sneaked**
Someone **sneaks** somewhere when they move there very quietly: *The cat sneaked into the kitchen and ate some cold chicken.*

sneeze *verb*: **sneezes, sneezed, sneezing, has sneezed**
You **sneeze** when air suddenly comes out of your nose and mouth making a loud noise that you can't control: *The dust in the room made everyone sneeze.*

sniff *verb*: **sniffs, sniffed, sniffing, has sniffed**
You **sniff** when you take a short breath through your nose: *She was sniffing and holding a handkerchief to her nose.* ❑ *The dog suddenly stopped and sniffed the ground.*

snore *verb*: **snores, snored, snoring, has snored**
Someone **snores** when they make a loud sound in their throat while they are sleeping: *He was snoring so loudly — we could hear him in the next room.*

snow *noun*
Snow is the small soft pieces of frozen water that fall from the sky

when it is very cold: *The countryside was covered with deep white snow.*

snow *verb*: **snows, snowed, snowing, has snowed**
It **snows** when small soft pieces of frozen water fall from the sky: *Do you think it will snow today?*

so *adverb and conjunction*
1 So means 'for that reason': *The car's broken down so I'll be late.* □ *There was no-one in, so I went away again.*
2 You use **so** in the same way as 'very': *I'm so happy we found you.* □ *Thank you so much for the lovely present.* □ *You've been so kind.*
3 You also use **so** in descriptions, when something is enough to cause something to happen: *It was so cold outside, even their beards had ice on them.* □ *I was so tired I feel asleep immediately.*
4 So is also used like 'also' when two people or things do the same thing: *He likes watching sport, and so do I.* □ *Cats eat meat and so do dogs.* □ *Peter will be there, and so will Beth.*
5 Something is **so** when it is the case or is a fact: *'I don't think she's very happy.' 'Is that so?'* □ *'Is she leaving?' 'I think so.'* □ *'Are you going home for the holidays?' 'I expect so.'*
6 You use **so** when you are telling someone the reason for an action: *I've put your coat on the heater so it will be dry for you.*

▷ **so that** or **so as to**
You use **so that** or **so as to** when you are telling someone the reason for an action: *I set the alarm clock so that I would get up*

in time. □ *He closed the curtains so as to keep out the light.*

soak *verb*: **soaks, soaked, soaking, has soaked**
1 Liquid **soaks** things when it makes them very wet: *The rain has soaked the football pitch.* □ *The lorry drove through the water and soaked us all.*
2 Liquid **soaks** through something when it passes through it: *The water has soaked through the ceiling.*

soap *noun*
Soap is stuff that you use to wash with; it makes bubbles when you mix it with water: *a bar of soap* □ *Always wash your hands with soap and water before touching food.*

sob *verb*: **sobs, sobbed, sobbing, has sobbed**
Someone **sobs** when they make noises while they are crying: *The little girl was sitting on the floor sobbing.*

soccer *noun*
Soccer is another name for a type of football; it is played with two teams of eleven players on a field that has a goal at each end.

sock *noun*: **socks**
A **sock** is a piece of clothing that covers your foot and ankle: *He was wearing bright red socks.* □ *a pair of socks.*

sofa *noun*: **sofas**
A **sofa** is a long soft seat with a back and arms, for two or more people: *Marjorie sat next to me on the sofa.*

soft *adjective*: **softer, softest**
1 Soft things are not hard or firm: *This bed is too soft for me.* □ *We had fresh soft bread and jam*

for breakfast.
2 Something is **soft** when it feels smooth and pleasant to touch: *The baby's skin is lovely and soft.* ❑ *She stroked the cat's long soft fur.*
3 Music or other sounds that are **soft** are not loud: *She has a very soft voice — it's difficult to hear what she's saying.*

---
meaning 1: the opposite is **hard**
meaning 3: the opposite is **loud**

---

softly *adverb*
1 Softly means 'in a gentle way': *She touched his cheek softly.*
2 Softly also means 'quietly': *She was singing softly to the baby.* ❑ *They crept softly along the corridor.*

software *noun*
The programs that are used to make a computer do particular tasks are called **software**: *He writes software for banks.*

soil *noun*
Soil is the dark brown stuff in which plants grow: *This soil is good for growing vegetables.*

sold *verb*
see **sell**: *Have you sold your house yet?* ❑ *The car was sold for £4000.*

soldier *noun*: **soldiers**
A **soldier** is a member of the army who fights in wars: *The soldiers waved to their families as the ship left the harbour.*

sole *noun*: **soles**
The **sole** of your foot or shoe is the part that touches the ground when you are walking: *These boots have got thick rubber soles.*

solid *adjective*
1 Something that is **solid** is hard and firm: *The water in the pond was frozen solid.* ❑ *This ice cream is completely solid.*
2 Something that is **solid** is made of the same material all the way through: *This bracelet is solid gold.* ❑ *They had to dig the tunnel through solid rock.*
3 Something that is **solid** is not hollow: *a solid cube.*

solo *noun*: **solos**
Someone who performs a **solo** sings or plays a musical instrument alone: *She sang a solo at the concert.*

solve *verb*: **solves, solved, solving, has solved**
You **solve** a problem when you find an answer to it: *He won enough money to solve all his problems.* ❑ *The mystery was never solved.*

some *determiner and pronoun*
1 Some is an amount of something: *We had some tea.* ❑ *I've made soup. Would you like some?*
2 You use **some** when you are talking about certain people or things, but not all of them: *Some people played tennis and some played golf.* ❑ *Only some farmers here grow rice.* ❑ *Some of the eggs were broken.*
3 You also use **some** when you can't say who or what you mean exactly: *Some man phoned about your library book.* ❑ *I can't come tonight. Shall we go some other evening instead?*

somebody *pronoun*
You use **somebody** to talk about a person without saying exactly who: *Will somebody come and help us?* ❑ *Has somebody been at my desk?*

some day or **someday** *adverb*
You use **some day** or **someday** to talk about a day or time in the future, though you don't know exactly when: *I'd like to go to Russia some day.* ❑ *He'll be a famous artist someday.*

somehow *adverb*
Somehow means 'in some way': *Somehow, he managed to escape.* ❑ *It's difficult, but we'll find the money somehow.*

someone *pronoun*
You use **someone** to talk about a person without saying exactly who: *Someone left the gate open and the dog escaped.* ❑ *Can you find someone to help you with the work?*

something *pronoun*
1 You use **something** to talk about an object, event, quality or action, but not one in particular: *I've got something in my eye* ❑ *There's something strange about him.* ❑ *Is there something I can do to help?*
2 You also use **something** when you don't want to, or cannot, say which you mean exactly: *I've got something to tell you.* ❑ *Can you give me something for a sore throat?*

sometime *adverb*
Sometime means 'at some time in the future': *We must visit Sarah sometime.* ❑ *Do you think he'll get a job sometime soon?*

sometimes *adverb*
Sometimes means 'on some occasions, but not all': *He sometimes helps in the kitchen, but not very often.* ❑ *Sometimes I feel very old.*

somewhere *adverb*
You use **somewhere** to talk about a place when you don't want to or cannot say which place in particular: *There's a restaurant somewhere along this street.* ❑ *They live somewhere in the north of Canada.*

son *noun*: **sons**
A **son** is a male child: *Your son looks like you.* ❑ *This is my oldest son, John.*

song *noun*: **songs**
1 A **song** is a piece of music with words for singing: *Sing us a song.* ❑ *He's written hundreds of popular songs.*
2 A bird's **song** is the sounds that it makes.

soon *adverb*
1 Soon means 'in a short time from now': *We'll soon be in Singapore.* ❑ *Her baby will be born quite soon.* ❑ *You'll soon be a teenager.*
2 Something happens too **soon** when it is too early: *It's too soon to know if he'll recover completely.* ❑ *The guests arrived too soon, and I wasn't ready.*

▷ **as soon as**
You use **as soon as** to talk about something that happens immediately after another thing: *I'll phone you as soon as I arrive.* ❑ *As soon as the doors were opened, people started to come in.*

▷ **as soon as possible**
You do something **as soon as possible** when you do it at the earliest time that you can: *Could you type this letter as soon as possible, please?*

sore *adjective*
A part of your body is **sore** when it hurts: *The dentist asked him if*

the tooth was sore. ❑ *I've got a sore throat.*

sorry *adjective*
1 You are **sorry** about something when you feel sad about it: *I was sorry to hear about the death of your husband.*
2 You are **sorry** for someone when you feel pity for them: *I feel sorry for Mary — she's been so unlucky recently.*
3 You say '**Sorry**' or '**I'm sorry**' to someone to apologize for something you have done: *He pushed me by accident and said, 'I'm sorry.'* ❑ *Sorry I'm late.*
4 You say '**Sorry?**' to someone when you haven't heard what they said: *'Sorry, what did you say?'*

sort *noun*: **sorts**
A **sort** is a type or kind: *What sort of computer have you got?* ❑ *This shop sells all sorts of kitchen equipment.* ❑ *Do you like this sort of music?* ❑ *It's a sort of love poem.*

sort *verb*: **sorts, sorted, sorting, has sorted**
You **sort** things when you put them into an order: *We'll have to sort these books by subject.* ❑ *He was sorting letters and putting them into boxes.*

▷ **sort out**
1 You **sort** things **out** when you put them in order: *Could you sort out this pile of papers, please?*
2 You **sort** a problem **out** when you deal with it and solve it: *He can't sort out his own problems.*

sound *noun*: **sounds**
1 Sound is what you hear, or what you sense through your ears: *They left, making no sound.*

2 A **sound** is a particular noise: *What was that sound?* ❑ *This doll makes a sound when you press its stomach.* ❑ *There are all sorts of strange sounds in this house at night.*

sound *verb*: **sounds, sounded, sounding, has sounded**
1 Something **sounds** when it makes a noise: *When the fire alarm sounds, please leave the building immediately.* ❑ *The driver sounded his horn.*
2 You say that something **sounds** a certain way if it seems that way to your ears: *We heard something outside the door that sounded like a cat.*

soup *noun*
Soup is a liquid food made with vegetables or meat, or both: *tomato soup* ❑ *We started the meal with soup.*

sour *adjective*
1 Sour foods have a sharp taste: *These grapes are sour.* ❑ *Add some lemon juice to the cream to give it a sour taste.*
2 Sour milk has gone bad: *The milk was sour so we had to throw it away.*

---

meaning 1: the opposite is **sweet**

---

source *noun*: **sources**
The **source** of something is the place where it has begun: *The source of the river is in those mountains over there.* ❑ *Turn off the gas before you look for the source of the leak.*

south *noun*
The **south** is the direction to your right when you are facing the rising sun: *London is in the*

south of Britain. ❑ *They crossed the United States from north to south.*

sow *verb*: **sows, sowed, sowing, has sowed** or **has sown**
You **sow** the seeds of plants when you put them in the ground so that they will grow: *The farmer was sowing the field with corn.*

rhymes with **toe**

space *noun*: **spaces**
1 Space is the enormous area that all the planets and stars are in: *In this story, men travel through space to find new planets.*
2 A **space** is an empty place: *There's a space here for you to sit down.* ❑ *He's got a space between his two front teeth.* ❑ *When you type the essay, leave spaces between each line.*
3 There is **space** when a place is big enough to do something: *There's space in this garden for the children to play.*

spaceship *noun*: **spaceships**
A **spaceship** is a vehicle that can travel through space: *In the film, seventeen spaceships attack the world's biggest cities.*

spade *noun*: **spades**
A **spade** is a tool with a square blade and a long handle, which you use for digging soil, especially in a garden: *The gardener was turning the soil over with a spade.*

spare *adjective*
1 Something is **spare** when it is extra or is not being used: *Are there any spare chairs in here?* ❑ *Take a spare pair of socks in case you get wet.*
2 Spare time is time when you don't have to work, and you can

do what you want: *What do you do in your spare time?* ❑ *She doesn't have a spare moment in the day.*

spark *noun*: **sparks**
1 A **spark** is a tiny piece of burning material that is thrown out by a fire: *A spark from the fire burnt a hole in the rug.*
2 A **spark** is also a tiny flash caused by electricity crossing between two points.

sparkle *verb*: **sparkles, sparkled, sparkling, has sparkled**
Something **sparkles** when it sends out tiny flashes of light: *The jewels sparkled in the shop window.*

spat *verb*
see **spit**: *I tried to give the baby the medicine, but he spat it out again.*

speak *verb*: **speaks, spoke, speaking, has spoken**
1 Someone **speaks** when they talk or say words: *Don't interrupt when someone else is speaking.* ❑ *Could I speak to Jerry, please?* ❑ *They were speaking very quietly.* ❑ *He spoke to the children about road safety.*
2 You **speak** a particular language when you are able to talk in that language: *He speaks five languages.* ❑ *What language do people speak in this part of China?* ❑ *She can speak English very well.*

special *adjective*
1 Something **special** is not ordinary: *She uses a special cream to make her skin soft.* ❑ *Tomorrow's a special day for the children — it's their first time in a plane.*

2 Something that is **special** is different from others: *This is a special tool that dentists use.* ❏ *Each of these men has a special job in the factory.*

spectacles *noun*

Spectacles are glasses that you wear to help you to see better: *She always wears her spectacles on the end of her nose.* [see picture at **glasses**]

speech *noun*: **speeches**

1 You have the power of **speech** when you can talk: *His speech isn't very clear. Do you think he's ill?*

2 You make a **speech** when you talk to an audience about something: *The president made a speech on TV last night.*

speed *noun*: **speeds**

The **speed** of something is the rate at which it moves: *What speed was he doing when he had the accident?* ❏ *The dog ran past me at a great speed.* ❏ *These two wheels turn at different speeds.* ❏ *The trains travel at speeds of up to 180 kilometres an hour.*

spell *noun*: **spells**

1 A **spell** is a period of time when something happens: *We've had a long spell of hot weather this month.* ❏ *He has had several spells of illness in the last year.*

2 Someone puts a **spell** on a person when they use magic on them: *He felt that she had put a spell on him. He couldn't behave in a normal way any more.*

spell *verb*: **spells, spelt** or **spelled, spelling, has spelt** or **has spelled**

1 You **spell** a word when you say all its letters in the correct order:

Could you spell your name for me, please?

2 A group of letters in a certain order **spells** a word when that is the word they form: *P, A, T spells 'pat'.*

spelling *noun*: **spellings**

1 Spelling is the ability to spell words in the correct way: *Your essay was quite good, but you'll have to improve your spelling.* ❏ *Our English teacher is giving us a spelling test tomorrow.*

2 A certain **spelling** of a word is one of the ways you can spell it: *Do you know the American spelling of this word?*

spelt *verb*

see **spell**: *Have you spelt his name correctly?* ❏ *'Receive' is spelt R, E, C, E, I, V, E.*

spend *verb*: **spends, spent, spending, has spent**

1 You **spend** money when you use it to pay for things: *How much have you spent today?* ❏ *She spends all her money on clothes and shoes.*

2 You **spend** time with someone when you take time to be with them for a period of time: *She complained that he didn't spend enough time with her.*

3 You **spend** time doing something when you do it for a period of time: *He spends hours watching television.* ❏ *We spent six weeks in France this year.*

spice *noun*: **spices**

Spices are various kinds of strong-tasting plants that you can add to food, usually in the form of a powder: *Pepper is a spice.* ❏ *There are six different spices in this Indian dish.*

spicy *adjective:* **spicier, spiciest**
Spicy food has a strong taste because it has spices in it: *They may not be able to eat it if it's too spicy.*

spider *noun:* **spiders**
A **spider** is a creature with eight legs; it catches insects in a web that it spins using threads from its body: *There's an enormous spider in the bath!* ❏ *That spider has caught a fly in its web.*

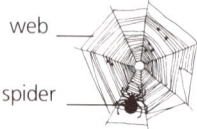
web
spider

spill *verb:* **spills, spilt** or **spilled, spilling, has spilt** or **has spilled**
You **spill** a liquid when you cause it to pour out of its container by accident: *Did someone spill red wine on the carpet?*

spill

spin *verb:* **spins, spun, spinning, has spun**
1 Something **spins** when it turns round very fast; you **spin** something when you make it turn round very fast: *The Earth spins as it travels round the Sun.* ❏ *The car spun round on the icy road.* ❏ *Can you spin a coin on the table, like this?*
2 Cotton or wool **is spun** when it is pulled and twisted so that it forms a long thin thread.
3 A spider **spins** its web when makes it using thread from its body.

spine *noun:* **spines**
Your **spine** is the line of bones down the middle of your back: *He injured his spine in a car accident.*

spit *verb:* **spits, spat, spitting, has spat**
1 Someone **spits** when they force liquid out of their mouth: *In many places, it is rude to spit in public.*
2 You **spit** out food or drink when you force it back out of your mouth: *I tried to give the baby his breakfast, but he just spat it out again.*

splash *verb:* **splashes, splashed, splashing, has splashed**
1 Liquid **splashes** when it is thrown out in tiny drops; something **splashes** you when it makes you wet in this way: *The mud from the lorry's wheels splashed all the people standing by the road.*
2 You **splash** in water or mud when you make it fly about in tiny drops: *The baby was splashing about in the bath.*

split *verb:* **splits, split, splitting, has split**
1 Something **splits** when it breaks open to form a long tear or crack: *The ripe fruits split open allowing the seeds to escape.* ❏ *His trousers have split.*
2 You **split** something when you divide it into smaller parts; you **split** people or things **up** when you separate them: *They split the stolen money between them.* ❏ *The teacher split them up because they were talking too much.*

split *noun:* **splits**
A **split** is a tear or a long narrow

opening: *There was a split in the pipe and oil was leaking out.*

spoil *verb*: **spoils, spoilt** or **spoiled, spoiling, has spoilt** or **has spoiled**
1 A person or thing **spoils** something when they damage it or make it less pleasant: *Don't play in the mud — you'll spoil your nice clean clothes.*
❑ *These new buildings spoil the view of the mountains.*
2 People, especially children, **are spoiled** when other people give them everything they want: *Their grandmother spoils them by giving them too many sweets.*

spoke and **spoken** *verb*
see **speak**: *'Did you speak to Sandra?' 'Yes, I spoke to her yesterday.'* ❑ *'Have you spoken to Sandra yet?' 'Yes, I've just spoken to her.'*

sponge *noun*: **sponges**
1 A **sponge** is a piece of soft light material which is full of holes; you use it for washing yourself: *A sponge holds a lot of water.*
2 A **sponge** is also a kind of light cake made with flour, eggs, sugar and fat: *Would you like a piece chocolate sponge?*

'spunj'

spoon *noun*: **spoons**
A **spoon** is a tool that you use for eating or serving food, made up of a bowl fixed to a handle: *This is a soup spoon, not a teaspoon.*

sport *noun*: **sports**
1 Sport refers to all the activities that people do to test their body, for pleasure for exercise or in competition with other people:

There's a lot of sport on TV tonight.
2 A **sport** is one of these activities, such as football, golf or tennis: *He's good at all sorts of sports.* ❑ *What's your favourite sport?*

sportsman or **sportwoman** *noun*: **sportsmen** or **sportswomen**
A **sportsman** or **sportswoman** is a man or a woman who takes part in sport, or in a particular sport: *The world's best sportsmen and sportswomen compete in the Olympic Games.*

spot *noun*: **spots**
1a A **spot** is a small round mark or stain: *There were spots of blood on the cloth.* ❑ *a white dog with black spots.* **b** A **spot** is also a drop of liquid: *Spots of rain were beginning to fall.*
2 Spots are small red lumps on your skin: *Teenagers often get spots on their faces.*
3 A **spot** is also a particular place: *This would be a good spot for a picnic.*

spotless *adjective*
Something that is **spotless** is very clean: *The kitchen should be spotless at all times.*

sprang *verb*
see **spring**: *The tiger sprang from the bushes.* ❑ *He sprang up from his chair when we came into the room.*

spray *verb*: **sprays, sprayed, spraying, has sprayed**
A liquid **is sprayed** when it is forced out of something in the form of very small drops: *They spray the grass with water in hot*

weather. ❑ *He's in the garden spraying the roses.*

spread *verb*: **spreads, spread, spreading, has spread**
1 Something **spreads** over an area when it moves so that it covers that area: *The mist spread over the valley.*
2 You **spread** something on a surface when you apply it with a knife so that it forms a covering: *He spread butter on his toast.*
3 A disease **spreads**, or **is spread**, when it is passed from one person or animal to the next: *The disease spread quickly from one person to the next.* ❑ *These flies spread disease.*
4 You **spread** something when you lay it out so that it is flat: *He took a blanket out of the bag and spread it on the sand.*
5 A bird **spreads** its wings when it stretches them out on either side of its body.

sprung *verb*
see **spring**: *These flowers have sprung up during the night.*

spun *verb*
see **spin**: *The cloth was spun from gold thread.* ❑ *This small spider has spun this huge web.*

spy *noun*: **spies**
A **spy** is a person who finds out secret information about another country: *They accused him of being an enemy spy.*

square *noun*: **squares**
1 A **square** is a flat shape with four sides of equal length: *He drew a square with a triangle on top.* ❑ *The carpet has a pattern of squares on it.* ❑ *He cut out a square shape.*
2 A **square** is also an open area

in a town or city that has buildings around all four sides: *a market square.*

squash *verb*: **squashes, squashed, squashing, has squashed**
Something **is squashed** when it is pressed by a heavy weight: *Johnny was squashed between two big fat men.* ❑ *I sat on the grapes and squashed them.*

squeak *verb*: **squeaks, squeaked, squeaking, has squeaked**
1 Something such as a hinge **squeaks** when it makes a short high sound, usually because it is old: *The gate squeaked as I opened it.*
2 A mouse **squeaks** when it makes a short high cry.

squeeze *verb*: **squeezes, squeezed, squeezing, has squeezed**
1 You **squeeze** something when you press it hard: *You can squeeze juice out of oranges with this machine.* ❑ *Squeeze the toothpaste tube from this end.*
2 Someone **squeezes** into a narrow space when they force their body into it: *He tried to squeeze through the gap.* ❑ *Six people squeezed into the small car.*

squirrel *noun*: **squirrels**
A **squirrel** is a small animal with brown or grey fur and a long thick tail.

❛s-**kwir**-el❜

stable *noun*: **stables**
A **stable** is a building where horses are kept.

stack *verb*: **stacks, stacked, stacking, has stacked**
You **stack** things, or you **stack**

them **up**, when you put one on top of the other to form a neat pile: *Could you stack these boxes in the corner, please?* ❑ *Beth stacked the books up on the floor.*

staff *noun*
The **staff** of a business or an organization are the people who work there: *His office has a staff of twenty.* ❑ *The school staff are always happy to meet parents.*

stage *noun*: **stages**
1 A **stage** is the platform in a theatre where the people who perform stand.
2 A **stage** is also one of the periods of time during which something grows or changes: *They built the enormous palace in several stages.* ❑ *We've nearly finished the first stage of the process.*

stagger *verb*: **staggers, staggered, staggering, has staggered**
Someone **staggers** when their legs are not steady and they can't walk properly: *He staggered into the house carrying a box on his shoulders.*

stain *noun*: **stains**
A **stain** is a mark on a surface where something has been spilt by accident: *There's a big red stain on the carpet where someone spilt a glass of wine.*

stairs *noun*
Stairs are the steps inside a building that you use to go from one floor to the next: *You can go up in the lift, or you can use the stairs.*

staircase *noun*: **staircases**
A **staircase** is a set of steps inside a building: *The hall had a*

huge staircase leading up to the first floor.

stale *adjective*
Food, especially bread, is **stale** when it is no longer fresh and soft: *He threw pieces of stale bread to the ducks.*

the opposite is **fresh**

stalk *noun*: **stalks**
A **stalk** is the stem of a plant, especially one to which fruits are attached: *Remove the stalks of the cherries before you make the jam.*

rhymes with **walk**

stall *noun*: **stalls**
A **stall** is a small shop in a market or in the street: *Let's set up a stall outside the house and try to sell the cakes.* ❑ *My brother has a hamburger stall in the local market.*

stamp *noun*: **stamps**
A **stamp** is a small piece of paper with a picture printed on it; you stick stamps on envelopes and parcels when you post them: *He collects old stamps.* ❑ *Can I have five stamps for these postcards to Spain, please?*

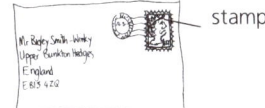
stamp

stamp *verb*: **stamps, stamped, stamping, has stamped**
1 You **stamp** on something when you bring your foot down hard on top of it: *He stamped on the beetle as it ran behind a cupboard.*
2 You **stamp** your foot when you bring it down hard on the ground,

because you are angry: *The child stamped his foot and shouted, 'It's not fair!'*

3 You **stamp** your feet on the ground when you step from one foot to the other: *They were stamping their feet, trying to keep warm.*

stand *verb*: **stands, stood, standing, has stood**

1a You **are standing** when you are on your feet with your body upright, not sitting or lying: *A group of girls stood outside the theatre.* ❑ *The baby deer was still too weak to stand.* ❑ *We were standing at the bus stop when it started to snow.* **b** You **stand** when you move into an upright position on your feet: *Everyone stood when the judge came into the court.*

2 You **stand** an object somewhere when you put it in an upright position there: *He stood the ladder against the wall.* ❑ *Stand the plant in a bucket of water for a few hours.*

3 The place where something **stands** is the place where it is, or the position it is in: *A large clock stood in the hall near the front door.* ❑ *Our old house once stood here.*

4a A door or a gate **is standing** open when it is open. **b** A building **is standing** empty when no-one is living in it or using it.

5a When you say you can't **stand** something, you mean that you don't like it at all: *Bill couldn't stand the pain any longer.* ❑ *How can you stand working with that horrible man?* **b** When you say you can't **stand** someone, you

mean that you don't like them at all: *I can't stand the woman who lives next door.*

▷ **stand back**
You **stand back** when you move backwards to make some space: *They ordered the people to stand back from the burning building.*

▷ **stand out**
Someone or something **stands out** when you can see them easily and clearly: *She always stands out in photographs with her blonde hair.*

▷ **stand up**
You **stand up** when you raise your body from a sitting or lying position so that you are upright and on your feet: *Everyone stood up when she came into the room.*

standard *noun*: **standards**
A **standard** is a level or quality: *Most parents want a high standard of education for their children.* ❑ *Their work was of a very poor standard.*

star *noun*: **stars**
1 A **star** is one of the bright points of light that you see in the sky at night: *On clear nights the sky is filled with stars.*
2 A **star** is also a shape made up of five pointed parts: *The American flag has fifty stars to represent each of the states.* ❑ *We made a star to put on the top of the tree.*
3a A **star** is a person who is very famous, especially an actor or singer. **b** The **star** of a play or film is the person who plays the most important part in it: *He was the star of several successful films.*

stare *verb*: **stares, stared, staring, has stared**

You **stare** at someone or something when you look at them for a long time: *Tom was staring out of the window.* ❑ *Everyone stared when I walked down the street with the pig.*

same as **gaze**

start *verb*: **starts, started, starting, has started**
You **start** to do something when you begin it; something **starts** when it begins: *When are you going to start studying for your exams?* ❑ *It started to snow.* ❑ *They started their journey at ten o'clock in the morning.* ❑ *People were starting to leave the room.*
2 A vehicle **starts** when its engine begins to work: *It was a very cold morning and the car didn't start.*

meaning 1: the opposite is **finish**

▷ **start off** or **start out**
You **start off** or **start out**, especially on a journey, when you begin: *We started off at ten o'clock.* ❑ *She's just starting out on her career.*

start *noun*
The **start** of something is its beginning: *Jack's car led the race from start to finish.*

starve *verb*: **starves, starved, starving, has starved**
1 People or animals **starve** when they die because they do not have enough to eat: *In winter, many small birds starve to death.*
2 People often say they **are starving** when they are very hungry: *'What's for dinner? I'm starving.'*

state *noun*: **states**
1 The **state** of something is the way it is or the way it looks at a particular time: *The house was in a very bad state when we bought it.* ❑ *She was in a state of shock.* ❑ *The country is in a very bad state.*
2 A **state** is a country or part of a country with its own system of government: *The European Union is made up of separate states.* ❑ *Which is the largest state in America?*

state *verb*: **states, stated, stating, has stated**
You **state** something when you say it or write it clearly: *You stated in your letter that you were interested in our new product.* ❑ *They asked the man to state his name and occupation.*

statement *noun*: **statements**
Someone makes a **statement** when they state something, especially in a clear or formal way: *I don't agree with your last statement.* ❑ *Did you make a statement to the police about the robbery?*

station *noun*: **stations**
A **station** is a place where trains or buses stop and passengers can get on or off.

stay *verb*: **stays, stayed, staying, has stayed**
1 Someone or something **stays** in a place or position when they remain there: *The rest of the family went on holiday, but I stayed at home.* ❑ *Stay where you are and don't move!* ❑ *Are you going to stay in bed all day?*
2 You **stay** with someone when you visit them and live with them for a short time; you **stay** in a

place when you live there for a short time: *They're staying with friends in Edinburgh.* ❑ *He's staying in a very grand hotel in Singapore.*

steady *adjective*: **steadier, steadiest**
1 Something is **steady** when it is firmly fixed or balanced so that it will not move or fall over: *The baby has started to walk, but he's not very steady on his feet yet.* ❑ *This table isn't very steady.*
2 Progress is **steady** when it continues at the same rate, not slower or faster than before: *He walked at a slow, steady pace.*

steak *noun*: **steaks**
A **steak** is a thick piece of meat, especially beef: *We had steaks and salad for lunch.*

steal *verb*: **steals, stole, stealing, has stolen**
A person **steals** when they take something without the owner's permission: *My car was stolen during the night.* ❑ *It's wrong to steal.* ❑ *He stole another chocolate from the box.* ❑ *Who's stolen my pen?*

steam *noun*
Steam is the clouds of tiny drops of liquid, that you can see rising from very hot liquids or hot food: *Clouds of steam rose from the factory chimney.* ❑ *The bathroom was filled with steam.*

steel *noun*
Steel is a very hard metal which is used for making vehicles, buildings, tools, and many other things.

steer *verb*: **steers, steered, steering, has steered**
You **steer** a vehicle when you make it move to the left or to the right by turning the steering wheel: *The racing drivers have to steer round corners at high speeds.*

steering wheel *noun*: **steering wheels**
A **steering wheel** is the wheel inside a vehicle that the driver holds; it is used to turn the vehicle's wheels to the left or to the right.

stem *noun*: **stems**
A **stem** is one of the straight narrow parts of a plant on which the flowers and leaves grow: *The flowers of this plant grow on short stems, close to the ground.*

same as **stalk**

step *noun*: **steps**
1a A **step** is the action of lifting your foot off the ground and putting it down again when you are walking, running or dancing: *Lily took a step back and nearly fell into the lake.* **b** A **step** is also the sound made by someone's foot coming down on the ground when they walk.
2 The **steps** of a dance are the special movements that you make with your feet: *Try to learn these simple steps.*
3 A **step** is a flat part of a stair that you put your foot on as you go up or down: *The postman left the parcel on the step outside the door.*
4 A **step** is also one of a series of actions involved in doing or achieving something: *This job was his first step to becoming an actor.* ❑ *What steps have you taken to solve the problem?*

step *verb*: **steps, stepped, stepping, has stepped**
You **step** when you lift your foot off the ground and put it down when you are walking, running or dancing: *I stepped on a pin and hurt my foot.*

stew *noun*: **stews**
A **stew** is a mixture of vegetables, or meat and vegetables, cooked slowly together in liquid in a pan: *a lamb stew.*

stick *noun*: **sticks**
1 A **stick** is a thin piece of dead wood: *We collected sticks from the forest to build a fire.*
2 A **stick** of something is a long thin piece of it: *a stick of chalk.*
3 A **stick** is also a straight piece of wood that you use to support yourself when you are walking: *His leg is getting better, but he has to walk with a stick.*
4 A **stick** is also a long piece of wood that is used for a special purpose: *a hockey stick* ❑ *a drumstick.*

stick *verb*: **sticks, stuck, sticking, has stuck**
1 You **stick** something into a surface when you push it into the surface: *He stuck the knife into the ground.* ❑ *She stuck a piece of old cloth into the hole.*
2a You **stick** one thing to another when you fasten them together using glue: *She was sticking stamps on a big pile of envelopes.* ❑ *This glue is strong enough to stick two pieces of wood together.*
b One thing **sticks** to another when it becomes attached firmly to that other thing: *These seeds stick to your clothes.* ❑ *It was hot and her clothes were sticking to*

her body.
3 Something **is stuck** when it is fixed in a certain position and can't be moved: *This window is stuck — I can't open it.* ❑ *Some of the lorries were stuck in the mud.*
4 You can also say that you **are stuck** when you can't continue because you do not understand something: *Could you help me with this maths problem? I'm stuck.*

sticky *adjective*: **stickier, stickiest**
Sticky things are covered with something that sticks: *She wiped her sticky fingers on her dress and took another cake.* ❑ *A stamp has a sticky surface on one side.*

stiff *adjective*: **stiffer, stiffest**
1 Something that is **stiff** is difficult to bend or move: *Put the photo between two pieces of stiff cardboard before you post it.* ❑ *I can't turn this tap on — it's too stiff.*
2 Parts of your body are **stiff** when you can't bend or move them easily: *He's getting old and his knees are stiff.*

still *adjective and adverb*
1 You are **still**, or you stay **still**, when you are quiet or remain in the same position without moving: *Could you please sit still for five minutes?* ❑ *The forest was still and silent.*
2 **Still** describes states or activities that continue in the same way as before: *We're still happy together, after forty years of marriage.* ❑ *He was watching TV when I left, and he was still there when I returned.*
3 **Still** is also used when you are comparing things: *He's rich, but*

his cousin is richer still.
4 Still also means 'even so': *People say he's bad, but I love him still.*

sting *verb*: **stings, stung, stinging, has stung**
1 An insect **stings** when it pricks your skin and puts poison into the wound it makes: *A wasp will sting you if you sit on it.* ❑ *He was was stung by a bee.*
2 Something **stings** your eyes or your skin when it causes you to feel a burning pain: *This cream stings my eyes.*

stir *verb*: **stirs, stirred, stirring, has stirred**
You **stir** a liquid when you mix it by moving a spoon around in it: *I put sugar in your tea, but I forgot to stir it.* ❑ *She stirred some cream into the soup.*

stitch *noun*: **stitches**
A **stitch** is a loop of thread which is used in sewing to fasten two pieces of cloth together: *Could you put one or two stitches here please? My sleeve's coming off.*

stitch *verb*: **stitches, stitched, stitching, has stitched**
You **stitch** something when you sew it: *She was stitching up the hem of her new dress.* ❑ *I think the doctor will have to stitch that cut — it looks very deep.*

stole and **stolen** *verb*
see **steal**: *Someone stole my bicycle yesterday.* ❑ *Who's stolen my pencil?*

stomach *noun*: **stomachs**
1 Your **stomach** is the part inside your body that food goes into when you swallow: *When our stomachs were full, we lay down and went to sleep.*
2 The front part of your body just

below your waist is also called your **stomach**: *He's got a very fat stomach.* ❑ *I've got a pain in my stomach.*

stone *noun*: **stones**
1 Stone is the very hard material that rocks are made of: *There's a high stone wall round the garden.* ❑ *The soil here is as hard as stone.*
2 A **stone** is a piece of this: *The boys were throwing stones into the lake.*

stood *verb*
see **stand**: *He stood still, listening.* ❑ *This is the place where the old house stood.*

stool *noun*: **stools**
A **stool** is a type of seat with legs but no back: *She was sitting on a high stool at the bar.*

stop *verb*: **stops, stopped, stopping, has stopped**
1 You **stop** doing something when you finish doing it, or you no longer do it: *We stopped talking and listened.* ❑ *Please stop writing now.*
2a Something **stops** when it does not continue any longer: *The rain stopped.* ❑ *That horrible noise has stopped.* **b** You **stop** something when you prevent it from continuing: *Use a handkerchief to stop the bleeding.*
3a You **stop** moving when you stand still and do not move: *When he heard my voice he stopped.*
b You **stop** a vehicle or a machine when you cause it to stand still: *Stop the car! I want to get out.* **c** You **stop** somewhere, or you **stop off** there, when you break your journey and stay there for a while: *We'll have to stop at the next town to get petrol.* ❑ *He*

sometimes stops off at his mother's house on his way home from work.

stop *noun*: **stops**
1 Something comes to a **stop** when it no longer moves: *The motorbike came to a stop outside the bank.*
2 A **stop** is a break made during a journey: *Sorry we're late. We had to make a couple of stops on the way home.*
3 A **stop** is also a place where a bus stops on its route: *I'm getting off at the next stop, so you can have my seat.*

store *noun*: **stores**
1 A **store** is a large shop: *Some of the bigger stores are open on Sundays.*
2 A **store** is a supply of something that you keep for the future: *I've got a store of pens here in my desk.*
3 A **store** is also a place where you keep things: *a store for books.*

store *verb*: **stores, stored, storing, has stored**
You **store** something when you keep it somewhere for use in the future: *Store the cake in a tin to keep it fresh.* ❏ *Store the wine in a cool dry place.*

storm *noun*: **storms**
A **storm** is a period of bad weather when there is very strong wind, rain and sometimes snow: *The ship sank in a storm at sea.* ❏ *The storm damaged many buildings.*

story *noun*: **stories**
A **story** is a description of real or imagined events: *He wants to write the story of his life.* ❏ *a children's story book* ❏ *Dad always told us a story before we went to sleep.*

stove *noun*: **stoves**
A **stove** is a cooker: *He put the pan of water on top of the stove.*

straight *adjective and adverb*: meaning 1: **straighter, straightest**
1 Something that is **straight** has no bends or curls in it: *The lorry passed us on a straight part of the road.* ❏ *She's got long straight hair.* ❏ *Hold your arms out straight in front of you.*
2 Straight means 'in a straight line, without changing direction': *He was looking straight at me.* ❏ *Turn left at the next street, and the museum is straight ahead of you.*
3 Straight also means 'immediately': *We're going out again straight after dinner.*

meaning 1: the opposite is **bent**, **curly** or **curved**

▷ **straight away**
You do something **straight away** when you do it immediately: *Could you check this letter for me straight away, please? I'm rather late.*

strange *adjective*: **stranger, strangest**
1 Something that is **strange** is odd or unusual: *It's strange that he hasn't telephoned.* ❏ *There's a strange noise coming from the car's engine.* ❏ *She gave me a very strange look.*
2 Something or someone is **strange** to you when you do not know them or you haven't seen them before: *There's a strange man outside. I think we should call the police.* ❏ *Everything in her new school was strange at first.*

stranger *noun*: **strangers**
1 A **stranger** is someone you

don't know or have never met before: *I'm quite shy — I don't like meeting strangers.*
2 You are a **stranger** in a place when you have never been there before and don't know it well: *'Where's the post office?' 'Sorry, I don't know. I'm a stranger here too.'*

strap *noun*: **straps**
A **strap** is a long narrow piece of material that is used for fastening or carrying things: *a handbag with a shoulder strap* ◻ *My watchstrap has broken.*

straw *noun*
1 Straw is the dry stalks of corn, that animals lie on when they are inside.
2 A **straw** is a thin tube that you can use to suck a drink into your mouth.

strawberry *noun*: **strawberries**
Strawberries are soft red fruits with many tiny seeds on their skin; they grow near the ground: *We had strawberries and cream for dessert.* ◻ *strawberry jam.*

stream *noun*: **streams**
A **stream** is a small river: *The small mountain stream joins the river here.* ◻ *Can we drink the water in this stream?*

street *noun*: **streets**
A **street** is a road with buildings on each side of it: *At night, the city streets were empty.* ◻ *We live in a very quiet street.* ◻ *Their office is in Fleet Street.*

strength *noun*
Strength is being strong: *She didn't have the strength to lift the heavy box.* ◻ *The strength of the wind was frightening.*

stretch *verb*: **stretches, stretched, stretching, has**
stretched
1 You **stretch** something when you make it longer and wider; something **stretches** when it becomes longer and wider: *These shoes are tight, but they'll stretch after a while.* ◻ *These trousers stretch when you sit down.*
2 Something **stretches** from one place to another when it covers the distance between them: *The mountains stretch from the north to the south of the country.* ◻ *The desert stretched for miles in front of them.*
3 You **stretch** part of your body when you push it outwards: *He yawned and stretched his arms out.* ◻ *Try this exercise if you need to stretch your legs.*

strict *adjective*: **stricter, strictest**
Someone who is **strict** expects other people to obey rules: *Her parents are very strict.* ◻ *There are strict rules in this company about how to dress.*

strike *verb*: **strikes, struck, striking, has struck**
1 You **strike** a person or thing when you hit them: *David struck the ball with his bat.* ◻ *He struck me twice across the face.* ◻ *He fell forward and his head struck the ground.*
2 A thought **strikes** you when it suddenly comes into your mind: *It suddenly struck me that I was completely wrong.*
3 A clock **strikes** when it makes a strong clear sound at a particular hour: *The clock in the hall struck twelve.*
4 You **strike** a match when you rub it against a rough surface to produce a flame: *Don't strike that*

match — there may be a gas leak
here.
5 Workers **strike** when they
refuse to work because they want
better working conditions.

strike *noun*: **strikes**
1 A **strike** is the act of hitting
something.
2 Workers go on **strike** when
they refuse to work because they
want better working conditions:
*The railway workers are going on
strike next week because they
want more money.*

string *noun*: **strings**
1 String is a thick thread which
is used for tying things: *The
parcel was tied with string. ⫿ a
piece of string ⫿ a ball of string*
2 The **strings** of a musical
instrument such as a violin or a
guitar, are the pieces of wire or
other material that are stretched
across it.

strip *noun*: **strips**
A **strip** of something is a long
narrow piece of it: *Could you
please write your name on this strip
of paper? ⫿ He owns a narrow strip
of land behind the house.*

strip *verb*: **strips, stripped,
stripping, has stripped**
1 You **strip** something, or you
strip it **off**, when you remove it:
*We'll have to strip off the old
wallpaper first.*
2 You **strip** when you take all your
clothes off: *We had to strip so that
the doctor could examine us.*

rhymes with **lip**

stripe *noun*: **stripes**
A **stripe** is a line that is a
different colour from the colour
around it: *He was wearing a dark
blue suit with thin white stripes.*

rhymes with **pipe**

stroke *verb*: **strokes, stroked,
stroking, has stroked**
You **stroke** something when you
pass your hand gently over it:
*She stroked my hand and told me
not to cry. ⫿ Can I stroke your
dog?*

stroke *noun*: **strokes**
1 A **stroke** is the action of striking
something: *John's taking lessons to
improve his tennis strokes.*
2 A **stroke** in swimming is one
of the various ways that you
move your arms and legs to travel
through the water: *You have to do
four different strokes in this race.*
3 A **stroke** is also something
that happens suddenly: *That was
a stroke of luck! ⫿ a stroke of
lightning.*
4 A **stroke** is also the sound that
a clock makes when it strikes: *We
arrived at the stroke of midnight.*

stroll *verb*: **strolls, strolled,
strolling, has strolled**
You **stroll** when you walk
without hurrying: *Let's stroll
down to the river after dinner.*

strong *adjective*: **stronger,
strongest**
1 A person or thing is **strong**
when they have a lot of power: *a
strong wind ⫿ He's a strong young
man.*
2 A **strong** smell or taste is very
powerful: *There's a strong smell of
gas in here. ⫿ I like strong cheese.*

meaning 1: the opposite is **weak**

struck *verb*
see **strike**: *The clock in the town
square struck eight. ⫿ The dog was
struck by a car.*

struggle *verb*: **struggles, struggled, struggling, has struggled**
1 You **struggle** when you twist and turn your body, trying to escape: *After some time, the fly stopped struggling and became still.*
2 You **are struggling** when you are finding something very difficult to do: *I'm struggling now — I think I need a rest.*
3 People **struggle** when they fight.

struggle is also a noun: *After a long struggle, they finally got their money back.*

stubborn *adjective*
A **stubborn** person refuses to do what other people tell them to do, or to follow advice: *We've told him it's dangerous, but he's very stubborn; he'll do it anyway.*

stuck *verb*
see **stick**: *I've stuck all the stamps on the envelopes.* ◻ *The lorry was stuck in a ditch.*

student *noun*: **students**
A **student** is a person who is studying, for example at a school, a college or a university: *He's my best student.* ◻ *a medical student.*

study *verb*: **studies, studied, studying, has studied**
You **study** when you spend time learning about a subject: *What are you studying at university?* ◻ *I'm studying English and French.*

study *noun*: **studies**
1 The **study** of a particular subject is the process of learning about it: *The study of numbers is called mathematics.*
2 Your **studies** are the subjects you study or the time you spend

studying: *You'll have to work hard at your studies if you want to get into college.*

stuff *noun*
1 **Stuff** is any kind of material for which you do not know the right word: *What's that stuff on the floor?* ◻ *They painted their faces with some red stuff.*
2 You also use **stuff** when you are talking about a number of things: *There's too much stuff in this cupboard.*

stuff *verb*
1 You **stuff** a cushion when you fill it with a soft material: *These cushions have been stuffed with feathers.*
2 You **stuff** things into a place when you push them into it carelessly: *He stuffed the papers into his pocket.*

stung *verb*
see **sting**: *I was stung on the nose by a bee.* ◻ *The cream stung my eyes.*

stupid *adjective*
1 A **stupid** person does not understand things very easily: *He was too stupid to understand.*
2 You do something **stupid** when you make a big mistake: *I was stupid to throw the letter away.*

the opposite is **clever** or **smart**

subject *noun*: **subjects**
1 A **subject** is something that you learn about, such as science, mathematics or a language: *He is studying eight different subjects at school.* ◻ *My favourite subject at school was English.*
2 The **subject** of a conversation or story is the person or thing that it is about: *Can we change*

the subject, please? ▫ 'What's the subject of the book you're reading?' 'It's about three young soldiers fighting a war.'

subtract verb: **subtracts, subtracted, subtracting, has subtracted**
You **subtract** a smaller number from a larger one when you take the smaller one away from the larger one.

the opposite is **add**

> ▸ 'Ten minus four' means the same as 'subtract four from ten'.

subtraction noun
Subtraction is the act of taking away a smaller number from a larger one: In the first class they learn how to do addition and subtraction.

the opposite is **addition**

succeed verb: **succeeds, succeeded, succeeding, has succeeded**
You **succeed** when you manage to do something that you have been trying to do: She's succeeded in getting the job. ▫ If you try hard, I'm sure you will succeed.

the opposite is **fail**

success noun: **successes**
Success, or a **success**, is the act of succeeding: The party was a great success. ▫ Have you had any success in finding a job?

the opposite is **failure**

successful adjective
1a A **successful** person has managed to do something, or has done very well in a particular way: He's a successful painter. ▫ She's been very successful in her

career. ▫ Were you successful in getting the job?
2 A **successful** event has gone well: We had a very successful meeting with our business partners.

such determiner and pronoun
1 Such means 'so great' or 'so much': He's such a nice man. ▫ Would you wear such a short skirt to the office?
2 Such means 'of that kind': I've never heard of such a thing before.

▷ **such as**
You use **such as** when you are giving an example of something: Do you have everything you need, such as pots and pans, and knives and forks?

suck verb: **sucks, sucked, sucking, has sucked**
1 You **suck** liquid when you take it into your mouth by drawing air in through your lips: The baby was sucking milk from the bottle.
2 You **suck** something when you put it in your mouth and make pulling movements with your lips and tongue: He's six years old, but he still sucks his thumb. ▫ If your throat hurts, try sucking this sweet.

sudden adjective
Something that is **sudden** happens very quickly, and might surprise you: There was a sudden noise, and I turned round. ▫ a sudden death ▫ Don't make any sudden movements — you'll frighten the deer.

suddenly adverb
Suddenly means 'in a sudden way': The bus stopped suddenly. ▫ Suddenly, the earth began to shake. ▫ I suddenly remembered I had seen him before.

suffer verb: **suffers, suffered, suffering, has suffered**
1a You **suffer** when you feel pain: *She suffered a lot of pain in the last few weeks of her life.*
b You also **suffer** when you feel very sad about something: *They made him suffer because he was different from them.*
2 You **suffer** from an illness when you have that illness: *He is suffering from flu.*

sugar noun
Sugar is the white or brown grains that you add to drinks and foods to make them taste sweeter: *Do you take sugar in your coffee?* ❑ *Try not to eat too much sugar — it's bad for you.*

suggest verb: **suggests, suggested, suggesting, has suggested**
You **suggest** something to someone when you mention an idea that you have about the best way to do something: *I suggest that you telephone again in half an hour.* ❑ *We were talking about our holiday plans when someone suggested Cornwall.*

suggestion noun: **suggestions**
Someone makes a **suggestion** when they mention an idea that they have about the best way to do something: *I don't know what to wear. Do you have any suggestions?*

suit noun: **suits**
1a A **suit** is a set of clothing for a man, made up of a jacket and trousers or a jacket and skirt: *He bought a new suit for the wedding.* ❑ *Molly was wearing a smart grey suit.*
2 A **suit** is also something you wear for a particular purpose:

How heavy is an astronaut's suit? ❑ *Can I dry my wet swimsuit here?*

suit verb: **suits, suited, suiting, has suited**
1 A colour or a piece of clothing **suits** you when it makes you look nice: *Green really suits you.*
2 An arrangement **suits** you when you are happy to agree to it: *Would it suit you if I called at 8 o'clock?*

suitable adjective
A **suitable** person or thing is right for a particular job or task: *He is the most suitable person for the job.* ❑ *I don't have any suitable clothes for a funeral.* ❑ *Is it a suitable time to talk to you?*

suitcase noun: **suitcases**
A **suitcase** is a container with flat sides and a handle; you use it to carry clothes when you are travelling: *Can I help you with your suitcase? It looks very heavy.*

sum noun: **sums**
1 A **sum** is a problem in arithmetic which you solve by adding, subtracting, dividing or multiplying numbers: *He did a quick sum on the back of an envelope.*
2 A **sum** is also an amount of money: *He was paid a small sum for the work.*
3 The **sum** of two or more numbers is the figure you get when you add them together: *The sum of two, six and ten is eighteen.*

summer noun
Summer is one of the seasons of the year, when the weather is warmest: *How long are your summer holidays?* ❑ *We went to Florida last summer.* ❑ *Do you*

remember those long hot summers in France?

sun *noun*
1 The **Sun** is the huge yellow ball in the sky that gives light and heat to the Earth: *The Earth goes round the Sun.*
2 The **sun** is the heat from the Sun: *We lay in the sun all day.*

Sunday *noun*
Sunday is the seventh day of the week, the day after Saturday: *We go to church every Sunday.*

sung *verb*
see **sing** : *Have you ever sung in front of an audience?* ❑ *The last song was sung by a group of small children.*

sunglasses *noun*
Sunglasses are spectacles made with dark glass; you wear them to protect your eyes from strong sunlight.

sunk *verb*
see **sink** : *The ship had sunk beneath the waves.*

sunlight *noun*
Sunlight is the light from the sun: *He opened the curtains and sunlight came into the room.* ❑ *The sunlight was too strong in this photo.*

sunny *adjective:* **sunnier, sunniest**
The weather is **sunny** when there is a lot of bright sunshine: *It's a beautiful sunny day — let's go for a walk.*

sunrise *noun*
Sunrise is the time when the sun rises in the morning: *The farmer gets up at sunrise to milk the cows.* ❑ *In summer, sunrise is at four o'clock in the morning.*

sunset *noun*: **sunsets**
Sunset is the time when the sun sets in the evening: *We got up at sunrise and went to bed at sunset.* ❑ *We get some beautiful sunsets here.*

sunshine *noun*
Sunshine is the light and heat of the sun: *The cat was sitting on the step enjoying the warm sunshine.*

supermarket *noun*: **supermarkets**
A **supermarket** is a large shop where you can buy food and other goods; in supermarkets, customers take the things they want from the shelves, and pay when they leave.

supper *noun*: **suppers**
Supper is a meal that people eat in the evening: *When we got home we had a light supper, and then went to bed.*

support *verb*: **supports, supported, supporting, has supported**
1 One thing **supports** another when it carries its weight: *He made a rough table with two rocks supporting a plank of wood.* ❑ *Will that thin branch support your weight?*
2 You **support** someone when you provide the money that they need to live: *He has to support a wife and three children.*

suppose *verb*: **supposes, supposed, supposing, has supposed**
1 You **suppose** that something is so when you think that it probably is so: *I suppose you're right.* ❑ *'Are you going to college next year?' 'I suppose so.'*
2 You also use **suppose** when

you are imagining an event and thinking about its effects: *Suppose you became rich — what would you do with the money?*

▷ **be supposed to**

1 You **are supposed to** do something when people expect you to do it, or you should do it: *You were supposed to bring a ball so that we could play football.*

2 Supposed to also means 'considered as': *It's supposed to be a very funny book.*

sure *adjective*

1 You are **sure** of something when you have no doubts about it: *Are you sure you locked the back door? ▢ How can you be sure that it's true? ▢ I wasn't sure that the letter would arrive in time.*

2 People also say '**sure**' to mean 'yes, of course' or 'yes, certainly': *'Could you help me with these bags?' 'Sure!'*

▷ **make sure**

You **make sure** of something when you check it: *Always make sure that the doors are locked when you go out.*

surface *noun*: **surfaces**

The **surface** of something is its outer covering, or the part that you can see: *There's something floating on the surface of the water. ▢ A snake's skin has a dry surface.*

surname *noun*: **surnames**

A person's **surname** is the name that they share with their whole family: *His first name is Robert and his surname is Douglas. ▢ Many Scottish surnames begin with 'Mac' or 'Mc'.*

surprise *noun*: **surprises**

1 Surprise is the feeling of slight shock that you get when

something happens that you weren't expecting: *I laughed and everyone looked at me in surprise.*

2 A **surprise** is an event that you weren't expecting: *It was a lovely surprise to see you all again. ▢ Mum's planning a surprise for Dad's bithday.*

surprise *verb*: **surprises, surprised, surprising, has surprised**

1 You say that something **surprises** you if it happens when you weren't expecting it: *It surprises me that he's behaved so badly. ▢ It doesn't suprise me that they're late.*

2 You **surprise** someone when you do something that they haven't been expecting: *He surprised the whole family when he passed his exams.*

surprised *adjective*

You look or feel **surprised** when something happens that you haven't been expecting: *a surprised look. ▢ 'How do you feel about passing your exams?' 'Surprised.'*

surprised

surprising *adjective*

A **surprising** event or situation is one that was not expected: *A surprising number of people came to see our small show.*

surround *verb*: **surrounds, surrounded, surrounding, has surrounded**

A person or thing **is surrounded** when they have something all round them: *After* the heavy rain, our house was surrounded by water. ❑ *The building was surrounded by policemen.* ❑ *A high wall surrounds the prison.*

suspect *verb*: **suspects, suspected, suspecting, has suspected**
You **suspect** someone of doing something when you think they have done it; you **suspect** that something is so when you think it is so: *The police suspect him of the robbery.* ❑ *I suspected that she was lying.*

swallow *verb*: **swallows, swallowed, swallowing, has swallowed**
You **swallow** something that you have in your mouth when you make it go down into your stomach: *Try to swallow the medicine quickly, without tasting it.*

swam *verb*
see **swim**: *The children played on the beach and swam in the sea.*

swan *noun*: **swans**
A **swan** is a large white or black bird with a long neck, which lives on or near water.

sweat *noun*
Sweat is the salty liquid that comes out of your skin when you are hot: *His forehead was dripping with sweat as he carried the heavy boxes into the house.*

sweat is also a verb: *He was sweating after playing football for an hour in the sun.*

sweater *noun*: **sweaters**
A **sweater** is a warm piece of clothing that you wear on the top part of your body; sweaters are usually made of wool: *Wear a*

warm sweater when you go out on the boat.

sweep *verb*: **sweeps, swept, sweeping, has swept**
You **sweep** a floor when you clean it using a brush: *When you've swept the floor, could you wash the dishes, please?*

sweet *adjective*: **sweeter, sweetest**
1 Sweet things taste like sugar or have sugar in them: *These little carrots taste very sweet.* ❑ *He had a cup of tea and a sweet biscuit.* ❑ *Try not to eat too many sweet foods.*
2 A **sweet** person or thing is very nice or attractive: *Look at this sweet little kitten.* ❑ *Thank you. You're very sweet.*

meaning 1: the opposite is **bitter** or **sour**

sweet *noun*: **sweets**
A **sweet** is a small piece of sweet food, such as a chocolate: *He spends all his money on sweets.*

swell *verb*: **swells, swelled, swelling, has swollen** or **has swelled**
Something **swells** when it increases in size: *My wrist swelled but I didn't break any bones.* ❑ *The river has swollen with the heavy rain.*

swept *verb*
see **sweep**: *Has the floor been swept?* ❑ *When you've swept the floor, have a rest.*

swim *verb*: **swims, swam, swimming, has swum**
People and animals **swim** when they travel through water using their arms and legs: *Can you swim?* ❑ *There's a pool at the*

hotel, but we prefer to swim in the sea. I go swimming three times a week.

❏ *Did you know that elephants can swim?*

swim *noun*
You have a **swim**, or you go for a **swim**, when you swim in water for a period of time: *We always have a swim before breakfast.*

swim

swimming pool *noun*: **swimming pools**
A **swimming pool** is a large container filled with water that people use to swim in.

swimming trunks *noun*: **swimming trunks**
Swimming trunks are the shorts that men and boys wear when they go swimming.

swimsuit *noun*: **swimsuits**
A **swimsuit** is a tight piece of clothing that women and girls wear when they go swimming.

swing *noun*: **swings**
A **swing** is a seat that hangs from two ropes or chains; you can sit on it and move backwards and forwards: *The children were playing on the swings in the park.*

swing *verb*: **swings, swung, swinging, has swung**
1 You **swing** something when you make it move through the air, backwards, forwards, or in a circle: *He swung the heavy hammer above his head and brought it down on the rock.*
2 Something **swings** when it moves from side to side, or backwards and forwards: *He pressed the button and the gates*

swung open. ❏ *A monkey uses its long arms to swing through the trees.*

switch *verb*: **switches, switched, switching, has switched**
To **switch** to something means to change to, or turn to that thing: *I've switched to a different kind of medicine.*

▷ **switch off**
You **switch off** a light or a machine when you press a switch so that it stops working: *Remember to switch the lights off when you leave.* ❏ *He switched off his computer and went home.*

▷ **switch on**
You **switch on** a light or a machine when you press a switch so that the light or machine begins to work: *He switched on the heater because he was cold.* ❏ *It's dark in here — could you switch the light on, please?*

swollen *verb*
see **swell**: *The boy's eye has swollen up.* ❏ *Put some ice on your swollen ankle.*

sword *noun*: **swords**
A **sword** is a weapon with a long sharp blade.

'sord'

swum *verb*
see **swim**: *He's never swum in the sea before.*

swung *verb*
see **swing**: *He swung the hammer above his head.* ❏ *Mary pushed the door and it swung open.*

system *noun*
A **system** is a way of working or of doing a particular task: *We have a special system for checking our work.*

Tt

table *noun*: **tables**
A **table** is a piece of furniture with legs and a flat top: *We all sat round the kitchen table.*

table tennis *noun*
Table tennis is a game that is played indoors on a table, using a light ball and a bat.

tablespoon *noun*: **tablespoons**
A **tablespoon** is a large spoon, used to serve food.

tail *noun*: **tails**
An animal's **tail** is the part, often long and thin, at the back or end of its body.

tail

tailor *noun*: **tailors**
A **tailor** is a person whose job is making clothes.

take *verb*: **takes, took, taking, has taken**
1 You **take** something when you reach out and get it: *She took the book from the shelf.* ❑ *Jim took another chocolate.*
2 You **take** something when you remove it: *Who has taken my rubber?*
3 You **take** something to a place when you take it with you when you go there: *I took the dog for a walk.* ❑ *I took the book to the library.*
4 You **take** a bus or a train when you travel on it: *He takes the train every morning at eight o'clock.*
5 You **take** a photograph when

you use a camera to get a picture: *She took a photograph of me in the garden.*
6 You **take** one number from another when you subtract it from the other one: *Take 10 from 12 and you are left with 2.*
7 You **take** something when you eat or drink it: *Do you take milk in your tea?*
8 You use **take** with other words to talk about an action: *He takes a walk every night.* ❑ *Come and take a look at this.*

▷ **take away**
1 You **take** something **away** when you remove it from one place and put it in another: *His mother took away all the empty plates.*
2 You **take** one number **away** from another when you subtract it from the other number: *Take three away from ten and you are left with seven.*

▷ **take down**
1 You **take** something **down** when you take it from a high place and put it in a lower place: *When they moved out of the flat, they had to take down all the paintings.*
2 You **take** something **down** when you make written notes about it: *The policeman took down everything the man said.*

▷ **take off**
1 You **take off** a piece of clothing when you remove it from your body: *Take off your dirty boots before you come inside.*

2 An aeroplane **takes off** when it leaves the ground and flies into the air: *The plane took off at midnight.*

▷ **take out**

1 You **take** something **out** when you take it from the place it is in: *He opened his suitcase and took out a clean shirt.* ❑ *The policeman took his notebook out of his pocket.*

2 You **take** someone **out** when you invite them to go somewhere with you, for example for a meal or a drink: *He took me out for dinner.*

▷ **take part**

You **take part** in something when you join in with other people who are doing it: *We take part in a quiz every Tuesday night.*

tale *noun*: **tales**
A **tale** is a story: *He told his grandchildren tales of his youth.*

talk *verb*: **talks, talked, talking, has talked**
You **talk** when you speak; you **talk** to someone when you have a conversation with them: *Stop talking.* ❑ *I was talking to Alan last night.*

talk *noun*: **talks**
1 A **talk** is a time that you spend having a conversation with someone: *I had a long talk with my boss this afternoon.*
2 Someone gives a **talk** when they speak to an audience: *Paul gave a talk on art at the university.*

tall *adjective*: **taller, tallest**
1 A **tall** person, building or plant is big in height: *He's very tall.* ❑ *There are a lot of tall trees in the forest.*
2 You use **tall** to talk about the height of a person or thing: *How tall is the Eiffel Tower?* ❑ *He's not much taller than me.*

the opposite is **short** or **small**

tame *adjective*
A **tame** animal is used to being with humans and is not dangerous: *The lions at the zoo are quite tame.*

the opposite is **wild**

tank *noun*: **tanks**
1 A **tank** is a container for holding liquid: *We filled up the tank with water.* ❑ *a petrol tank.*
2 A **tank** is also a large heavy vehicle used by the army.

tanker *noun*: **tankers**
A **tanker** is a ship or lorry that is used to carry oil or other liquids: *an oil tanker.*

tap *noun*: **taps**
1 A **tap** is a device attached to a pipe that you turn to make water or gas flow, or stop flowing: *Did I turn the tap off?*
2 A **tap** is also a light knock: *He gave me a tap on the shoulder.*

tap *verb*: **taps, tapped, tapping, has tapped**
You **tap** something when you knock it lightly: *He tapped at the window.*

tape *noun*: **tapes**
1 **Tape** is thin narrow plastic which is used to record sound and pictures: *I've got their new album on tape.*
2 A **tape** is a length of this, in a cassette: *Would you lend me your Beatles tape?*

tape recorder *noun*: **tape recorders**
A **tape recorder** is a machine

which you use to record and play music and other sounds on tape.

tart *noun*: **tarts**
A **tart** is a pie made with pastry and filled with fruit: *Have a piece of apple tart.*

task *noun*: **tasks**
A **task** is a piece of work or a duty that you must do: *She gave me a list of tasks to do while she was away.*

taste *noun*
1 The **taste** of something is the way it seems to you when you put it on your tongue: *This fish has a very salty taste.* □ *I don't like the taste of this cheese.*
2 Taste is the ability that you have to recognize food or drink when you put it on your tongue: *The senses of taste and smell are connected.*
3 Your **taste** is the type of choice you make when you are buying or selecting something: *She has good taste in clothes.*

taste *verb*: **tastes, tasted, tasting, has tasted**
1 You **taste** something when you notice its special qualities when you put it on your tongue: *Can you taste the onion in this sauce?*
2 You **taste** something when you try a little of it to see if you like it: *Just taste a little of this soup. You might like it.*

taught *verb*
see **teach**: *He taught me how to play chess.*

taxi *noun*: **taxis**
A **taxi** is a car with a driver which you can hire to take you somewhere: *We got a taxi to the airport.*

same as **cab**

tea *noun*: **teas**
1 Tea is a drink that you make by adding boiling water to the dried leaves of a tea plant: *Would you like a cup of tea?*
2 Tea is also a meal eaten in the early evening: *We had sandwiches and biscuits for tea.*

teach *verb*: **teaches, taught, teaching, has taught**
Teachers **teach** when they tell people about a subject and help them to learn: *She teaches English at the local school.*

the opposite is **learn**

teacher *noun*: **teachers**
A **teacher** is a person who teaches: *She's a maths teacher.*

team *noun*: **teams**
A **team** is a group of people who play a sport or work together: *He plays for the local football team.*

teapot *noun*: **teapots**
A **teapot** is a container in which you make tea.

tear¹ *noun*: **tears**
Tears are drops of liquid that fall from your eyes when you cry.

rhymes with **near**

tear² *noun*: **tears**
A **tear** is a hole in something, especially in a piece of material: *Don't buy that jacket; it's got a tear on the collar.*

rhymes with **hair**

tear *verb*: **tears, tore, tearing, has torn**
1 You **tear** something when you make a hole in it: *I've torn my dress on that bush.*
2 You also **tear** something when

you pull it apart: *I tore the newspaper in half.*

rhymes with **hair**

▷ **tear up**
You **tear** something **up** when you pull it apart into little pieces: *She tore up my letter.*

tease *verb*: **teases, teased, teasing, has teased**
Someone **teases** you when they laugh at you or make fun of you in a playful way: *Everyone teased Charles about his big ears.*

teaspoon *noun*: **teaspoons**
A **teaspoon** is a small spoon, used to stir tea or coffee.

teenager *noun*: **teenagers**
A **teenager** is someone who is aged between 13 and 19.

teeth *noun*
see **tooth**: *He has lovely white teeth.*

telegram *noun*: **telegrams**
A **telegram** is a message sent over a long distance through wires or by radio, and delivered in printed form: *They sent us a telegram. They're arriving tomorrow.*

telephone *noun*: **telephones**
A **telephone** is a device that you use to speak to someone who is some distance away: *The telephone's ringing. I'll get it.* ❑ *Could I use your telephone?* [see picture at **phone**]

usually shortened to **phone**

telephone *verb*: **telephones, telephoned, telephoning, has telephoned**
You **telephone** someone when you speak to them using the

telephone: *Elaine telephoned you last night, but you weren't in.*

usually shortened to **phone**

television *noun*: **televisions**
1 A **television** is a device that can receive and show pictures and sound from signals broadcast from a long distance away: *They've got a new television.*
2 Television is the system by which these sounds and pictures are received and shown: *What's on television tonight?*

meaning 1: also called a **television set**
meanings 1 and 2: called **TV** for short

tell *verb*: **tells, told, telling, has told**
1 You **tell** someone something when you give them information: *Can you tell me when the next train leaves, please?* ❑ *She's told everyone your secret.* ❑ *Have they told you if you've got the job?* ❑ *No-one told us that we needed money.*
2 You **tell** someone a story when you say it or read it to them: *Tell us a ghost story.*
3 Someone **tells** the truth when they say things that are true; someone **tells** lies when they say things that are not true.
4 You can **tell** what something is, or what is happening, when you can see or judge it correctly: *I can't tell what it is — it's too far away.* ❑ *Can you tell what they're saying?*
5 You can **tell** the difference between people or things when you can see the difference between them: *I can't tell the*

difference between these two wines.
6 You **tell** the time when you say what time a clock or watch shows: *Has your little girl learnt how to tell the time yet?*

temper *noun*
You are in a good **temper** when you feel happy; you are in a bad **temper** when you feel annoyed: *She's been in a bad temper all morning.*

▷ **lose your temper**
You **lose your temper** when you suddenly become angry: *I'm sorry I lost my temper yesterday.*

temperature *noun*: temperatures
1 The **temperature** of a place is how hot or cold it is there, measured in degrees: *What's the temperature in Paris today?* ❑ *Keep the food at a low temperature.*
2 You have a **temperature** when your body is warmer than usual, because you are ill: *She's got a temperature and she feels sick.*

temple *noun*: temples
A **temple** is a place where people go to pray.

ten *noun and adjective*: tens
1 Ten is the number 10: *Seven plus three is ten.*
2 Ten is the time of 10 o'clock: *The film ends at ten.*
3 Ten is also the age of ten; someone who is **ten** is ten years old: *He'll be ten on his birthday.*

ten *determiner and pronoun*
Ten means 'ten in number': *The tickets cost ten pounds each.* ❑ *We have thirty boxes but we need another ten.*

tennis *noun*
Tennis is a game for two or four players, in which you have to hit a ball over a net using a racket: *They have a tennis court in their garden.* ❑ *They play tennis in the summer and football in the winter.*

tent *noun*: tents
A **tent** is a kind of shelter made of strong cloth supported by poles: *The children are sleeping in a tent in the garden tonight.*

tenth *determiner and adjective*
The **tenth** person or thing is the one that comes after ninth.

term *noun*: terms
A **term** is one of the periods that the school year is divided into: *There are three terms in each school year in Britain.*

terrible *adjective*
Something that is **terrible** is very bad: *What is that terrible smell?* ❑ *I've made a terrible mistake.*

terrify *verb*: terrifies, terrified, terrifying, has terrified
Someone or something **terrifies** you if they make you feel very frightened: *The loud noises terrified the children.*

terrified *adjective*
You are **terrified** if you are very frightened: *Six terrified children were allowed to leave the plane.*

test *noun*: tests
A **test** is a set of questions that you have to answer, to show how much you know about a particular subject: *We have an English test every week.*

test *verb*: tests, tested, testing, has tested
1 You **test** someone when you ask them questions to see how much they know about a

particular subject: *We were tested on English verbs.*

2 You **test** something when you find out how well it works, or if it is all right: *Would you like to test the machine before you buy it?*

than *conjunction*

You use **than** when you are comparing things: *Amy is much younger than Matt.* ❑ *It's colder today than yesterday.* ❑ *I'd rather go to the cinema than the theatre.*

thank *verb*: **thanks, thanked, thanking, has thanked**

You **thank** someone who has done something for you when you show them that you are pleased: *I must thank Ken for the beautiful flowers.*

▷ **thank you** or **thanks**

You say **thank you** or **thanks** to someone to show you are pleased with something they have done: *Thanks very much for all your help.*

that *determiner, pronoun and conjunction.*

1 You use **that** when you want to show which person, place or thing you mean: *Who's that boy over there?* ❑ *I like that sweater.* ❑ *That's the ferry over there.* ❑ *Isn't that James in the photograph?*

2 You also use **that** when you are talking about a person or thing already mentioned or known about: *Is that what you meant?* ❑ *Where's that pencil I was using earlier?* ❑ *Who was that on the phone?* ❑ *'You look nice.' 'That's very kind of you.'* ❑ *What was that you said?* ❑ *Is there something that you would prefer to do?*

3 You use **that** when you are saying what you or someone else

thinks, says or feels: *I thought that he looked rather sad.* ❑ *I'm hoping that you can help me.* ❑ *It's a shame that you can't come to the party.* ❑ *William said that he would be back soon.*

4 You use **that** with 'so' to say what the result of something is: *He laughed so much that he cried.* ❑ *It was so cold that we decided to come home.*

the *determiner*

1 You use **the** to talk about particular people, animals or objects: *Have you seen the newspaper?* ❑ *I'm going to the doctor's tomorrow morning.* ❑ *Could you close the window, please?*

2 The is used in front of names of things of which there is only one: *the Moon.* ❑ *the Atlantic Ocean.* ❑ *the Nile.*

3 You use **the** before adjectives ending in '-est' and before words such as 'most', 'first' and 'last': *Who was the last person to use the shower?* ❑ *She's the kindest person I've ever met.*

theatre *noun*: **theatres**

A **theatre** is a building with a stage inside, where plays are performed: *Eva is going to the theatre tonight.*

theft *noun*

Theft is stealing: *He was charged with theft.*

their *determiner*

Their means 'belonging to them': *That's their dog, isn't it?* ❑ *Have you been to their new house?* ❑ *They were going to see their parents.*

rhymes with **hair**

theirs *pronoun*
You use **theirs** to talk about something that belongs to two or more people: *Which books are theirs?*

them *pronoun*
You use **them** when you talk about two or more people or things: *We're going to see them later this evening.* ❏ *I need those addresses. What did you do with them?*

themselves *pronoun*
1 You use **themselves** after the verb when the people who do an action are the same people who are affected by that action: *They built a hut to protect themselves from the wind.*
2 People do something **themselves** when they do it without help from anyone else: *Did they really build the house themselves?*
3 You can use **themselves** to show who you mean more clearly: *It was the women themselves who started to change things.*

then *adverb*
1 Then means 'at a particular time', either in the past or in the future: *I was at school then.* ❏ *Do you think you'll be finished by then?*
2 Then also means 'after that': *I saw Clive and then I went home.* ❏ *First you chop the vegetables, then you boil them in water for ten minutes.*

there *adverb*
1 You use **there** to talk about a place which is some distance away from where you are: *Look over there.* ❏ *'She lives in Oxford.'*

'I'm going there this afternoon.'
2 You use **there is** or **there are** to talk about what exists: *Are there enough books for everyone?* ❏ *There isn't any wine left.* ❏ *There are 100 centimetres in one metre.*

meaning 1: the opposite is **here**

therefore *adverb*
Therefore means 'for that reason': *Tony has worked hard and therefore he deserves a reward.*

these *determiner and pronoun*
You use **these** to talk about several people or things that are not far away from you: *I like these curtains.* ❏ *These pictures belong to Rosie.* ❏ *These are difficult times for everyone.*

the opposite is **those**

they *pronoun*
You use **they** to talk about two or more people or things: *Paul and Emma said they were arriving at 7.30.* ❏ *These apples taste nice, don't they?*

they'd *verb*
They'd is short for **they had** or **they would**: *They said they'd like to come to the party.*

they'll *verb*
They'll is short for **they will**: *They'll give us a lift to the cinema.*

they're *verb*
They're is short for **they are**: *They're both 19 years old.*

they've *verb*
They've is short for **they have**: *They've already left.*

thick *adjective:* **thicker, thickest**
1 A material is **thick** if it measures quite a lot from one side to the other: *This rope will be strong enough — it's quite thick.*

2 You say that something is a certain measurement **thick** when that is the distance between its two sides: *The snow was three centimetres thick.*
3 Thick describes something made up of parts that are very close together: *She has beautiful thick hair.*
4 Liquid is **thick** when it has only a small amount of water in it: *This soup is too thick — I'll add some water.*
5 Thick fog or smoke is difficult to see through.

meaning 1: the opposite is **thin**

thief *noun*: **thieves**
A **thief** is someone who steals: *Have they caught the thief yet?*

thigh *noun*: **thighs**
Your **thighs** are the parts of your legs above your knees and below your hips. [see picture at **leg**]

thin *adjective*: **thinner, thinnest**
1 Something that is **thin** doesn't measure very much from one side to the other: *This dress is too thin for wearing in the winter.*
2 Someone who is **thin** doesn't have much fat on their body: *She couldn't eat much, and became very thin.*

meaning 1: the opposite is **thick**

thing *noun*: **things**
1 A **thing** is an object or something that is not alive: *What's this thing on your desk?*
2 A **thing** is also a fact, idea, action or event: *Things have changed a lot recently.* ❑ *What's the best thing to do?* ❑ *That's a stupid thing to say.*

think *verb*: **thinks, thought, thinking, has thought**

1 You **think** when you use your mind, especially to make decisions: *I'll think about it and let you know.* ❑ *I didn't think of that.*
2 You **think** something when that is your opinion: *I think he's a good writer.*
3 You are **thinking** of doing something when you are planning to do it: *We're thinking of buying a new car.*
4 You **think** of something when you remember it: *I can't think of his name.*

third *determiner*
The **third** person or thing is the one which comes after the second: *The third person to arrive was Fred.* ❑ *This is the third time he's been late this week.*

third *adverb*
You come **third** in a competition or exam when two people finish before you, or do better than you: *He came third in the race.*

thirst *noun*
Thirst is the feeling you have when you need a drink.

thirsty *adjective*: **thirstier, thirstiest**
You are **thirsty** when you need something to drink: *You get very thirsty when you stand in the sun all day.*

thirteen *noun and adjective*: **thirteens**
1 Thirteen is the number 13: *Twelve plus one is thirteen.*
2 Thirteen is also the age of thirteen; someone who is **thirteen** is thirteen years old: *Her brother is thirteen.*

thirteen *determiner and pronoun*
Thirteen means thirteen in

number: *The tickets cost thirteen pounds.* ❑ *Ten people died in the crash and thirteen were injured.*

thirty *noun and adjective*: **thirties**
1 Thirty is the number 30: *Seventy take away forty is thirty.*
2a Thirty is also the age of thirty; someone who is **thirty** is thirty years old: *Her sister is thirty.* **b** A person in their **thirties** is between 30 and 39 years old.
3 The years in any century between 30 and 39 are often called 'the **thirties**'.

thirty *determiner and pronoun*
Thirty means thirty in number: *The books cost thirty pounds.* ❑ *There were thirty people on the bus.* ❑ *There were a hundred people there; thirty were women and children.*

this *determiner*
1 You use **this** to point out a person or thing that is near you: *This pen is mine.* ❑ *This road leads to the beach.* ❑ *This is a really good book.* ❑ *This is Anna, my sister.*
2 You also use **this** to talk about a period of time that belongs to the present or to today: *I got up late this morning.* ❑ *We're going to Frankfurt this week.* ❑ *This has been the hottest day of the summer.*

thorn *noun*: **thorns**
A **thorn** is a sharp point which grows on the stem of some plants, such as roses.

those *determiner and pronoun*
You use **those** to talk about things which are some distance away from where you are: *Look at those beautiful flowers.* ❑ *Are those your brothers?* ❑ *Are these chairs the same as those over there?*

though *conjunction*
You use **though** to show a difference in two statements that you have made: *We waited for five minutes, though it seemed like hours.*

same as **although**

thought *verb*
see **think**: *I thought I saw George yesterday.* ❑ *He thought about it for a while.*

thought *noun*: **thoughts**
A **thought** is an idea: *I had a sudden thought.*

thousand *noun*: **thousands**
A **thousand** or one **thousand** is the number 1000: *A hundred multiplied by ten is a thousand.*

thousand *determiner and pronoun*
A **thousand** means one thousand in number: *The painting cost a thousand pounds.* ❑ *Five thousand people lost their jobs.*

▷ **thousands of**
You use **thousands of** when you are talking about a very large number of people or things: *Thousands of people came to the concert.*

thread *noun*
Thread is cotton in a long thin form; you use it with a needle to sew: *She used some black thread to mend the shirt.*

rhymes with **bed**

three *noun and adjective*: **threes**
1 Three is the number or figure 3: *Two plus one is three.*

2 Three is the time of 3 o'clock: *He'll be arriving at three.*
3 Three is also the age of three; someone who is **three** is three years old: *She'll be three on Saturday.*

three *determiner and pronoun*
Three means three in number: *The potatoes cost three pounds.* ❑ *We need three more people.*

threw *verb*
see **throw**: *He threw the ball and it hit the window.*

throat *noun*: **throats**
Your **throat** is the part at the back of your mouth which leads down to your stomach: *Have you got anything for a sore throat?*

through *preposition and adverb*
1 One thing goes **through** another when it passes from one side to the other, or from one end to the other: *It takes twenty minutes to go through the tunnel.* ❑ *Just go through the door at the end of the corridor.* ❑ *Something flew through the air and landed on my desk.*
2 You go **through** things when you deal with them one at a time: *Could you go through these letters for me, please?*
3 Through means 'from the beginning to the end': *I read through his essay.* ❑ *She glanced through the magazine.*

throw *verb*: **throws, threw, throwing, has thrown**
You **throw** something you are holding when you let it go using your strength to make it move or fly through the air: *He threw a cushion at me.* ❑ *Throw me the ball, please.*

▷ **throw away**
You **throw away** something that you don't need when you get rid of it, by putting it in the bin: *He has thrown away all of his old toys.* ❑ *She threw away her old jacket and bought a new one.* ❑ *You use this type of camera once and then you throw it away.*

thumb *noun*: **thumbs**
Your **thumb** is the shortest and thickest finger on your hand, set apart from the other fingers: *He has broken his thumb.* [see picture at **hand**]

thunder *noun*
Thunder is the loud noise that you hear after flashes of lightning, during a storm.

Thursday *noun*
Thursday is the fourth day of the week, the day after Wednesday: *We're going to the cinema on Thursday.*

tick *noun*: **ticks**
1 A **tick** is a mark (✓) that you write to show that something is correct, or that something has been done: *Put a tick beside all the right answers.*
2 A **tick** is also the regular noise that a watch or a clock makes: *They sat and listened to the tick of the clock.*

tick *verb*: **ticks, ticked, ticking, has ticked**
1 You **tick** something that has been written when you put a mark (✓) beside it: *She ticked all the correct answers.*

throw

2 A clock or watch **ticks** when it makes a regular faint noise: *'Is that clock working?' 'Yes, it's ticking.'*

ticket *noun*: **tickets**
1 A **ticket** is a small piece of paper that allows you to travel on a bus, a train or a plane: *How much is a train ticket to London from Edinburgh?*
2 A **ticket** is also a small piece of paper that allows you to see a film, a play or a sports match: *Have you got a ticket for the football match on Saturday?*

tickle *verb*: **tickles, tickled, tickling, has tickled**
You **tickle** someone when you touch them lightly on their body to produce a feeling which makes them laugh: *I tickled him on the feet to wake him up.*

tide *noun*: **tides**
The **tide** is the regular rise and fall of the sea; it reaches its highest and lowest level twice every day: *The tide is coming in.*

tidy *adjective*: **tidier, tidiest**
1 A place is **tidy** when it is neat, with everything in its proper place: *This room looks very tidy.*
2 A **tidy** person is neat, and likes to keep things in their proper place: *Kate's very tidy, and she never loses things.*

tidy *verb*: **tidies, tidied, tidying, has tidied**
You **tidy** a place when you put everything in its proper place: *I must tidy the house before the guests arrive.*

tie *verb*: **ties, tied, tying, has tied**
1 You **tie** one thing to another when you join them using string or rope: *They tied his hands and*

feet together. ❑ *Tie the herbs together before putting them in the pan.*
2 You **tie** shoelaces when you fasten them into a bow or a knot: *You haven't tied your shoelaces.*

tie *noun*: **ties**
A **tie** is a long narrow piece of material that a man wears round his neck, with a shirt: *He's wearing a dark blue tie.*

tiger *noun*: **tigers**
A **tiger** is a large wild animal which belongs to the cat family; it has yellow-orange fur with black stripes.

tight *adjective*: **tighter, tightest**
1 Something that is **tight** fits very closely, or too closely: *Make sure the lid is tight.* ❑ *These old jeans are too tight for me now.*
2 You hold something **tight** if you hold on to it very firmly: *Hold on tight and I'll try to pull you up.*

till *conjunction*
Till means 'until': *I'm very busy. Can you wait till tomorrow?*

timber *noun*
Timber is wood used for building: *Cut the timber into lengths of 3 metres.*

time *noun*: **times**
1 The **time** is the hour and minute at any point in the day: *What time does the train arrive?* ❑ *What time is it?*
2 **Time** is also the number of minutes or hours that you spend doing something: *Do we have time to eat?* ❑ *Mary and I spent a long time talking yesterday.*
3 The **time** that something happens is the hour, day or week when it takes place: *They invited*

us to the party, but we were on holiday at the time.
4 The number of **times** that you do something is the number of occasions that you do it: *How many times has he been to Russia?* ❑ *I met his parents for the first time yesterday.*

▷ **in time**
You arrive **in time** for something when you are early enough for it: *She arrived just in time for the meeting.*

▷ **on time**
Something that arrives or is done **on time** arrives or is done at the expected time, and is not late: *The bus never arrives on time.*

times *verb*
Times means 'multiplied by': *Four times five is twenty.*

timetable *noun*: **timetables**
1 A **timetable** is a list that shows when buses, trains, boats or planes leave and arrive at particular places: *Have you got a timetable for trains from London to Oxford?*
2 In schools, a **timetable** is a list which shows the times at which particular classes are taught.

timid *adjective*
A **timid** person is shy: *He's a very timid little boy; he doesn't like parties much.*

tin *noun*: **tins**
1 Tin is a silver-coloured metal: *The soldiers drank from tin mugs.*
2 A **tin** is a metal container, used for storing food: *a tin of soup.*

tinned *adjective*
Tinned foods are stored in tins: *tinned soup* ❑ *tinned fruit.*

tiny *adjective*: **tinier, tiniest**
Something that is **tiny** is very

small: *They eat huge numbers of tiny fish every day.*

the opposite is **huge** or **enormous**

tip *noun*: **tips**
1 The **tip** of something is the very end of it: *He burnt the tip of his tongue.*
2 You give someone such as a waiter or a taxi-driver a **tip** when you give them extra money to keep for themselves: *We gave the driver a tip and thanked him for his help.*

tip *verb*: **tips, tipped, tipping, has tipped**
1 Something **tips** when it rolls on to one side: *The boat tipped to the left, and then to the right.*
2 You **tip** something, or **tip** something **up**, when you lift up one side of it: *She tipped up the table, and the pile of papers fell to the floor*
3 You **tip** someone such as a waiter or a taxi-driver when you give them extra money: *Is it normal to tip someone who serves you in a pub?*

tiptoe *verb*: **tiptoes, tiptoed, tiptoeing, has tiptoed**
You **tiptoe** when you walk very quietly on the front part of your feet: *She tiptoed round the house, so as not to disturb anyone.*

tired *adjective*
You are **tired** when you feel that you want to have a rest or go to sleep: *He was very tired after his long journey.*

▷ **tired of**
You are **tired of** something when you have had it for so long that you don't want it any more; you

are **tired of** doing something when you have done it so many times that you don't want to do it any more: *I'm tired of all my clothes.* ❑ *She's tired of answering his telephone.*

title *noun*: **titles**
1 The **title** of a book or a play is its name: *The title of the film is 'Star Wars'.*
2 A **title** is also a word that you use before a person's surname, such as Mr, Mrs, Dr, Ms and Sir: *May I introduce Mrs Mary White.*

to *preposition*
1 You use **to** to describe movement in a particular direction: *She goes to work by train every day.* ❑ *Does this bus go to Oxford Street?*
2 To also means 'until': *We work from 9 o'clock to 5 o'clock.*
3 You give something **to** someone when you hand them it: *I gave my keys to Barry.*
4 You use **to** with other words to show a connection: *Have you sent that letter to Mum yet?* ❑ *I saw her talking to Noel.* ❑ *He was very rude to his teacher.*
5 When you are telling the time, **to** means 'before': *It's ten minutes to six.*
6 You use **to** after some verbs: *He said he was going to leave at 7 o'clock.* ❑ *He promised to finish it on Monday.* ❑ *I have to do some shopping.*

toad *noun*: **toads**
A **toad** is an animal similar to a frog but bigger.

toast *noun*
Toast is bread that has been heated until it is brown and crisp: *He spread jam on his toast.*

tobacco *noun*
Tobacco is the dried leaves of a certain plant; it is smoked in cigarettes, cigars and pipes.

today *noun*
Today is the present day: *I'm going on holiday today.*

toe *noun*: **toes**
Your **toes** are the five separate parts at the end of your foot: *Babies often like playing with their toes.* [see picture at **foot**]

together *adverb*
1 Two or more people are **together** when they are with each other or in a group: *The two boys are always together.* ❑ *They want to be together for the rest of their lives.*
2 Two or more people do something **together** when they do it at the same time: *We all arrived together.* ❑ *They travel to work together every morning.*
3 You join things **together** when you attach one to the other: *I stuck the pieces of the broken vase together.*

toilet *noun*: **toilets**
1 A **toilet** is a container that you use to get rid of solid or liquid waste from your body.
2 A **toilet** is also a room with this in it: *Where is the toilet?* ❑ *She went into the men's toilet by mistake.*

told *verb*
see **tell**: *I told him about the new film.* ❑ *You've told me that joke before.*

tomato *noun*: **tomatoes**
A **tomato** is a soft round red fruit that people often eat in salads: *I'll have a cheese and tomato sandwich, please.*

tomorrow *noun*
Tomorrow is the day after today: *I'll see you tomorrow.*

tongue *noun*: **tongues**
Your **tongue** is the soft piece of flesh inside your mouth which you use to speak and to taste food.

tonight *noun*
Tonight means 'this evening': *I'll see you tonight.*

too *adverb*
1 You use **too** when you want to add something to what has been said before: *I'm fourteen and Peter is too.* ❑ *'Who left early?' 'I did and Jane did too.'* ❑ *I'm tired, and I'm hungry too.*
2 Too also means more than is needed or wanted: *I've eaten too much.* ❑ *It's too cold to go outside without a jacket.* ❑ *He works too hard.*

took *verb*
see **take**: *He took his children to the zoo.*

tool *noun*: **tools**
A **tool** is something that you use to help you do a job, such a hammer or a spade: *We keep the garden tools in a shed.*

tooth *noun*: **teeth**
1 A **tooth** is one of the hard white objects in your mouth, which you use for biting and chewing.
2 A **tooth** is also one of the separate parts of a comb.

toothache *noun*
You have **toothache** when you have a pain in a tooth.

toothbrush *noun*: **toothbrushes**
A **toothbrush** is a small brush that you use to clean your teeth.

toothpaste *noun*
Toothpaste is a special kind of soft paste that you put on a toothbrush, to clean your teeth.

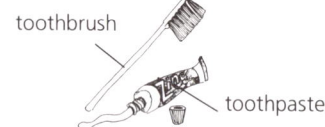

toothbrush   toothpaste

top *noun*: **tops**
1 The **top** of something is the highest part of it: *He was the first to reach the top of the mountain.*
2 The **top** of something is the lid which fits over the end of it: *Where's the top of my pen?*
3 The **top** of something is the upper surface of it: *We keep them on the top of the cupboard.*
4 A **top** is a piece of clothing that you wear on the upper part of the body: *I bought a new black top yesterday.*

meaning 1: the opposite is
bottom

top *adjective*
1 Top describes people or things that are at the highest level or position: *They live on the top floor of the building.* ❑ *He's one of the top men in the government*
2 You get **top** marks in a test or exam when you get higher marks than everyone else.

▷ **on top of**
One thing is **on top of** another when it is resting on its surface: *The books were in a pile on top of the cupboard.*

torch *noun*: **torches**
A **torch** is a small electric light that you can carry about with you.

tore and **torn** *verb*
see **tear**: *Mr Chung tore the page in half.* ❑ *I've torn my jeans.*

toss *verb*: **tosses, tossed, tossing, has tossed**
1 You **toss** something when you throw it: *He angrily tossed her bags into the car.*
2 A boat **tosses** when it moves from side to side because of the movement of the sea: *The little boat tossed about on the stormy sea.*
3 You **toss** a coin when you throw it up into the air and guess which side of it will be facing upwards when it lands, as a way of making a decision: *They tossed a coin to see who would go first.*

total *noun*: **totals**
A **total** is the result of adding several numbers or prices together: *The bill came to a total of $50.*

total *adjective*
Total means 'complete' or 'whole': *What was the total cost?* ❑ *The whole day was a total waste of time.*

totally *adverb*
Totally means 'completely': *The building was totally empty.*

touch *verb*: **touches, touched, touching, has touched**
1 You **touch** something when you put your hands on to it, to feel it or to hold it: *He touched the vase very carefully.* ❑ *The sign said 'Do not touch'.*
2 Two things **touch** when they are so close to each other that they press against one another: *Their shoulders touched.*

touch *noun*
1 Touch is the ability that you

have to recognize things by feeling them with your fingers: *It was dark and he had to use touch to find his way round the room.*
2 A **touch** is an act of touching: *She felt a light touch on her arm.*

tough *adjective*: **tougher, toughest**
1 Something that is **tough** is very hard, strong and difficult to break: *These boots are very tough.*
2 Tough meat is difficult to chew.

   'tuf '

tour *noun*: **tours**
1 A **tour** is a trip in which you visit lots of different places: *They're going on a tour of the USA.*
2 A **tour** is also a trip around one place: *I'll give you a tour of the house later.*

   rhymes with **poor**

tour *verb*: **tours, toured, touring, has toured**
You **tour** when you go on a trip and visit lots of different places: *They are touring Europe by car.*

   rhymes with **poor**

tourist *noun*: **tourists**
A **tourist** is a person who spends their holiday visiting places in another country or area: *Paris is full of tourists, especially during the summer.*

towards or **toward** *preposition*
You move **towards** or **toward** something when you move in its direction: *He put on his coat and moved towards the door.* ❑ *She turned toward me and smiled.*

towel *noun*: **towels**
A **towel** is a large piece of thick material which you use to dry

yourself after washing or swimming.

tower noun: **towers**
A **tower** is a tall narrow part of a building, or a tall narrow building: *You get a wonderful view from the top of the tower.*

town noun: **towns**
1 A **town** is a place with streets and buildings, where a lot of people live and work: *He lives in the town of Falkirk, in Scotland.*
2 Town is the centre of a city or town, where most of the shops and businesses are: *We had lunch in town.*

toy noun: **toys**
Toys are things like dolls and teddies, which children play with: *There were toys all over the floor in the child's bedroom.*

trace noun: **traces**
A **trace** of something is a very small amount of it: *There were traces of last night's dinner on the table.* ❏ *They found traces of oil in the drinking water.*

track noun: **tracks**
1 A **track** is a mark left on the ground by a person, animal or vehicle: *We could see the tracks of the car's tyres in the snow.*
2 A rough path or road is called a **track**: *a mountain track.*
3 A **track** is a special kind of circular course for athletes to run round: *A running track is usually 400 metres long.*

tractor noun: **tractors**
A **tractor** is a vehicle that is used on farms to pull other machines.

trade noun
1 Trade is the buying and selling of goods: *He made his money*

through trade with foreign countries.
2 A particular **trade** is the business of buying and selling things of a certain kind: *He works in the tourist trade.*
3 A person's **trade** is their job, especially a job for which they need to have a particular skill: *He learned his trade from his father, who was also a plumber.*

traffic noun
Traffic is the vehicles which move on the roads: *Sorry I'm late — there was so much traffic on the roads.*

traffic lights noun
Traffic lights are the red, orange and green lights on roads which tell drivers when they must stop and when they can go: *The accident happened when the traffic lights were switched off.*

train noun: **trains**
A **train** is a vehicle with several carriages that are pulled along a railway by an engine: *We caught the 4 o'clock train to London.*

train verb: **trains, trained, training, has trained**
1 You **train** a person or an animal when you teach them skills: *He trained his dog to fetch his slippers.*
2 You **train** to do a particular job when you learn how to do it: *He's training to be a teacher.*

translate verb: **translates, translated, translating, has translated**
You **translate** words or a piece of writing when you change them from one language into another: *Can you translate this word?* ❏ *He translated the story into Chinese.*

transparent *adjective*
Something is **transparent** when you can see through it: *The box has a transparent lid.*

trap *noun*: **traps**
A **trap** is a device used to catch wild animals: *The farmer set a trap for the rabbit.* ❏ *a mouse trap*

trap *verb*: **traps, trapped, trapping, has trapped**
1 You **trap** an animal when you catch it in a trap: *They dug a hole in the ground to trap the tiger.*
2 You **trap** a person when you trick them into doing something: *He trapped Robert into telling him the truth.*
3 You **are trapped** somewhere when you are stuck there and you cannot escape: *They were trapped in the burning house.* ❏ *His leg was trapped under a heavy piece of wood.*

travel *verb*: **travels, travelled, travelling, has travelled**
You **travel** when you go to a place, or you go to several different places: *Jack travels to London every day for his job.* ❏ *They spent six months travelling round the US.* ❏ *Is this the safest way to travel?*

tray *noun*: **trays**
A **tray** is a flat piece of metal, wood or plastic that you use to carry food and drinks on: *She carried the tea and coffee on a tray.*

treat *verb*: **treats, treated, treating, has treated**
1 The way you **treat** a person or an animal is the way you behave towards them: *She treats her dogs like babies.* ❏ *She treats her mother badly.*

2 A doctor **treats** a patient, or their illness, when they do things to try to cure the illness: *The doctor treated him with various drugs, but none of them worked.*

treatment *noun*
1 Your **treatment** of a person or animal is the way that you behave towards them: *His treatment of his family is terrible.*
2 A doctor gives a patient **treatment** when they try to make the patient feel better or cure their illness: *Paul was given treatment for his back pain.*

tree *noun*: **trees**
A **tree** is a large plant, with a wooden trunk and branches: *They have a lot of apple trees in their garden.*

triangle *noun*: **triangles**
A **triangle** is a flat shape with three sides and three sharp points: *He divided the square into four triangles.*

trick *noun*: **tricks**
1 A **trick** is a clever act which you do to puzzle or surprise people: *The elephant can stand on its front legs and do tricks.*
2 A **trick** is also something done to deceive people: *It was a clever trick, and some people believed him.*

▷ **play a trick**
You **play a trick** on someone when you do or say something to them that surprises or fools them: *Nelly was always playing tricks on Patrick.*

trick *verb*: **tricks, tricked, tricking, has tricked**
You **trick** someone when you deceive them, or you play a trick

on them: *They tricked her into letting them into the house.*

tried *verb*
see **try** : *I tried to push the car, but it was too heavy.* ❑ *Have you tried this new cheese?*

trip *noun*: **trips**
A **trip** is a short journey to a place and then back again: *We went on a trip to the beach.*

trip *verb*: **trips, tripped, tripping, has tripped**
You **trip** when you catch your foot on something and nearly fall over: *She tripped on the stairs.*

▷ **trip up**
Someone or something **trips** you **up** when they make you fall over or nearly fall over: *She tried to trip him up with her foot.*

trolley *noun*: **trolleys**
A **trolley** is a kind of small cart which runs on wheels and is used to carry things.

trouble *noun*
1 You have **trouble** doing something when you find it difficult: *He's been having trouble sleeping since the accident.*
2 You are in **trouble** when you are having problems, or when you are going to be punished for something you have done wrong: *He's always in trouble at school.*
3 A **trouble** is something which causes a problem: *Forget your troubles and enjoy the party.*

trousers *noun*
Trousers are a piece of clothing which covers your bottom and both of your legs: *He's wearing a new pair of trousers.*

truck *noun*: **trucks**
A **truck** is a lorry: *The truck was carrying timber.*

true *adjective*
Something that is **true** is right and correct; a **true** story is a story about events that really happened: *Is it true that Martin has got a new job?* ❑ *This book I'm reading is a true story.*

the opposite is **false**

trumpet *noun*: **trumpets**
A **trumpet** is a musical instrument which you play by blowing hard into it.

trumpet

trunk *noun*: **trunks**
1 The **trunk** of a tree is its main stem.
2 An elephant's long curved nose is called a **trunk**.
3 A **trunk** is also a large strong box for carrying or storing things in.

trunks *noun*
Trunks are pants or shorts which boys and men wear when they are swimming.

trust *verb*: **trusts, trusted, trusting, has trusted**
You **trust** someone when you know that they tell the truth and that they will not do anything to harm you: *I told her all my secrets because I trusted her.*

truth *noun*
The **truth** is the correct facts about something: *Tell me the truth — did you steal that car?*

try *verb*: **tries, tried, trying, has tried**
1 You **try** to do something when you do your best to make it happen: *I'll try to be there on time.* ❑ *Try harder. You can do it.*

2 You **try** doing something when you do it to see if it has the effect that you want: *Have you tried taking something for that headache?*

3 You **try** food when you taste it to see if you like it: *Try this cheese. I think you'll like it.*

▷ **try on**
You **try on** clothes when you put them on to find out if they fit, usually before you buy them: *I tried on the shoes, but they were too big.*

▷ **try out**
You **try** something **out** when you test it to see how well it works, or what it is like: *We're going to try out that new café for lunch.*

try *noun*: **tries**
A **try** is an act of trying: *I'll have a try, but I don't think I'll be able to do it.*

T-shirt or **tee-shirt** *noun*: **T-shirts** or **tee-shirts**
A **T-shirt** is a top with short sleeves, usually made from cotton, that you pull over your head: *She's wearing a blue T-shirt and jeans.*

tube *noun*: **tubes**
1 A **tube** is a long hollow pipe: *Water is pumped along the tube and into a bottle.*
2 A **tube** is also a container made of soft metal or plastic which contains a thick cream or paste: *tubes of toothpaste.*

Tuesday *noun*
Tuesday is the second day of the week, the day after Monday: *We go to see my aunt every Tuesday.*

tune *noun*: **tunes**
A **tune** is a piece of music: *He played a tune on the piano.*

tunnel *noun*: **tunnels**
A **tunnel** is a long narrow corridor that goes under a hill or under an area of water: *The train goes through a tunnel under the sea.*

turkey *noun*: **turkeys**
1 A **turkey** is a large bird with a long neck and a heavy body; people keep turkeys for their meat.
2 Turkey is the meat of this bird, used as food.

turn *noun*: **turns**
It is your **turn** to do something when it is your chance or your duty to do it: *It's my turn to play on the computer now.* ❑ *It's your turn to wash the dishes tonight.*

turn *verb*: **turns, turned, turning, has turned**
1 You **turn** when you move so that you are facing in the opposite direction: *He turned and walked away.* ❑ *Turn left at the top of the road.*
2 You **turn** something when you move it round: *He turned the handle and pushed the door open.*
3 One thing **turns** into another when it becomes that other thing: *Water turns to ice at 0°.*
4 You **turn** something when you move its position: *She turned the box upside down.*

▷ **turn off**
You **turn** something **off** when you stop electricity, gas, water or another kind of power flowing to it: *Did you turn the lights off?* ❑ *He turned off the television and began to read the newspaper.*

▷ **turn on**
You **turn** something **on** when you make electricity, gas, water or

another kind of power flow to it:
*He turned on the cooker and
began to make the dinner.*

▷ **turn up**
1 Someone **turns up** when they
arrive: *He turned up 15 minutes
late.*
2 Someone or something **turns
up** when they are found: *I'm sure
the money will turn up sooner or
later.*
3 You **turn** something such as a
radio or television **up** when you
make its volume louder: *Could
you turn the television up? I can't
hear it properly.*

twelve *noun and adjective:*
twelves
1 Twelve is the number 12:
Seven plus five is twelve. ❑ *Two
twelves are twenty-four.*
2 Twelve is the time of 12
o'clock: *Lunch is at twelve o'clock.*
3 Twelve is also the age of
twelve; someone who is twelve is
twelve years old: *His brother will
be twelve in January.*

twelve *determiner and pronoun*
Twelve means twelve in number:
*The tickets cost twelve pounds
each.* ❑ *We need to collect twelve
books.*

twelfth *determiner and adjective*
The **twelfth** person or thing is
the one that comes after the
eleventh.

twenty *noun and adjective:*
twenties
1 Twenty is the number 20:
Seven plus thirteen is twenty.
2 Twenty is also the age of
twenty; someone who is **twenty**
is twenty years old: *He didn't go
to college until he was twenty.*
4 People call the years between

20 and 29 in any century 'the
twenties': *They wore dresses like
this in the twenties.*

twenty *determiner and pronoun*
Twenty means twenty in
number: *The books cost twenty
pounds.* ❑ *'How many people
were hurt?' 'About twenty, I
think.'*

twice *adverb*
Something happens **twice** when
it happens two times: *We've been
to see that film twice.* ❑ *He only
did it twice.*

twig *noun:* **twigs**
A **twig** is a very small, thin
branch of a tree: *We collected
dead twigs to start the fire with.*

twin *noun:* **twins**
A **twin** is one of two children
born to the same mother at the
same time: *Do you like being a
twin?*

twist *verb:* **twists, twisted,
twisting, has twisted**
1 You **twist** something when you
turn it or wind it round: *'How do
you open this bottle?' 'Twist the
lid.'*
2 You **twist** one thing round
another when you turn it round
it: *She was twisting her hair round
her fingers.*
3 Something **twists** when it
turns one way and then another:
The path twisted down to the sea.
4 You **twist** a part of your body
when you hurt it by bending it
the wrong way: *He fell and
twisted his ankle.*

two *noun and adjective:* **twos**
1 Two is the number 2: *Two plus
one is three.*
2 Two is the time of 2 o'clock:
He'll be arriving at two.

3 Two is also the age of two; someone who is **two** is two years old: *She'll be two tomorrow.*

two *determiner and pronoun*
Two means two in number: *You owe me two pounds.* ❑ *We need two more people.*

type *noun*: **types**
A **type** of something is a kind or sort of it: *What type of job do you do?* ❑ *What's your favourite type of fruit?*

type *verb*: **types, typed, typing, has typed**

You **type** when you write something using a typewriter or a computer: *Please type your essay if you can.*

typewriter *noun*: **typewriters**
A **typewriter** is a machine with keys that you press to produce letters printed on paper.

tyre *noun*: **tyres**
A **tyre** is a thick round piece of rubber which is filled with air and fits round the outside of a vehicle's wheel: *Sorry we're late — we had a flat tyre.*

Uu

ugly *adjective:* **uglier, ugliest**
Someone or something that is
ugly is not pleasant to look at:
What an ugly view.

the opposite is **beautiful** or
pretty

umbrella *noun:* **umbrellas**
An **umbrella** is a shelter that you
hold over your head to keep you
dry when it is raining: *I left my
umbrella on the bus.*

umbrella

unable *adjective*
You are **unable** to do something
when you cannot do it: *Mr
Merton is unable to come to the
meeting.*

uncle *noun:* **uncles**
Your **uncle** is the brother of your
mother or father, or your aunt's
husband: *Here's a photo of my
uncle and my two cousins.*

under *preposition*
1 One thing is **under** another if it
is below it: *The dog hid under the
table.* ❑ *The key was under the
mat.*
2 One thing goes **under** another
if it passes below it: *The road
goes under the bridge.*
3 Something is **under** an amount
when it is less than that amount:
The whole meal cost under £10.
4 Someone works **under** another
person when they work for them:

*She has three people working
under her.*

under *adverb*
1 Under means 'beneath': *The
fence was too high so we
squeezed under.*
2 Under also means less than a
particular amount: *Children of
twelve and under travel free.*

underground *adjective and
adverb*
Underground means 'below the
surface of the ground': *We went
for a trip on an underground
railway.* ❑ *These men work
underground all day, digging for
gold.*

underground *noun*
The **underground** is an
underground railway: *She goes to
work on the underground.*

underneath *preposition*
1 One thing is **underneath**
another when it is below it: *He
found his book underneath a pile
of magazines.*
2 One thing goes **underneath**
another when it passes below it:
*A tunnel goes underneath the sea
from England to France.*

underneath *adverb*
Underneath means 'beneath':
*The fence was too high so we
squeezed underneath.*

understand *verb:* **understands,
understood, understanding, has
understood**
You **understand** something
when you know what it means:
Do you understand this sentence?

❑ *I didn't understand what he was saying.*

undo *verb*: **undoes, undid, undoing, has undone**
You **undo** something that is fastened when you open it or loosen it: *He tried to undo the knot in the rope.*

undress *verb*: **undresses, undressed, undressing, has undressed**
Someone **undresses** when they take off all of their clothes: *He undressed and climbed into the bath.*

uneven *adjective*
An **uneven** surface is not flat or level: *This road is very uneven.*

unfair *adjective*
Something or someone that is **unfair** does not treat people in the same way: *It's unfair to give presents to some children and not to others.*

unfriendly *adjective*
An **unfriendly** person behaves in an unpleasant way and isn't nice to other people: *She seems unfriendly at first, but she's just shy.*

unhappy *adjective:* **unhappier, unhappiest**
1 You are **unhappy** if you are sad: *Nick was very unhappy when his dog died.*
2 You are **unhappy** with someone or something when you are not pleased with them: *He was very unhappy with the situation at work.*

uniform *noun*: **uniforms**
A **uniform** is a special set of clothes which every member of a group has to wear: *Do you have*

to wear a school uniform? ❑ *a policeman's uniform.*

unit *noun*: **units**
1 A **unit** is an amount that you use for measuring things: *A metre is a unit of length.*
2 A **unit** is also one section of something: *The history course is divided into ten units.*
3 A **unit** is an amount that you use to talk about money: *The unit of money in Britain is the pound.*

universe *noun*
The **universe** is the Earth, the Sun, the Moon and all the other planets and stars in space.

university *noun*: **universities**
A **university** is a place where you go to study at the highest level after leaving school: *He's going to university to study French.* ❑ *Bob has got a job now, but Bill is still at university.*

unless *conjunction*
1 **Unless** means 'if .... not': *Don't come unless I telephone.* [= Come only if I telephone.]
2 **Unless** also means 'except when': *We always go for a walk on Sundays, unless it's raining.*

unload *verb*: **unloads, unloaded, unloading, has unloaded**
You **unload** a vehicle or a ship, when you remove all the things that it is carrying: *Can you help me unload the shopping from the car?*

unpack *verb*: **unpacks, unpacked, unpacking, has unpacked**
You **unpack** when you take things out of a suitcase or bag: *We were too tired to unpack, so we went straight to bed.*

untidy *adjective:* **untidier, untidiest**

1 A place is **untidy** when there are lots of things lying about and nothing is in its proper place: *My desk is always so untidy.* ❏ *What an untidy room!*

2 An **untidy** person is someone who is not very neat: *His hair was untidy and his clothes weren't very clean.*

untie *verb*: **unties, untied, untying, has untied**
You **untie** something when you undo the knot that ties it: *She untied his shoelaces for him.*

until *conjunction*
1 Something happens **until** a certain time when it happens up to that time and no longer: *I waited until eleven o'clock, but he didn't arrive.* ❏ *He ate until he felt sick.*

2 Something that doesn't happen **until** a certain time takes place at that time and not before: *He won't be here until tonight.*

unusual *adjective*
Something that is **unusual** is strange or rare: *It's unusual for Simon to arrive so early.* ❏ *That's a very unusual necklace.*

unwrap *verb*: **unwraps, unwrapped, unwrapping, has unwrapped**
You **unwrap** something when you take off the material it is wrapped in: *He unwrapped the parcel.*

up *preposition and adverb*
1 You go **up** when you move towards a higher place; you go **up** something when you move towards the top: *He climbed up the ladder.*

2 **Up** means 'towards a higher level': *She pointed up at the bird*

sitting on the branch.

3 You stand **up** when you get on to your feet after sitting or lying down: *He stood up and walked round the room.*

4 You are **up** when you are not in bed: *I was up at five o'clock this morning.*

5 You walk **up** to someone or something when you walk towards them: *He walked up to me and introduced himself.*

6 You use **up** to show that an action has the effect of increasing something: *Turn the volume up — I can't hear it.* ❏ *Prices have gone up again.*

meanings 1 and 6: the opposite is **down**

uphill *adjective and adverb*
You go **uphill** when you move up a slope: *The journey was uphill all the way.* ❏ *an uphill journey.*

upper *adjective*
The **upper** part of something is the part of it that is higher than the rest: *He lives on the upper floor.* ❏ *She has a bruise on her upper arm.*

the opposite is **lower**

upright *adjective and adverb*
Upright means 'standing straight up': *He sat in an upright position.* ❏ *She stood her bike upright against the wall.*

upset *verb*: **upsets, upset, upsetting, has upset**
1 You **upset** someone if you make them sad; something **upsets** you if it makes you sad: *The bad news upset her.* ❏ *I'm sorry, I didn't mean to upset you.*

2 You **upset** something when you knock it over: *The dog ran* *around the room and upset the vase.*

upset *adjective*
You are **upset** when you are unhappy: *She was very upset when her grandmother died.*

upside down *adverb*
Something is **upside down** when the part of it that is usually at the top is at the bottom: *I knew he wasn't really reading — he was holding the book upside down.*

upside down

upstairs *adverb*
1 You go **upstairs** when you go to a higher floor: *I'll go upstairs and get that book.*
2 Something that is **upstairs** is on a higher floor: *The bedroom is upstairs.*

up-to-date *adjective*
Something that is **up-to-date** is very modern: *He has an up-to-date computer.*

upwards or **upward** *adverb*
You go **upwards** or **upward** when you move or look towards a higher level: *He looked upwards and saw the sun.* ❑ *As they went upward they could see the whole valley below them.*

urgent *adjective*
Something that is **urgent** is very important and needs attention immediately: *I have an urgent message for Mr Hastings.*

us *pronoun*
You use **us** to talk about yourself and at least one other person: *His*

happy face surprised all of us. ❑ *Do you want to come with us tonight?*

use *verb*: **uses, used, using, has used**
You **use** something when you do a job with it: *He used blue paint to decorate the living room.* ❑ *Do you want to use my pen?* ❑ *Paul's using the telephone at the moment.*

'yooz'

▷ **used to**
1 You are **used to** something when you know it very well, or when you have always done it: *I'm not used to being on my own.* ❑ *She soon got used to her new school.*

'yoost'

2 You say that you **used to** do something when you did it often in the past; you say that something **used to** be a certain way when things were once like that: *I used to be afraid of spiders, but now I don't mind them.* ❑ *There used to be a cinema here, but not any more.*

'yoost'

▷ **use up**
You **use up** something when you use it all, so that there is none left: *I've used up all the milk.*

use *noun*: **uses**
1 The **use** of something is the act of using it: *We cannot allow the use of guns.*
2 Something that has a **use** can be used for a reason: *This knife has a lot of uses.*
3 You have the **use** of something if you are able to use it: *He lost the use of both his legs in the*

accident. ❑ *We had the use of the house while they were on holiday*

'yoos'

useful *adjective*
Something is **useful** if you are able to use it and it does the job well: *This ladder is very useful.* ❑ *a useful tool.*

useless *adjective*
Something is **useless** if it does not have any use or does not do what it is supposed to do: *This knife is useless — it's completely blunt.*

usual *adjective*
Usual describes things which happen in the same way as they always have: *I'll see you at the usual time tomorrow.* ❑ *I had my usual cup of coffee and slice of toast, then went to work.*

▷ **as usual**
Things happen **as usual** when they happen in the same way as they always have: *He was late as usual.*

usually *adverb*
Something that **usually** happens is the case on most occasions: *We usually go on holiday in June.* ❑ *Where's Jenny? She usually arrives before me.*

Vv

vacant *adjective*
A room or a seat is **vacant** if no-one is using it: *There were no vacant seats on the train.* ❑ *Does the hotel have any vacant rooms?*

vacation *noun*: **vacations**
A **vacation** is a holiday: *She's been on vacation to the USA.*

valley *noun*: **valleys**
A **valley** is an area of flat low land between hills: *They live in a cottage in the valley.*

valuable *adjective*
Something is **valuable** if it is worth a lot of money: *She has a lot of valuable jewellery.*

value *noun*
1 The **value** of something is the amount of money that it is worth: *What is the value of that necklace?*
2 The **value** of something is how useful it is: *This keyboard is of no value to me because I haven't got a computer.*

van *noun*: **vans**
A **van** is a vehicle which is like a large car; it is used to carry goods: *We managed to fit all the furniture into one van.*

variety *noun*: **varieties**
1 A **variety** of things is a selection of different kinds of them: *There was large variety of gifts to choose from.*
2 A **variety** is a sort or kind of something: *There are many varieties of dog in the world.* ❑ *We grow three varieties of cabbage.*

various *adjective*
Various means 'several different': *Various people phoned this morning.* ❑ *There are various flowers in this part of the garden.*

vase *noun*: **vases**
A **vase** is a container for putting flowers in: *We looked for a vase to put the roses in.*

‘ **vaaz** ’

vegetable *noun*: **vegetables**
A **vegetable** is a plant that you can eat, such as a potato, a carrot or an onion: *He grows carrots and other vegetables in his garden.*

vehicle *noun*: **vehicles**
A **vehicle** is a machine such as a car, a bus, a train, a lorry or a bicycle, which is used to carry people or goods.

very *adverb and adjective*
1 Very means 'extremely'; it is used to make a word stronger: *It's very cold today.* ❑ *It's very nice of you to help me.* ❑ *He seems very pleased with his present.*
2 Very also means 'extreme': *We climbed to the very top of the hill.* ❑ *We stayed till the very end.*

vest *noun*: **vests**
1 A **vest** is a piece of clothing without any sleeves; you wear it on the upper part of your body under your clothes.
2 In the United States, a **vest** is a waistcoat.

vet *noun*: **vet**
A **vet** is a doctor for animals: *We took the cat to the vet because she seemed ill.*

video *noun*: **videos**
1 A **video** is a copy of a film or television programme, stored on a cassette.
2 A **video** is also a video cassette.
3 A **video** is also a video recorder.

video cassette *noun*: **video cassettes**
A **video cassette** is the special cassette on to which you record a film or television programme.

often shortened to **video**

video recorder *noun*: **video recorders**
A **video recorder** is a machine that allows you to watch videos on the television.

often shortened to **video**

view *noun*: **views**
A **view** from a place, especially a window, is everything that you can see from it: *They had a view of the sea from their hotel window.* ❑ *We had a great view of the city from the top of the tower.*

village *noun*: **villages**
A **village** is a small group of houses and shops; a village is smaller than a town.

vinegar *noun*
Vinegar is a liquid with a sharp taste, used in cooking, and to help to keep food for longer.

violent *adjective*
A **violent** person or thing uses or has great force: *There was a really violent storm last night.* ❑ *He's a very violent criminal.*

violin *noun*: **violins**
A **violin** is a musical instrument with four strings; you hold it

under your chin and play it using a rod called a 'bow': *He's learning to play the violin.*

violin

visible *adjective*
Something is **visible** if you can see it: *The mountains are just visible from my window.*

the opposite is **invisible**

visit *verb*: **visits, visited, visiting, has visited**
1 You **visit** someone when you go to them and spend some time with them: *We're visiting my aunt this weekend.* ❑ *The children went to visit their grandmother when he was in hospital.*
2 You **visit** a place when you go there for a short time: *We visited the Eiffel Tower when we were in Paris.*

visit *noun*: **visits**
A **visit** is the act of going to see a person or place: *We went on a visit to Buckingham Palace.*

voice *noun*: **voices**
Your **voice** is the sound that comes from your mouth when you speak or sing: *He has a very loud voice.* ❑ *She spoke to me in an angry voice.* ❑ *These boys have beautiful voices.*

volume *noun*: **volumes**
1 A **volume** is a book: *The library has over a million volumes.*
2 The **volume** on a television, radio or CD player is the strength of the sound which comes from it: *Could you turn the volume up?*

I can't hear it.
3 The **volume** of a container is the amount of space it has inside it: *What is the volume of this box?*

voyage *noun*: **voyages**
A **voyage** is a long journey, especially on the sea: *They went on a voyage round the world.*

Ww

wade *verb*: **wades, waded, wading, has waded**
You **wade** through water or mud when you walk through it by pushing your legs forward against it: *She had to wade across the river.* ❑ *John waded into the water to get the boat back.*

wag *verb*: **wags, wagged, wagging, has wagged**
1 An animal **wags** its tail when it moves it from side to side: *The dog barked and wagged its tail when the doorbell rang.*
2 You **wag** your finger at someone when you shake it up and down to show that you are angry with them: *She wagged a finger at me. 'You're not paying attention,' she said.*

wage *noun*: **wages**
A person's **wage** is the money they earn for the work that they do: *The company pays very high wages.* ❑ *When he left school, his first weekly wage was only $30.*

wagon *noun*: **wagons**
1 A **wagon** is any vehicle with four wheels used for carrying heavy loads.
2 A railway **wagon** is an open railway carriage that is used for carrying goods: *The train pulled six wagons full of coal.*

waist *noun*: **waists**
Your **waist** is the part round the middle of your body, where you wear a belt: *I had a very small waist when I was a young girl.*

waistcoat *noun*: **waistcoats**
A **waistcoat** is a piece of clothing for your upper body; it does not have sleeves, and is often worn under a jacket: *This suit is made up of a jacket, trousers, and a waistcoat.*

wait *verb*: **waits, waited, waiting, has waited**
1 You **wait** when you stay where you are until someone or something comes: *Where do we wait for the bus?* ❑ *A lot of people were waiting outside the theatre.* ❑ *Wait a moment; I've had an idea.* ❑ *Stephen shouted 'Wait!'*
2 Waiters **wait** on other people when they bring them food or drinks.

waiter *noun*: **waiters**
A **waiter** is a man who serves people with food and drink, especially in a restaurant: *I asked the waiter to bring us some water.*

waitress *noun*: **waitresses**
A **waitress** is a woman who serves guests with food and drink, especially in a restaurant: *We called the waitress over and gave her our order.*

wake *verb*: **wakes, woke, waking, has woken**
1 You **wake**, or you **wake up**, when you stop sleeping: *He woke the next morning to find that the snow had all gone.* ❑ *I went to bed late and didn't wake up until 9 o'clock in the morning.*
2 Someone or something **wakes** you, or **wakes** you **up**, when they do something that stops you

sleeping: *Don't make so much noise! You'll wake the neighbours.* ❑ *They woke us up at five o'clock every morning.*

walk *verb*: **walks, walked, walking, has walked**
People or animals **walk** when they move along putting one foot in front of the other: *The baby can't walk yet, but he can crawl.* ❑ *Jackie walks to school, but Jane goes by car* ❑ *Don't walk so fast!* ❑ *We've missed the bus so we'll have to walk.*

rhymes with **talk**

walk *noun*: **walks**
1 A **walk** is a period of walking, or a journey made on foot: *Let's go for a walk through the fields.* ❑ *It's only a short walk to Tessa's flat.*
2 A **walk** is also a way of walking: *I recognized his unusual walk.*

rhymes with **talk**

walking stick *noun*: **walking sticks**
A **walking stick** is a stick that people use to lean on while they are walking, especially if their legs are weak or injured: *The old man walks with the help of a walking stick.*

wall *noun*: **walls**
1 A **wall** is one of the upright sides of a building or a room: *We painted the outside walls of the cottage white.* ❑ *I put the picture on the wall in the kitchen.*
2 A **wall** is also a structure made of stone or brick; it is used to separate one area from another: *The boys climbed over the garden wall.* ❑ *The prison is surrounded by a high wall.*

rhymes with **tall**

wallet *noun*: **wallets**
A **wallet** is a small flat case used for holding paper money: *Don't leave your wallet in your back pocket; someone might steal it.*

wallpaper *noun*
Wallpaper is strong paper used for decorating walls inside a building: *Do you think six rolls of wallpaper will be enough?*

wander *verb*: **wanders, wandered, wandering, has wandered**
You **wander** when you move about from place to place, without going to anywhere in particular: *He wandered about the city looking at the old houses, the temples and the street markets.*

want *verb*: **wants, wanted, wanting, has wanted**
1 You **want** something when you wish to have it or do it: *What do you want for your birthday?* ❑ *I want a new watch.* ❑ *He wanted to work in the United States.* ❑ *Do you want to come to the beach?*
2 You **want** someone to do something when you wish that they would do it: *I want you to explain everything to me.* ❑ *She doesn't want us to go with her.*

war *noun*: **wars**
There is **war**, or a **war**, when two or more countries fight each other: *Do you think there will be a war?* ❑ *The boys' father was killed in the war.*

the opposite is **peace**

ward *noun*: **wards**
The rooms in hospitals with beds for patients are called **wards**: *There are lots of bright pictures on the walls in the children's ward.*

wardrobe *noun*: **wardrobes**
A **wardrobe** is a large cupboard in which you hang clothes.

warehouse *noun*: **warehouses**
A **warehouse** is a large building used for storing goods.

warm *adjective*: **warmer, warmest**
1 Something that is **warm** is between hot and cold: *The children were outside enjoying the warm weather.* ◻ *My feet are quite warm but my hands are cold.*
2 Warm clothing protects you from cold: *You'll need to wear a warm jacket when you go sailing.*
3 Warm also means 'friendly': *The local people gave us a very warm welcome.* ◻ *She has a nice warm smile.*

the opposite is **cool**

warm *verb*: **warms, warmed, warming, has warmed**
You **warm** yourself when you make your body, or part of your body, warm: *Come and warm yourself by the fire.*

▷ **warm up**
1 You **warm** cold food **up** when you heat it gently: *She warmed the pies up in the oven.*
2 Something **warms** you **up** when it makes your body feel warm: *We drank hot soup to warm us up.*
3 A sportsman or sportswoman **warms up** when they do gentle exercises before an event or match: *If you don't warm up*

properly before a match, you might injure yourself.

warmth *noun*
Warmth is pleasant heat: *He could feel the warmth of the sun on his back.*

warn *verb*: **warns, warned, warning, has warned**
Someone **warns** you about danger or something bad when they tell you it is going to happen, or may happen: *They warned him of the danger, but he didn't listen.* ◻ *No-one warned me that the work was so difficult.* ◻ *A red light warns you when the car's getting too hot.*

warning *noun*: **warnings**
You receive a **warning** when someone or something lets you know about a danger: *She ignored the doctor's warnings, and continued to smoke.* ◻ *The red light is a warning that a train is coming.*

was *verb*
You use **was** with **I**, **he**, **she** and **it** to describe people, things and events in the past: *It was a very good film.* ◻ *Was she a friend of yours?* ◻ *She was my best friend at school.* ◻ *My mother was born in India.* ◻ *It was about ten o'clock when they arrived.*

▸ **was** belongs to the verb **be**
▸ **was not** can be shortened to **wasn't**

wash *verb*: **washes, washed, washing, has washed**
1 You **wash** something when you clean it using soap and water: *Have you washed your face and hands this morning?* ◻ *He washed his socks in the sink.* ◻ *I didn't*

hear the phone; I was washing my hair. ❑ I'll wash the dishes.

2 Water **washes** over something when it flows over it: He lay on the beach and let the waves wash over him.

▷ **wash up**

You **wash up** after a meal when you wash the dishes that you have used: If you wash up, I'll dry the dishes.

wash noun

You have a **wash** when you wash yourself: Is there time to have a wash before dinner?

washing noun

1 Washing is dirty clothes that need to be washed; you do the **washing** when you wash clothes: At the end of the week there was a huge pile of washing to do. ❑ We usually do the washing at the weekend.

2 Clothes that have just been washed are also called **washing**: She's outside, hanging the washing on the line.

washing machine noun: **washing machines**

A **washing machine** is an electric machine that washes clothes: You mustn't put that woollen sweater in the washing machine.

washing-up noun

You do the **washing-up** when you wash dirty dishes after a meal: It's your turn to do the washing-up.

wasn't verb

Wasn't is short for **was not**: I went to his house but he wasn't there. ❑ Len wasn't earning very much money. ❑ It was a really good film, wasn't it?

wasp noun: **wasps**

A **wasp** is a flying insect that has a long yellow and black striped body; like a bee, it can sting: There's a wasps' nest in that tree. ❑ A wasp stung me on the arm.

waste verb: **wastes, wasted, wasting, has wasted**

1 People **waste** something when they use up more of it than they need: They said that the factories wasted too much water. ❑ You're wasting electricity; you only need one light.

2 You **waste** something when you don't use it in a useful way: We wasted three hours waiting for the bus. ❑ He's wasted all that paper.

waste noun

You say something is a **waste** when it is not used in a useful way: Don't watch TV so much — it's a waste of time.

watch noun: **watches**

1 A **watch** is a small clock that you wear on your wrist or carry in your pocket: They gave her a gold watch when she left the company. ❑ My grandfather always carried his watch in his waistcoat pocket.

2 You keep a **watch** on someone or something when you watch them closely to make sure that they are all right: Could you keep a watch on the children while I'm out, please?

watch verb: **watches, watched, watching, has watched**

1 You **watch** someone or something when you look at them doing something for a period of time: We watched the boats going up and down the river. ❑ He was watching me from the window.

2 You **watch** a film or the TV when you pay attention to it: *Did you watch the news on TV last night?*
3 You **watch** a person or animal when you guard them or look after them: *Will you watch the baby for five minutes?*

▷ **watch out**
You say '**watch out!**' to warn someone that they may be in danger: *Watch out! That ladder's going to fall!*

water *noun*
Water is the transparent liquid that is in rivers, lakes and the sea, and which falls from the sky as rain: *All plants and animals need water to live.* □ *They had no clean water and many of them became ill.* □ *I'll just put these flowers in water.* □ *The water level in the river is very low because there hasn't been any rain for a month.* □ *Could I have a glass of water, please?* □ *You can't drink sea water.* □ *The water's lovely and warm. Come and have a swim.*

water *verb*: **waters, watered, watering, has watered**
You **water** plants when you pour water on the earth around them to keep them alive: *Could you water my plants while I'm on holiday, please?*

waterfall *noun*: **waterfalls**
A **waterfall** is water in a river that flows over the edge of a high rock and falls to the bottom: *Which is the highest waterfall in Africa?*

waterproof *adjective*
Material that is **waterproof** does not allow water to pass through it: *The fishermen were wearing*

waterproof jackets and trousers. □ *Is this tent waterproof?*

wave *verb*: **waves, waved, waving, has waved**
1 You **wave** when you raise your hand and move it from side to side; people wave to say hello or goodbye to someone who is some distance away: *The children waved goodbye from the train.* □ *He waved to me as he drove past.*

wave

2 You **wave** something that you are holding in your hand when you move it around in the air: *The old man waved his stick in the air and shouted at the children.*

wave *noun*: **waves**
1 A **wave** is the action of waving: *There's Peter over there. Give him a wave.*
2 A **wave** is also one of the ridges that form on the surface of water and move across it one after the other: *During the storm the waves on the sea were more than 10 metres high.* □ *There's a special machine for making waves in the swimming pool.*
3 Someone with a **wave** or **waves** in their hair has hair that is not completely straight.

wavy *adjective*: **wavier, waviest**
A **wavy** line, or **wavy** hair, is not completely straight: *Her hair isn't curly — it's wavy.*

wax *noun*
Wax is the material that is used

to make candles: *In the past, people sealed letters with hot wax.*

way *noun*: **ways**
1a The **way** to a place is the route that you take to get there: *What's the best way to get to London?* ❑ *They got couldn't find the way home.* ❑ *The accident happened when she was on her way to the office.* **b** A **way** is also a direction in which you move or look: *We were going the same way, so we walked together.* ❑ *He was looking the other way and didn't see the car.*
2 Something that is a long or short **way** is a long or short distance from where you are: *He walked a short way along the path and then stopped.* ❑ *Is it a long way to your house from here?*
3a A **way** of doing something is a method of doing it: *You can make bread in several different ways.* ❑ *Is this the best way to put up a tent?* **b** The **way** you do or say something is the manner in which you do or say it: *He treated the animals in a very cruel way.* ❑ *Try to tell him the bad news in a gentle way.*
4 Something is the right or the wrong **way** round when it is in the right or the wrong position: *He was wearing his hat the wrong way round.*
5 Someone's **ways** are their particular habits or types of behaviour: *She has a way of staring at people.* ❑ *That's just one of his funny ways.*

▷ **give way**
Something **gives way** when it breaks and falls down, usually because it is too weak to carry a

weight: *The table will give way if you put any more food on it.*

▷ **in the way**
Something is **in the way** when it blocks you: *I couldn't see the film because his head was in the way.*

▷ **lose your way**
You **lose your way** when you do not know where you are, or which way to go: *Sorry we're late; we lost our way.*

▷ **make way**
You **make way** for someone when you move so that that they can pass you: *We moved back to make way for the president's car.*

we *pronoun*
We is the word you use when you are talking about yourself and one or more other people: *We all eat dinner together at seven o'clock in the evening.*

weak *adjective*: **weaker, weakest**
A **weak** person or thing does not have much power or strength: *His legs are still very weak after the illness.*

the opposite is **strong**

weaken *verb*: **weakens, weakened, weakening, has weakened**
Something **weakens** when it becomes less strong or powerful: *The illness weakened the old man's heart.*

weakness *noun*: **weaknesses**
1 Weakness is the state of being weak: *You will suffer from some weakness for a while after the illness.*
2 You have a **weakness** for something when you like it, even though it may not be good for

you: *I've got a weakness for sweet things.*

wealth *noun*
Someone who has **wealth** has lots of money or owns many valuable things: *His enormous wealth made him a very powerful man.*

wealthy *adjective:* **wealthier, wealthiest**
Someone who is **wealthy** has a lot of money or owns a lot of valuable things: *the wealthy countries of the world.*

same as **rich**
the opposite is **poor**

weapon *noun:* **weapons**
A **weapon** is something that people use to fight with: *The bank robbers were carrying weapons.*

wear *verb:* **wears, wore, wearing, has worn**
You are **wearing** a piece of clothing when it is covering part of your body: *He wasn't wearing a tie.* □ *What are you going to wear for their wedding?*

▷ **wear down**
Something **is worn down** when it becomes smaller because something is rubbing it or hitting it: *The sea water has worn down these rocks.*

▷ **wear off**
The effect of something **wears off** when it gradually disappears: *When the effects of the drug wear off you may feel some pain again.*

▷ **wear out**
Things **wear out** when you use them again and again until you cannot use them any more: *These shoes wore out after only six months.*

weather *noun*
The **weather** is the amount of heat, cold, rain, sunshine or wind in a particular area: *What's the weather like outside?* □ *The weather changed and it became much colder.* □ *The weather is much warmer today, isn't it?*

web *noun:* **webs**
A **web** is a very fine net that a spider makes; it uses it to trap the insects it eats. [see picture at **spider**]

we'd
We'd is short for **we would**, **we should**, or **we had**: *We'd like to buy a house in the country.* □ *We'd be very glad to accept your invitation.* □ *When we'd eaten our lunch we went out for a walk.*

wedding *noun:* **weddings**
A **wedding** is the ceremony that takes place when two people become husband and wife: *After the wedding we all took photographs.*

Wednesday *noun*
Wednesday is the third day of the week, the day after Tuesday: *Joan was on holiday last Wednesday.* □ *His birthday is on a Wednesday this year.*

'wenz-day

weed *noun:* **weeds**
A **weed** is any wild plant that is growing where you don't want it, for example in a garden.

week *noun:* **weeks**
1 A **week** is a period of seven days: *It took a week for the parcel to arrive.* □ *They are having two weeks' holiday in Egypt.*
2 A **week** is also the period from one Sunday to the following

Saturday: *My birthday is next week, on Tuesday.*

3 The working **week** or the school **week** is the number of days in a week that people spend at work or at school: *He's been away from school for a week.*

weekday *noun*: **weekdays**
A **weekday** is any of the days of the week except Saturday and Sunday: *The new office is open every weekday until five o'clock.*

weekend *noun*: **weekends**
The **weekend** is Saturday and Sunday: *He works most weekends.* ❏ *We like to relax at home at weekends.*

weekly *adverb and adjective*
Something that happens **weekly** happens once a week: *Do they pay you weekly or monthly?* ❏ *She's at her weekly dance class.* ❏ *a weekly newspaper.*

weep *verb*: **weeps, wept, weeping, has wept**
Someone who **is weeping** is crying: *She wept all day when the dog died.* [see picture at **cry**]

same as **cry**

weigh *verb*: **weighs, weighed, weighing, has weighed**
You **weigh** something when you find out how heavy it is by putting it on scales; someone or something **weighs** a certain amount when that is how heavy they are: *The nurse weighs the baby when it is born.* ❏ *The shopkeeper weighed the apples.* ❏ *How much do you weigh?* ❏ *This suitcase weighs a lot.*

weight *noun*: **weights**
1 The **weight** of something is the amount that it weighs: *His weight hasn't changed since he was a young man.* ❏ *What's the weight of this basket of grapes?*

2 Something that is a **weight** is heavy: *The baby's becoming such a weight now.*

welcome *noun*: **welcomes**
A certain kind of **welcome** is the way that people greet you: *Everyone in the village gave us a very warm welcome.*

welcome *verb*: **welcomes, welcomed, welcoming, has welcomed**
People **welcome** you when they greet you, usually in a friendly way: *I'd like to welcome you all to our party.*

welcome *adjective*
1 You say '**welcome**' to a visitor to show them that you are glad they have come: *Welcome to Edinburgh. I hope you had a good journey.* ❏ *When we arrived everyone shouted 'Welcome back!'*

2 Something that is **welcome** is received and accepted with pleasure: *The money we won was very welcome.*

3 You say that someone is **welcome** in a place when you are happy for them to be there: *You're always welcome here.*

▷ **you're welcome**
You reply '**you're welcome**' to someone who has just said 'thank you' to you: *'Thanks very much for all your help.' 'You're welcome.'*

we'll
We'll is short for **we shall** or **we will**: *We'll probably be a bit late.* ❏ *We'll finish the work tomorrow.*

well *adjective*: **better**
A person who is **well** is healthy or has nothing wrong with them:

You look pale. Are you feeling well? □ *He phoned to say he wasn't very well.*

well *adverb*: **better, best**
1 a You do something **well** when you do it in a good or satisfactory way: *You dance very well.* **b** You do **well** when you are successful: *He's doing very well at college.*
2a You do something **well** when you do it completely: *Mix the flour and water well.* **b** You know someone **well** when you know a lot about them: *I've met your sister, but I don't know her well.*

▷ **as well**
As well means 'too' or 'also': *Dad's going to Hong Kong, and we're going as well.*

▷ **as well as**
As well as means 'and' or 'not only': *He's a good tennis player as well as a good golfer.*

▷ **well done!**
You say '**well done!**' to someone who has been successful or who has done a good piece of work.

▷ **well off**
People who are **well off** have plenty of money: *He's quite well off now; he's just bought a car and a big new house.*

well
People often say '**well**' at the beginning of a statement or question: *Well, what are we going to do now?* □ *'Did you go to the meeting yesterday?' 'Well, yes, but no-one else was there.'*

well *noun*: **wells**
A **well** is a deep hole in the ground from which you get water or oil.

went *verb*
see **go**: *We went fishing last Saturday.*

wept *verb*
see **weep**: *Veronica wept when she saw the poor children.* □ *He wept when his dog died.*

were *verb*
You use **were** with **we**, **you** and **they** to describe people, things and events in the past: *We were driving home when it started to snow.* □ *When were you last in Singapore?* □ *There were about a thousand people at the concert.*

▸**were** belongs to the verb **be**.
▸**were not** can be shortened to **weren't**.

we're
We're is short for **we are**: *We're getting married next week.* □ *We're lost. Can you help us, please?*

weren't
Weren't is short for **were not**: *Why weren't you at work yesterday?*

west *noun*
The **west** is the direction in which the sun sets: *They live in the west of Ireland.* □ *There was a light breeze blowing from the west.* □ *The front of the house faces west.*

wet *adjective*: **wetter, wettest**
1 Something that is **wet** is covered or soaked with water: *The car skidded on the wet road.* □ *He hung the wet clothes on the washing line.*
2 The weather is **wet** when it is raining: *It's too wet to play tennis today.*
3 Wet paint is paint that has not

yet dried: *The sign on the gate read 'Wet paint'.*

the opposite is **dry**

we've
We've is short for **we have**: *We've been to Manchester today.*

whale *noun*: **whales**
A **whale** is a very large animal which lives in the sea; it comes to the surface to breathe: *The blue whale is the largest animal on the Earth.*

what *pronoun and determiner*
1 You use **what** when you are asking questions about things: *What's the time?* ❑ *What does he do for a living?* ❑ *What kind of car is this?* ❑ *What's your son's name?*
2 You also use **what** to mean 'the thing that…' or 'the things that…': *Is this what you were looking for?* ❑ *Tell me what you want.* ❑ *What I need is a bigger desk.*
3 People say '**What** a…' at the beginning of a statement to show that they are pleased, surprised or angry: *What a wonderful party!* ❑ *What a good day that was!* ❑ *What a fool I've been!*

▷ **what about**
You say '**what about**…?' when you are making a suggestion: *'What shall we eat tonight?' 'What about fish?'*

whatever *pronoun and determiner*
1 You use **whatever** to mean 'anything that' or 'everything that': *He always agrees with whatever she says.* ❑ *Whatever he does, he always does it well.*
2 Whatever also means 'no matter what': *Whatever happens, I will always be here for you.*

wheat *noun*
Wheat is a type of cereal plant that produces grain which is used to make flour: *a field of wheat* ❑ *They make their bread with wheat flour.*

wheel *noun*: **wheels**
1 A **wheel** is one of the circular objects on a vehicle; when the wheels turn, the vehicle can move along the ground: *A bicycle has two wheels and a car usually has four.* ❑ *A car has tyres on its wheels.*
2 A **wheel** is also any circular object that looks like this: *a steering wheel* ❑ *Inside a watch there are little wheels and a spring.*

wheelbarrow *noun*: **wheelbarrows**
A **wheelbarrow** is a cart with one wheel at the front and handles at the back.

wheelchair *noun*: **wheelchairs**
A **wheelchair** is a chair with wheels; people who have difficulty walking use a wheelchair to move around: *After a few months she was able to get out of her wheelchair and stand for a short time.* [see picture at **chair**]

when *adverb and conjunction*
1 You use **when** in questions to mean 'at what time': *When will you be ready to go out?* ❑ *When were you born?* ❑ *When does the next train arrive?*
2 When is also used to talk about a particular time, and means 'at the time that…': *When he arrives, we can all have lunch.* ❑ *When it rains, water comes in through the roof.*

whenever *adverb and conjunction*
Whenever means 'at any time that' or 'at every time that': *We always visit the museums whenever we are in London.* ❑ *Whenever I phone him he's not at home.*

where *adverb, pronoun and conjunction*
1 You use **where** in questions to talk about the place at which a person or thing is, or the place they are coming from, or going to: *Where's John?* ❑ *Where is the nearest post office?* ❑ *'Where's your car?' 'It's over there.'* ❑ *Where is all this water coming from?*
2 You also use **where** when you are saying something about a particular place or situation: *This is the village where my father was born.* ❑ *This is where the story gets exciting.*

wherever *adverb and conjunction*
Wherever means 'no matter which place or situation that' or 'in every place or situation that': *Wherever we are, we always telephone each other every day.* ❑ *Wherever possible, young children should be kept with their parents.*

whether *conjunction*
1 When people use **whether** with words like 'know' 'ask' and 'decide' it means the same as 'if': *Do you know whether this is the train for Brighton?*
2 You also use **whether** to talk about a choice between two things: *We couldn't see whether he was angry or not.* ❑ *Whether it's*

raining or sunny, I'm going for a walk tomorrow.

which *determiner and pronoun*
1 You use **which** in questions when you are asking someone to name or choose from a group: *Which house is yours?* ❑ *Which is the fastest car?* ❑ *I didn't know which one to choose.* ❑ *Which of these boys is your son?* ❑ *Which hand do you write with?*
2 You also use **which** when you are giving more information about something: *This is the house which we stayed in when we were on holiday.* ❑ *He said he could drive, which was a lie.*

whichever *determiner and pronoun*
Whichever means 'no matter which' or 'any one that': *Whichever hotel you choose, make sure it has a bathroom.* ❑ *Take whichever of these CDs you want.*

while *conjunction*
1 While means 'during the time that': *Will you be visiting Edinburgh while you are in Scotland?* ❑ *I read the newspaper while Chris was making supper.*
2 While also means 'although': *While I understand your reasons, I still don't agree.*

while *noun*
A **while** is a period of time: *She'll feel better again in a while.* ❑ *We waited inside for a while but the rain didn't stop.*

whip *noun*: **whips**
A **whip** is a long thin strip of leather or rope that is fixed to a handle; it is used for hitting people or animals with: *The jockey used his whip to make the horse run faster.*

whiskers *noun*
Whiskers are the long strong hairs growing from the sides of an animal's face: *Our cat has long white whiskers.*

whisper *verb*: **whispers, whispered, whispering, has whispered**
You **whisper** when you speak very quietly, using your breath, rather than your voice: *She whispered something in his ear.* ❑ *They were whispering together at the back of the class.*

whisper *noun*: **whispers**
You speak in a **whisper** when you speak very quietly: *I could hear them talking in whispers outside my bedroom door.*

whistle *verb*: **whistles, whistled, whistling, has whistled**
1 A person **whistles** when they make a high loud sound by blowing air through their lips: *He was whistling a tune while he worked.* ❑ *Someone whistled outside the house, and I looked out of the window.*
2 Something **whistles** when it makes a high loud sound: *The wind was whistling through the trees.*

  'wis-el **'**

whistle *noun*: **whistles**
1 A **whistle** is the sound of someone or something whistling: *The man gave a loud whistle and the dog came running towards him.*
2 A **whistle** is also a device or an instrument that makes a high loud sound: *The referee blew his whistle at the end of the match.*

  'wis-el **'**

white *noun and adjective*: **whites**
1 White is the colour of milk or snow: *He has beautiful white teeth.* ❑ *The bride wore a long white dress.*
2 People with **white** skin have light-coloured skin: *People with very white skin have to protect themselves when they go out in the sun.*
3 The **white** of an egg is the part that surrounds the yolk; it turns white when you cook the egg.

who *pronoun*
1 You use **who** when you are asking the name of a person or people: *Who made that rude noise?* ❑ *Who is that beautiful woman over there?* ❑ *Who did you see at the party?*
2 You use **who** when you want to describe a person, or explain which person you mean, or to add some more information about a person: *It was Marion who told me about the accident.* ❑ *This is a painting by Van Gogh, the artist who cut off his ear.*

whoever *pronoun*
Whoever means 'no matter which person' or 'the person that': *Whoever phones, tell them I'm not in.* ❑ *Whoever painted that house didn't do it very well.*

whole *noun*
1 The **whole** of something is all of it: *We spent the whole of our holiday lying on the beach.*
2 A **whole** is a complete thing, especially one that is made up of parts that go together: *Two halves make a whole.*

  'hole '

whole *adjective*
1 The **whole** thing is all of it: *He*

ate the whole cake by himself.
❑ *He spent his whole life trying to find a cure for the disease.*
2 Something that is **whole** is complete: *These snakes can swallow a rabbit whole.*

'hole'

whom *pronoun*
1 You use **whom** to ask to which person something is done: *To whom was the parcel sent?*
2 You also use **whom** when you are describing a person or explaining which person you mean: *The man to whom I gave the message said he was your assistant.*

'hoom'

whose *pronoun*
1 You use **whose** when you are asking which person something belongs to: *Whose house is this?* ❑ *The man asked me whose son I was.*
2 You also use **whose** when you are describing a person or explaining which person you mean: *This is the man whose family owns all the land round here.* ❑ *They've invited all the parents whose children are coming to this school next year.*

'hooz'

why *adverb and pronoun*
1 You use **why** in questions to mean 'for what reason': *Why is this door locked?* ❑ *Why did you say that?* ❑ *Why are you shouting?* ❑ *Do you know why they didn't come?*
2 You also use **why** after 'reason': *Can you think of a reason why she's late?*

wicked *adjective*
You can describe a person or their behaviour as **wicked** if they are very bad or cruel: *It's wicked of them to ignore these people who need help.*

same as **bad** or **evil**
the opposite is **good** or **kind**

wide *adjective:* **wider, widest**
1 Something that is **wide** is a large distance from one side to the other: *This part of the city has very wide streets.* ❑ *The river gets wider as it flows through the valley.*
2 You also use **wide** when you are saying how much something measures from one side to the other: *The lake is 30 kilometres long and 5 kilometres wide.* ❑ *The cloth for the curtains is 3 metres wide.*

same as **broad**
meaning 1: the opposite is **narrow**

width *noun*
The **width** of something is the amount it measures from one side to the other: *Did you measure the width in inches or centimetres?* ❑ *This rug is about a metre in width.*

wife *noun:* **wives**
A man's **wife** is the woman he has married: *He and his wife share the housework.* ❑ *What was your wife's surname before she married you?*

wig *noun:* **wigs**
A **wig** is a covering of false hair that is worn on the head: *He wore a black wig and a false moustache. No-one recognized him.*

wild *adjective*
1 Wild animals are are not used to living near or with people: *In winter we put food in the garden for the wild birds.* ❏ *wild horses.*
2 Wild plants are plants that grow in a natural state: *She picked a bunch of wild flowers in the wood.*

meaning 1: the opposite is **tame**

wildlife *noun*
Wildlife is animals, birds and insects that live in a natural state, and are not kept by human beings: *We are gradually destroying the world's wildlife.*

will *verb*: will, would
1 People say they **will** do something when they are going to do it, or when they agree to do it: *I will be in the office tomorrow.* ❏ *'Will you be there on time?' 'Yes, I will.'*
2 You use **will** in questions when you are asking what someone is going to do or what is going to happen: *Will the plane be stopping at Amsterdam before it goes on to Hamburg?* ❏ *Will you be there at seven o'clock?*
3 You use **will** when you are ordering someone to do something: *Will you stop making that noise!*
4 You also use **will** to offer to do something; you use **will not** or **won't** to say that someone refuses to do something: *I'll do the washing up. You just relax.* ❏ *I've discussed it with her, but she won't change her mind.*

> ▸ **I will, you will, he will, she will, we will** and **they will** can be shortened to **I'll, you'll,**

> **he'll, she'll, we'll** and **they'll**.
> ▸ **will not** can be shortened to **won't**.

willing *adjective*
You are **willing** to do something when you want to do it or are happy to do it: *They are always willing to help.* ❏ *She's a very willing student.*

win *verb*: wins, won, winning, has won
1 Someone **wins** a competition or a race when they come first, before all the others: *Moira won the piano competition.* ❏ *Who won the 400 metres race?*
2 You **win** a prize when you receive a gift to show that you have been successful in a competition: *She always wins first prize for her cakes.* ❏ *Dad won a teddy bear at the fair.*

meaning 1: the opposite is **lose**

wind *noun*: winds
The **wind**, or a **wind**, is air that blows across the Earth in a certain direction: *There wasn't much wind, and the sailing boats weren't moving very fast.* ❏ *A warm wind blew from the west.*

❛**win-d**❜

wind *verb*: winds, wound, winding, has wound
1 You **wind** something when you twist it round and round: *The sailor was winding a length of rope round his arm.* ❏ *The nurse wound a long bandage round his head.*
2 You **wind** a watch or clock when you make it work by turning the small screw which makes the spring inside tight.
3 A road **winds** when it twists

and turns: *A rough path wound up the side of the mountain.*

rhymes with **find**

▷**wind up**
You **wind up** a clock or a watch when you turn the screw on it to make it work: *Could you remember to wind up the clock every morning, please?*

window *noun*: **windows**
A **window** is an opening in the wall of a building or in the side of a vehicle, with glass fitted in it so that you can see through it: *We opened all the windows because it was such a lovely day.* ❑ *You can drive through the park and see wild animals through your car windows.*

windy *adjective*: **windier, windiest**
The weather is **windy** when a strong wind is blowing: *It was wet and very windy yesterday.*

wine *noun*: **wines**
Wine is a strong drink made with the juice of grapes or other fruits: *I had a glass of wine with my lunch.* ❑ *Do you prefer red or white wine?*

wing *noun*: **wings**
1 A bird's or insect's **wings** are the parts of its body that it uses to fly with: *I think this bird has broken one of its wings.* ❑ *Many butterflies have bright colours on their wings.*
2 An aeroplane's **wings** are the two parts at each side which keep it in the air when it is flying.

wing

wing

wink *verb*: **winks, winked, winking, has winked**
You **wink** when you shut one of your eyes and open it again quickly, as a friendly or a secret sign: *'Let's leave Mum to do all the work,' said Dad, winking at me.*

winner *noun*: **winners**
The **winner** of a race or a competition is the person who has won it: *The winner of the singing contest will get a gold cup.*

winter *noun*
Winter is one of the four seasons of the year, coming between autumn and spring: *Winter is the coldest season of the year.*

wipe *verb*: **wipes, wiped, wiping, has wiped**
1a You **wipe** something when you clean dirt from it using a cloth: *She wiped the marks off the table with a cloth.* ❑ *He quickly wiped his face and hands with a damp cloth.* **b** You **wipe** liquid **up** when you remove it from a surface with a cloth: *Could you please wipe up the coffee that you've spilt on the table?*
2 You **wipe** your eyes when you dry tears from them; you **wipe** your skin when you dry it using a cloth, a handkerchief or your hand: *She stopped crying and wiped her eyes with a handkerchief.* ❑ *A nurse wiped the sweat from the patient's forehead.*

▷**wipe out**
People or things **are wiped out** when they are all destroyed: *The disease wiped out whole villages.*

wire *noun*: **wires**
1 Wire is metal in a very long thin form: *a wire fence.*
2 A **wire** is a piece of this used

for carrying electricity or for making things: *One of the wires in the plug is loose.*

wise *adjective:* **wise, wiser, wisest**
A **wise** person makes sensible decisions, usually because they have a lot of knowledge or experience; a **wise** decision is a sensible decision: *You were wise to refuse.* ❑ *Are you really leaving? Do you think that's wise?*

the opposite is **foolish**

wish *verb:* **wishes, wished, wishing, has wished**
1 You **wish** for something when you want it very much; you **wish** something would happen when you want it to happen very much, even when it is impossible: *She watched the other children and wished for a friend.* ❑ *I wish I had more money.* ❑ *I wish I wasn't so shy.*
2 You **wish** someone luck or happiness when you say that you hope that they will have it: *I wish you lots of luck in your exams.* ❑ *He wished me a happy New Year.*

wish *noun:* **wishes**
1a A **wish** is something that you want, or want to happen: *He said he had no wish to leave home.*
b You make a **wish** when you say that you want something, or want something to happen: *Make a wish when you blow out the candles on your birthday cake.*
2 You give someone your good **wishes** when you tell them that you hope they will be happy and successful: *Give your mother my best wishes.*

with *preposition*
1 People or things are **with** others when they are in their company, or are beside them or among them: *She was dancing with my brother.* ❑ *The boys often play with each other.* ❑ *She put the rice in the cupboard with the other food.*
2 You do something **with** a particular thing when you use that thing to do it: *She tied up her hair with ribbons.* ❑ *Wash your face with soap and water.*
3 You use **with** when you are describing a quality that someone or something has: *Helen's the girl with the long fair hair and blue eyes.* ❑ *The cat is black with white ears.* ❑ *A lorry is a vehicle with wheels.* ❑ *Our house is the one with the green door.* ❑ *She's the one with the loud voice.*
4 You also use **with** when you are talking about the cause of something: *He was shaking with fear.* ❑ *The fans were all jumping up and down with joy.*
5 You use **with** after 'cover' and 'fill': *His clothes were covered with blood.* ❑ *She filled the tank with petrol.*
6 You leave something **with** someone when you leave it in their care: *Can I leave the baby with you for a couple of hours?*
7 You use **with** to say how something should be done: *Sing this part with lots of feeling.*
8 You use **with** in sentences that refer to particular people or actions: *Be very careful with that vase.* ❑ *What's the matter with you?* ❑ *What shall I do with this old coat?*

within *preposition*
1 Something is **within** a place when it is inside it: *They always stayed within the walls of the city.*
2 Something that happens **within** a certain period of time, happens during that time and for no longer: *Please reply to this letter within seven days.* ❑ *Within a month, he had a new job.*

without *preposition*
1 Without means 'not having': *How can we live without any money?*
2 Without is also used to talk about something that you do not use or need: *In summer, I sleep without any blankets on my bed.* ❑ *You can't eat soup without a spoon.*
3 You do something **without** someone when they are not with you when you do it; you do something **without** their help when they don't give you any help: *If you're late we'll go without you.* ❑ *She can't walk downstairs without help.*
4 You also use **without** when you are talking about not doing something: *You can't go without saying goodbye.* ❑ *They want to have money without working.*

woke and **woken** *verb*
see **wake**: *A noise outside woke me.* ❑ *I was woken up by the noise.*

wolf *noun*: **wolves**
A **wolf** is a wild animal like a large dog; wolves live with others in groups called 'packs'.

woman *noun*: **women**
A **woman** is an adult female human being: *Both married and single women will receive the same amount of money.*

won *verb*
see **win**: *He won the singing competition.* ❑ *She won first prize.*

wonder *verb*: **wonders, wondered, wondering, has wondered**
1 You **wonder** something when you ask yourself about it: *I wonder when I'll see him again.* ❑ *I was wondering if you would like to come to my party.*
2 You **wonder** about something that puzzles you or surprises you when you think about it and try to work it out: *Have you ever wondered why he has so much money?*

wonder *noun*
1 Wonder is a feeling that you have when you see something very strange or unusual: *The children watched the magic tricks with wonder.*
2 A **wonder** is something that people admire because it is so unusual: *Ayers Rock in Australia is one of the natural wonders of the world.*

wonderful *adjective*
You describe a person or thing as **wonderful** when you think they are very good or very great: *We had a wonderful holiday in Greece.* ❑ *She's a wonderful cook.*

won't
Won't is short for **will not**: *Those trousers won't fit you. They're too big.* ❑ *I promise I won't tell anyone your secret.*

wood *noun*
1 Wood is the hard material that trees are made of; it is used to make furniture and paper, it is

used in building, and as a fuel for burning on fires: *Paul was cutting up wood for the fire.* ❏ *Is this table made of wood or plastic?*

2 A **wood** is a type of wood that comes from a particular tree.

3 A **wood** is also a group of trees growing close together: *There isn't much sunlight in the middle of the wood.*

wooden *adjective*
Wooden things are made of wood: *She used a wooden spoon to stir the mixture.* ❏ *We found some old wooden toys in the back of the cupboard.*

wool *noun*
Wool is the soft thick hair of sheep which is cut off their backs and used to make thread for knitting and weaving: *How much wool do you need to make a man's sweater?* ❏ *This carpet is made of wool.*

woollen *adjective*
Woollen things are made of wool: *The fishermen wear thick woollen jumpers to keep out the cold.*

word *noun*: **words**
A **word** is a group of letters that have a meaning: *What does this word mean?* ❏ *There are thousands of words in this dictionary.*

wore *verb*
see **wear**: *Richard wore his army uniform when he got married.*

work *noun*
1 Work is tasks that you have to do; doing work uses energy and time: *They've done a lot of work on their house.* ❏ *Digging the garden is very hard work.* ❏ *Have you done enough work?*

2a A person's **work** is their job; someone who has no **work** doesn't have a job: *Typing letters isn't part of my work.* ❏ *He's looking for work at the moment.*
b You go to **work** when you go to the place where you do your job; you are at **work** when you are at the place where you do your job: *He goes to work at half past seven every morning.*

meaning 1: the opposite is **rest**

work *verb*: **works, worked, working, has worked**
1 People **work** when they do a job or do various tasks: *He's working in the garden shed.* ❏ *Ann works in a factory.*
2 Something **works** when it does what it is supposed to do: *My computer isn't working properly.* ❏ *Do you think this plan will work?* ❏ *The punishment didn't work and he started behaving badly again.*

meaning 1: the opposite is **rest**

▷ **work out**
You **work** something **out** when you think about it carefully until you find the right answer: *I can't work out why it's so expensive.* ❏ *He worked out that we needed another £200.*

worker *noun*: **workers**
A **worker** is a person who has a job, especially in a factory: *The car workers are on strike again.*

workman *noun*: **workmen**
A **workman** is a man who does jobs such as building and repairing roads and houses: *The workmen have arrived to dig up the pavements.*

world *noun*: **worlds**
1 The **world** is the planet that we

live on: *People all over the world watched the match on television.* □ *Tokyo is one of the biggest cities in the world.*
2 Other **worlds** are other planets: *Do you think there are people living on different worlds?*

worm *noun*: **worms**
A **worm** is a creature with no legs and a long narrow body made up of sections; it lives in soil: *Several types of worm live in the soil.*

worn *verb*
see **wear**. *Do you want this dress? I've never worn it.*

worn *adjective*
Something that is **worn** has become damaged because it has been used a lot: *You need a new jacket — that one is very worn.* □ *He was wearing a worn pair of jeans.*

worried *adjective*
You are **worried** when you feel anxious about something: *Don't look so worried. I'm sure everything will be all right.* □ *He has a worried look on his face.* □ *We're all very worried about losing our jobs.*

worry *verb*: **worries, worried, worrying, has worried**
You **worry** about something when you feel anxious and upset about it: *Don't worry too much about the exams.* □ *She's always happy — nothing seems to worry her.* □ *Mum worries that we aren't eating properly.*

worry *noun*: **worries**
1 Worry is the unpleasant feeling that you get when you are worried: *All this worry will make her ill.*

2 A **worry** is something that causes you to feel anxious and upset: *I'm going on holiday to forget all my worries.*

worse *adjective*
One thing is **worse** than another when it is bad compared with that other thing: *His spelling is worse than mine.* □ *'Are you feeling better.' 'No, I'm feeling a lot worse.'*

the opposite is **better**

worst *adjective*
The **worst** thing is worse than all the others: *This is the worst film I've ever seen!* □ *I've seen some bad films, but this is the worst.*

the opposite is **best**

worth *adjective*
1 Something is **worth** a particular price if people will buy it for that amount: *This painting is worth a million dollars.* □ *Is this picture worth much?*
2 An activity is **worth** doing if it is interesting or useful: *It's worth saving some money every month.*

worth *noun*
1 The **worth** of something is its value: *I'd like to know the worth of this piece of old jewellery.*
2 A person's or a thing's **worth** is their usefulness: *She's really shown her worth in the last few weeks.*

would *verb*
1 see **will**. *He said he would phone me the following week.*
2 You use **would** when you are imagining situations: *If I had a car I would take you to the airport myself.* □ *I wouldn't be happy if I lived in a city.*
3 People use **would** with 'like'

when they are talking about what they want: *I would like to go to America next year.* ❑ *Would you like some more soup?*

> ▸ **I would, you would, he would, she would, we would** and **they would** can be shortened to **I'd, you'd, he'd, she'd, we'd** and **they'd**.

wouldn't
Wouldn't is short for **would not**: *I wouldn't like to be famous.*

wound *noun*: **wounds**
A **wound** is an injury, especially where the skin is cut by a weapon: *The soldier died of his wounds.* ❑ *The wound on his hand took a long time to heal.*

> ‘ **woond** ’

wound *verb*: **wounds, wounded, wounding, has wounded**
A person or animal **is wounded** when they are injured by a weapon: *Her father was wounded during the war.*

wound *verb*
see **wind**: *The fisherman wound the rope round a pole.* ❑ *He wound up his watch*

> ‘ **wownd** ’

> ▸When a word starts with '**wr**...', the '**w**' is not pronounced.

wrap *verb*: **wraps, wrapped, wrapping, has wrapped**
You **wrap** something when you put paper or some other material all round it: *She wrapped the glasses in newspaper.* ❑ *The old man wrapped himself in a blanket.*

> ‘ **rap** ’

▹ **wrap up**
1 You **wrap** something **up** when

you put something such as paper all round it: *Molly wrapped the presents up in bright paper.*
2 You **wrap up** when you put warm clothes on: *Remember to wrap up well — it's cold outside.*

wreck *verb*: **wrecks, wrecked, wrecking, has wrecked**
Something **is wrecked** when it is destroyed: *Ken's sudden illness wrecked all our plans.*

> ‘ **rek** ’

wrinkle *noun*: **wrinkles**
Material or skin that has **wrinkles** has small folds or lines in it: *The old man's face was covered with wrinkles.* ❑ *After the journey their clothes were full of wrinkles.*

> ‘ **ring**-kl ’

wrist *noun*: **wrists**
Your **wrist** is the part of your body where your hand joins your arm: *They tied his wrists together so that he couldn't escape.* [see picture at **arm**]

> ‘ **rist** ’

write *verb*: **writes, wrote, writing, has written**
1 You **write** when you put letters and words on paper with a pen or pencil: *She wrote her name and address on a piece of paper.* ❑ *The policeman was writing something in his notebook.* ❑ *The children learn to read and write when they are five.*
2 You **write** a story, a book, a poem or a play when you invent it and write it down: *My sister writes children's stories.* ❑ *He's written some very good travel books.*
3 You **write** to someone when

you write a letter and send it to them: *Have you written to your aunt yet?*

▷ **write back**
You **write back** to someone who has sent you a letter when you send them a reply: *He wrote to me a few times, but I never wrote back.*

▷ **write down**
You **write** something **down** when you make a note of it so that you can refer to it later: *The policeman was writing down everything I said.*

writer *noun*: **writers**
A **writer** is a person who writes books and stories, or who writes for magazines or newspapers: *Roald Dahl was a very successful writer of children's books.*

writing *noun*
1 Writing is words that are written on paper: *I couldn't read his writing.*
2 Writing is the process or skill of putting words down on paper using a pen or pencil: *No-one taught me reading and writing. I learnt it by myself.*
3 Writing is also the skill of making up stories or of producing reports for magazines and newspapers: *He earns a lot from his writing.*

written *verb*
see **write**: *Have you written to your mother yet?*

wrong *adjective*
1 Something that is **wrong** is not correct or accurate: *He gave several wrong answers and failed the test.* ❑ *We got on the wrong train.* ❑ *I thought he was honest, but I was wrong.*
2 Behaviour that is **wrong** is not good or not right: *It's wrong to steal.* ❑ *It was wrong to take the car without asking.*
3 Something goes **wrong** with a machine when it stops working properly: *Something went wrong with the computer.* ❑ *There's something wrong with the car. It's making a funny noise.*

rhymes with **long**

meanings 1 and 2: the opposite is **right**

wrote *verb*
see **write**: *My friend wrote a letter to me.* ❑ *I wrote my telephone number in his notebook.*

Xx

X-ray *noun*: **X-rays**
An **X-ray** is a special kind of photograph which shows the bones inside a person's body: *The*

X-ray of Pete's arm shows that he has broken his wrist.

'**eks**-ray'

Yy

yacht *noun*: **yachts**
A **yacht** is a type of sailing boat.

'**yot**'

yard *noun*: **yards**
1 A **yard** is a unit of length that measures a little less than one metre: *She can run 100 yards in 15 seconds.*
2 A **yard** is also the area around a building, usually without any grass: *The boys played football in the yard.*

yawn *verb*: **yawns, yawned, yawning, has yawned**
You **yawn** when you open your mouth very wide and take a deep breath, usually when you are tired: *George yawned and said he was going to bed.*

yawn

year *noun*: **years**
A **year** is a period of 365 days or twelve months: *The Earth takes a year to travel round the Sun.*

□ *She is a year older than me.*
□ *Where did you go on holiday this year?* □ *They've been married for a year.*

▷ **all year round**
Something happens **all year round** when it happens for the whole year: *In some countries it is warm all year round.*

yearly *adverb and adjective*
1 Something happens **yearly** when it happens once a year: *He goes to the dentist twice yearly.*
2 A **yearly** amount of money is the amount that is paid for a whole year: *They pay a yearly rent of £5000.*

yell *verb*: **yells, yelled, yelling, has yelled**
You **yell** when you shout very loudly: *'Where are you?' he yelled.*
□ *Stop yelling — I can hear you quite well.*

yellow *noun and adjective*: **yellows**
Yellow is the colour of the sun and the yolk of an egg: *We painted the walls yellow.* □ *a yellow dress* □ *The paint on the walls was a pale yellow.*

yes
You say **yes** to show that you agree with something, or to show that you will do something: *'You're American, aren't you?' 'Yes, that's right.'* □ *'Could you help me with these bags?' 'Yes, of course.'*

yesterday *noun*
Yesterday is the day before today: *What did you do yesterday?* □ *We arrived home from our holiday yesterday.*

yet *adverb*
You say that something has not happened **yet**, if it has not taken place in the time up until now: *I haven't seen her yet but she is here.* □ *Has the film started yet?*

yoghurt *noun*: **yoghurts**
Yoghurt is a half-liquid food made from milk, often with fruit added: *We had strawberry yoghurt for breakfast.*

yolk *noun*: **yolks**
The **yolk** of an egg is the yellow part in the middle of it.

you *pronoun*
You refers to the person or people that you are talking to: *I saw you in town yesterday.* □ *Would you like a cup of tea?* □ *Have you heard about Tony's new job?* □ *You are both invited to my party.*

you'd
You'd is short for **you would** and **you had**: *You'd better hurry or you'll be late.* □ *You said you'd telephone Gill.*

you'll *verb*
You'll is short for **you will**: *You'll have plenty of time if you leave now.*

young *adjective*: **younger, youngest**
An **young** person or animal has not lived for a long time: *The younger children went to bed at nine.* □ *Young people are looking for something different.*

the opposite is **old**

your *determiner*
Your means 'belonging to you': *Don't forget your keys.* □ *I haven't met your mother.*

you're
You're is short for **you are**: *You're fifteen, aren't you?* □ *You're going to be late.*

yours *pronoun*
You use **yours** to talk about something that belongs to the person you are talking to: *Is this pen yours?* □ *I've met Mike's parents but I haven't met yours.*

yourself *pronoun*: **yourselves**
1 You use **yourself** in sentences where the person you are talking to is affected by their own action: *Be careful. Don't hurt yourself.* □ *Make yourselves comfortable.*
2 You do something **yourself** if you do it without help from anyone else: *Did you really do that yourself?* □ *You'll be able to finish it yourselves.*

youth *noun*
1 A person's **youth** is the time when they were young: *I used to play football a lot in my youth.*
2 A **youth** is a young man: *a handsome youth.*

you've
You've is short for **you have**: *You've taken the wrong coat.* □ *You've got a black mark on your trousers.*

Zz

zero *noun*: **zeros**
1 Zero is the number 0: *2 minus 2 equals zero.* ❑ *'What's their telephone number?' 'Six zero double one.'* [= 6011]
2 Zero degrees (0°) is the temperature at which water freezes: *It's very cold today — five degrees below zero.*

zigzag *noun*: **zigzags**
A **zigzag** is a line which has lots of sharp points: *The path formed a zigzag as it went up the side of the hill.*

zip or **zipper** *noun*: **zips** or **zippers**

A **zip** or **zipper** is a device for fastening clothes; it is made of two rows of metal teeth which fit into each other when it is closed: *The dress has a zip up the back.*

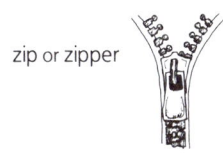
zip or zipper

zoo *noun*: **zoos**
A **zoo** is a public place where people can go and look at wild animals.

Irregular verbs

infinitive	past tense	past participle
be	was, were	been
bear	bore	borne
beat	beat	beaten
become	became	become
begin	began	begun
bend	bent	bent
bind	bound	bound
bite	bit	bitten
bleed	bled	bled
blow	blew	blown
break	broke	broken
bring	brought	brought
broadcast	broadcast	broadcast
build	built	built
burn	burnt, burned	burnt, burned
burst	burst	burst
buy	bought	bought
catch	caught	caught
choose	chose	chosen
come	came	come
cost	cost	cost
creep	crept	crept
cut	cut	cut
deal	dealt	dealt
dig	dug	dug
do	did	done
draw	drew	drawn
dream	dreamt, dreamed	dreamt, dreamed
drink	drank	drunk
drive	drove	driven
eat	ate	eaten
fall	fell	fallen
feed	fed	fed
feel	felt	felt
fight	fought	fought
find	found	found
fly	flew	flown
forbid	forbade	forbidden
forget	forgot	forgotten
forgive	forgave	forgiven

infinitive	past tense	past participle
freeze	froze	frozen
get	got	got
give	gave	given
go	went	gone
grind	ground	ground
grow	grew	grown
hang	hung	hung
have	had	had
hear	heard	heard
hide	hid	hidden
hit	hit	hit
hold	held	held
hurt	hurt	hurt
keep	kept	kept
kneel	knelt, kneeled	knelt, kneeled
know	knew	known
lay	laid	laid
lead	led	led
lean	leant, leaned	leant, leaned
leap	leapt, leaped	leapt, leaped
learn	learnt, learned	learnt, learned
leave	left	left
lend	lent	lent
let	let	let
lie	lay	lain
light	lit	lit
lose	lost	lost
make	made	made
mean	meant	meant
meet	met	met
mistake	mistook	mistaken
pay	paid	paid
put	put	put
read	read	read
ride	rode	ridden
ring	rang	rung
rise	rose	risen
run	ran	run
saw	sawed	sawn
say	said	said
see	saw	seen
sell	sold	sold
send	sent	sent
set	set	set
sew	sewed	sewn

infinitive	past tense	past participle
shake	shook	shaken
shine	shone	shone
shoot	shot	shot
show	showed	shown, showed
shrink	shrank	shrunk
shut	shut	shut
sing	sang	sung
sink	sank	sunk
sit	sat	sat
sleep	slept	slept
slide	slid	slid
smell	smelt, smelled	smelt, smelled
sow	sowed	sown
speak	spoke	spoken
spell	spelt, spelled	spelt, spelled
spend	spent	spent
spill	spilt, spilled	spilt, spilled
spin	spun	spun
spit	spat	spat
split	split	split
spoil	spoilt, spoiled	spoilt, spoiled
spread	spread	spread
stand	stood	stood
steal	stole	stolen
stick	stuck	stuck
strike	struck	struck
sweep	swept	swept
swell	swelled	swollen, swelled
swim	swam	swum
swing	swung	swung
take	took	taken
teach	taught	taught
tear	tore	torn
tell	told	told
think	thought	thought
throw	threw	thrown
understand	understood	understood
undo	undid	undone
upset	upset	upset
wake	woke	woken
wear	wore	worn
weep	wept	wept
win	won	won
wind	wound	wound
write	wrote	written